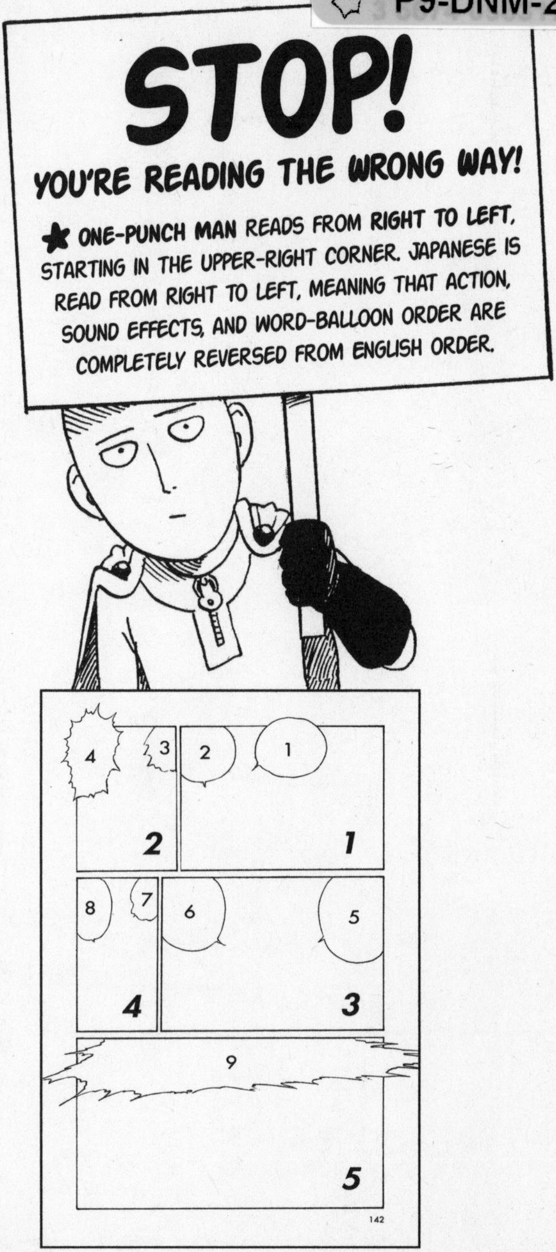
STOP!
YOU'RE READING THE WRONG WAY!
★ ONE-PUNCH MAN READS FROM RIGHT TO LEFT, STARTING IN THE UPPER-RIGHT CORNER. JAPANESE IS READ FROM RIGHT TO LEFT, MEANING THAT ACTION, SOUND EFFECTS, AND WORD-BALLOON ORDER ARE COMPLETELY REVERSED FROM ENGLISH ORDER.

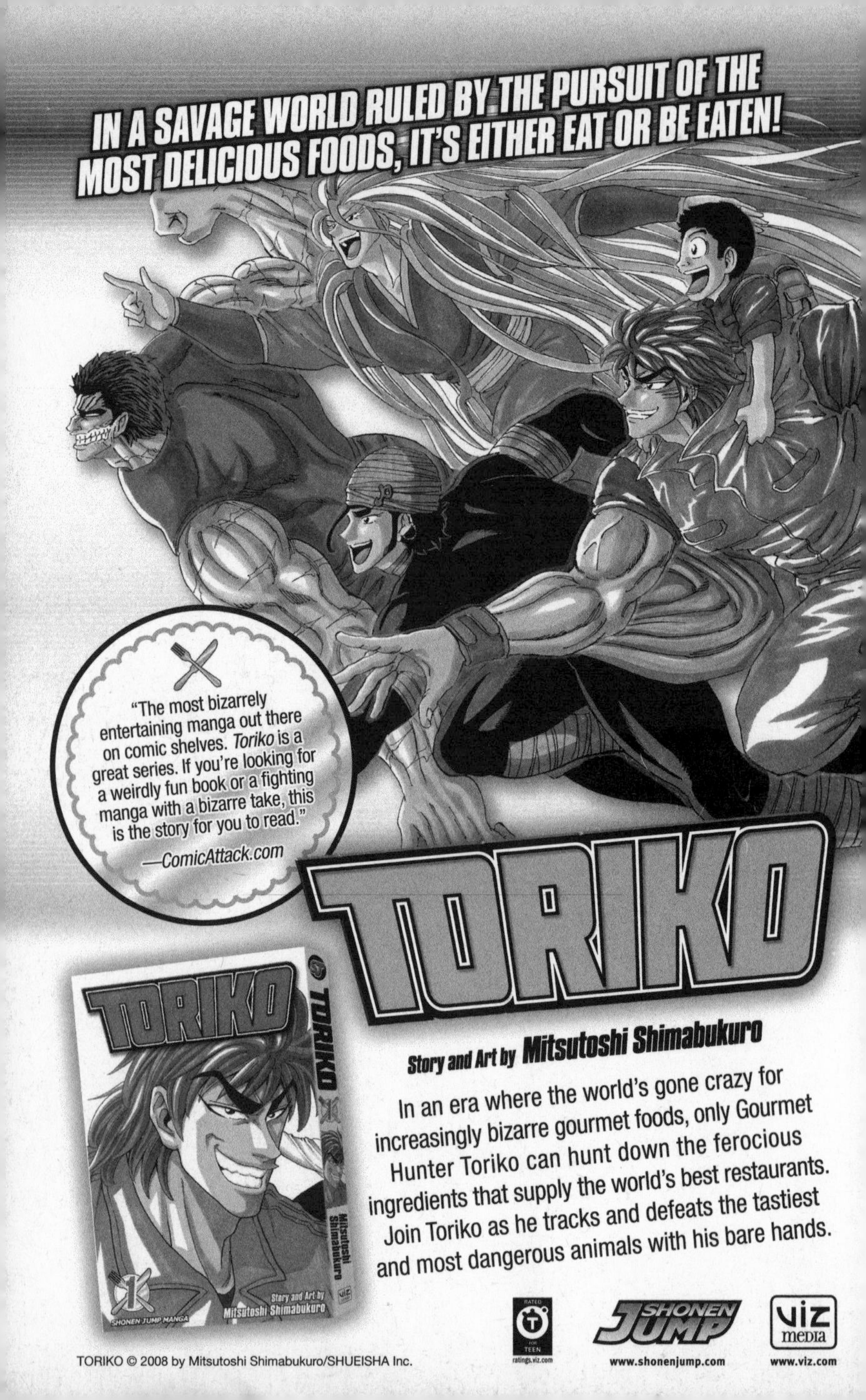
IN A SAVAGE WORLD RULED BY THE PURSUIT OF THE MOST DELICIOUS FOODS, IT'S EITHER EAT OR BE EATEN!
"The most bizarrely entertaining manga out there on comic shelves. Toriko is a great series. If you're looking for a weirdly fun book or a fighting manga with a bizarre take, this is the story for you to read."
—ComicAttack.com
TORIKO
TORIKO
Mitsutoshi Shimabukuro
Story and Art by Mitsutoshi Shimabukuro
SHONEN JUMP MANGA
Story and Art by Mitsutoshi Shimabukuro
In an era where the world's gone crazy for increasingly bizarre gourmet foods, only Gourmet Hunter Toriko can hunt down the ferocious ingredients that supply the world's best restaurants. Join Toriko as he tracks and defeats the tastiest and most dangerous animals with his bare hands.
TORIKO © 2008 by Mitsutoshi Shimabukuro/SHUEISHA Inc.
RATED T FOR TEEN
ratings.viz.com
SHONEN JUMP
www.shonenjump.com
viz media
www.viz.com

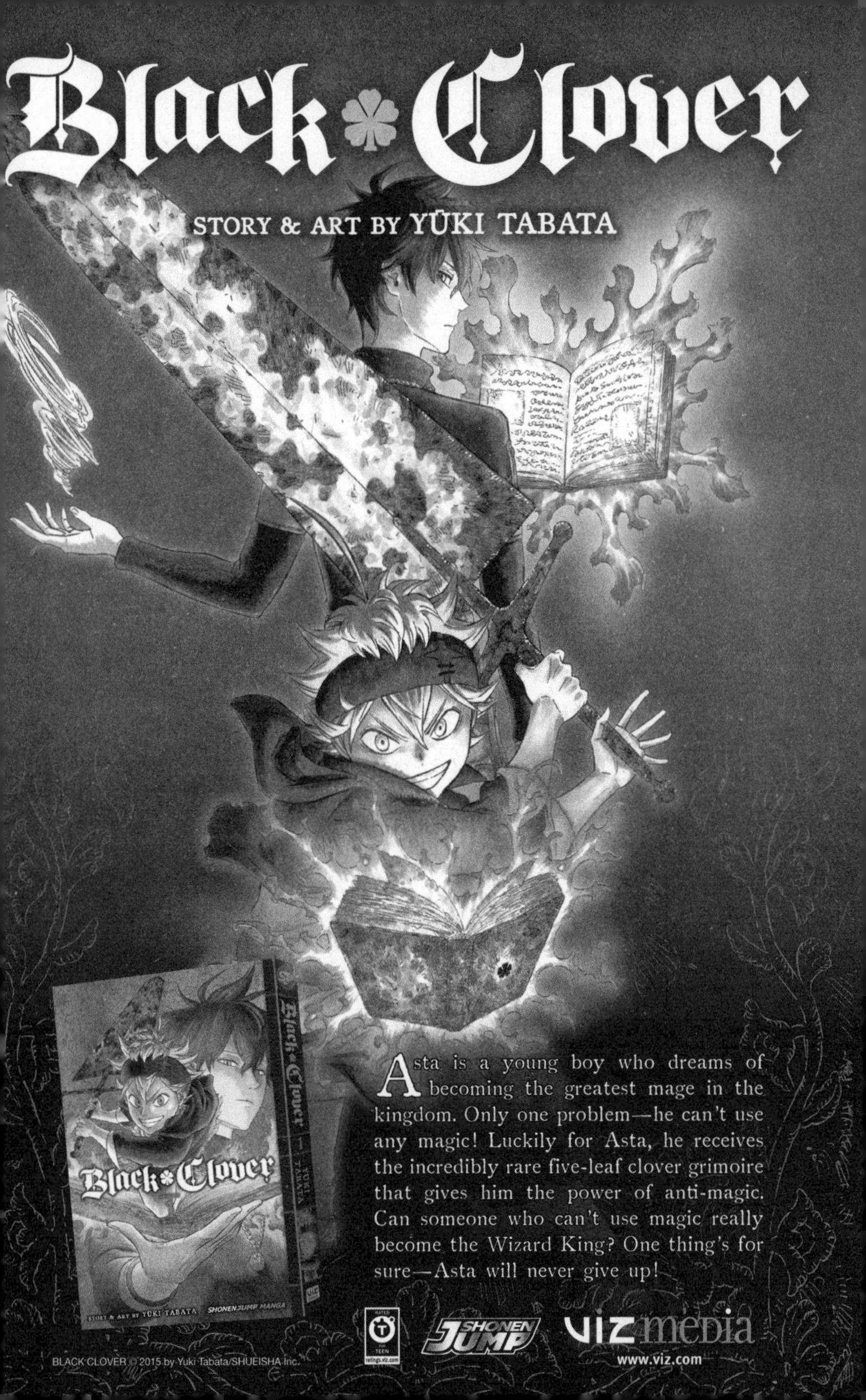
Black Clover
STORY & ART BY YŪKI TABATA
Asta is a young boy who dreams of becoming the greatest mage in the kingdom. Only one problem—he can't use any magic! Luckily for Asta, he receives the incredibly rare five-leaf clover grimoire that gives him the power of anti-magic. Can someone who can't use magic really become the Wizard King? One thing's for sure—Asta will never give up!
RATED T FOR TEEN ratings.viz.com
SHONEN JUMP
VIZ media
www.viz.com
BLACK CLOVER © 2015 by Yuki Tabata/SHUEISHA Inc.

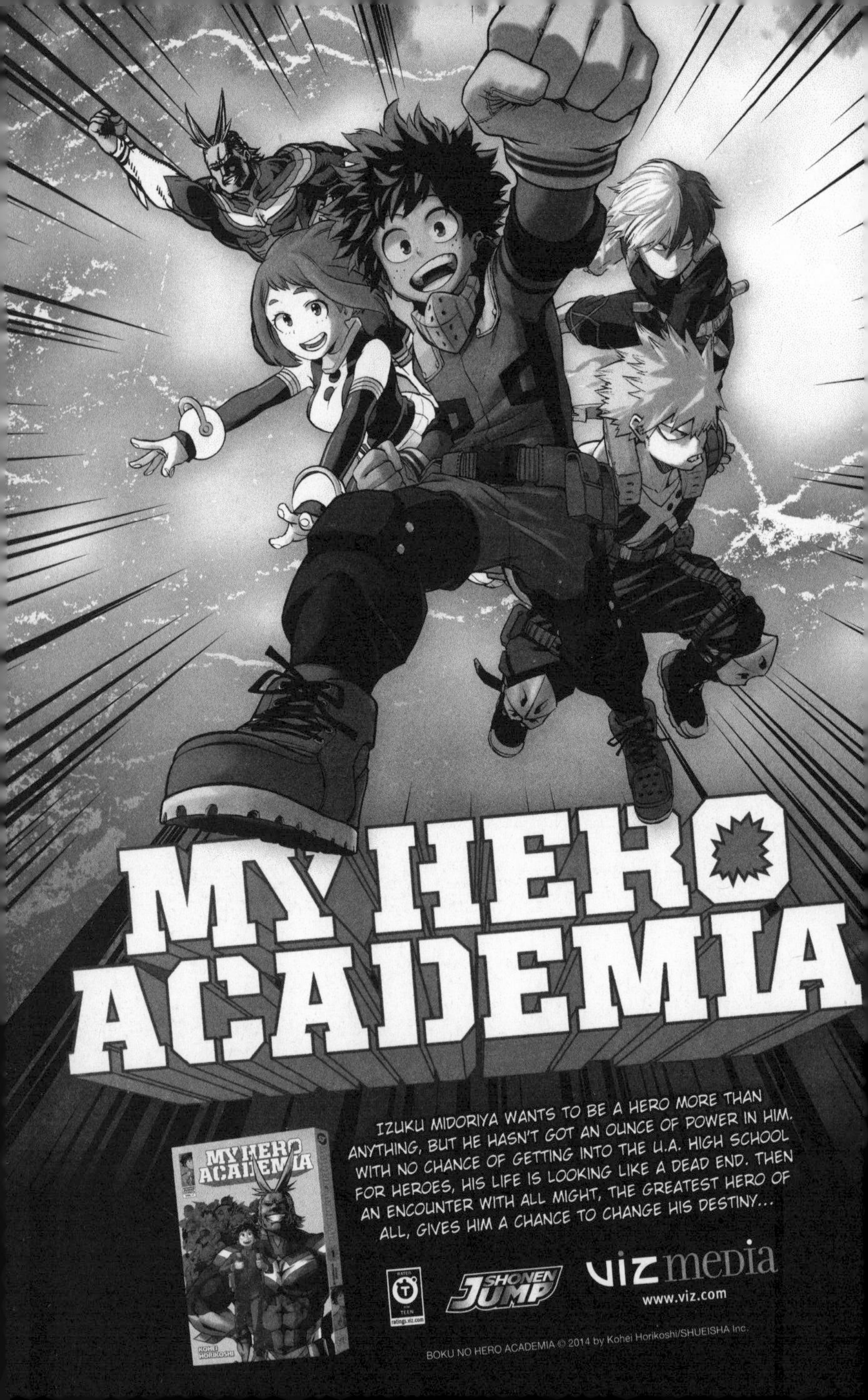
MY HERO ACADEMIA
IZUKU MIDORIYA WANTS TO BE A HERO MORE THAN ANYTHING, BUT HE HASN'T GOT AN OUNCE OF POWER IN HIM. WITH NO CHANCE OF GETTING INTO THE U.A. HIGH SCHOOL FOR HEROES, HIS LIFE IS LOOKING LIKE A DEAD END. THEN AN ENCOUNTER WITH ALL MIGHT, THE GREATEST HERO OF ALL, GIVES HIM A CHANCE TO CHANGE HIS DESTINY...
MY HERO ACADEMIA
KOHEI HORIKOSHI
RATED T TEEN ratings.viz.com
SHONEN JUMP
VIZ media
www.viz.com
BOKU NO HERO ACADEMIA © 2014 by Kohei Horikoshi/SHUEISHA Inc.

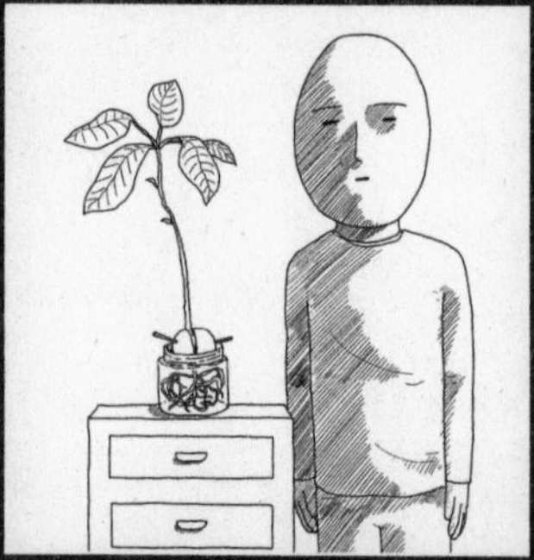

O N E

I'm growing an avocado tree. It's growing quickly and appears to be full of life.

—ONE

Manga creator ONE began *One-Punch Man* as a webcomic, which quickly went viral, garnering over 10 million hits. In addition to *One-Punch Man*, ONE writes and draws the series *Mob Psycho 100* and *Makai no Ossan*.

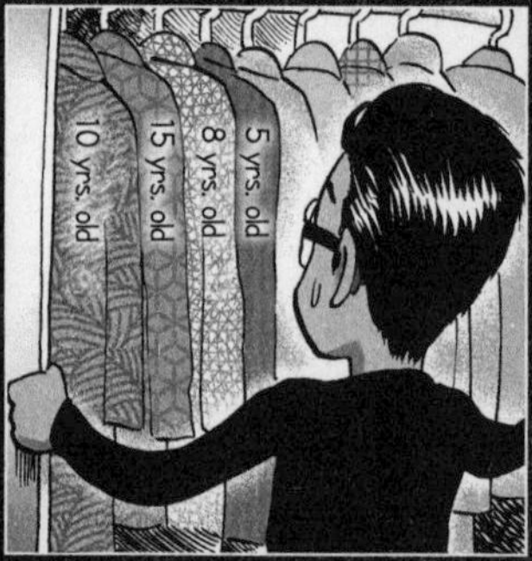
5 yrs. old
8 yrs. old
15 yrs. old
10 yrs. old

YUSUKE MURATA

I rarely clean out my closet, so it's full of old clothes. I really should do something about that.

—Yusuke Murata

A highly decorated and skilled artist best known for his work on *Eyeshield 21*, Yusuke Murata won the 122nd Hop Step Award (1995) for *Partner* and placed second in the 51st Akatsuka Award (1998) for *Samui Hanashi*.

ONE-PUNCH MAN | 12

ONE + YUSUKE MURATA

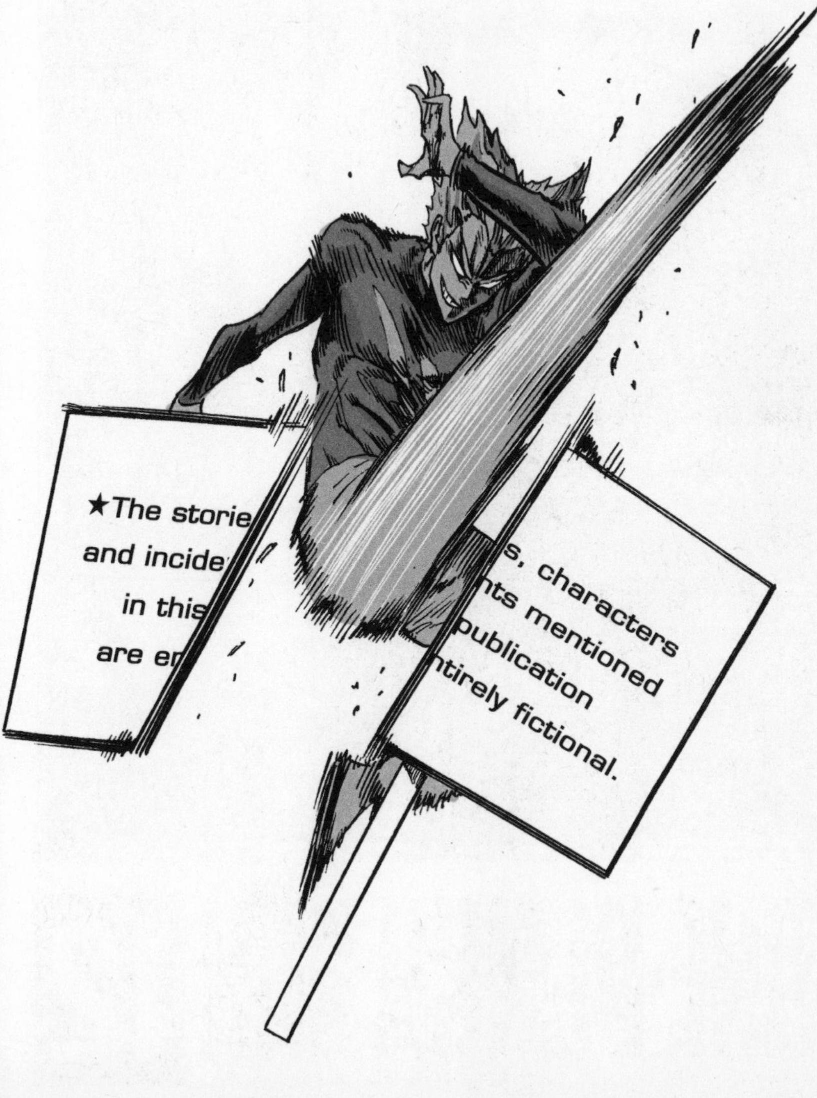
★The storie
and incide
in this
are en
s, characters
nts mentioned
publication
ntirely fictional.

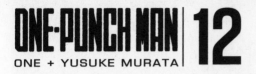

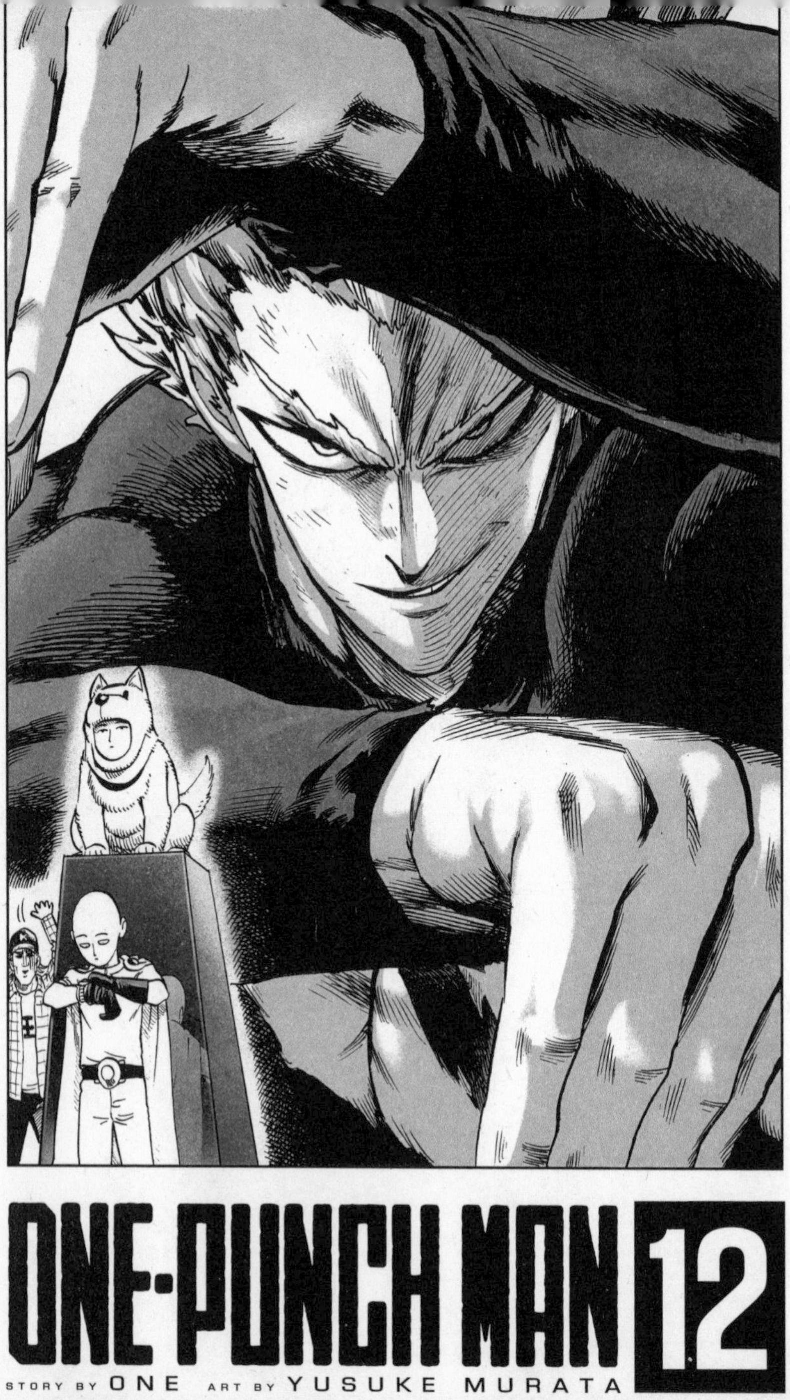

ONE-PUNCH MAN 12

STORY BY ONE ART BY YUSUKE MURATA

CHARACTERS

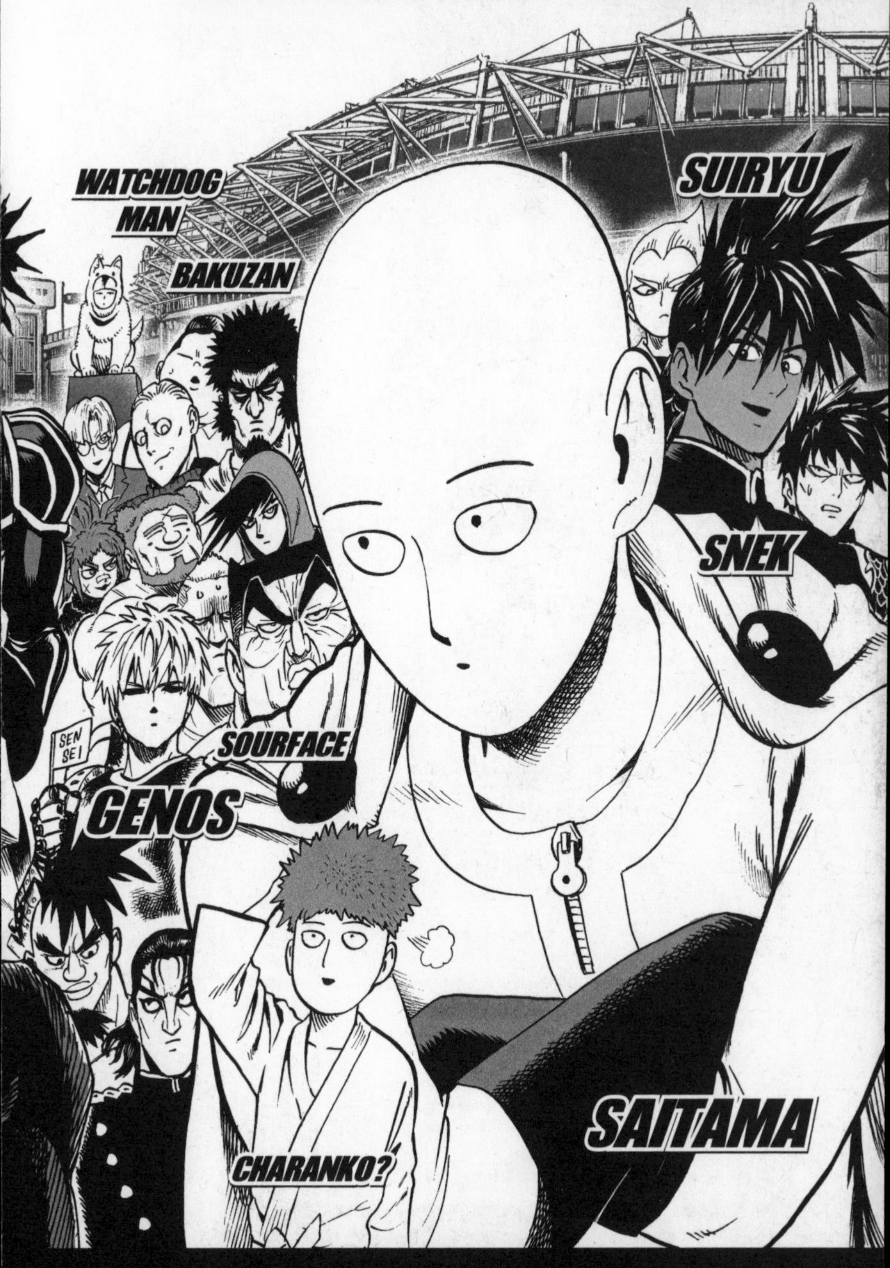
SUIRYU
SNEK
SAITAMA
WATCHDOG MAN
BAKUZAN
SOURFACE
SEN SEI
GENOS
CHARANKO?

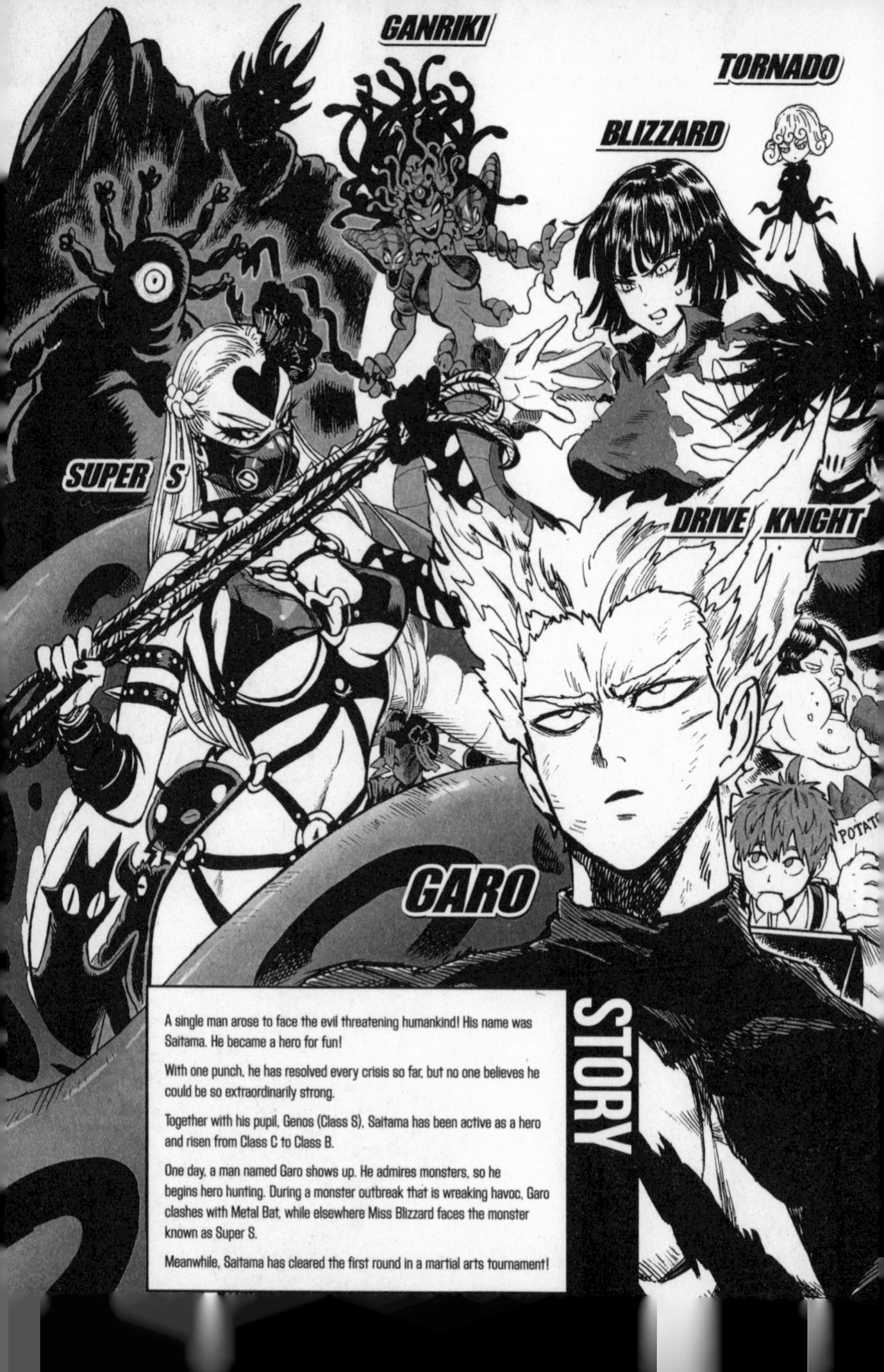
GANRIKI
TORNADO
BLIZZARD
SUPER S
DRIVE KNIGHT
GARO
POTATO

STORY

A single man arose to face the evil threatening humankind! His name was Saitama. He became a hero for fun!

With one punch, he has resolved every crisis so far, but no one believes he could be so extraordinarily strong.

Together with his pupil, Genos (Class S), Saitama has been active as a hero and risen from Class C to Class B.

One day, a man named Garo shows up. He admires monsters, so he begins hero hunting. During a monster outbreak that is wreaking havoc, Garo clashes with Metal Bat, while elsewhere Miss Blizzard faces the monster known as Super S.

Meanwhile, Saitama has cleared the first round in a martial arts tournament!

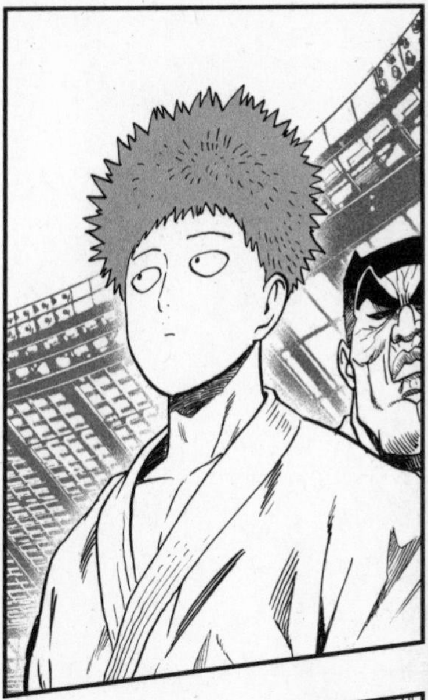

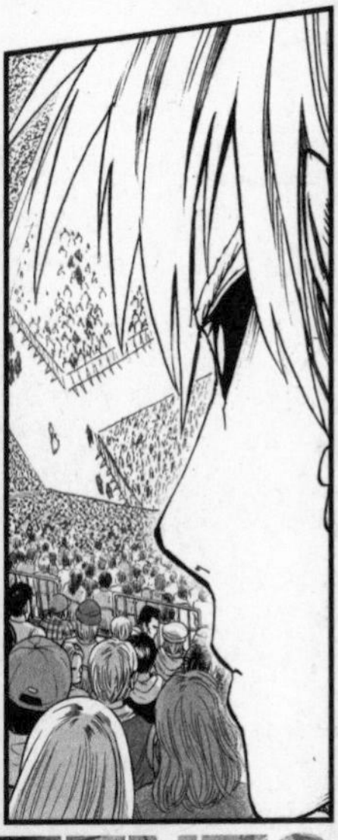

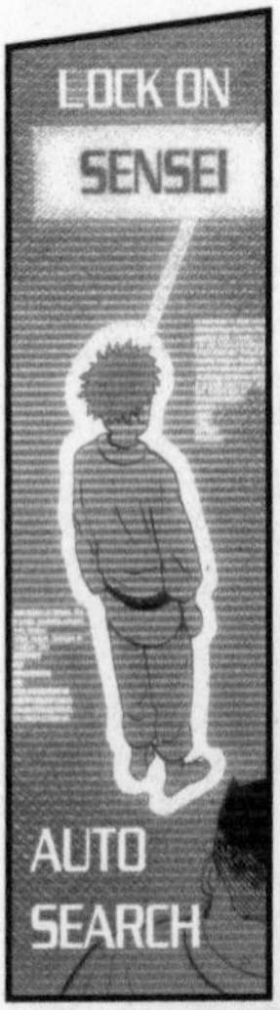
LOCK ON
SENSEI
AUTO
SEARCH

CONTENTS

ONE-PUNCH MAN VOLUME TWELVE

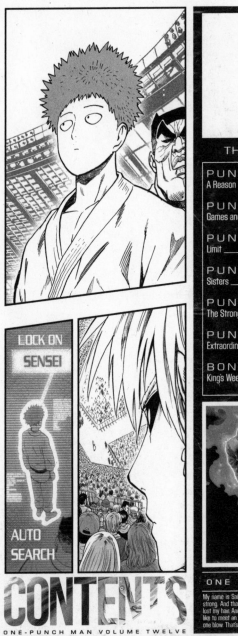

12

THE STRONG ONES

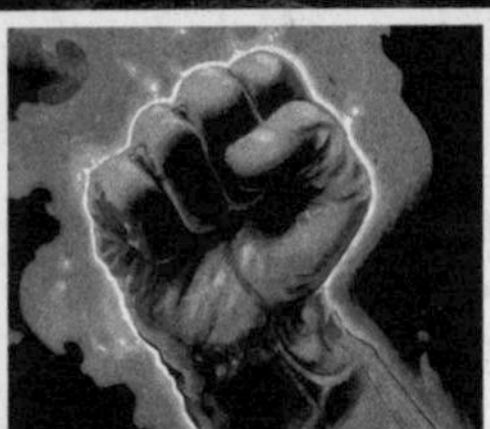

ONE-PUNCH MAN

ONE + YUSUKE MURATA

My name is Saitama. I am a hero. My hobby is heroic exploits. I got too strong. And that makes me sad. I can defeat any enemy with one blow. I lost my hair. And I lost all feeling. I want to feel the rush of battle. I would like to meet an incredibly strong enemy. And I would like to defeat it with one blow. That's because I am One-Punch Man.

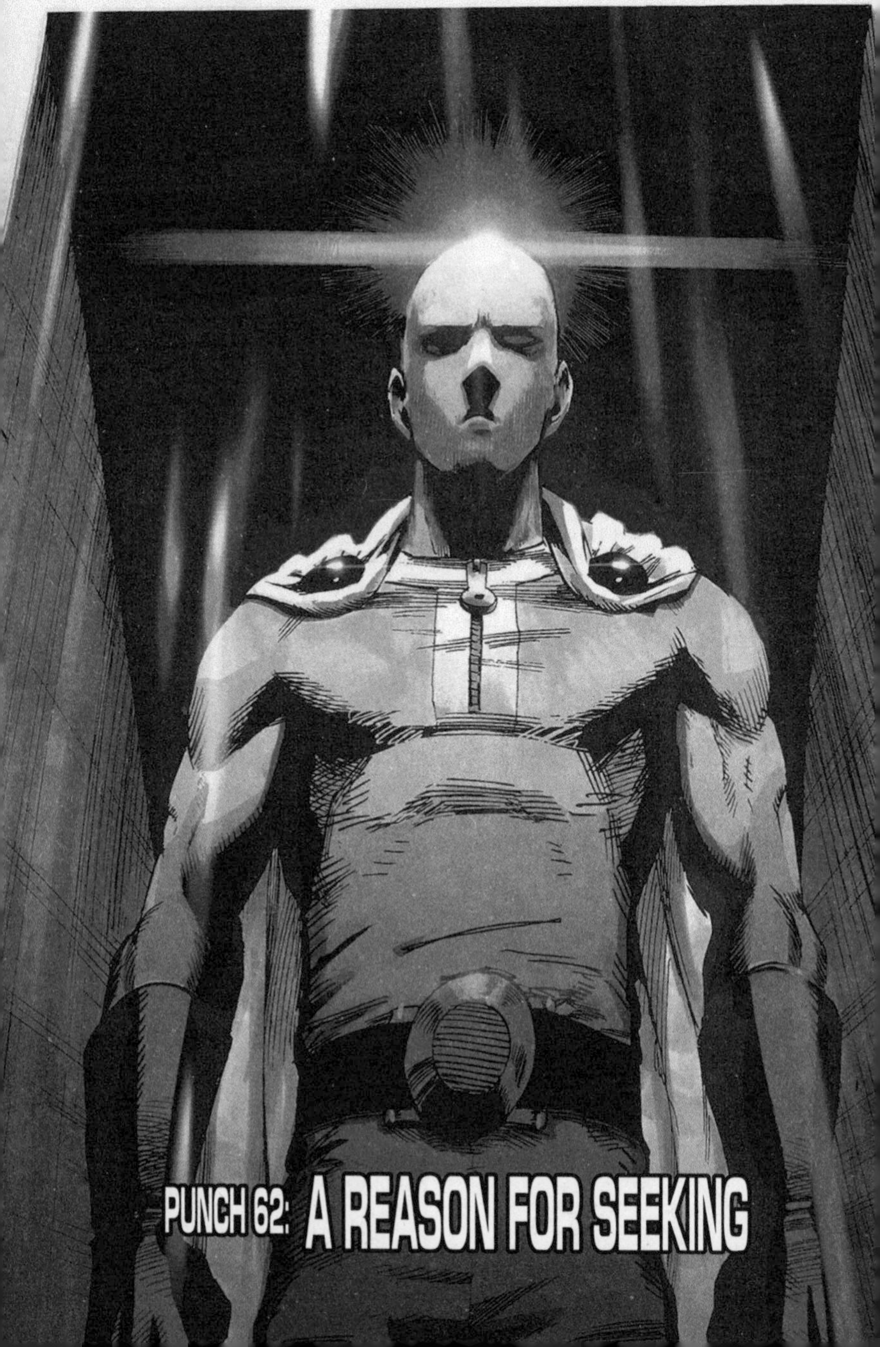
PUNCH 62: A REASON FOR SEEKING

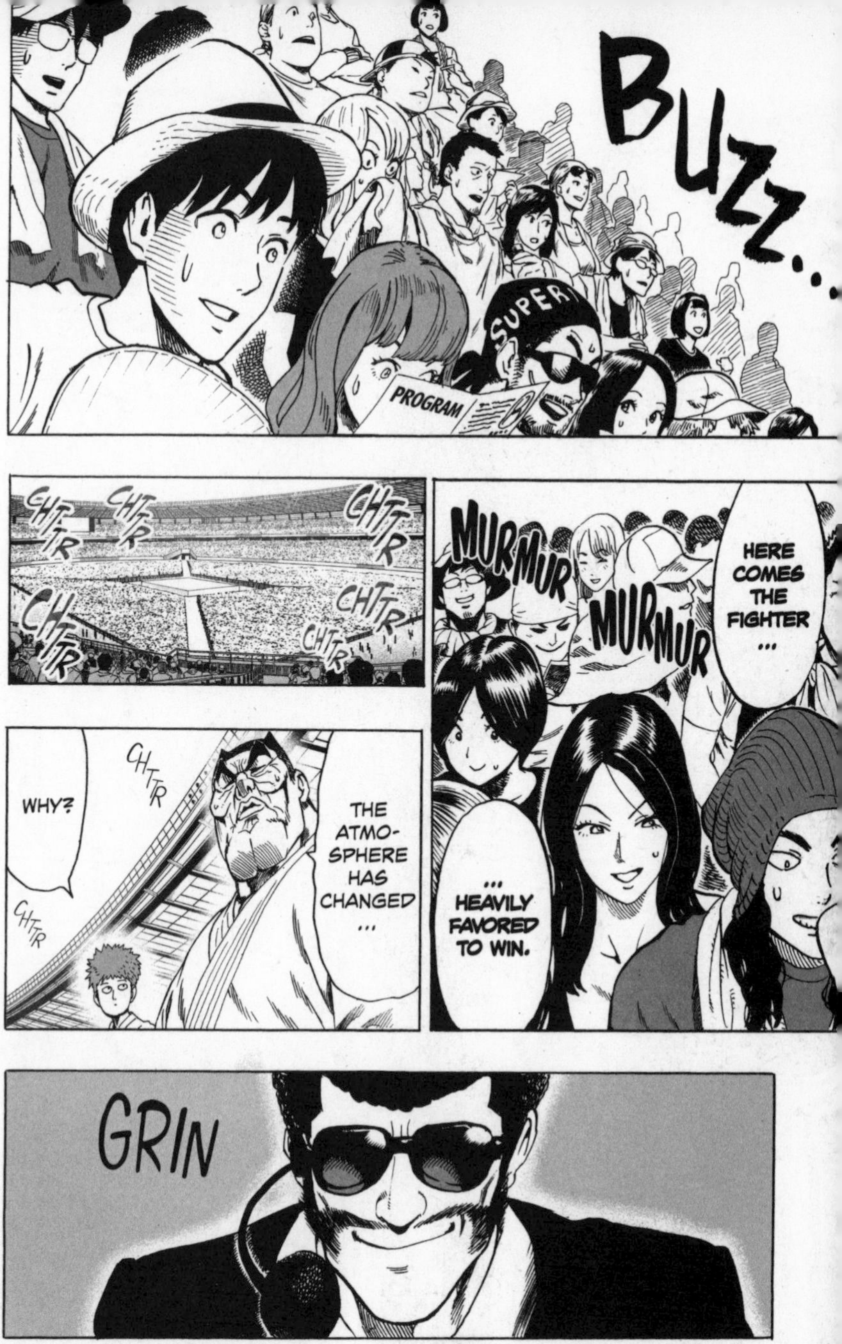
BUZZ...
SUPER
PROGRAM
HERE COMES THE FIGHTER ...
MURMUR
MURMUR
... HEAVILY FAVORED TO WIN.
CHTTR
CHTTR
CHTTR
CHTTR
CHTTR
CHTTR
THE ATMOSPHERE HAS CHANGED ...
CHTTR
WHY?
CHTTR
GRIN

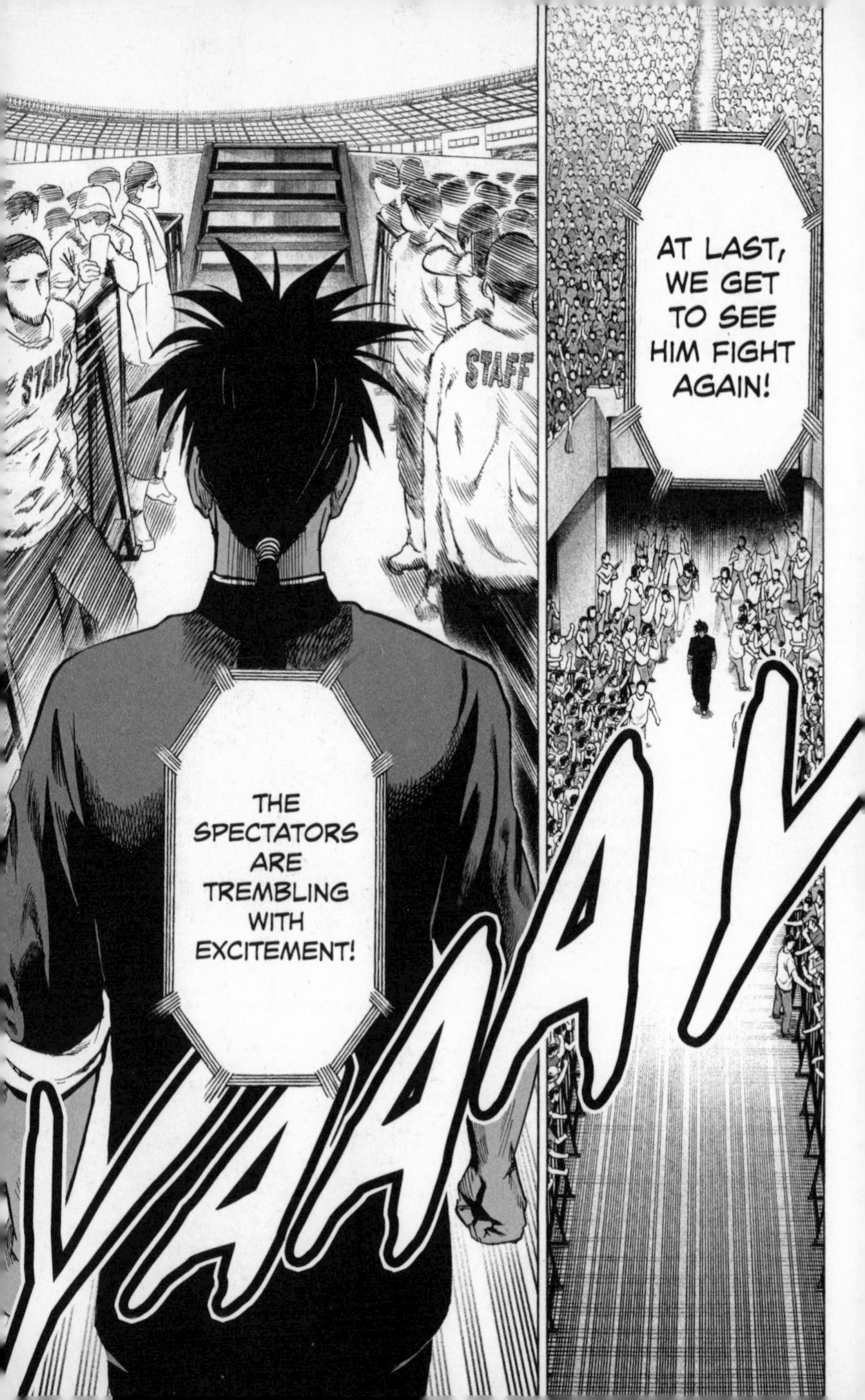
AT LAST, WE GET TO SEE HIM FIGHT AGAIN!
THE SPECTATORS ARE TREMBLING WITH EXCITEMENT!
YAAAY

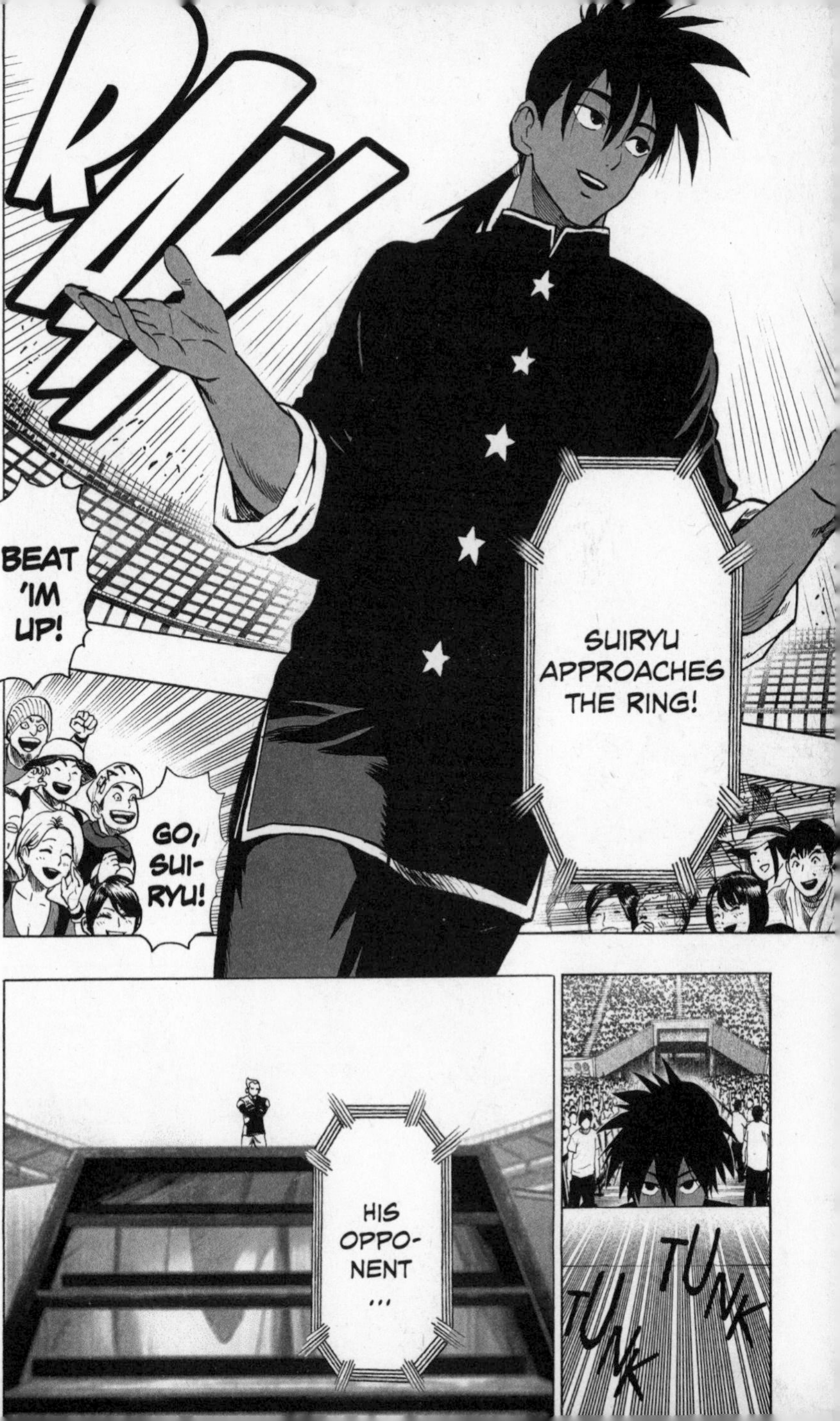
SUIRYU APPROACHES THE RING!
BEAT 'IM UP!
GO, SUI-RYU!
TUNK TUNK
HIS OPPO-NENT ...

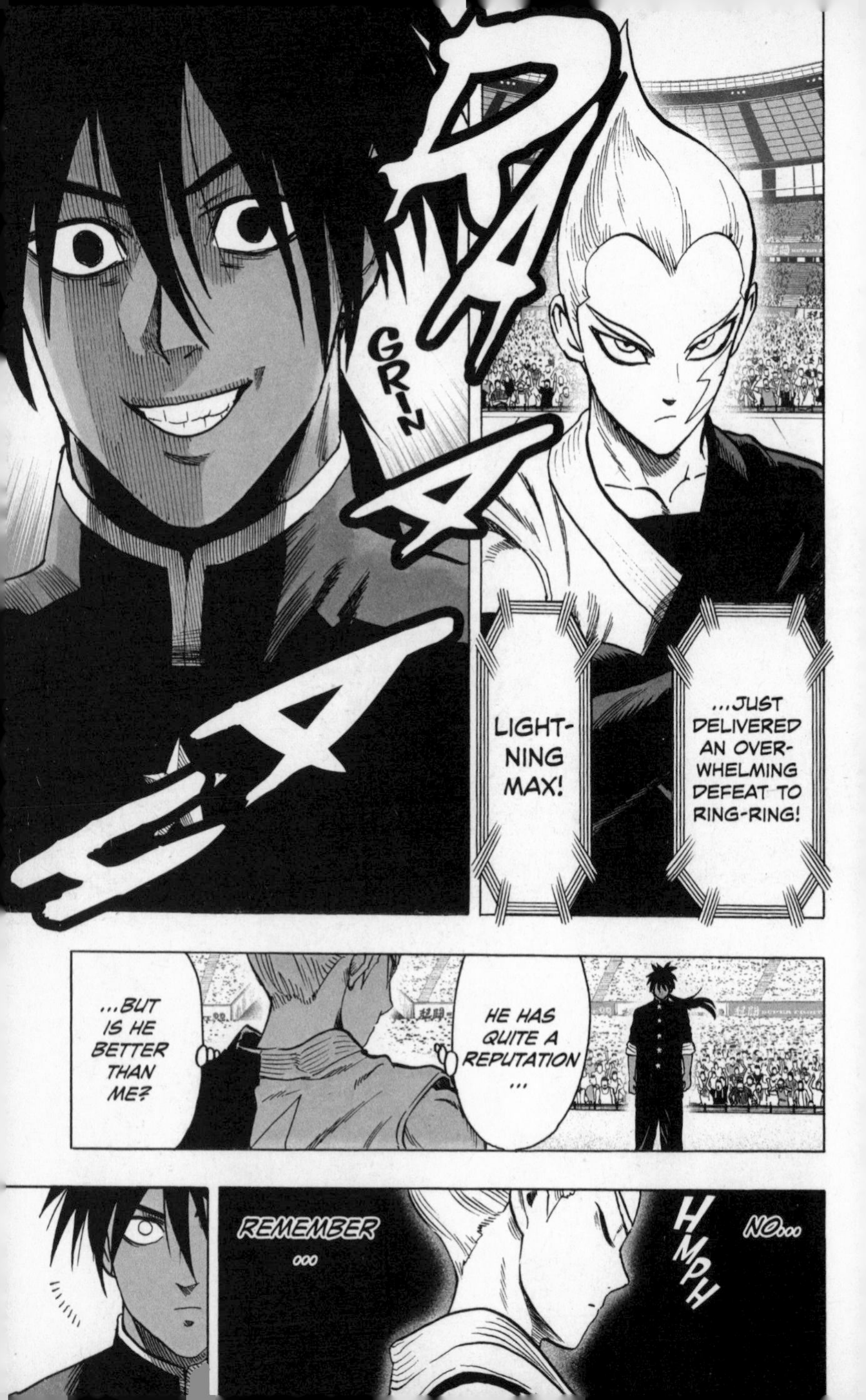
LIGHT-NING MAX!
...JUST DELIVERED AN OVER-WHELMING DEFEAT TO RING-RING!
DA
GRIN
HE HAS QUITE A REPUTATION ...
...BUT IS HE BETTER THAN ME?
NO...
HMPH
REMEMBER ...

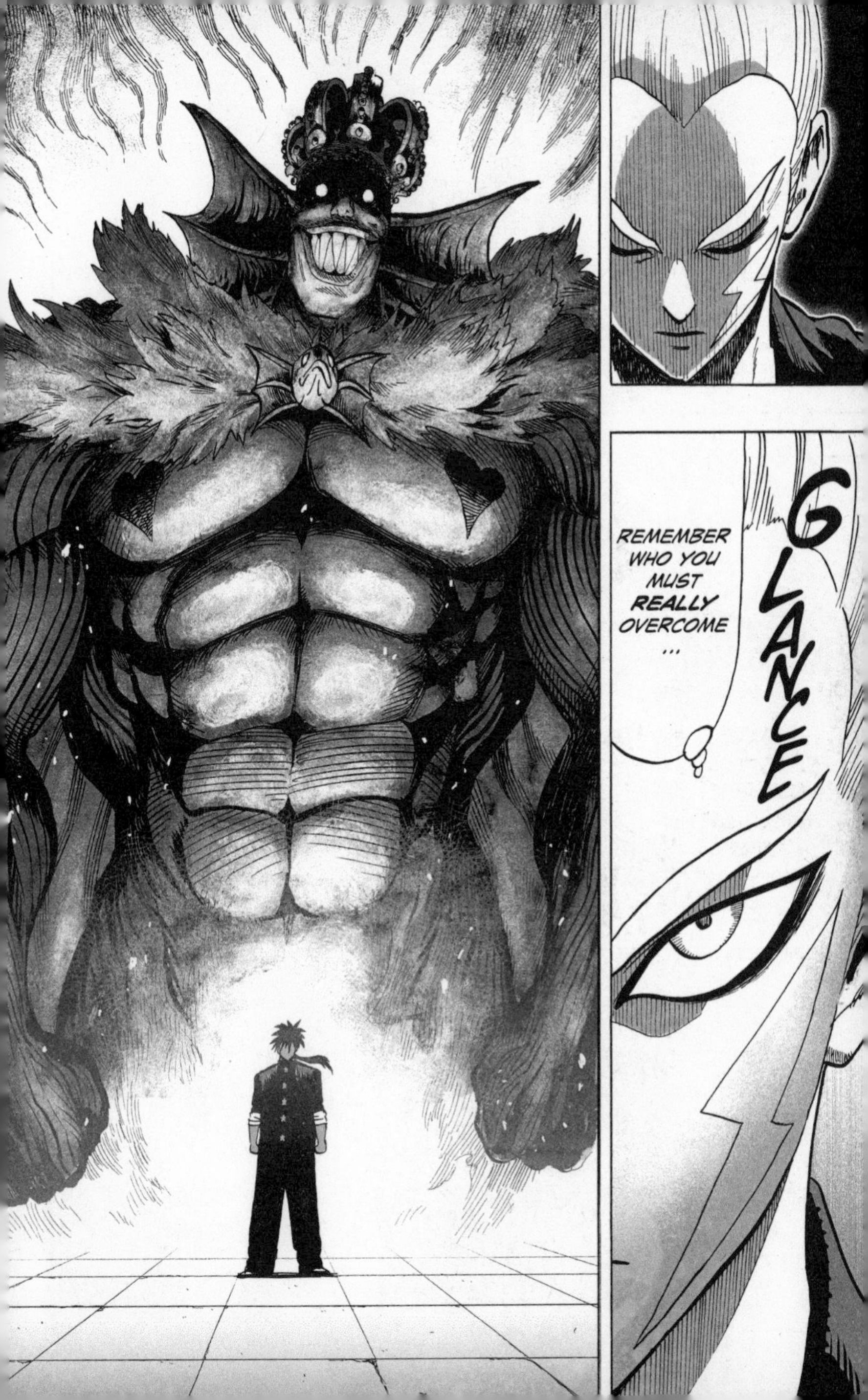
REMEMBER WHO YOU MUST REALLY OVERCOME ...
GLANCE

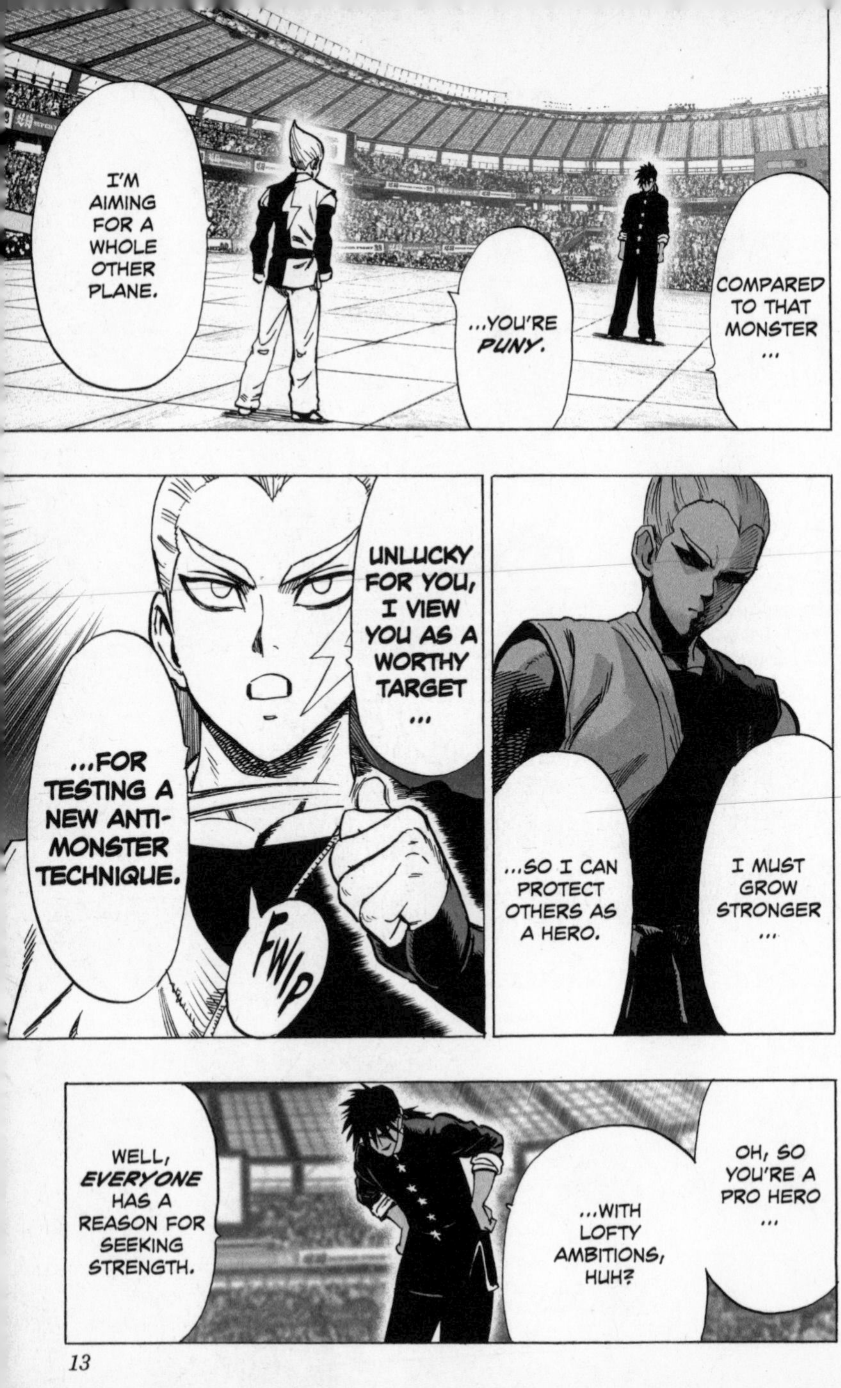
COMPARED TO THAT MONSTER ...
...YOU'RE PUNY.
I'M AIMING FOR A WHOLE OTHER PLANE.
I MUST GROW STRONGER ...
...SO I CAN PROTECT OTHERS AS A HERO.
UNLUCKY FOR YOU, I VIEW YOU AS A WORTHY TARGET ...
...FOR TESTING A NEW ANTI-MONSTER TECHNIQUE.
FWIP
OH, SO YOU'RE A PRO HERO ...
...WITH LOFTY AMBITIONS, HUH?
WELL, EVERYONE HAS A REASON FOR SEEKING STRENGTH.

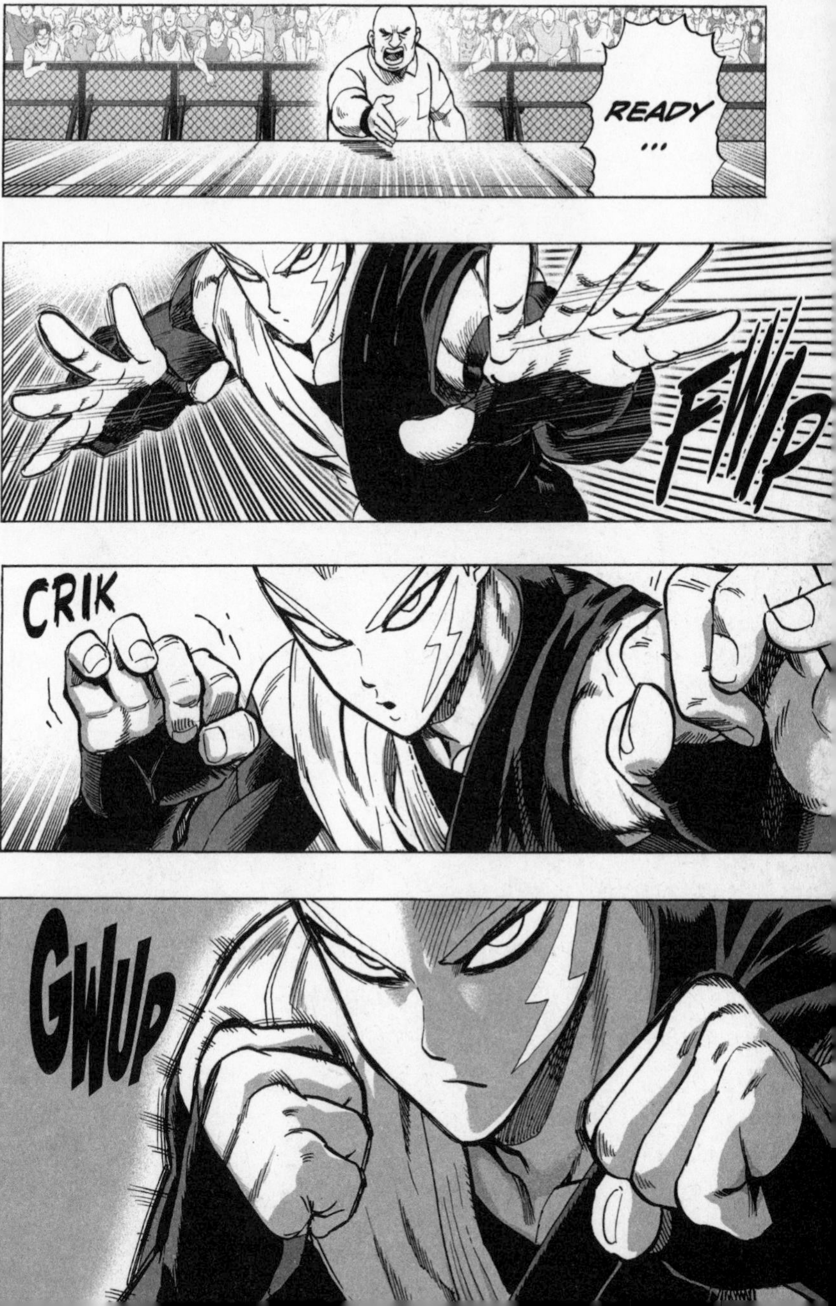
READY ...
FWP
CRIK
GWUP

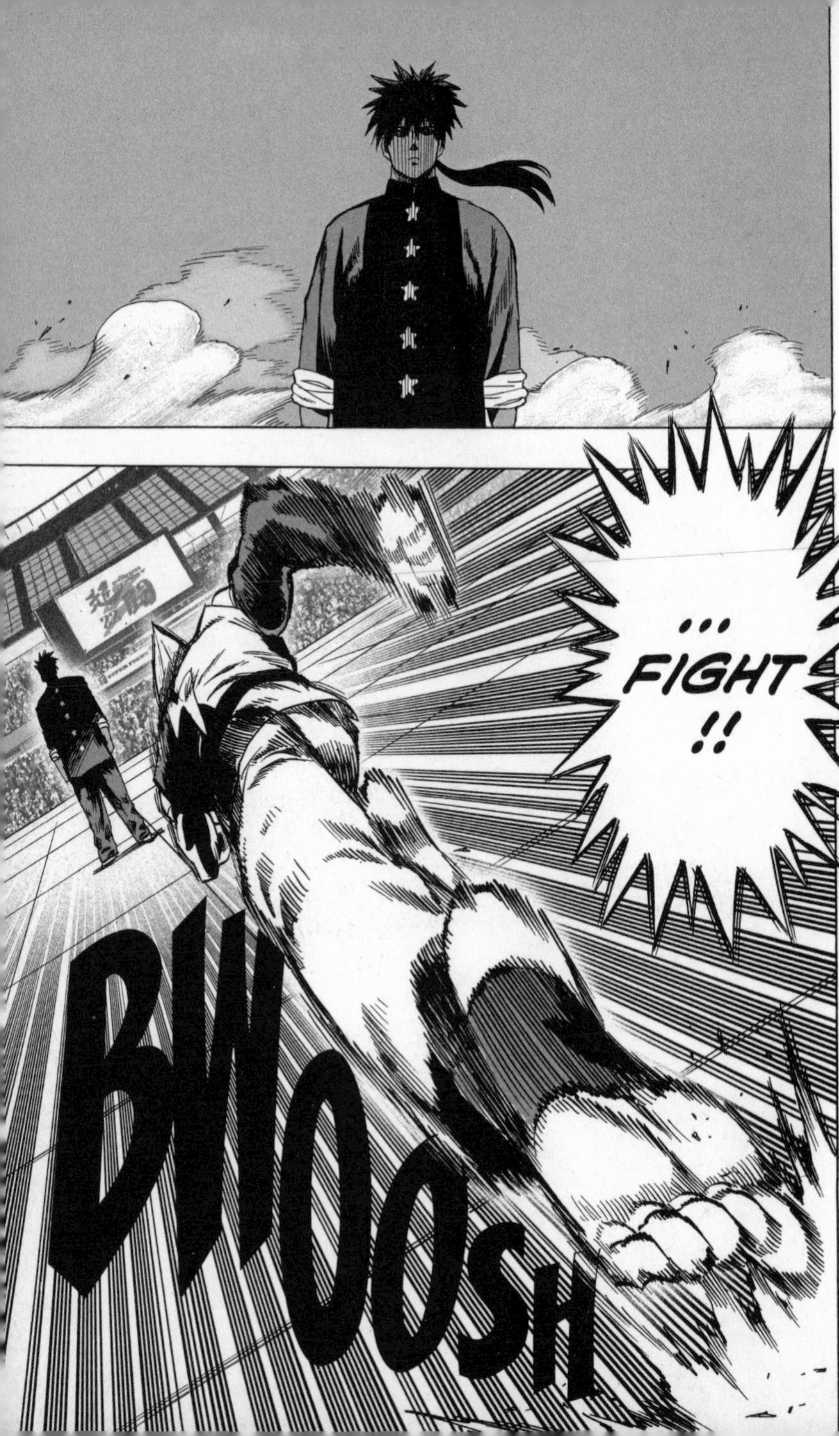
... FIGHT !!
BWOOSH

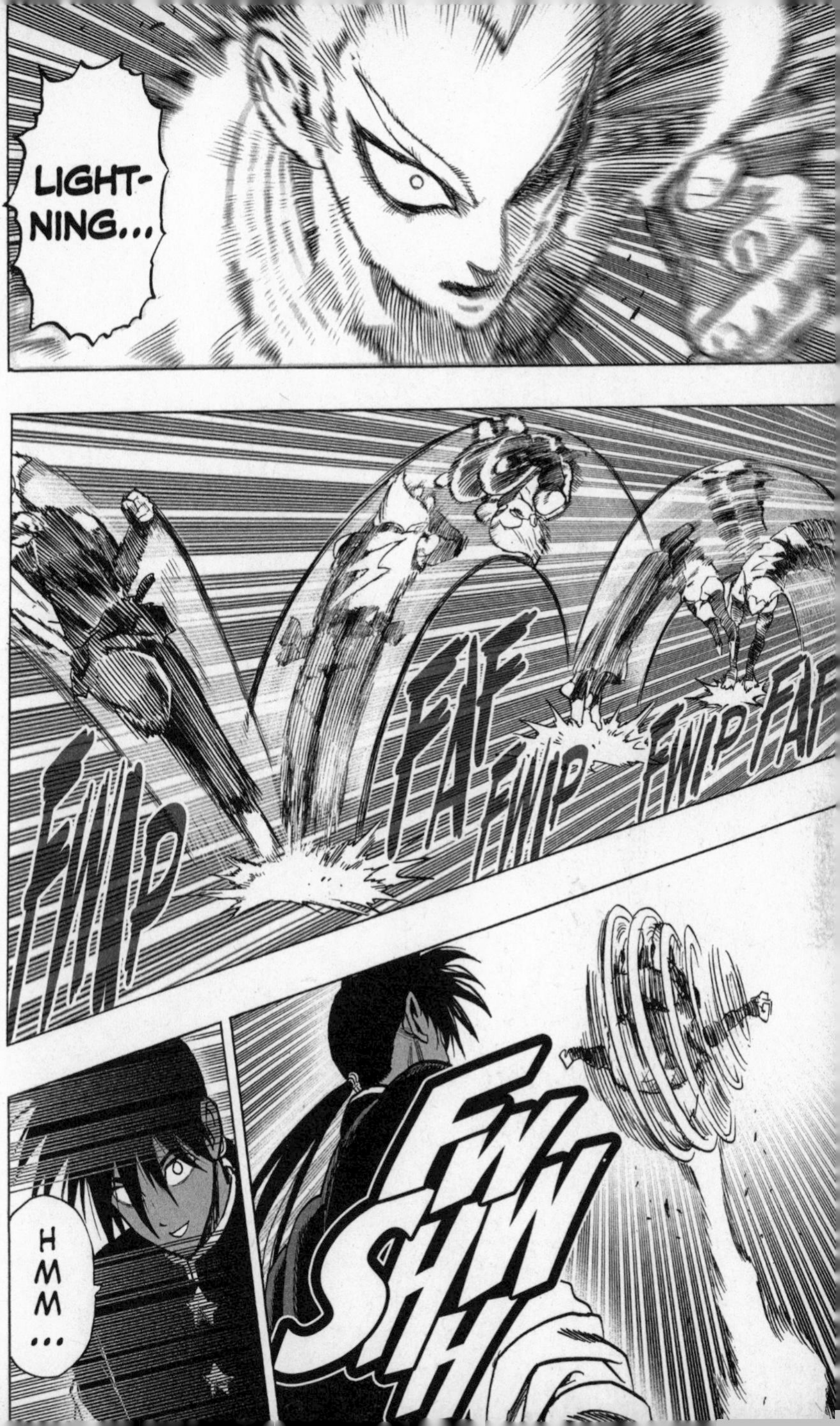
LIGHT-
NING...
FWIP FAF
FWIP
FAF
FWIP
FWSHH
HMM...

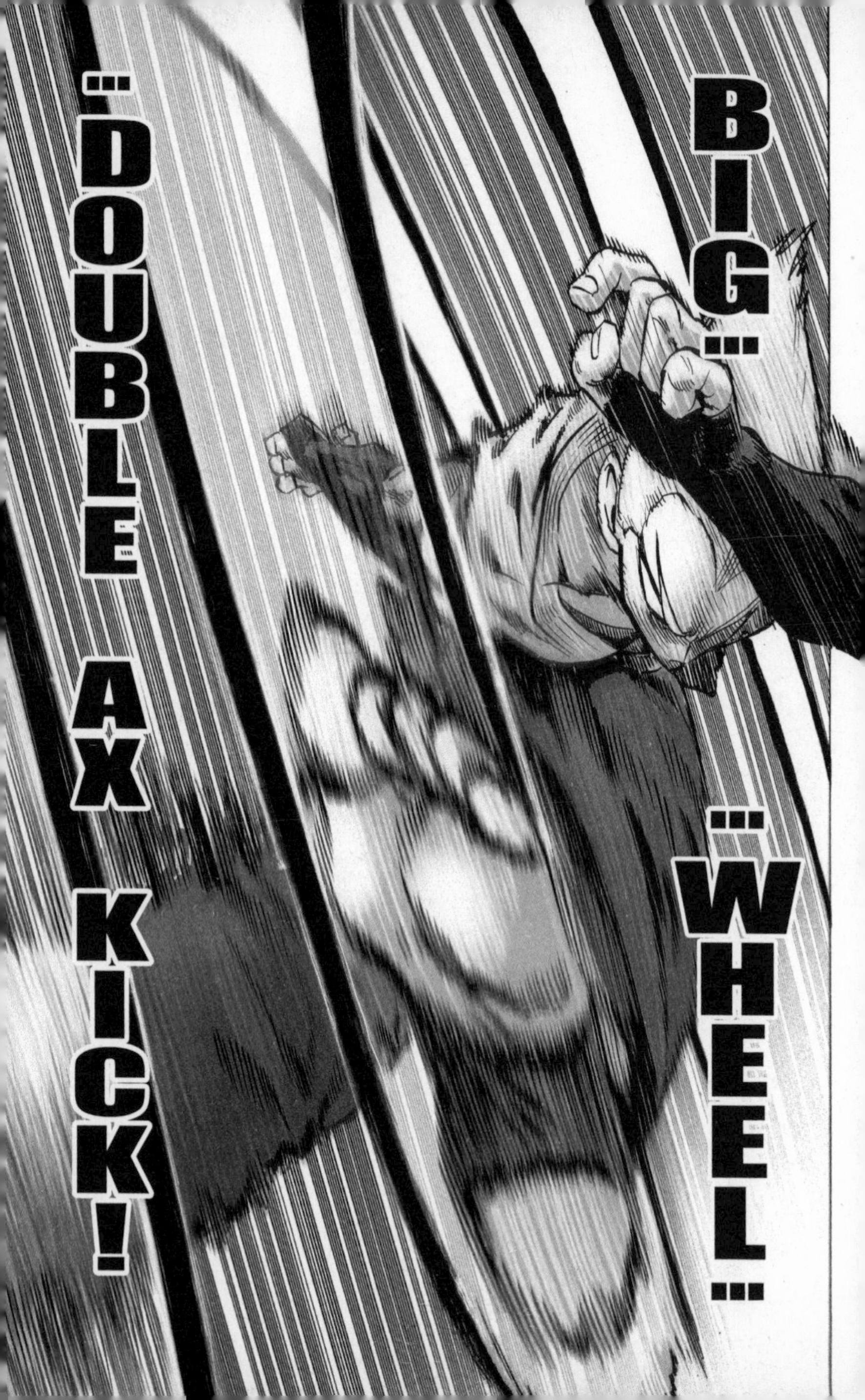
BIG... ...WHEEL...
...DOUBLE AX KICK!

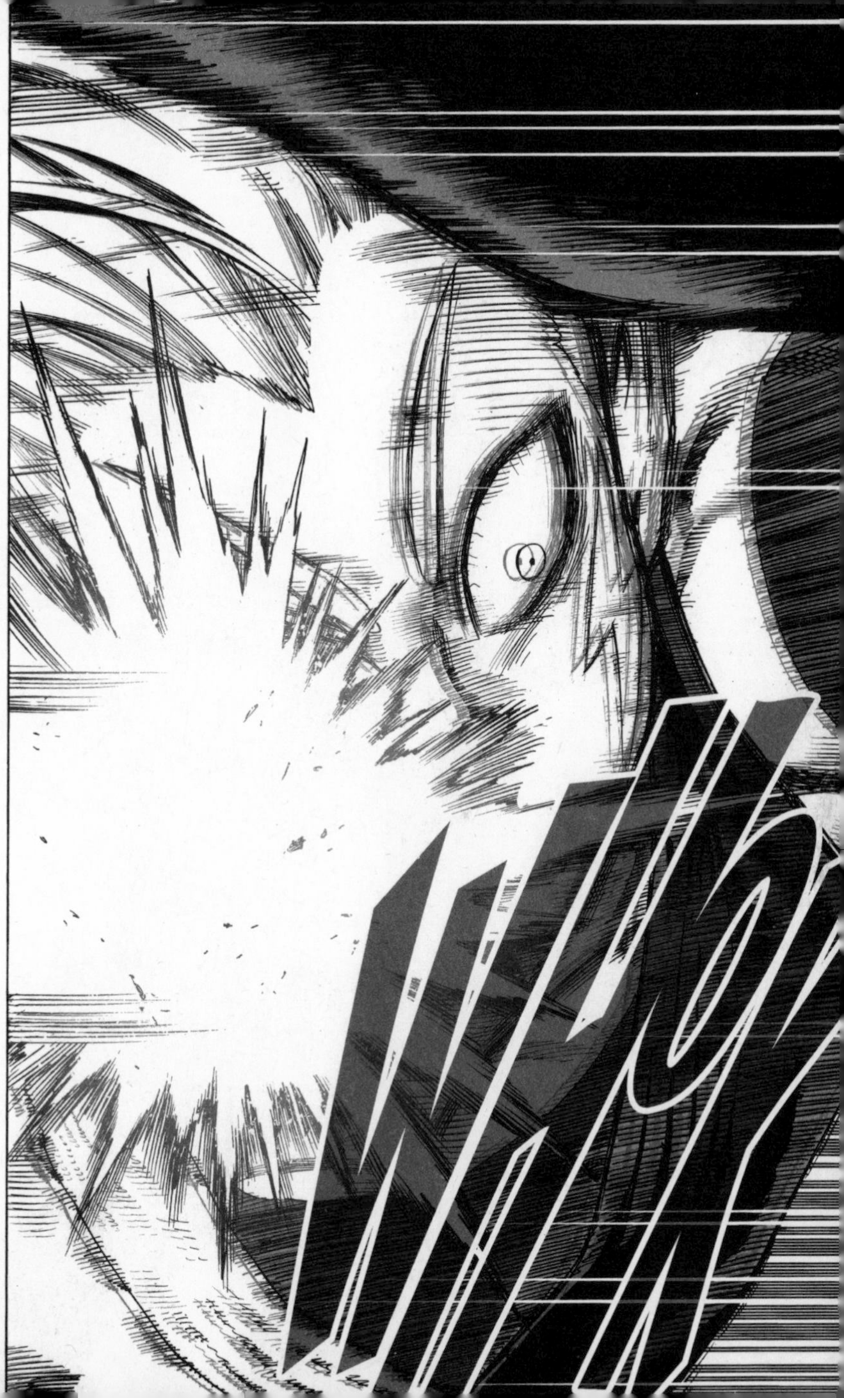

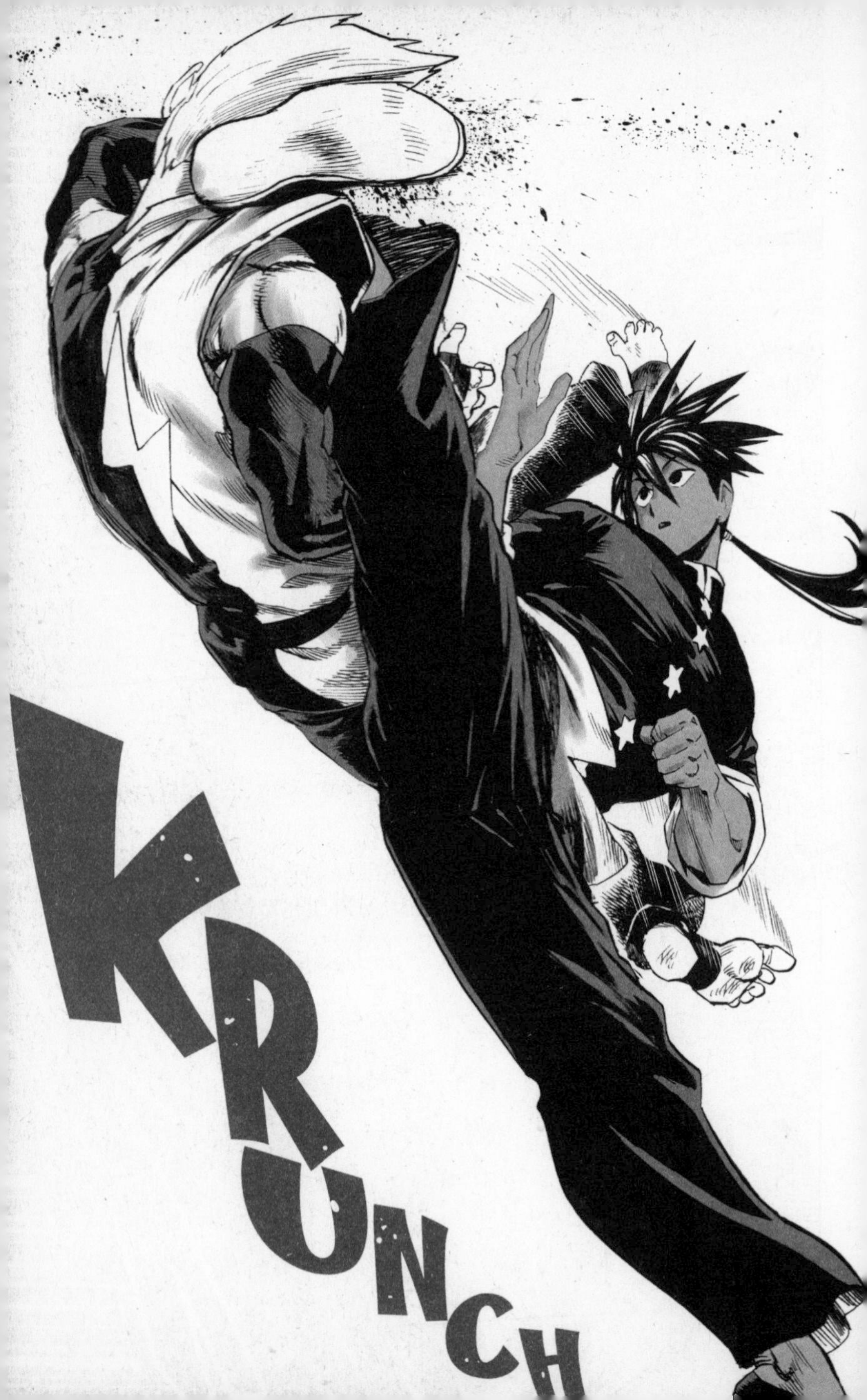
KRUNCH

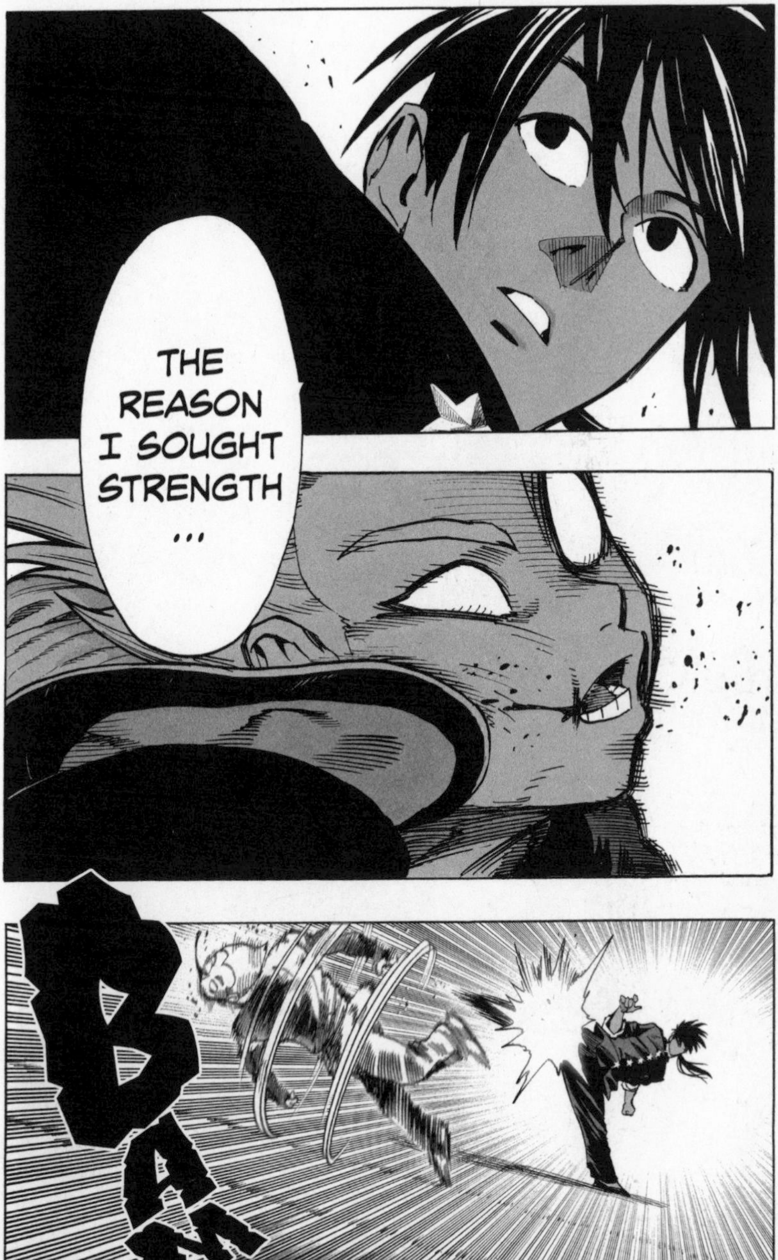
THE REASON I SOUGHT STRENGTH ...
BAM

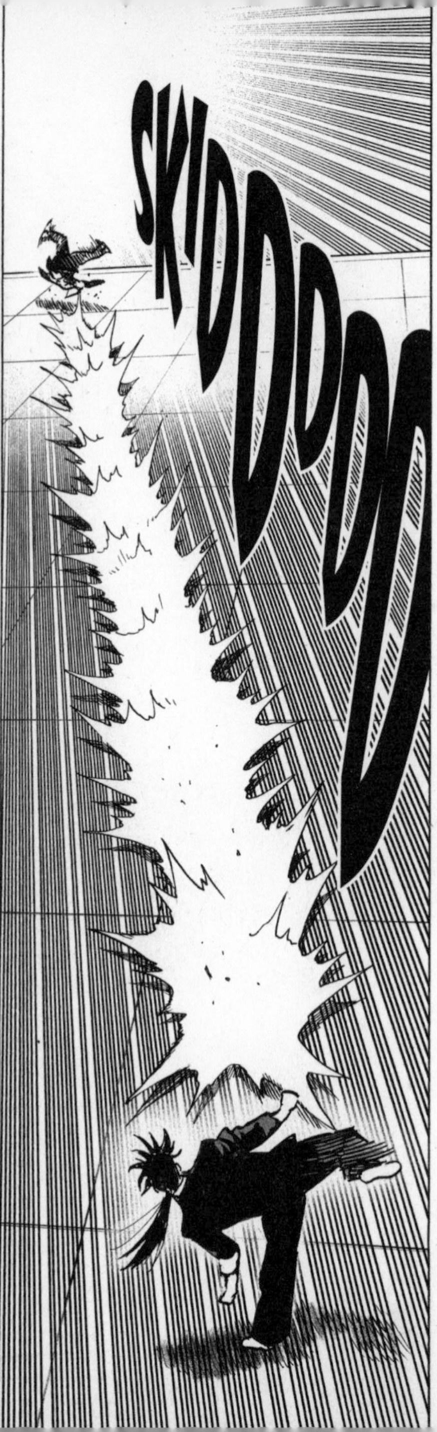
SKIDDDDD
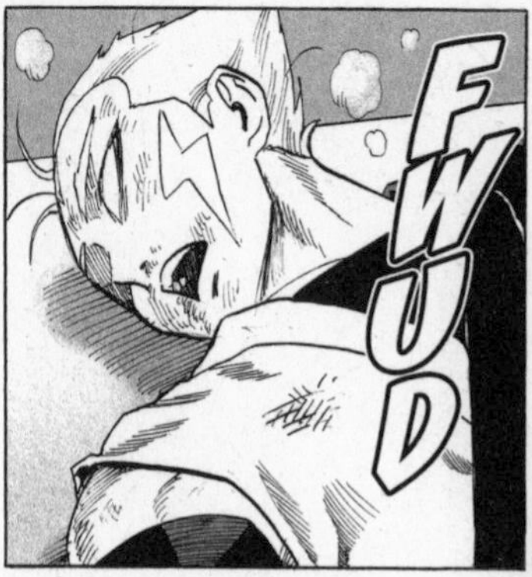
FWUD
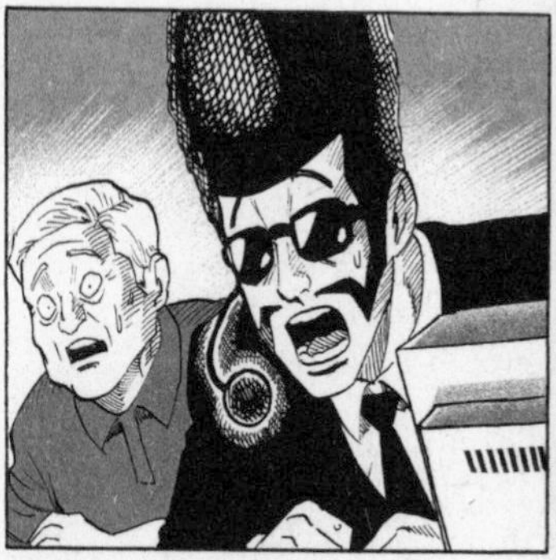
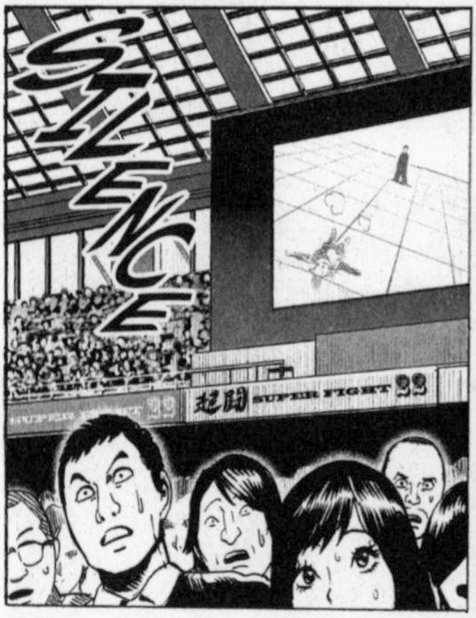
SILENCE
超闘 SUPER FIGHT 99

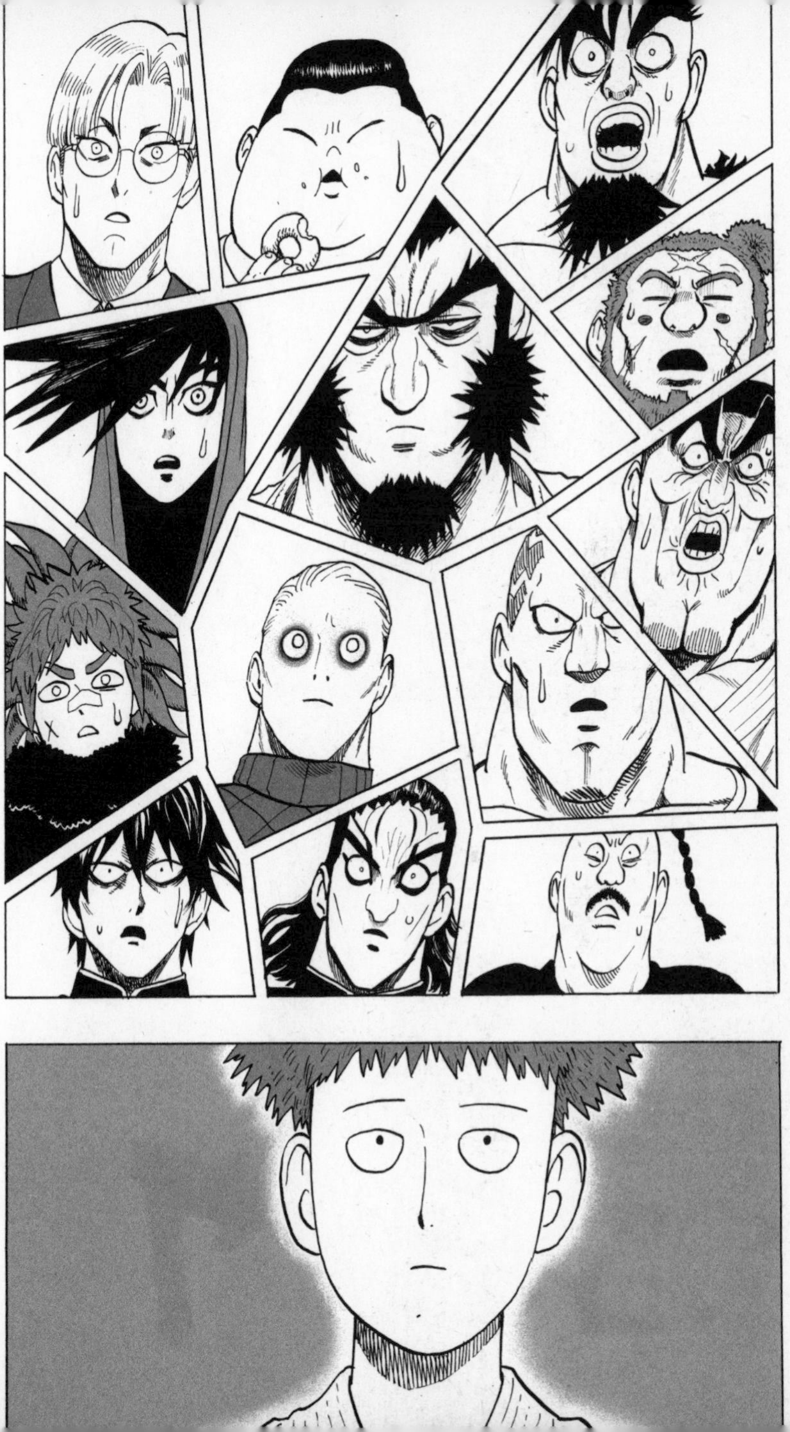

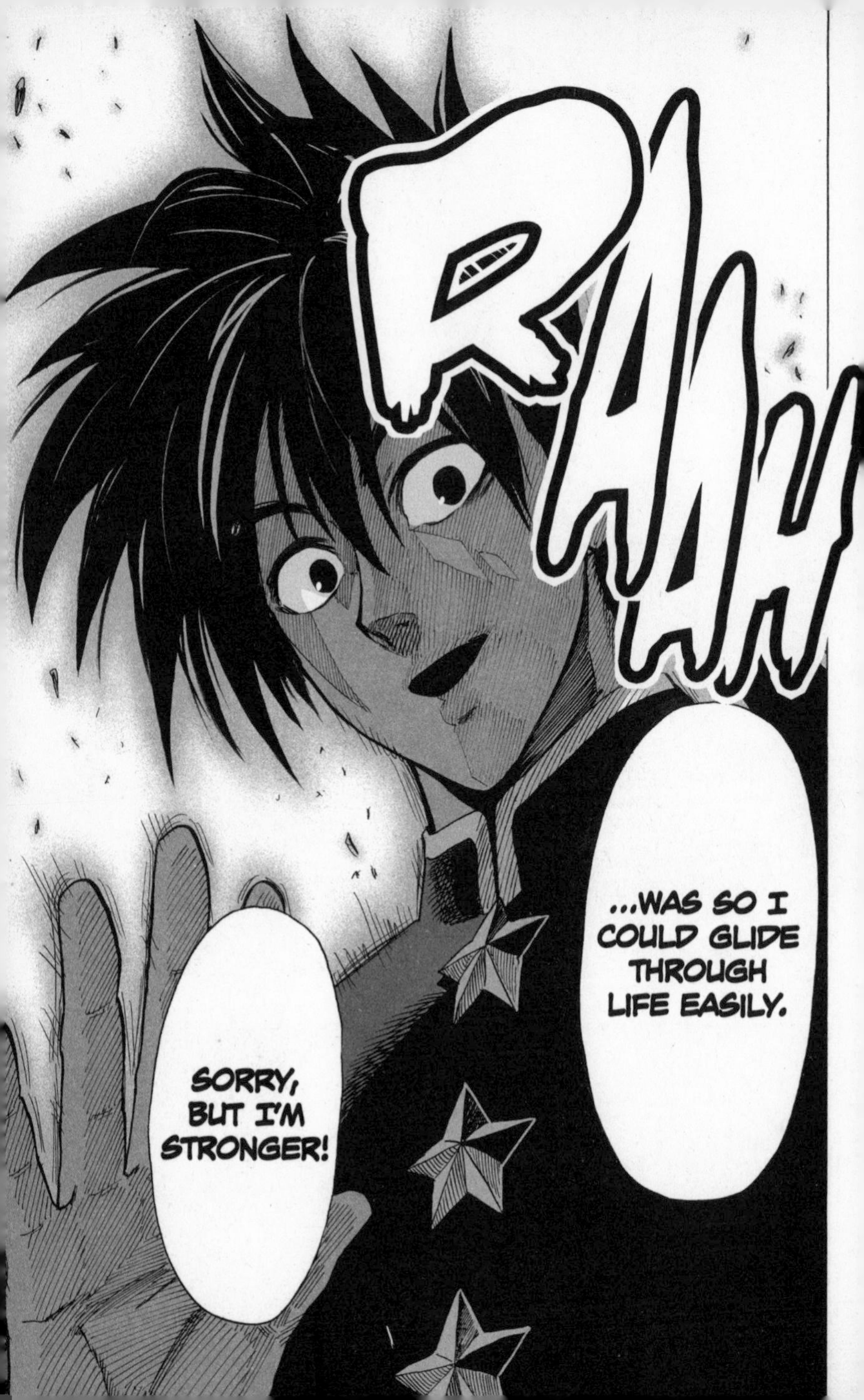
RAAH
...WAS SO I COULD GLIDE THROUGH LIFE EASILY.
SORRY, BUT I'M STRONGER!

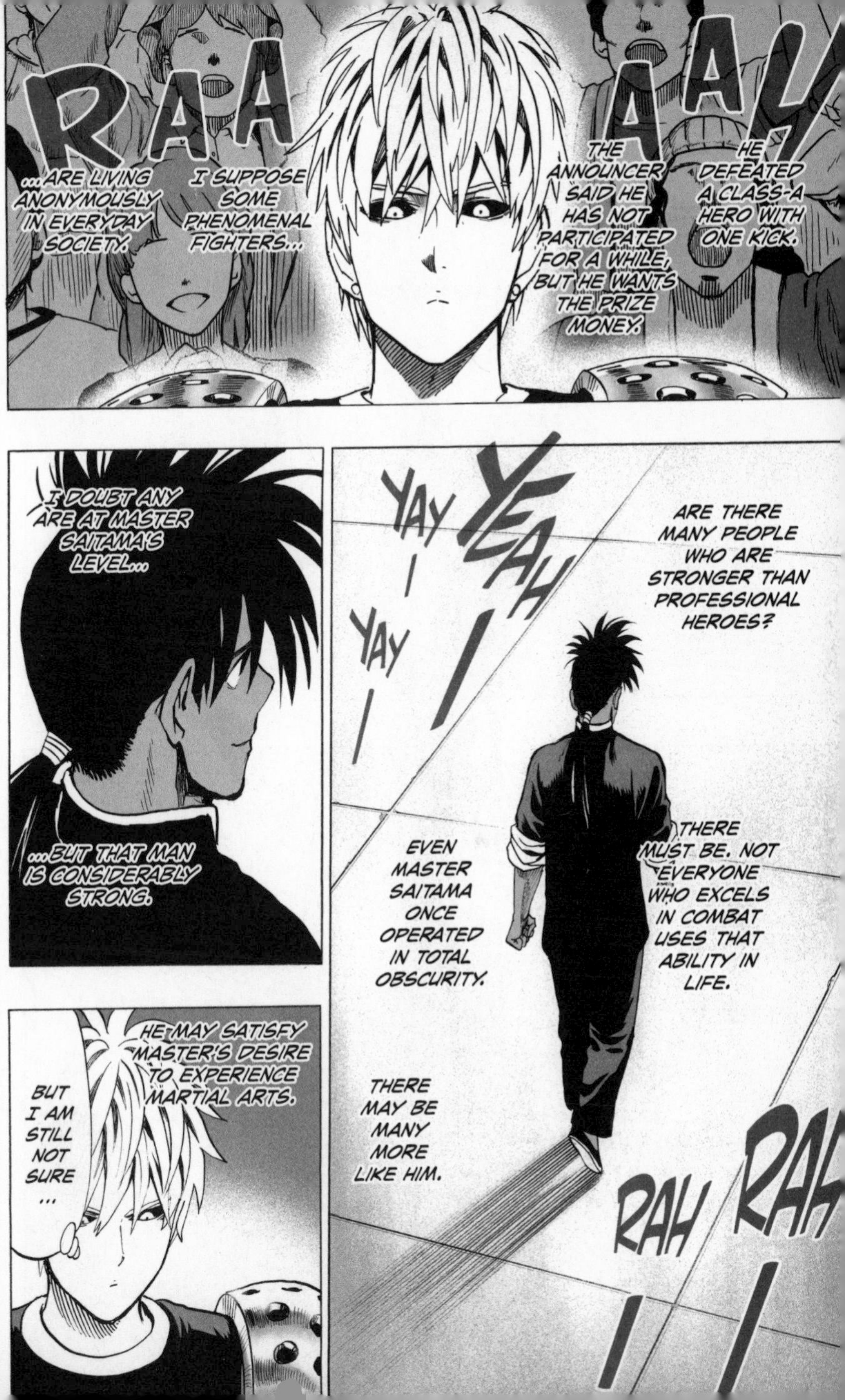
RAA AAH
HE DEFEATED A CLASS-A HERO WITH ONE KICK.
THE ANNOUNCER SAID HE HAS NOT PARTICIPATED FOR A WHILE, BUT HE WANTS THE PRIZE MONEY.
I SUPPOSE SOME PHENOMENAL FIGHTERS...
...ARE LIVING ANONYMOUSLY IN EVERYDAY SOCIETY.
YEAH!
YAY! YAY!
ARE THERE MANY PEOPLE WHO ARE STRONGER THAN PROFESSIONAL HEROES?
THERE MUST BE. NOT EVERYONE WHO EXCELS IN COMBAT USES THAT ABILITY IN LIFE.
EVEN MASTER SAITAMA ONCE OPERATED IN TOTAL OBSCURITY.
THERE MAY BE MANY MORE LIKE HIM.
RAH RAH!!
I DOUBT ANY ARE AT MASTER SAITAMA'S LEVEL...
...BUT THAT MAN IS CONSIDERABLY STRONG.
HE MAY SATISFY MASTER'S DESIRE TO EXPERIENCE MARTIAL ARTS.
BUT I AM STILL NOT SURE ...

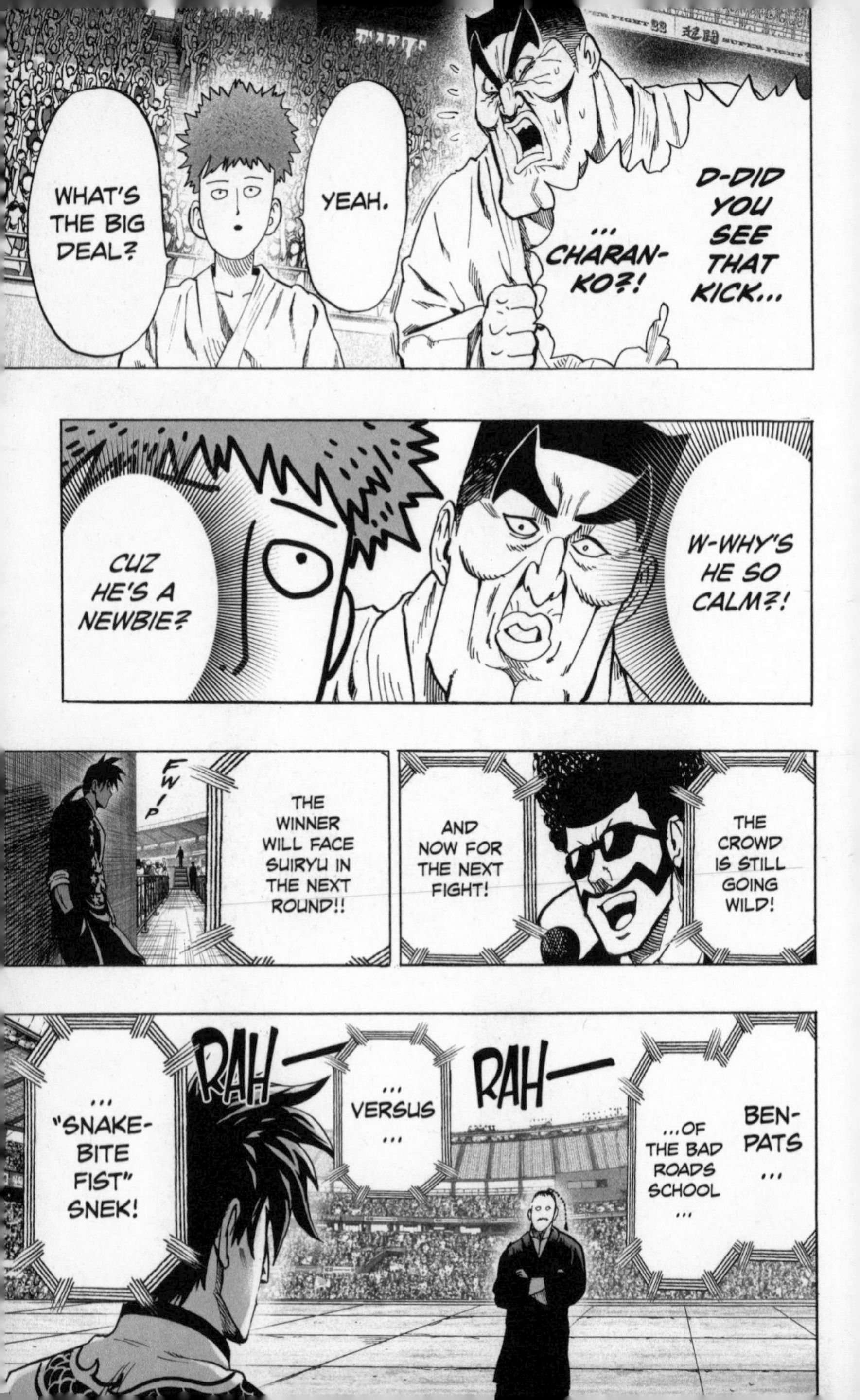
D-DID YOU SEE THAT KICK...
...CHARAN-KO?!
YEAH.
WHAT'S THE BIG DEAL?
W-WHY'S HE SO CALM?!
CUZ HE'S A NEWBIE?
THE CROWD IS STILL GOING WILD!
AND NOW FOR THE NEXT FIGHT!
THE WINNER WILL FACE SUIRYU IN THE NEXT ROUND!!
FWIP
BEN-PATS...
...OF THE BAD ROADS SCHOOL...
RAH—
RAH—
...VERSUS...
..."SNAKE-BITE FIST" SNEK!

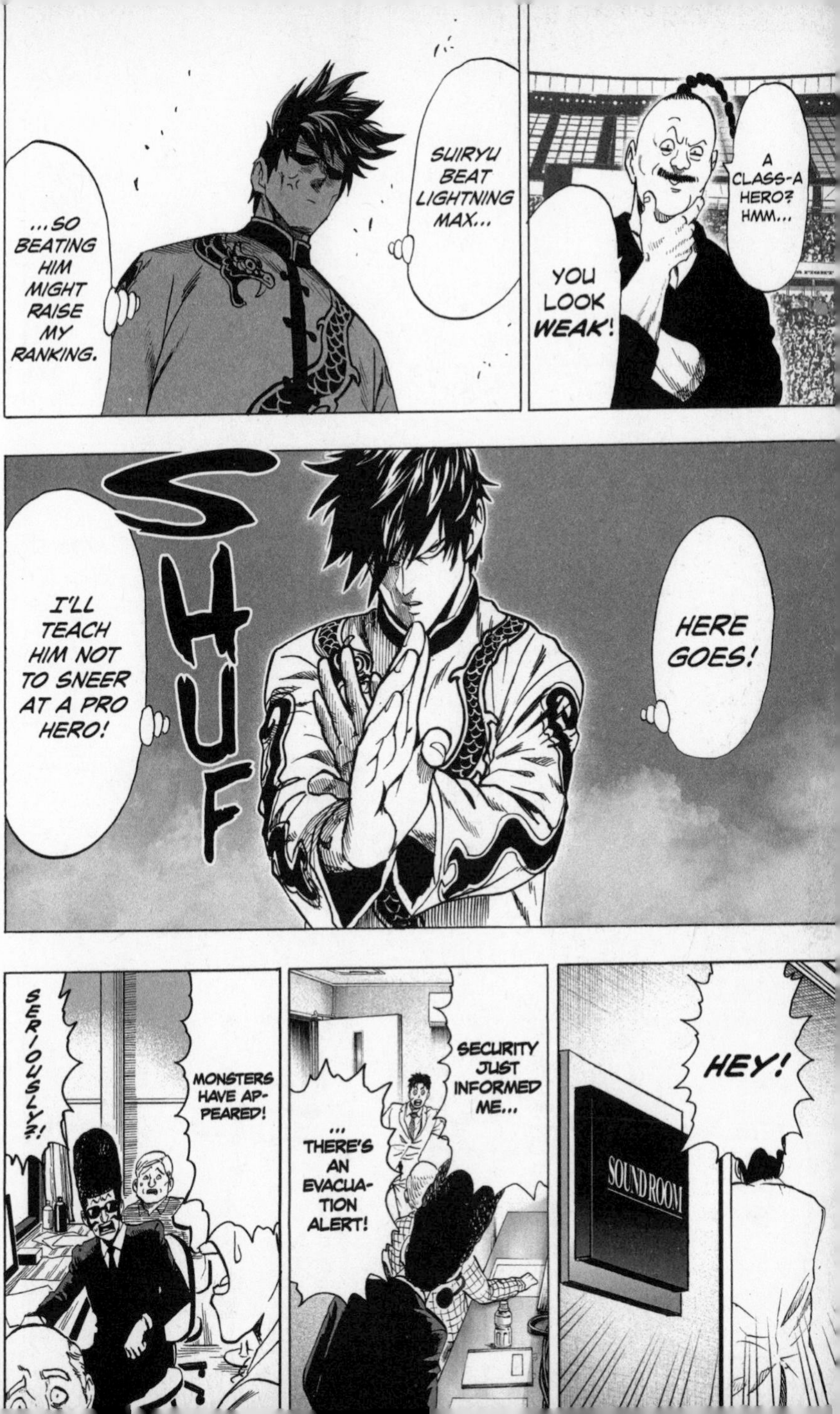
A CLASS-A HERO? HMM...
YOU LOOK WEAK!
SUIRYU BEAT LIGHTNING MAX...
...SO BEATING HIM MIGHT RAISE MY RANKING.
HERE GOES!
SHUF
I'LL TEACH HIM NOT TO SNEER AT A PRO HERO!
HEY!
SOUND ROOM
SECURITY JUST INFORMED ME...
...THERE'S AN EVACUATION ALERT!
MONSTERS HAVE APPEARED!
SERIOUSLY?!

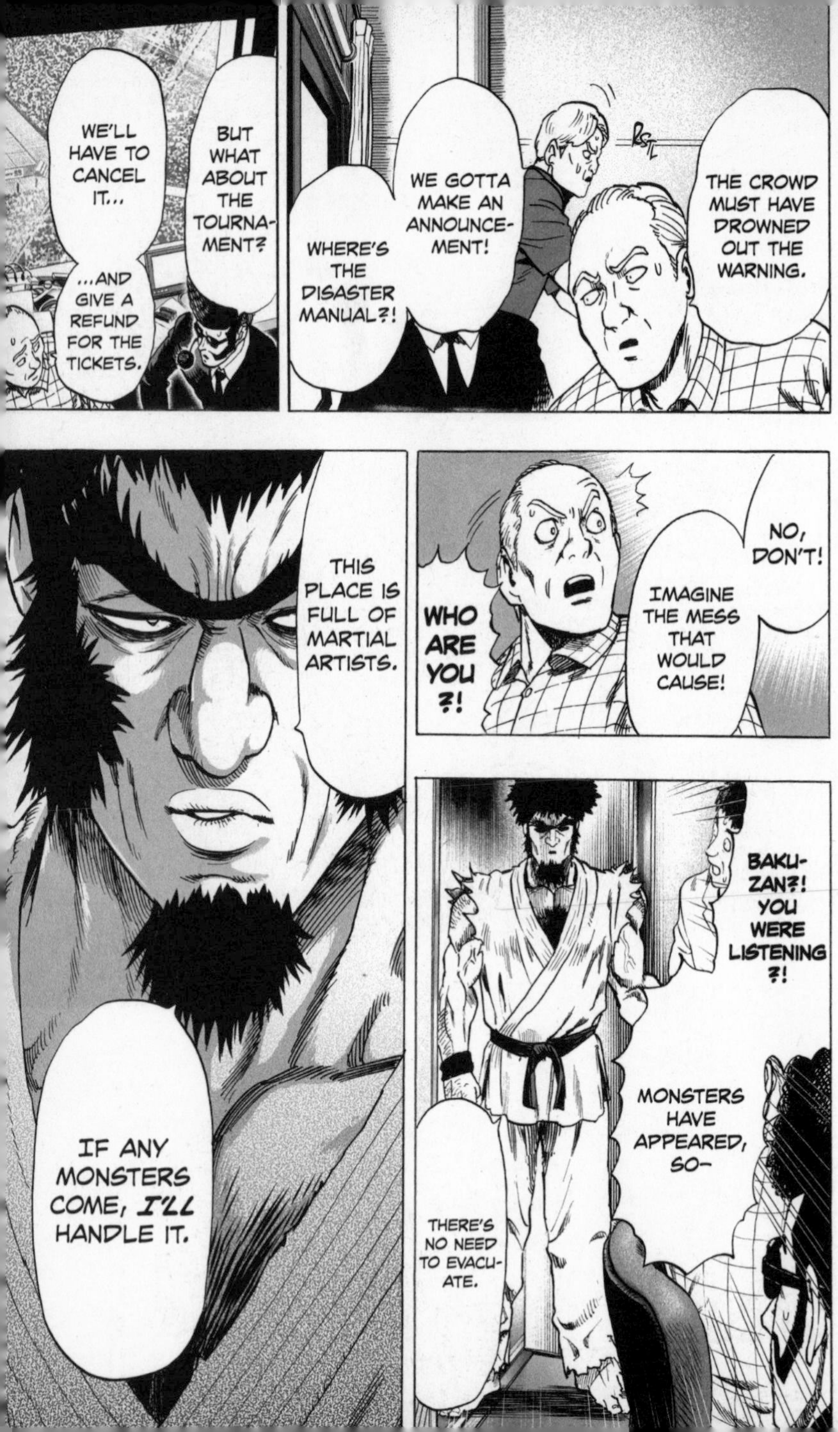
THE CROWD MUST HAVE DROWNED OUT THE WARNING.
RSTL
WE GOTTA MAKE AN ANNOUNCEMENT!
WHERE'S THE DISASTER MANUAL?!
BUT WHAT ABOUT THE TOURNAMENT?
WE'LL HAVE TO CANCEL IT...
...AND GIVE A REFUND FOR THE TICKETS.
NO, DON'T!
IMAGINE THE MESS THAT WOULD CAUSE!
WHO ARE YOU?!
BAKUZAN?! YOU WERE LISTENING?!
MONSTERS HAVE APPEARED, SO—
THERE'S NO NEED TO EVACUATE.
THIS PLACE IS FULL OF MARTIAL ARTISTS.
IF ANY MONSTERS COME, *I'LL* HANDLE IT.

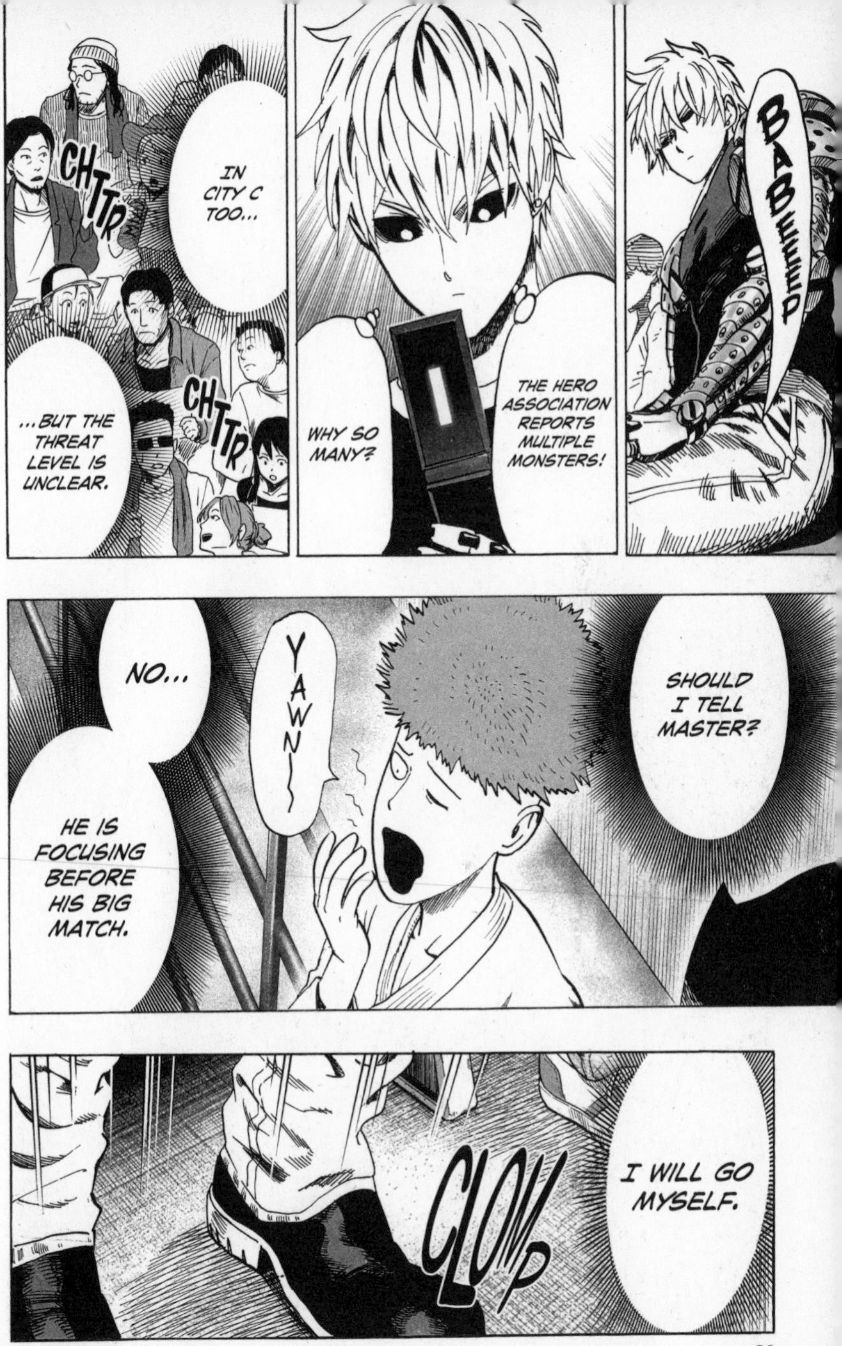
BABEEEP
THE HERO ASSOCIATION REPORTS MULTIPLE MONSTERS!
WHY SO MANY?
IN CITY C TOO...
CHTTR
CHTTR
...BUT THE THREAT LEVEL IS UNCLEAR.
SHOULD I TELL MASTER?
YAWN
NO...
HE IS FOCUSING BEFORE HIS BIG MATCH.
I WILL GO MYSELF.
CLOMP

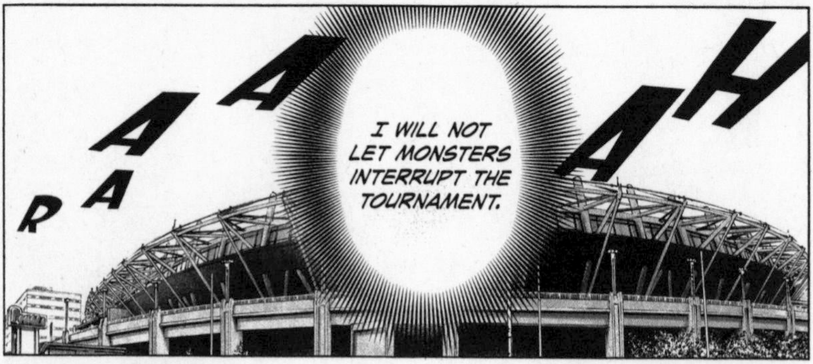
RAAAAAH
I WILL NOT LET MONSTERS INTERRUPT THE TOURNAMENT.

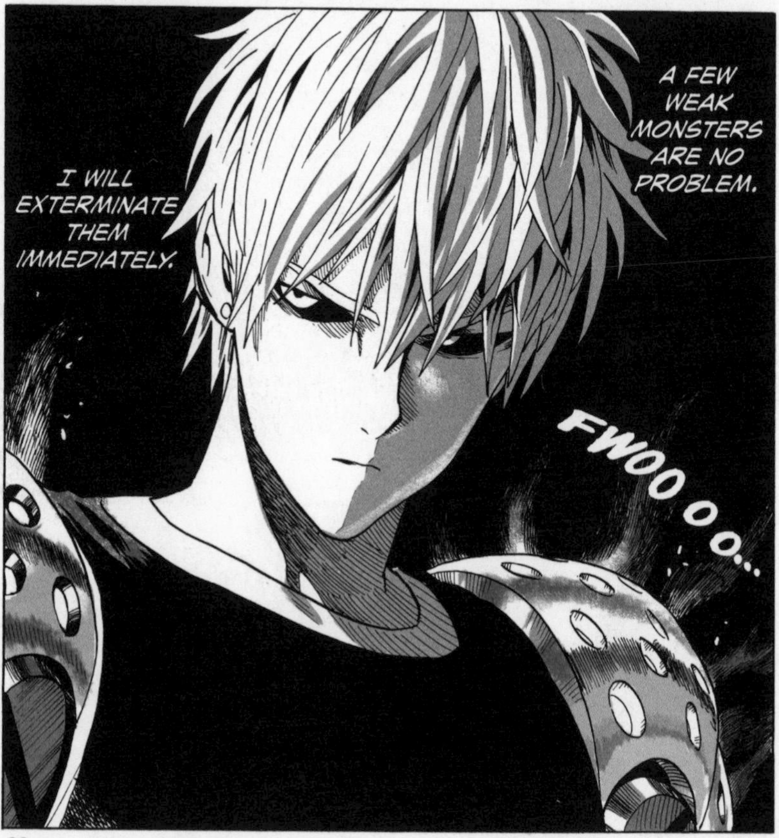
A FEW WEAK MONSTERS ARE NO PROBLEM.
I WILL EXTERMINATE THEM IMMEDIATELY.
FWOOOOO...

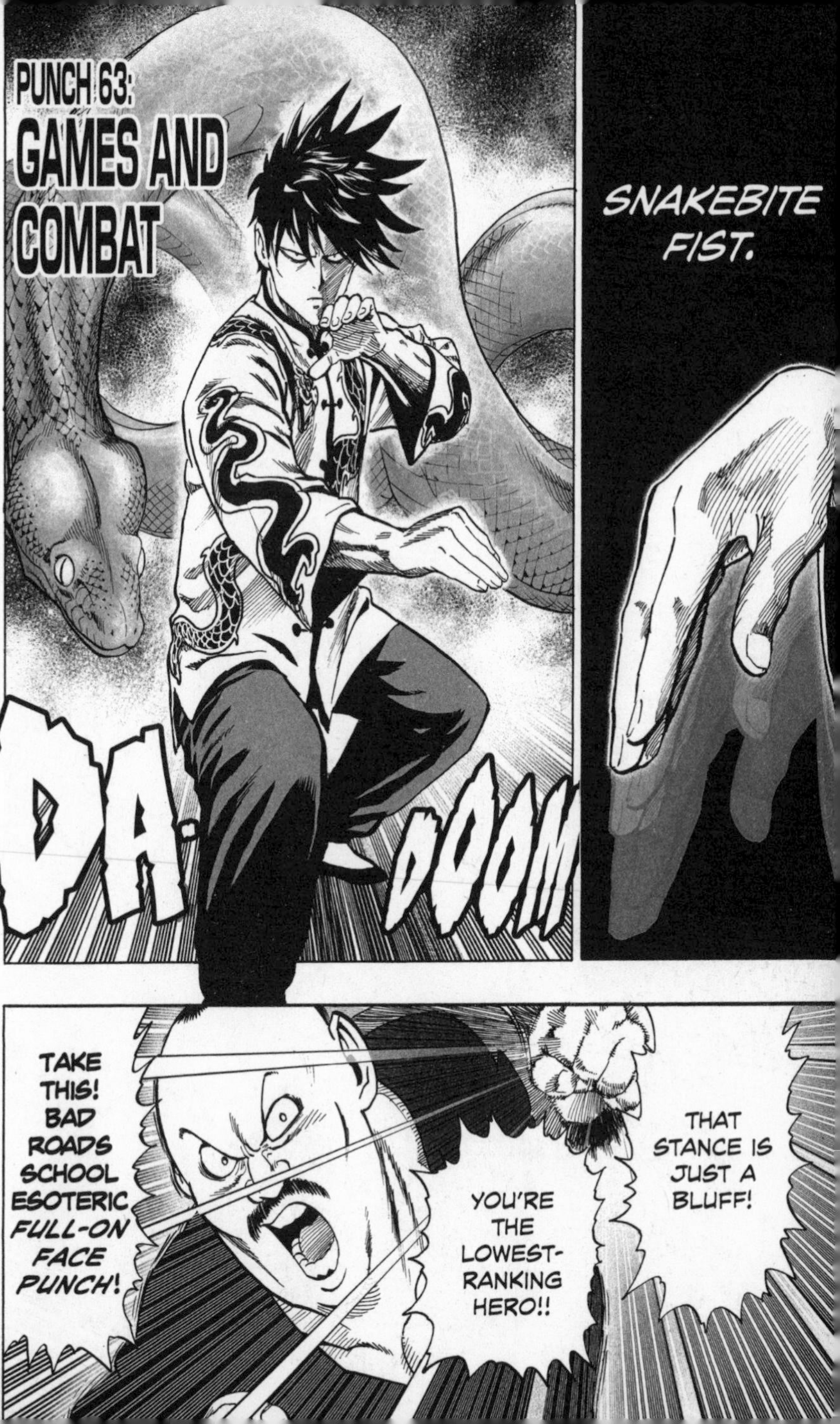
SNAKEBITE FIST.
PUNCH 63: GAMES AND COMBAT
DA-DOOM
THAT STANCE IS JUST A BLUFF!
YOU'RE THE LOWEST-RANKING HERO!!
TAKE THIS! BAD ROADS SCHOOL ESOTERIC *FULL-ON FACE PUNCH*!

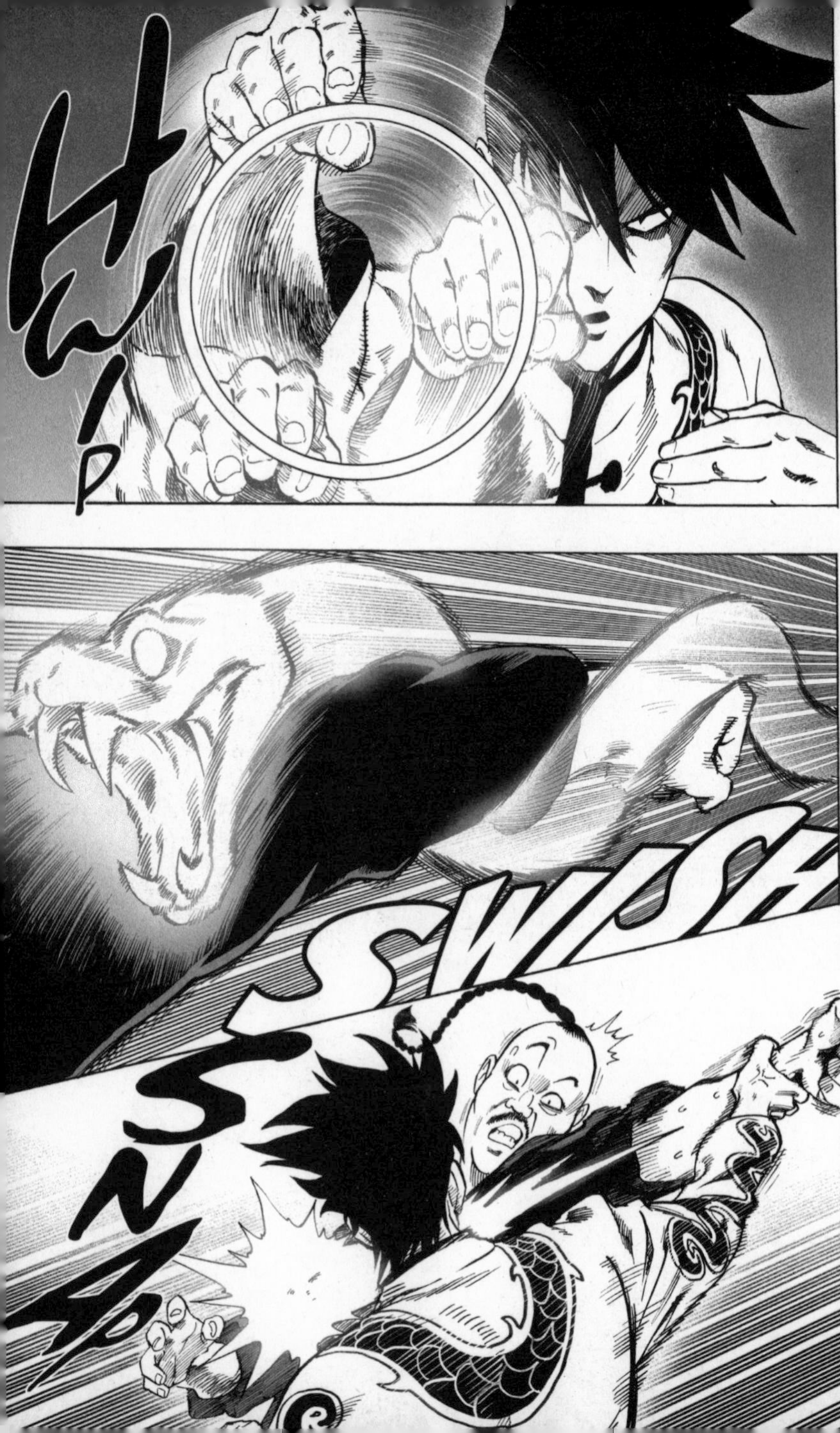
SWISH
SNAP

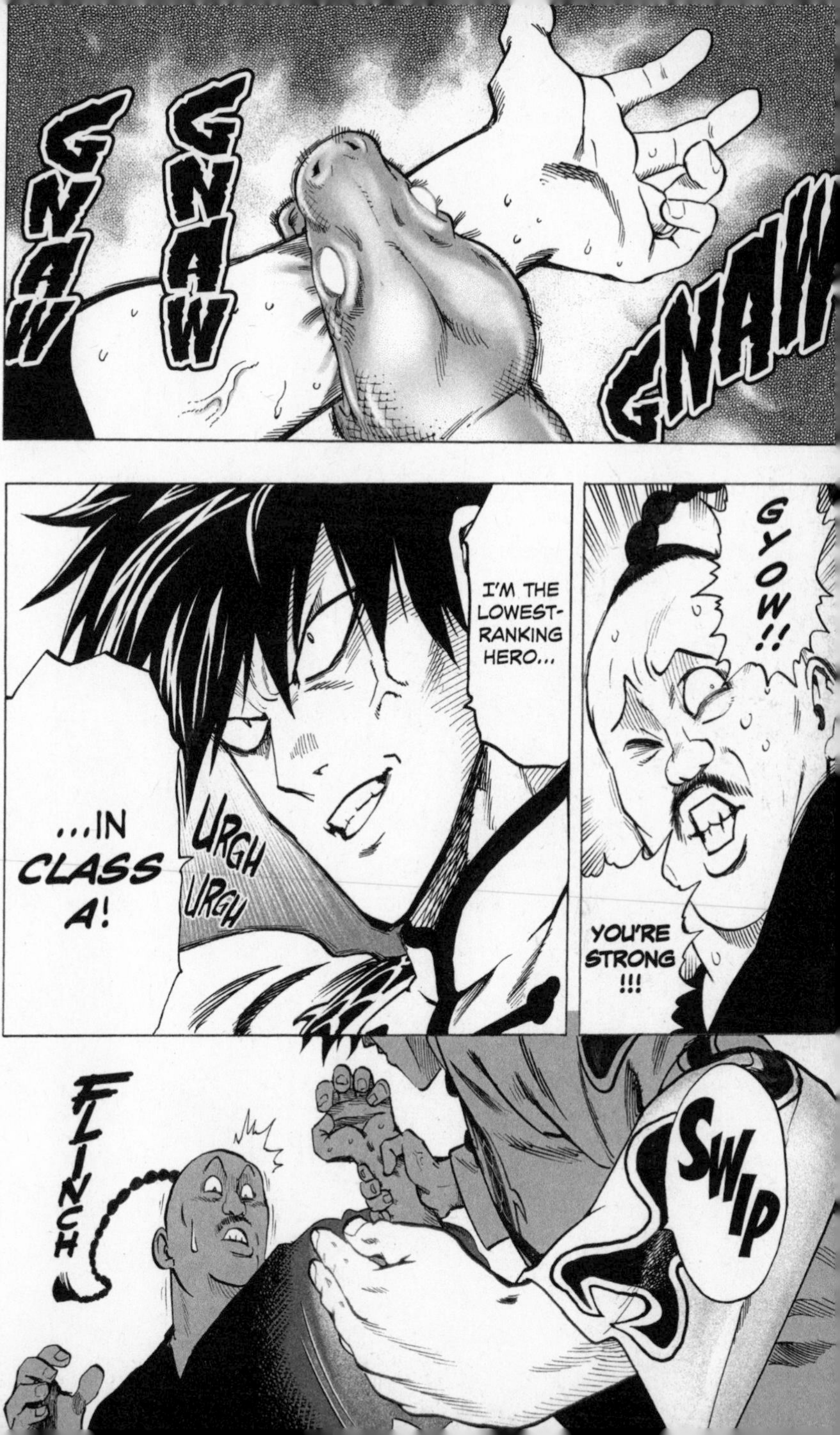
GNAW
GNAW
GNAW
GYOW!!
YOU'RE STRONG!!!
I'M THE LOWEST-RANKING HERO...
URGH
URGH
...IN CLASS A!
SWIP
FLINCH

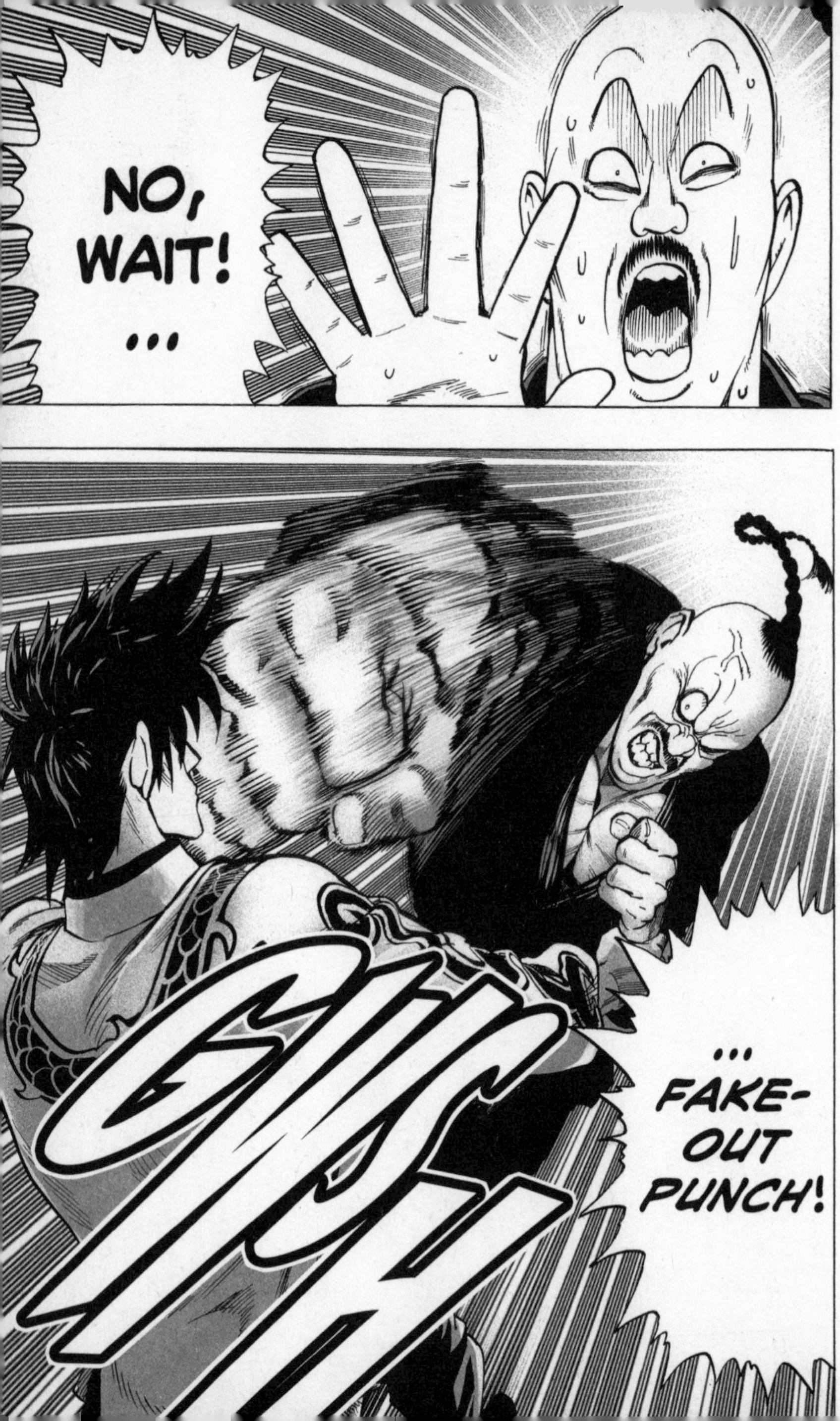
NO, WAIT! ...
... FAKE-OUT PUNCH!

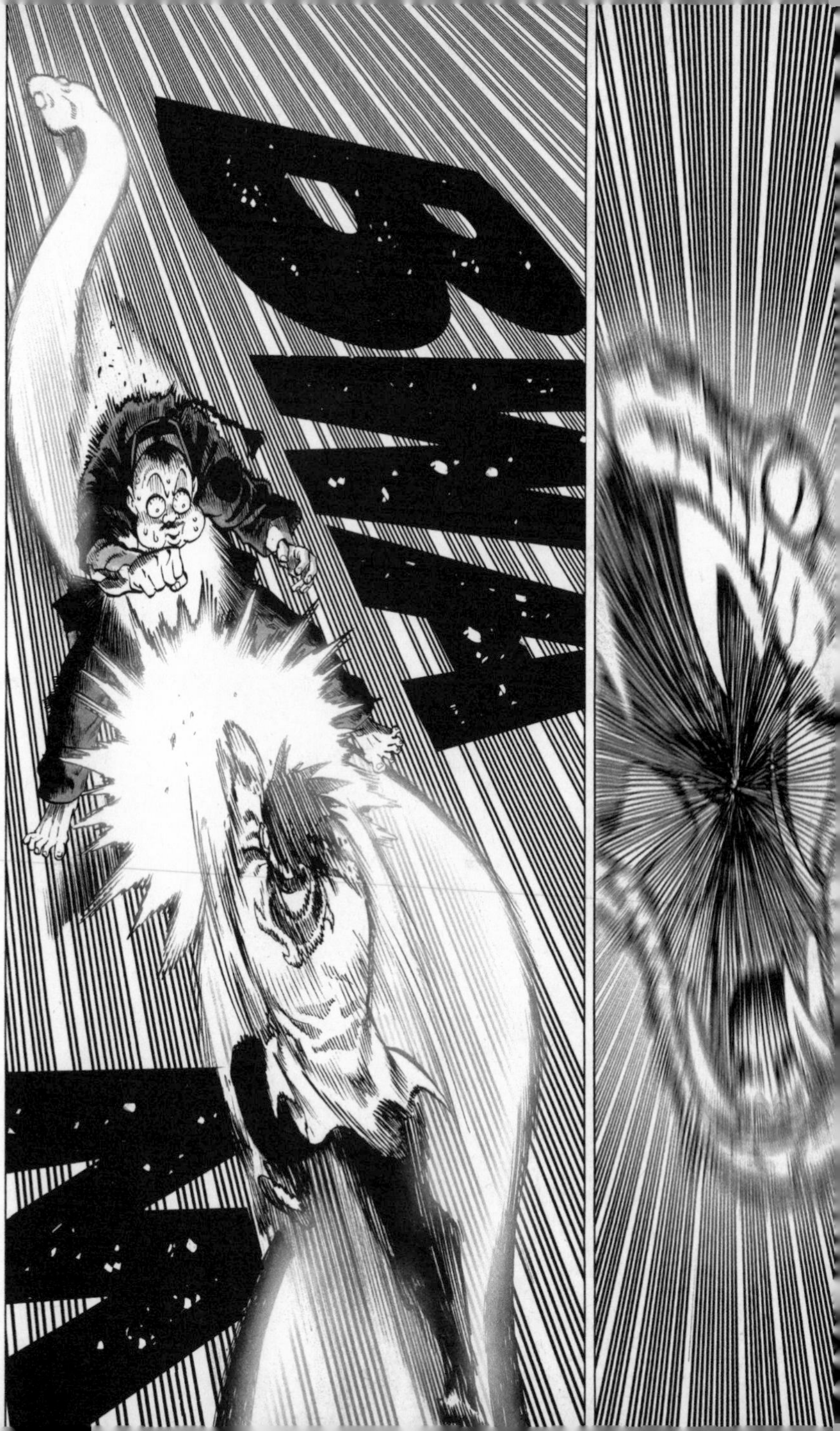

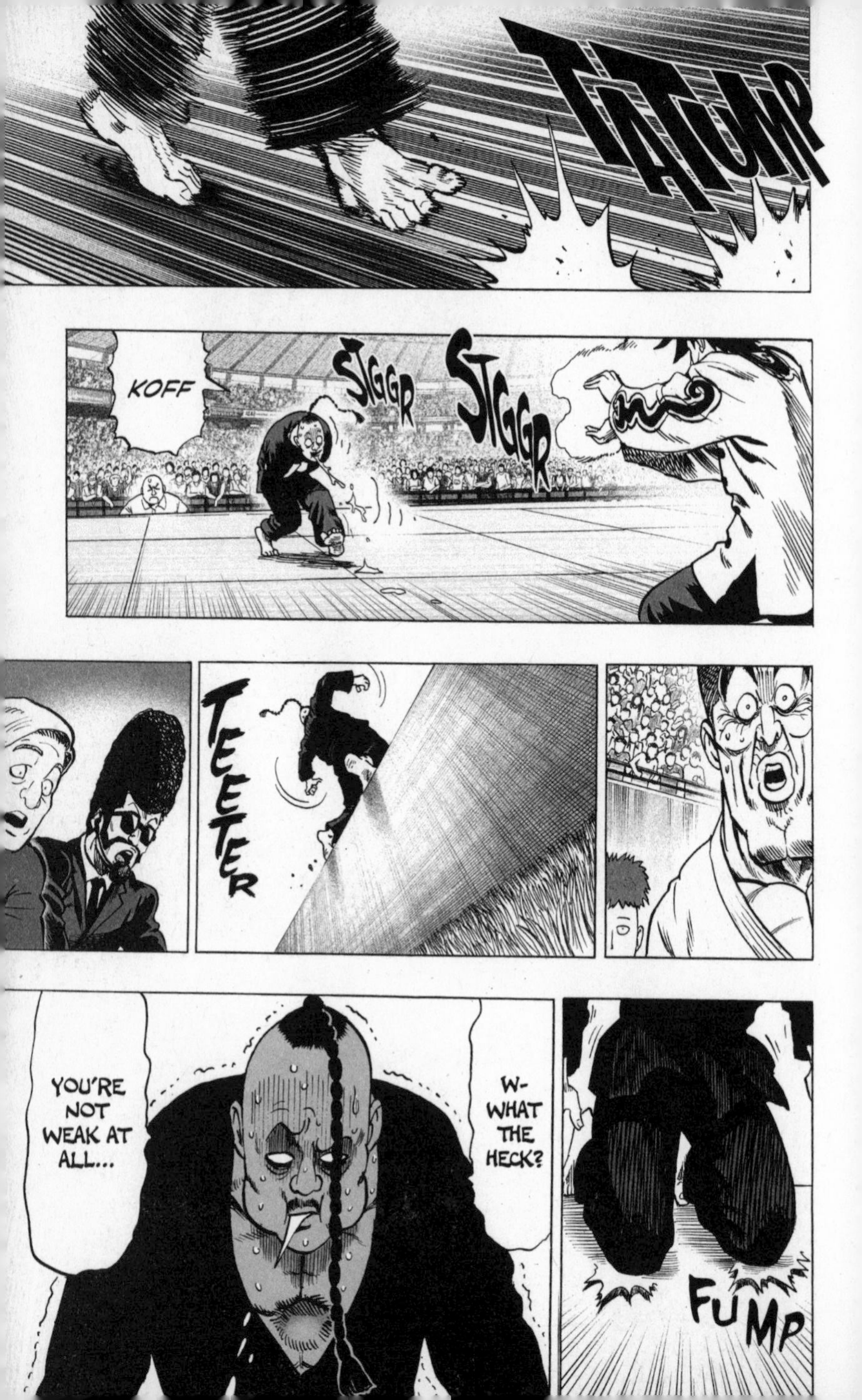
THUMP
STGGR
STGGR
KOFF
TEETER
FUMP
W- WHAT THE HECK?
YOU'RE NOT WEAK AT ALL...

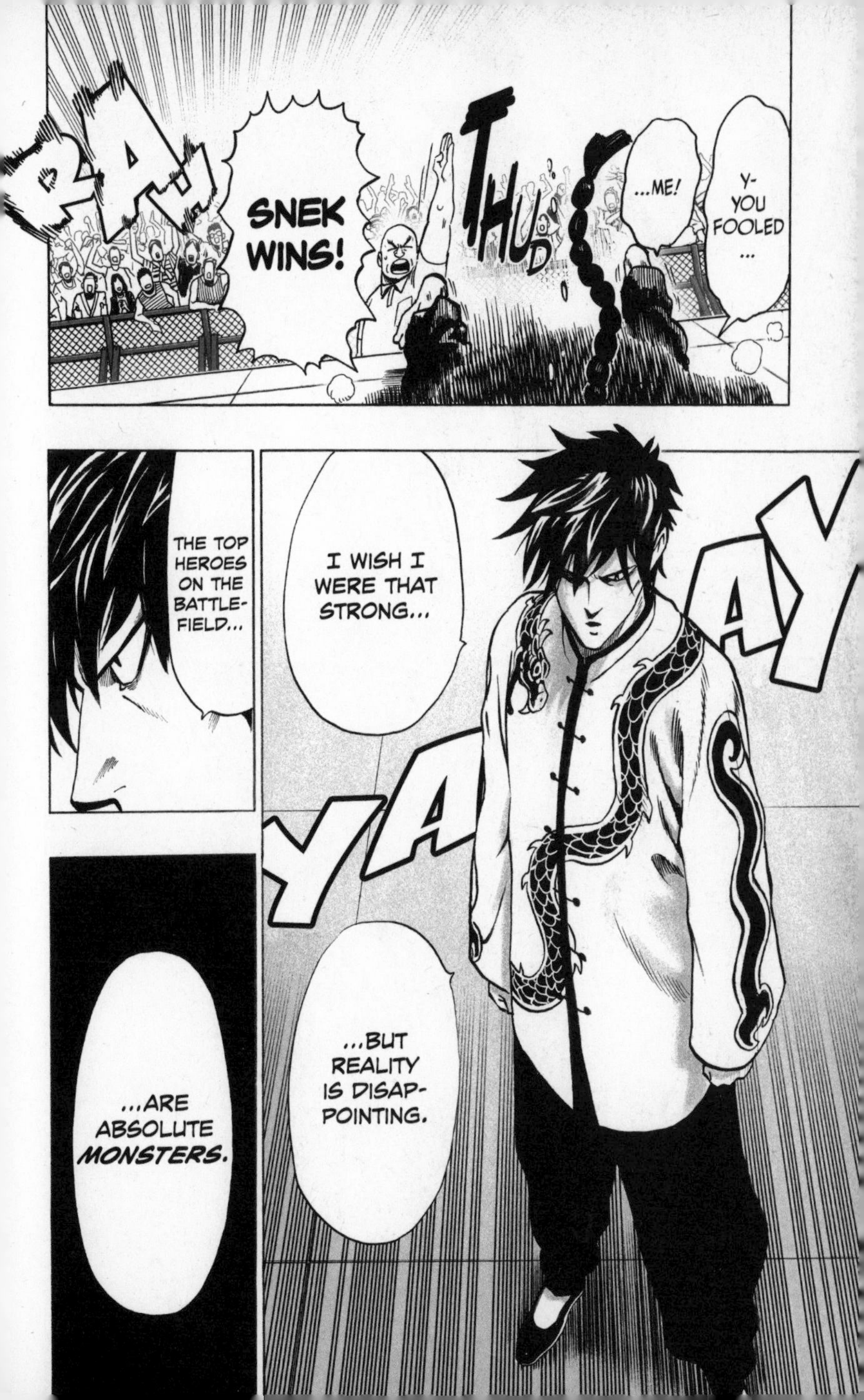
Y- YOU FOOLED ...
...ME!
THUD
SNEK WINS!
RA!
I WISH I WERE THAT STRONG...
YAAY
...BUT REALITY IS DISAP-POINTING.
THE TOP HEROES ON THE BATTLE-FIELD...
...ARE ABSOLUTE MONSTERS.

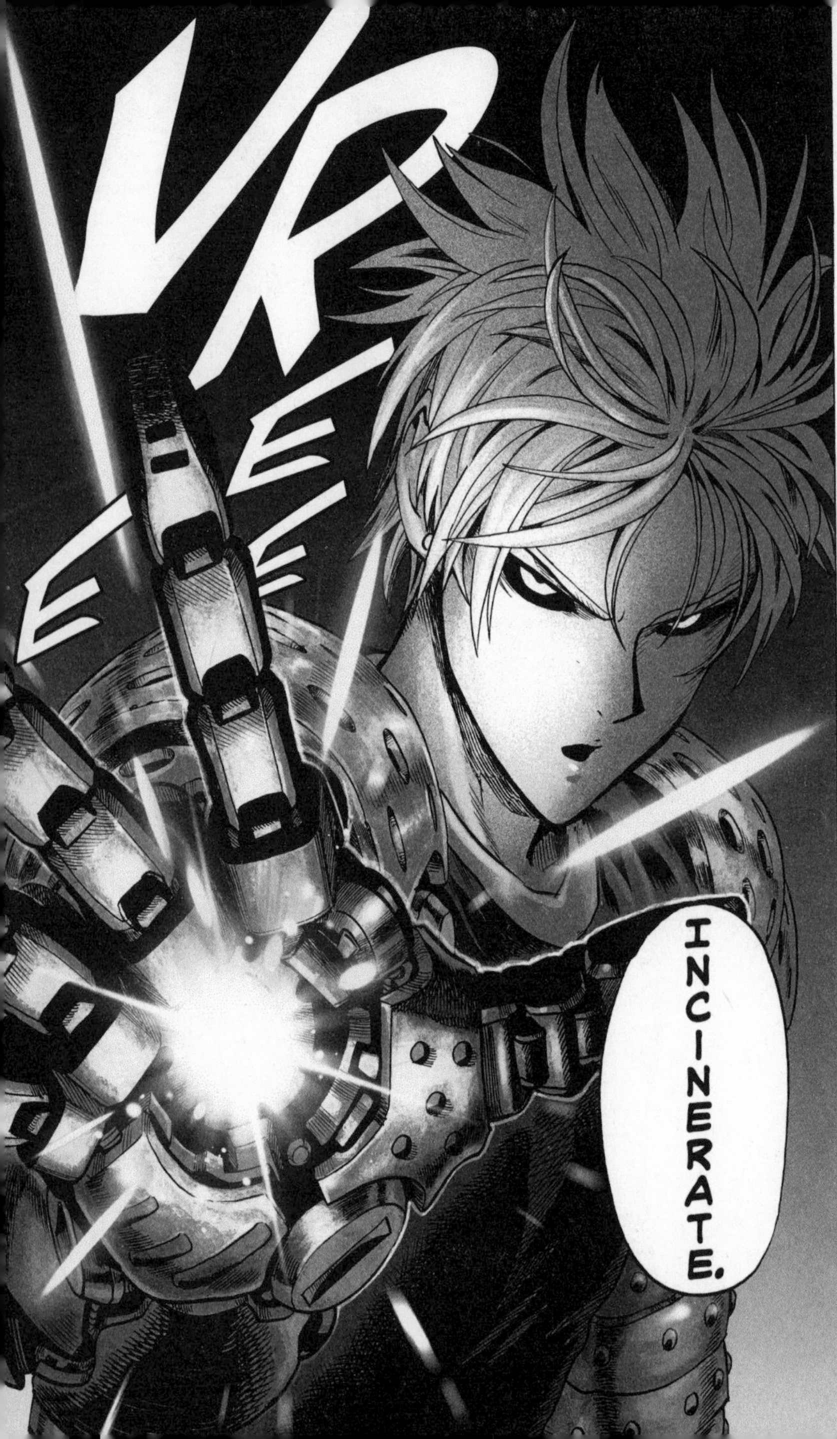
INCINERATE.

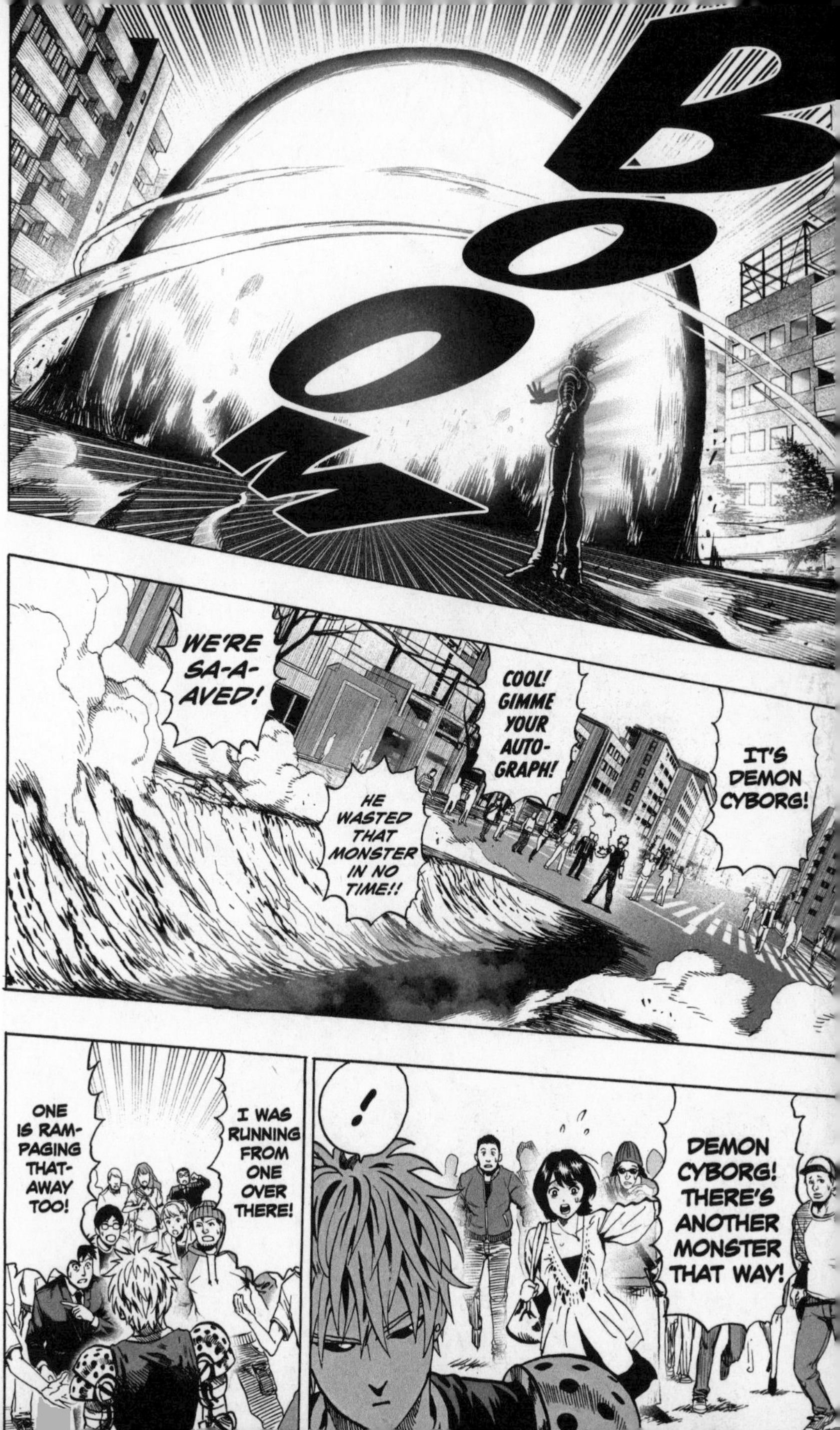
BOOM
IT'S DEMON CYBORG!
COOL! GIMME YOUR AUTO-GRAPH!
HE WASTED THAT MONSTER IN NO TIME!!
WE'RE SA-A-AVED!
DEMON CYBORG! THERE'S ANOTHER MONSTER THAT WAY!
!
I WAS RUNNING FROM ONE OVER THERE!
ONE IS RAM-PAGING THAT-AWAY TOO!

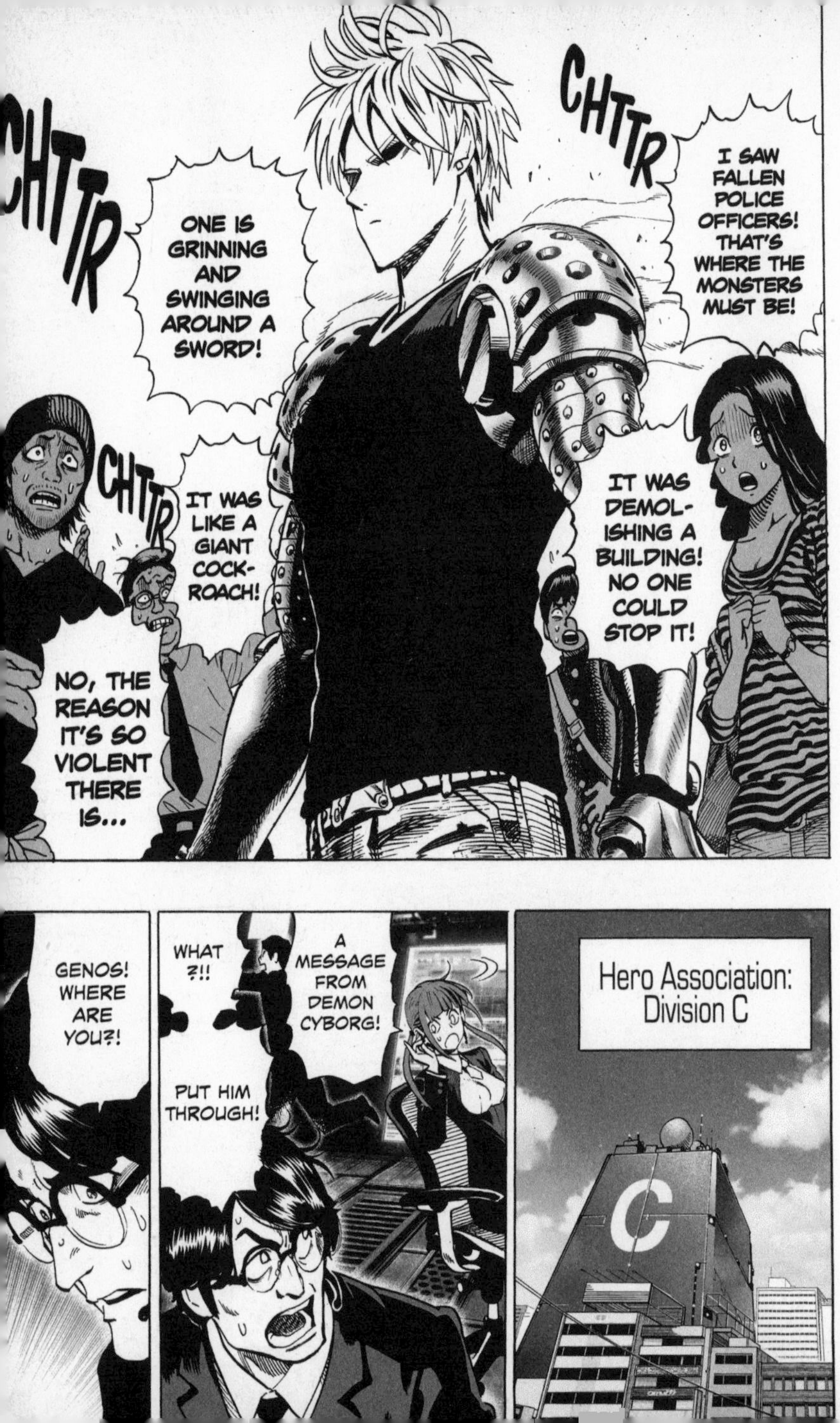
CHTTR
I SAW FALLEN POLICE OFFICERS! THAT'S WHERE THE MONSTERS MUST BE!
CHTTR
ONE IS GRINNING AND SWINGING AROUND A SWORD!
IT WAS DEMOL-ISHING A BUILDING! NO ONE COULD STOP IT!
CHTTR
IT WAS LIKE A GIANT COCK-ROACH!
NO, THE REASON IT'S SO VIOLENT THERE IS...
Hero Association: Division C
A MESSAGE FROM DEMON CYBORG!
WHAT?!!
PUT HIM THROUGH!
GENOS! WHERE ARE YOU?!

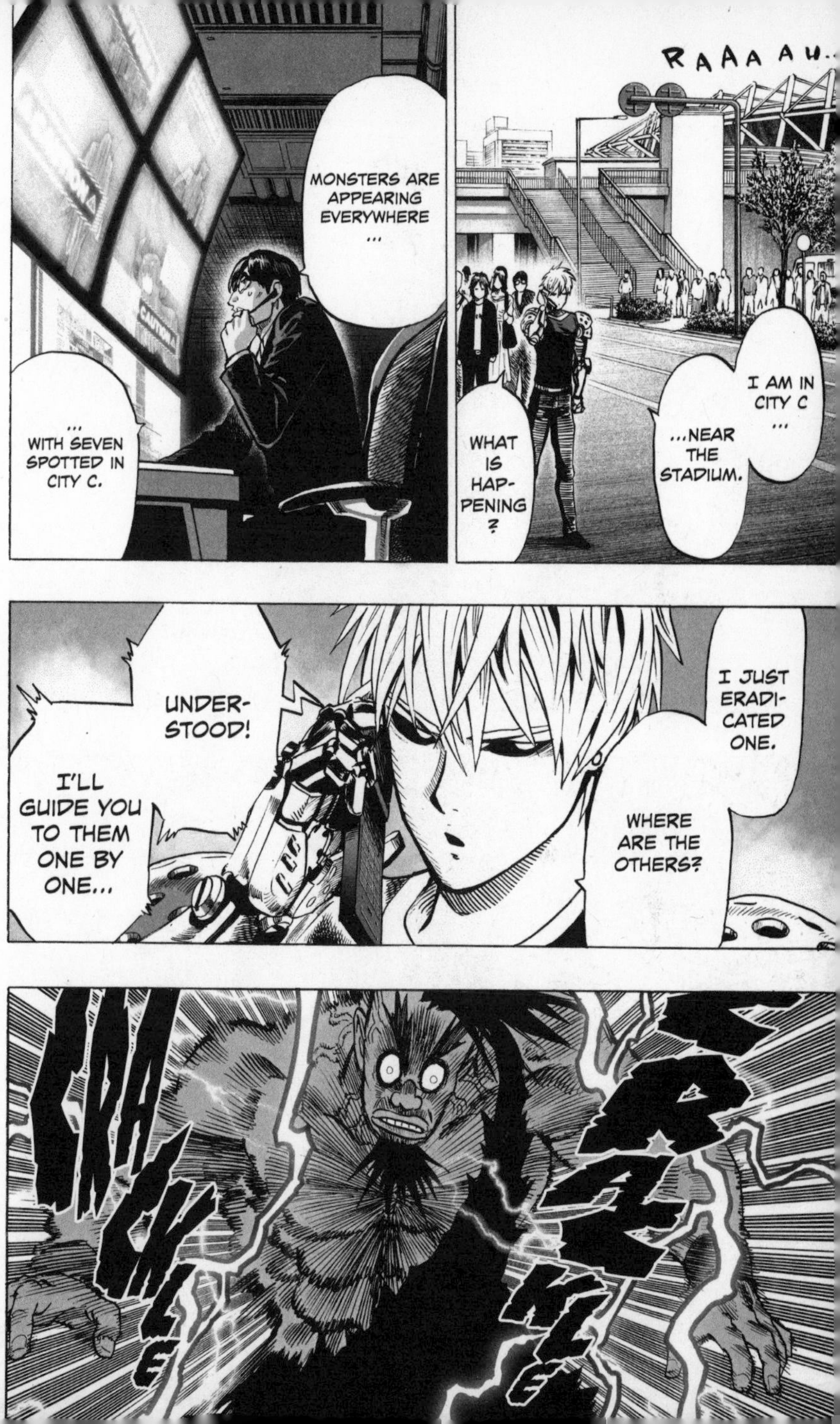
RAAAAH..
I AM IN CITY C ...
...NEAR THE STADIUM.
WHAT IS HAPPENING?
MONSTERS ARE APPEARING EVERYWHERE ...
... WITH SEVEN SPOTTED IN CITY C.
I JUST ERADICATED ONE.
WHERE ARE THE OTHERS?
UNDERSTOOD!
I'LL GUIDE YOU TO THEM ONE BY ONE...

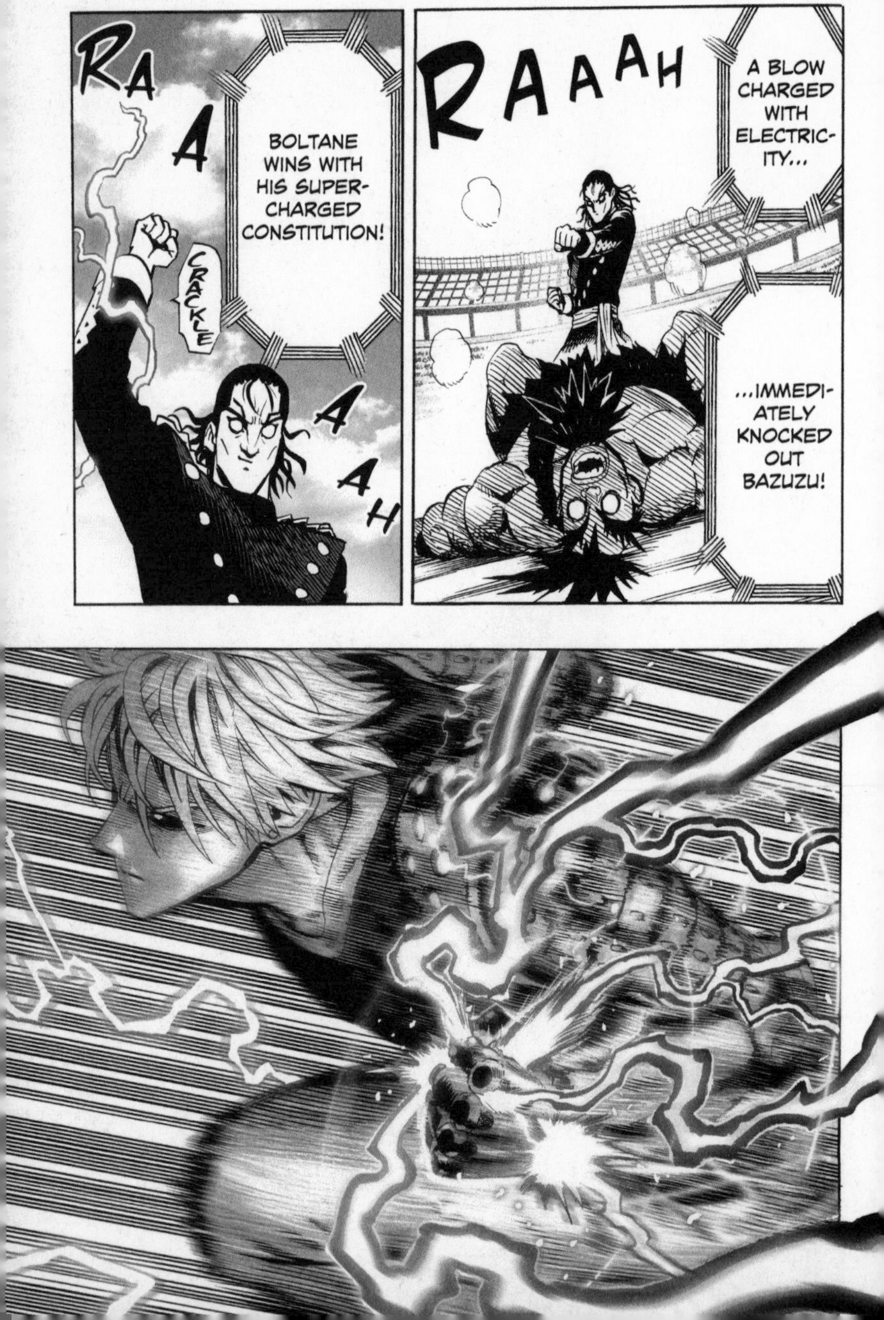
RAAAH
A BLOW CHARGED WITH ELECTRICITY...
...IMMEDIATELY KNOCKED OUT BAZUZU!
RAAAAH
BOLTANE WINS WITH HIS SUPERCHARGED CONSTITUTION!
CRACKLE

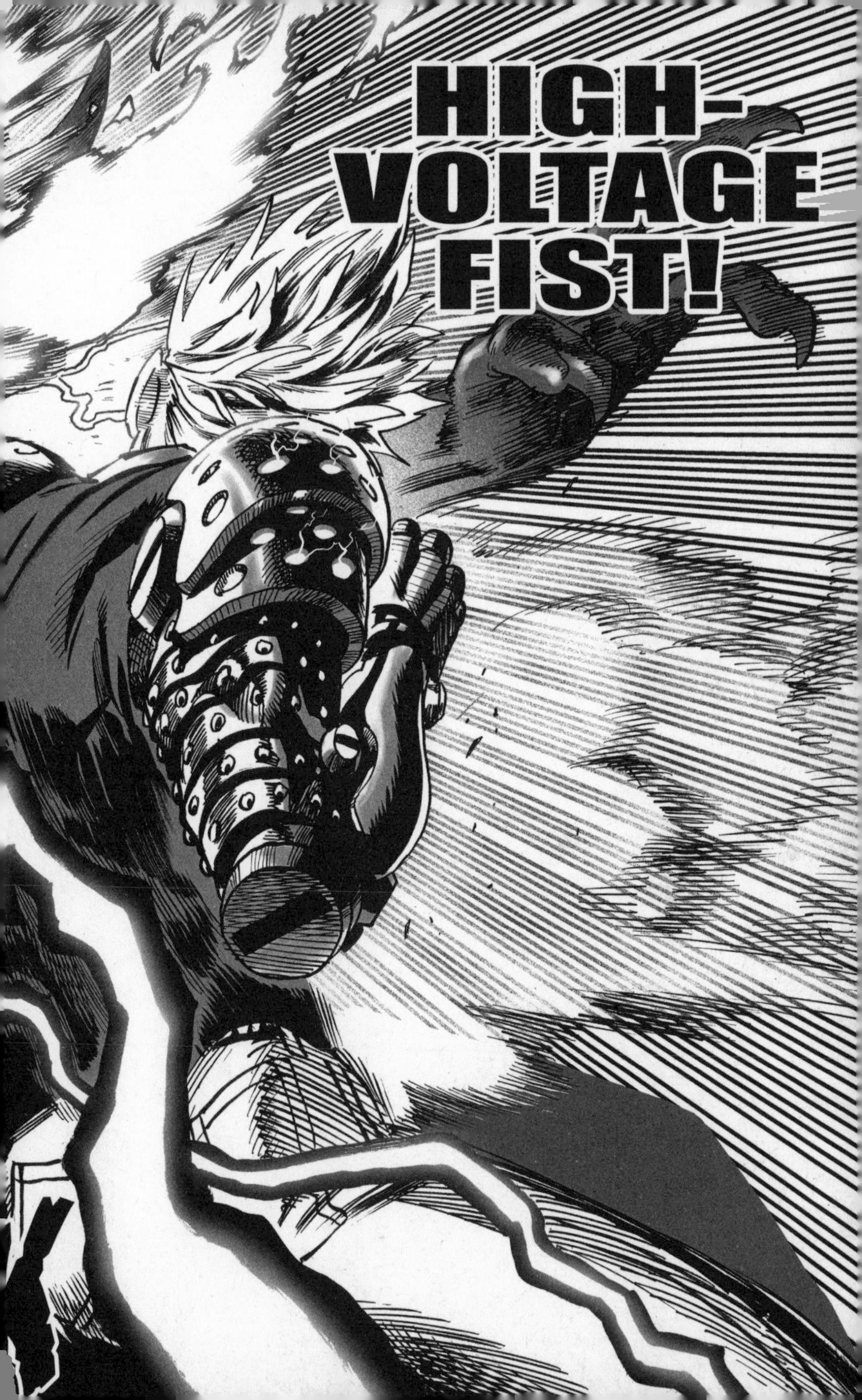
HIGH-
VOLTAGE
FIST!

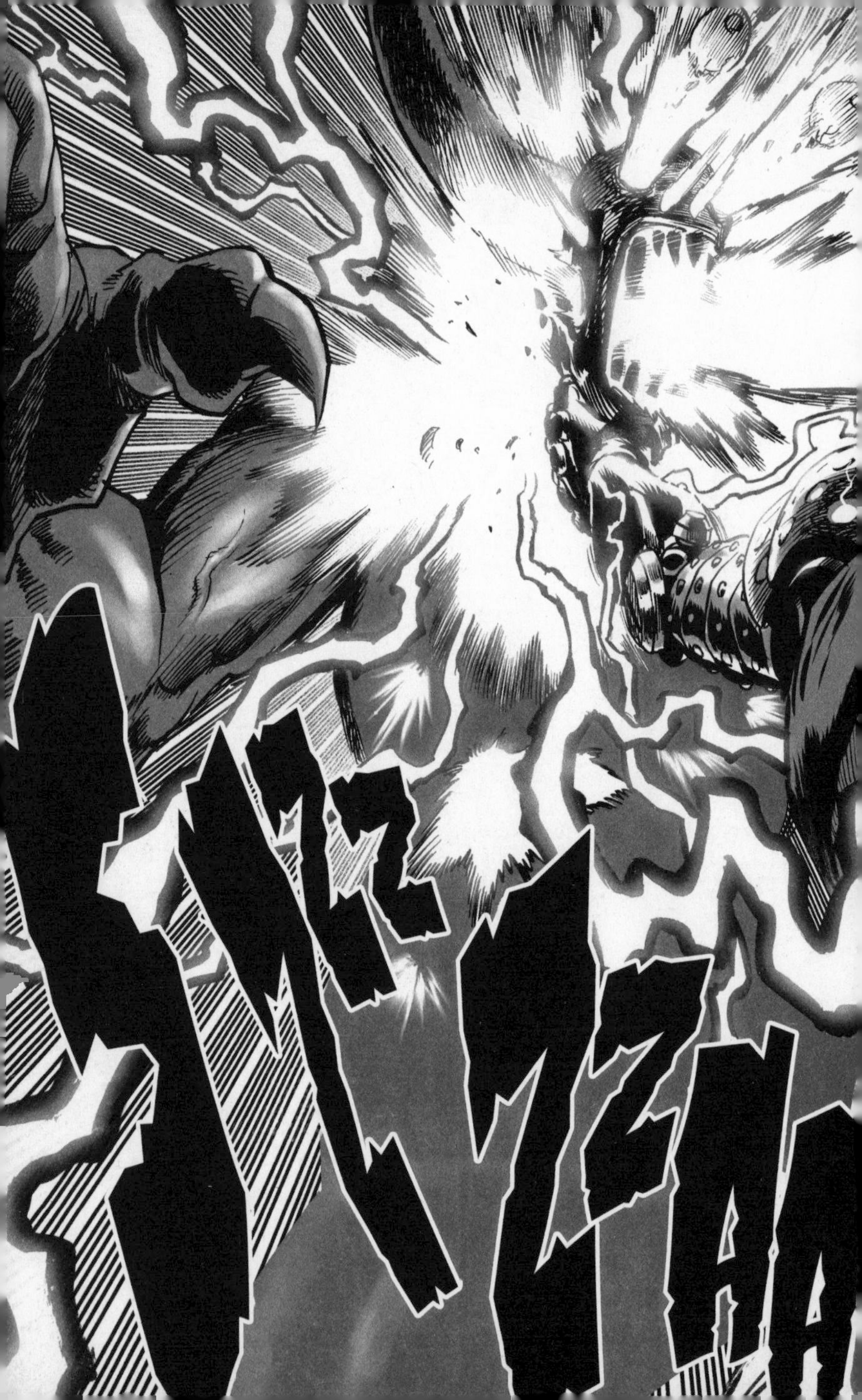

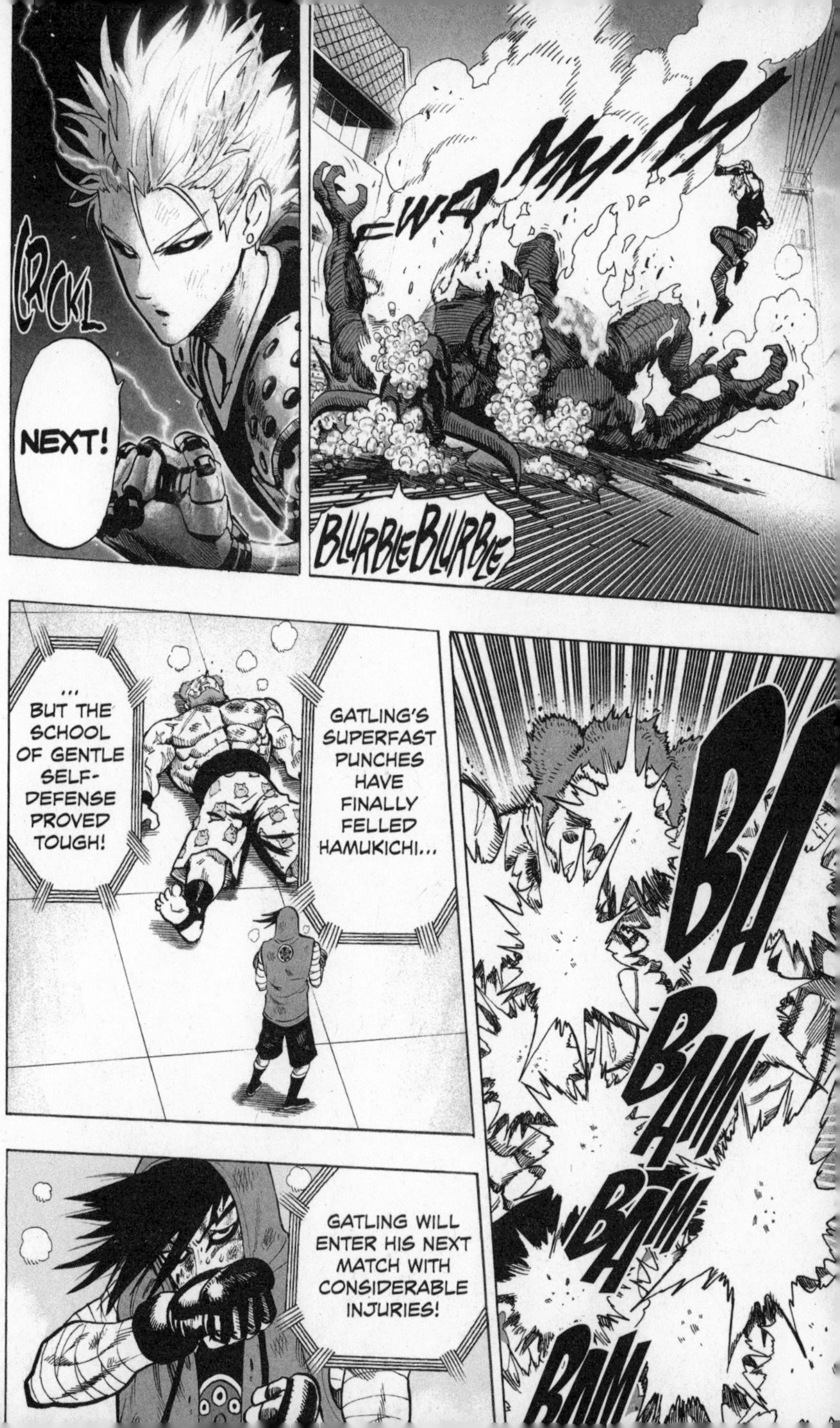
FWAMMMM
BLURBLEBLURBLE
CRCKL
NEXT!
BA BAM BAM BA BAM
GATLING'S SUPERFAST PUNCHES HAVE FINALLY FELLED HAMUKICHI...
... BUT THE SCHOOL OF GENTLE SELF-DEFENSE PROVED TOUGH!
GATLING WILL ENTER HIS NEXT MATCH WITH CONSIDERABLE INJURIES!

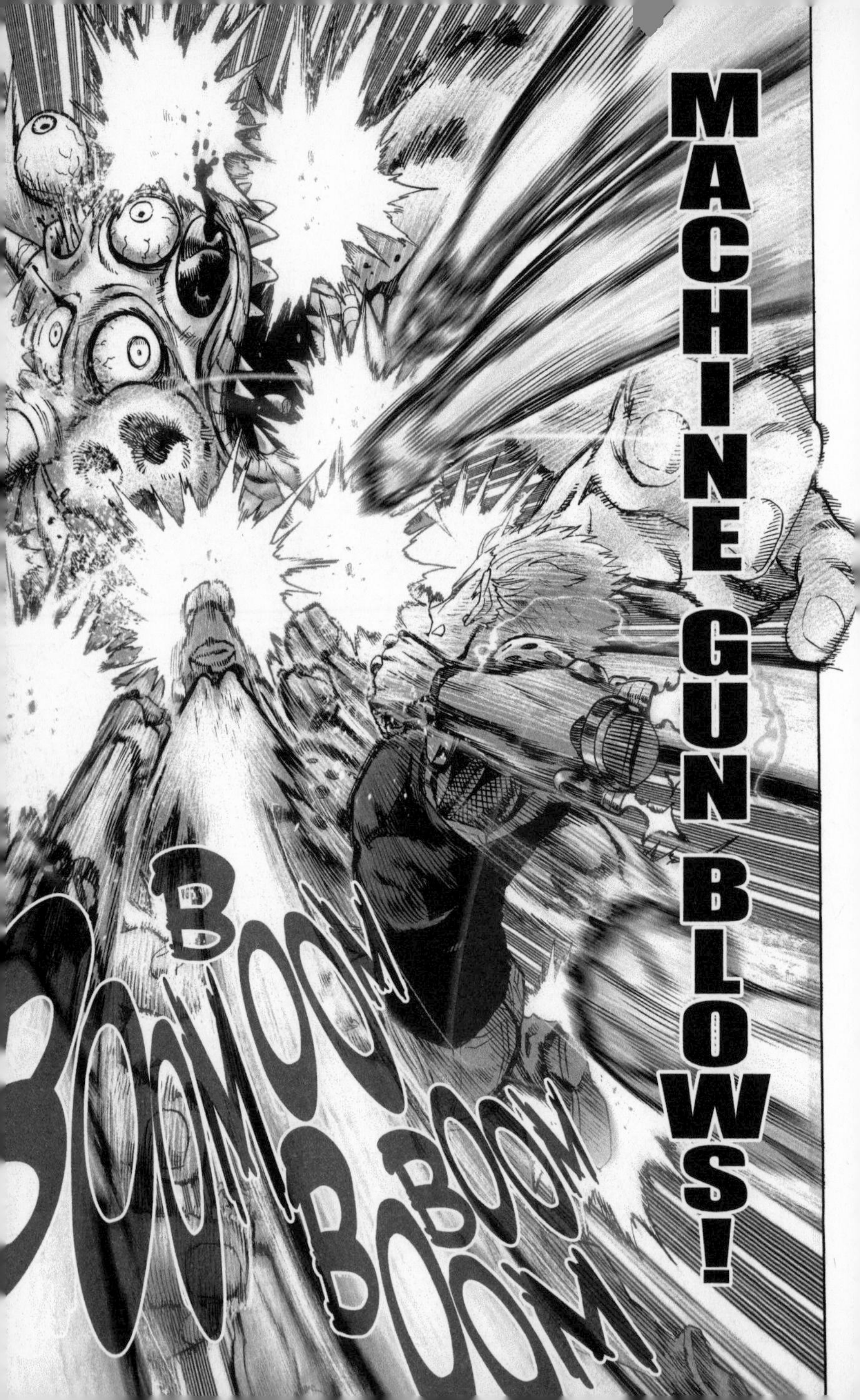
MACHINE GUN BLOWS!
BOOM BOOM
BOOM BOOM

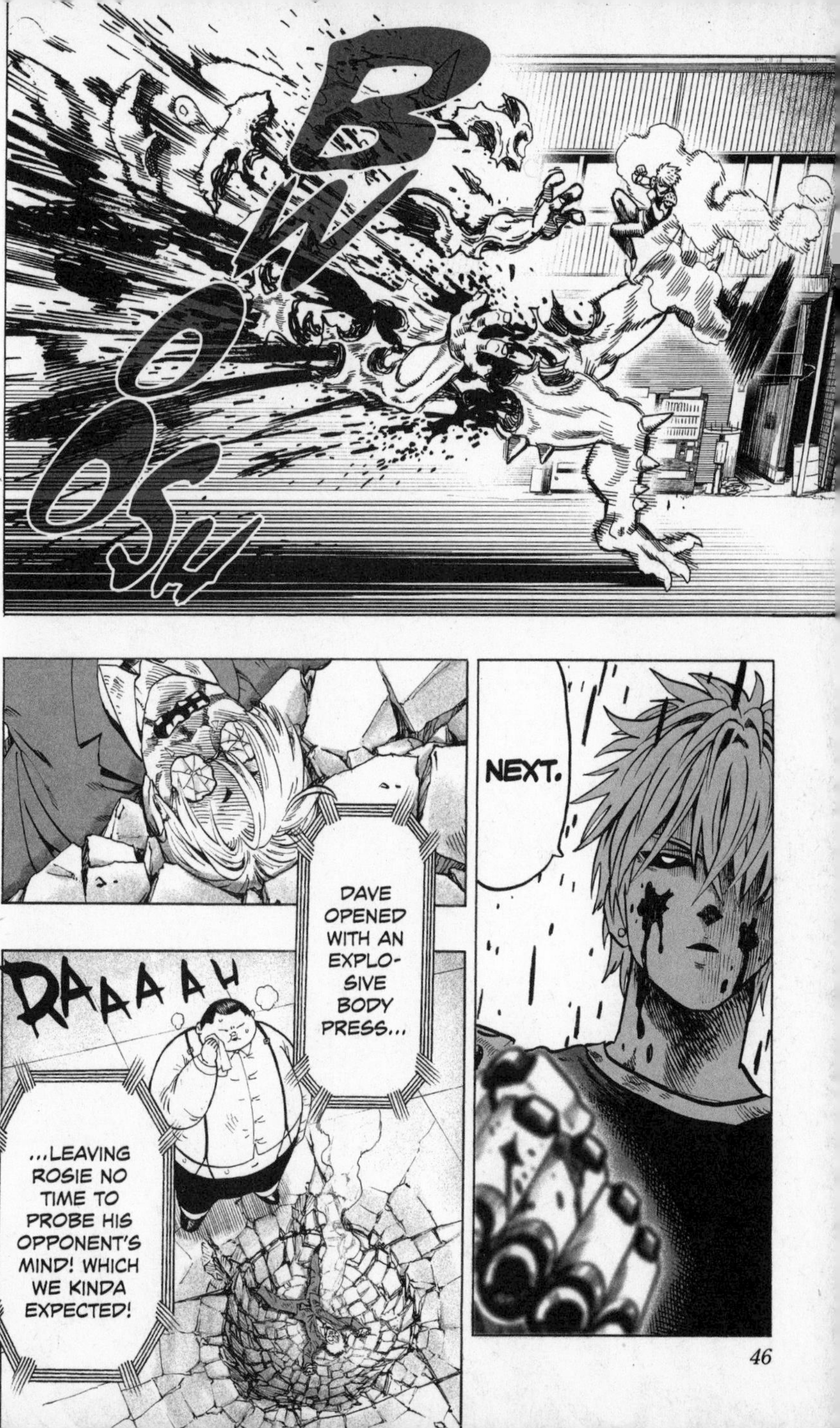
BWOOSH
NEXT.
DAVE OPENED WITH AN EXPLOSIVE BODY PRESS...
DAAAAH
...LEAVING ROSIE NO TIME TO PROBE HIS OPPONENT'S MIND! WHICH WE KINDA EXPECTED!

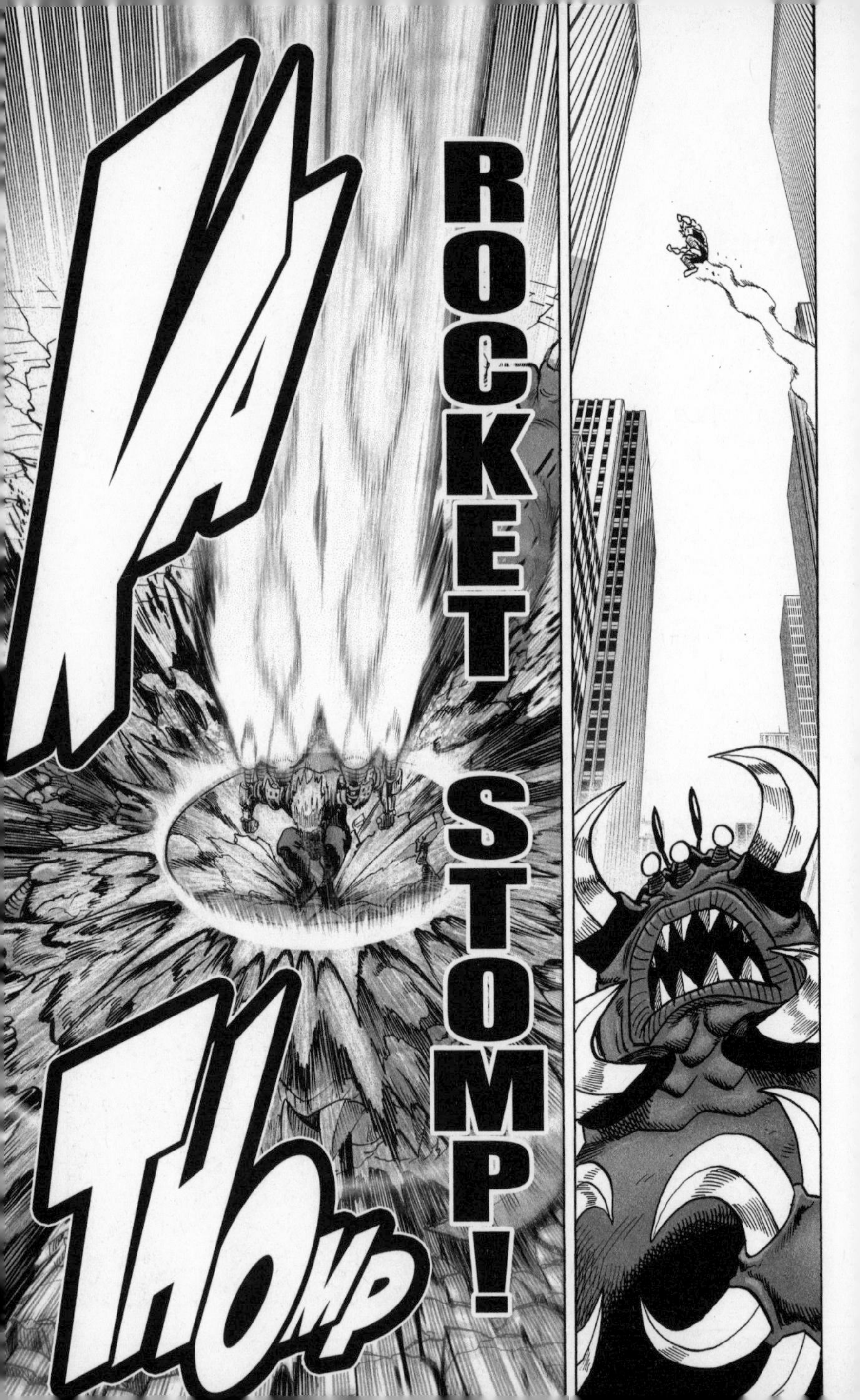
KA
ROCKET STOMP!
THOMP

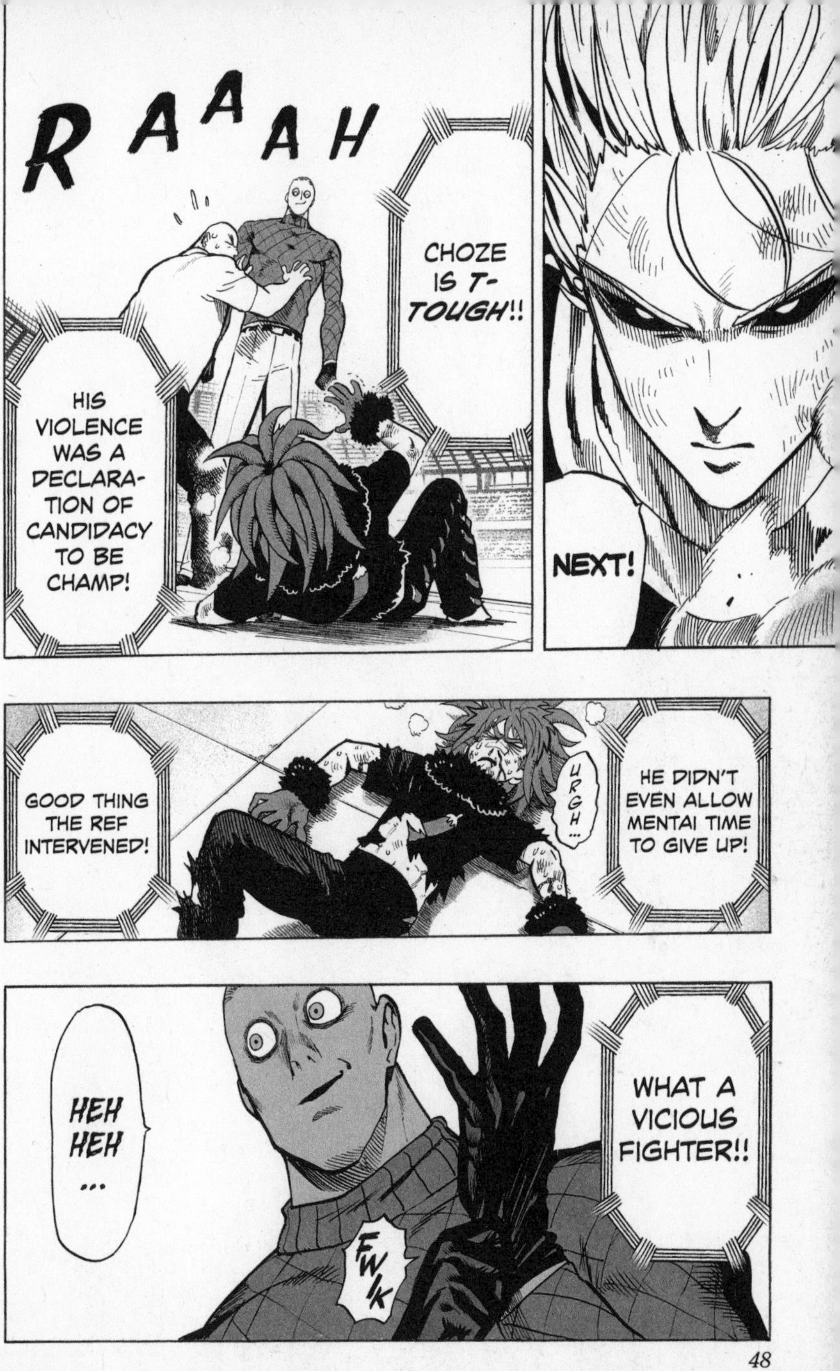
NEXT!
RAAAH
CHOZE IS T-TOUGH!!
HIS VIOLENCE WAS A DECLARATION OF CANDIDACY TO BE CHAMP!
HE DIDN'T EVEN ALLOW MENTAI TIME TO GIVE UP!
URGH...
GOOD THING THE REF INTERVENED!
WHAT A VICIOUS FIGHTER!!
FWIK
HEH HEH...

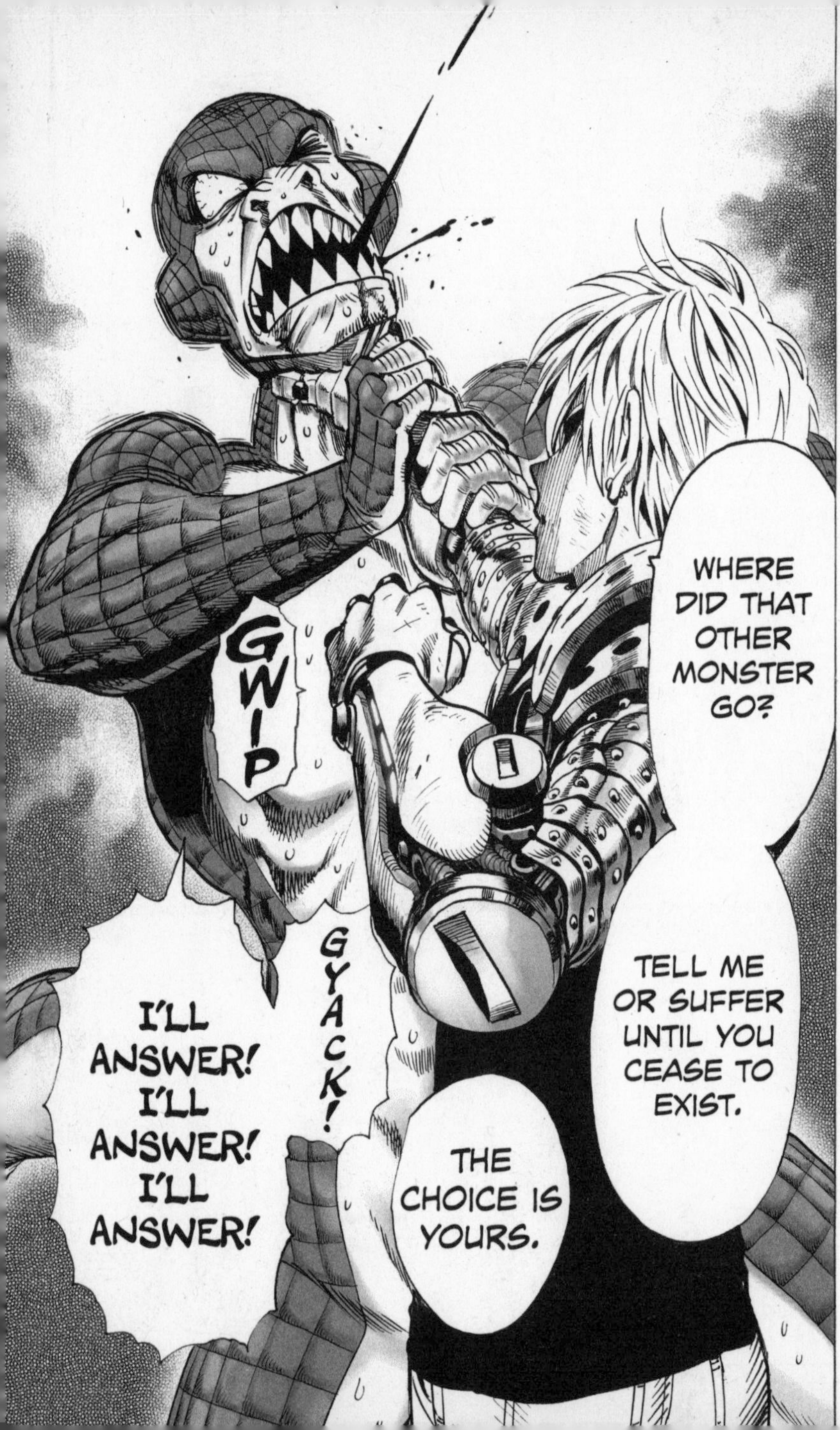
WHERE DID THAT OTHER MONSTER GO?
TELL ME OR SUFFER UNTIL YOU CEASE TO EXIST.
THE CHOICE IS YOURS.
GWIP
GYACK!
I'LL ANSWER! I'LL ANSWER! I'LL ANSWER!

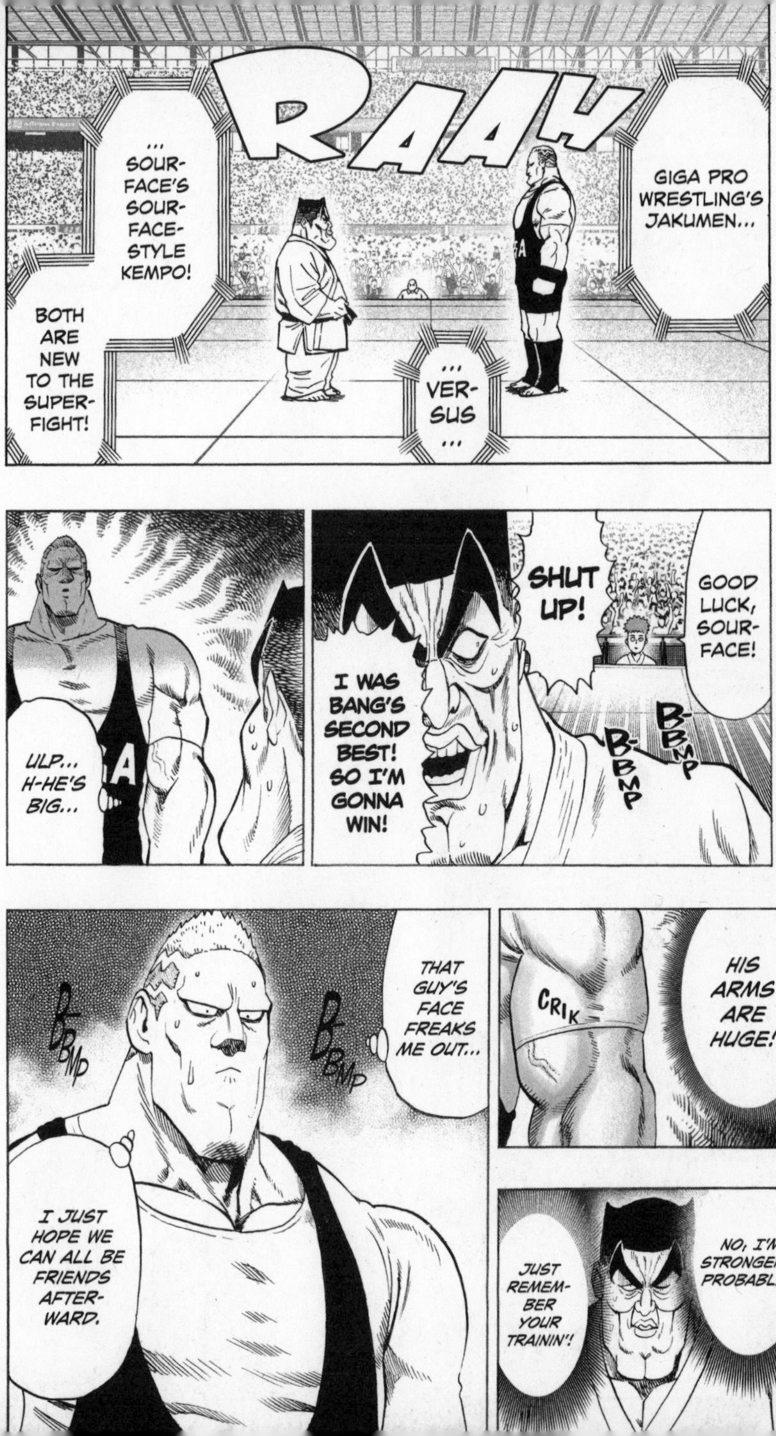
RAAH
GIGA PRO WRESTLING'S JAKUMEN...
...VERSUS...
...SOURFACE'S SOURFACE-STYLE KEMPO!
BOTH ARE NEW TO THE SUPERFIGHT!
GOOD LUCK, SOURFACE!
SHUT UP!
B-BBMP
B-BBMP
I WAS BANG'S SECOND BEST! SO I'M GONNA WIN!
ULP... H-HE'S BIG...
HIS ARMS ARE HUGE!
CRIK
NO, I'M STRONGER... PROBABLY...
JUST REMEMBER YOUR TRAININ'!
THAT GUY'S FACE FREAKS ME OUT...
BBMP
BBMP
I JUST HOPE WE CAN ALL BE FRIENDS AFTERWARD.

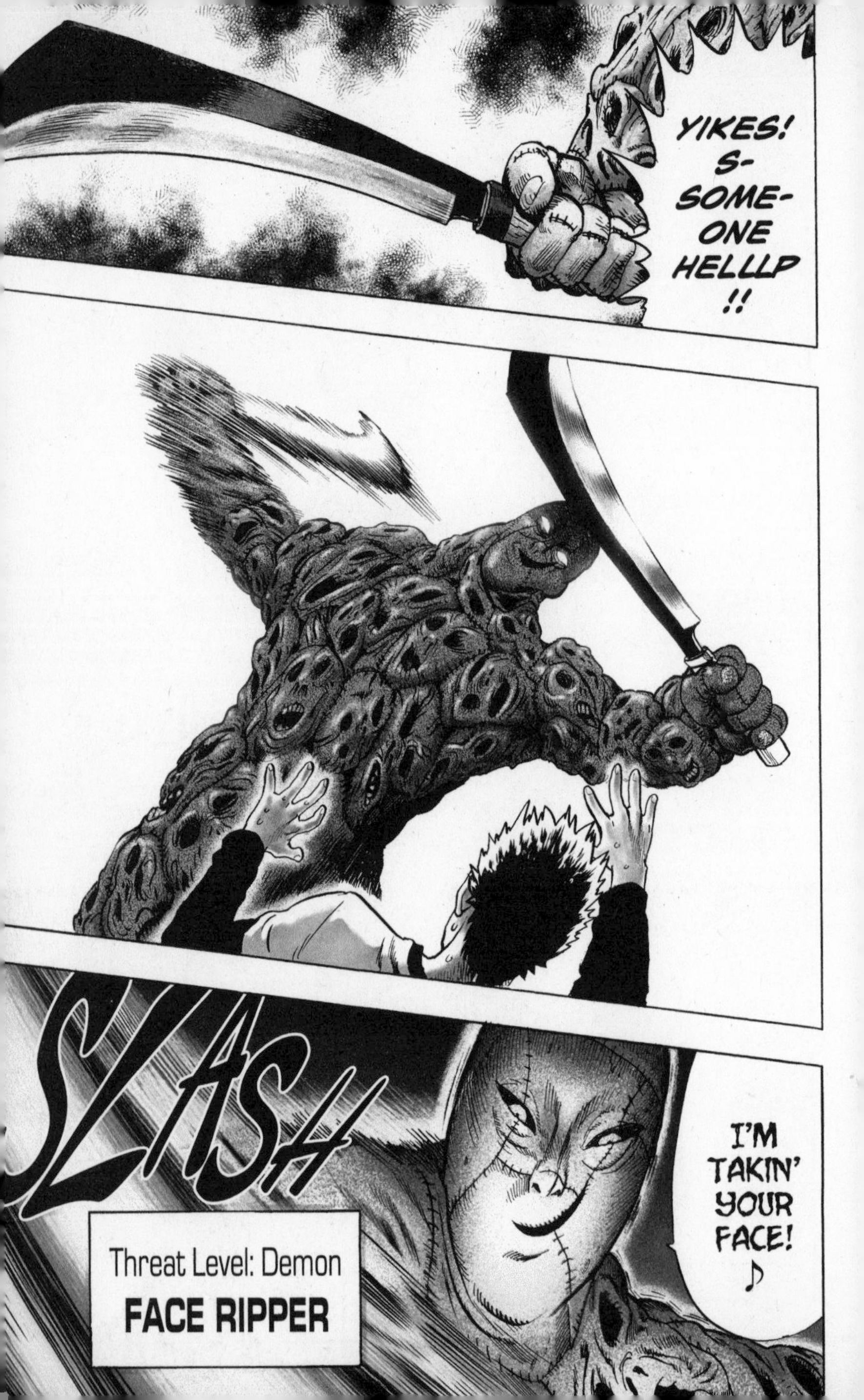
YIKES! S-SOMEONE HELLLP!!
SLASH
I'M TAKIN' YOUR FACE! ♪
Threat Level: Demon
FACE RIPPER

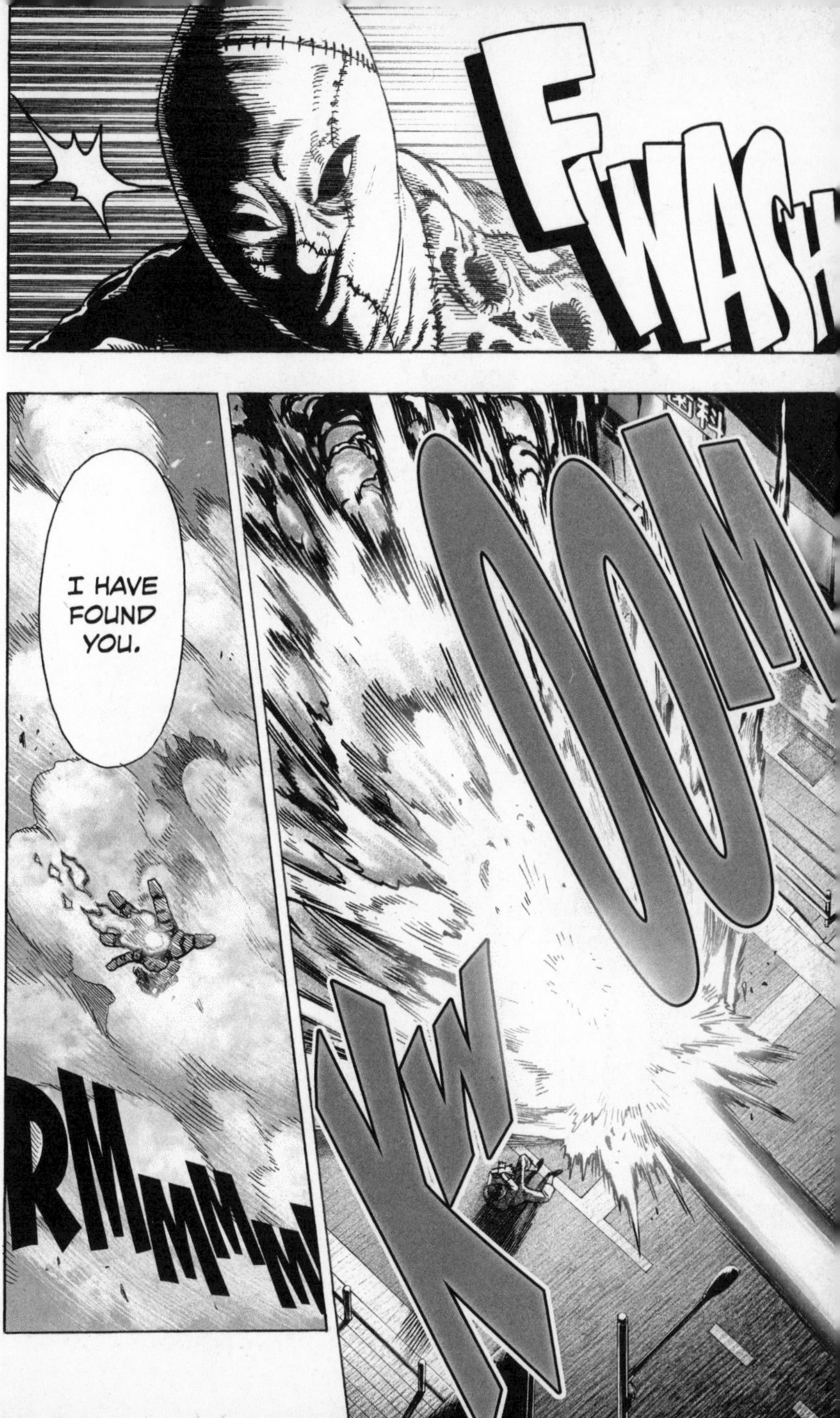
FWASH
KWOOM
I HAVE FOUND YOU.
RMMMMM

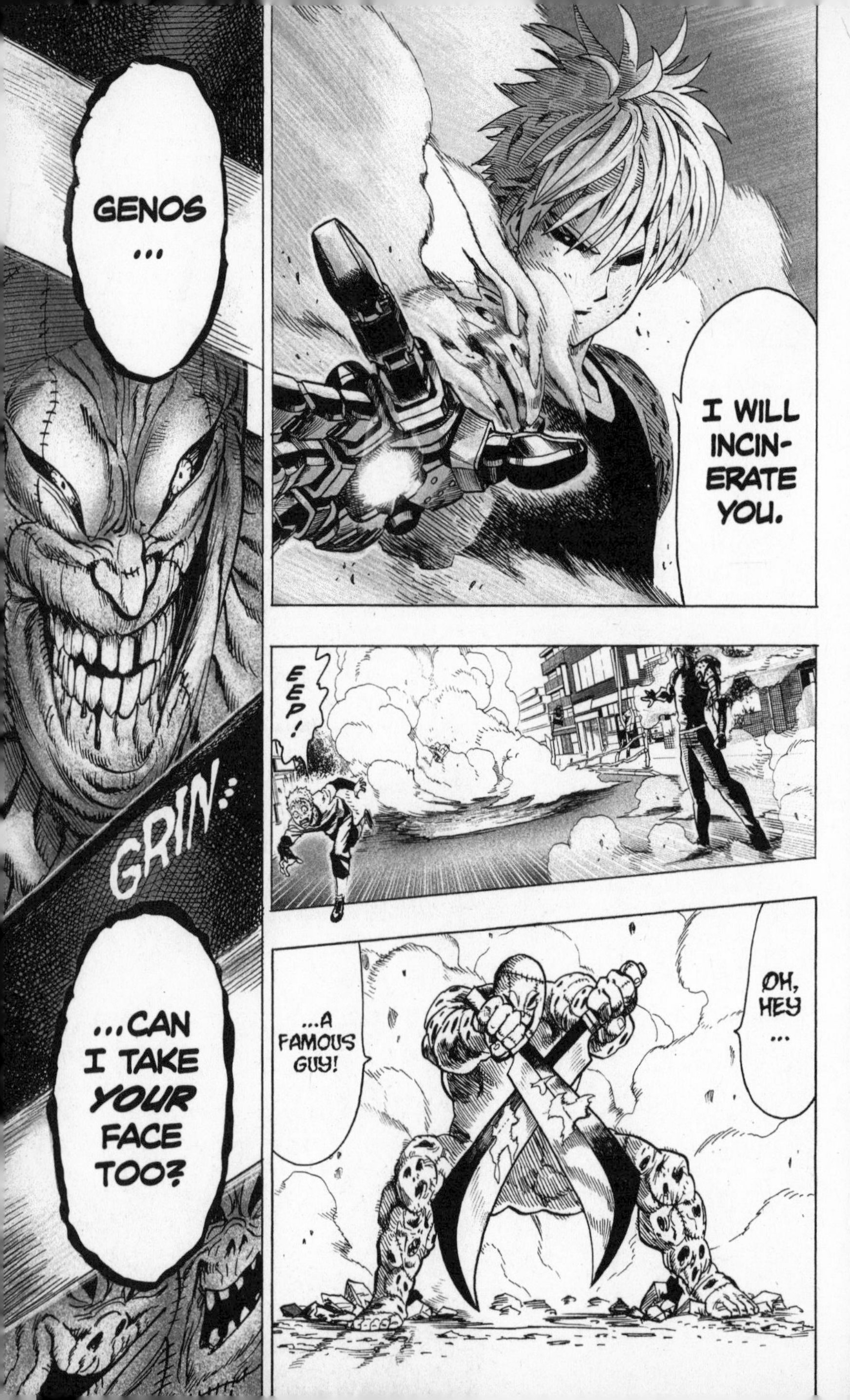
I WILL INCINERATE YOU.
EEP!
OH, HEY...
...A FAMOUS GUY!
GENOS...
GRIN
...CAN I TAKE *YOUR* FACE TOO?

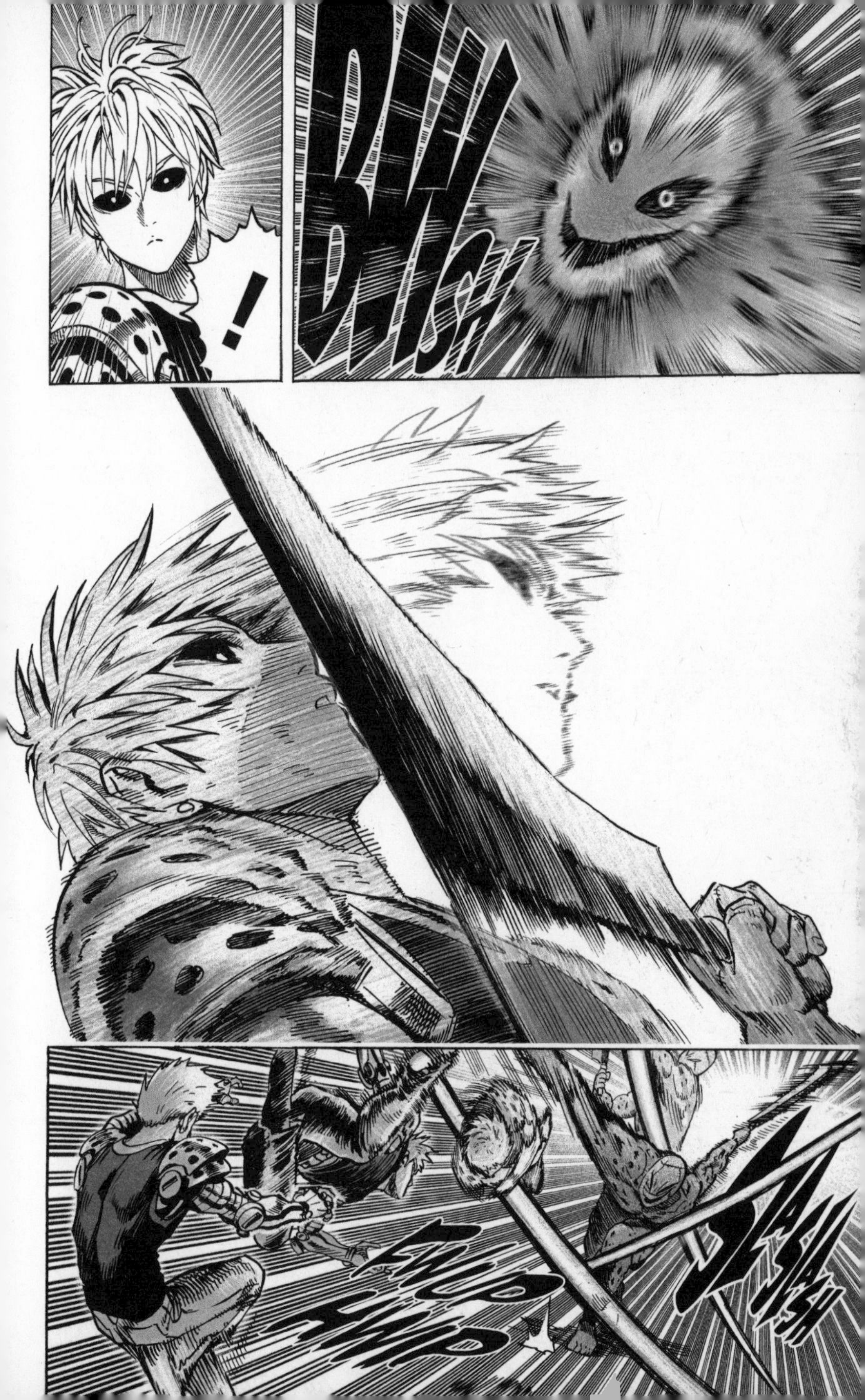
WHSH
!
WHIP WHIP

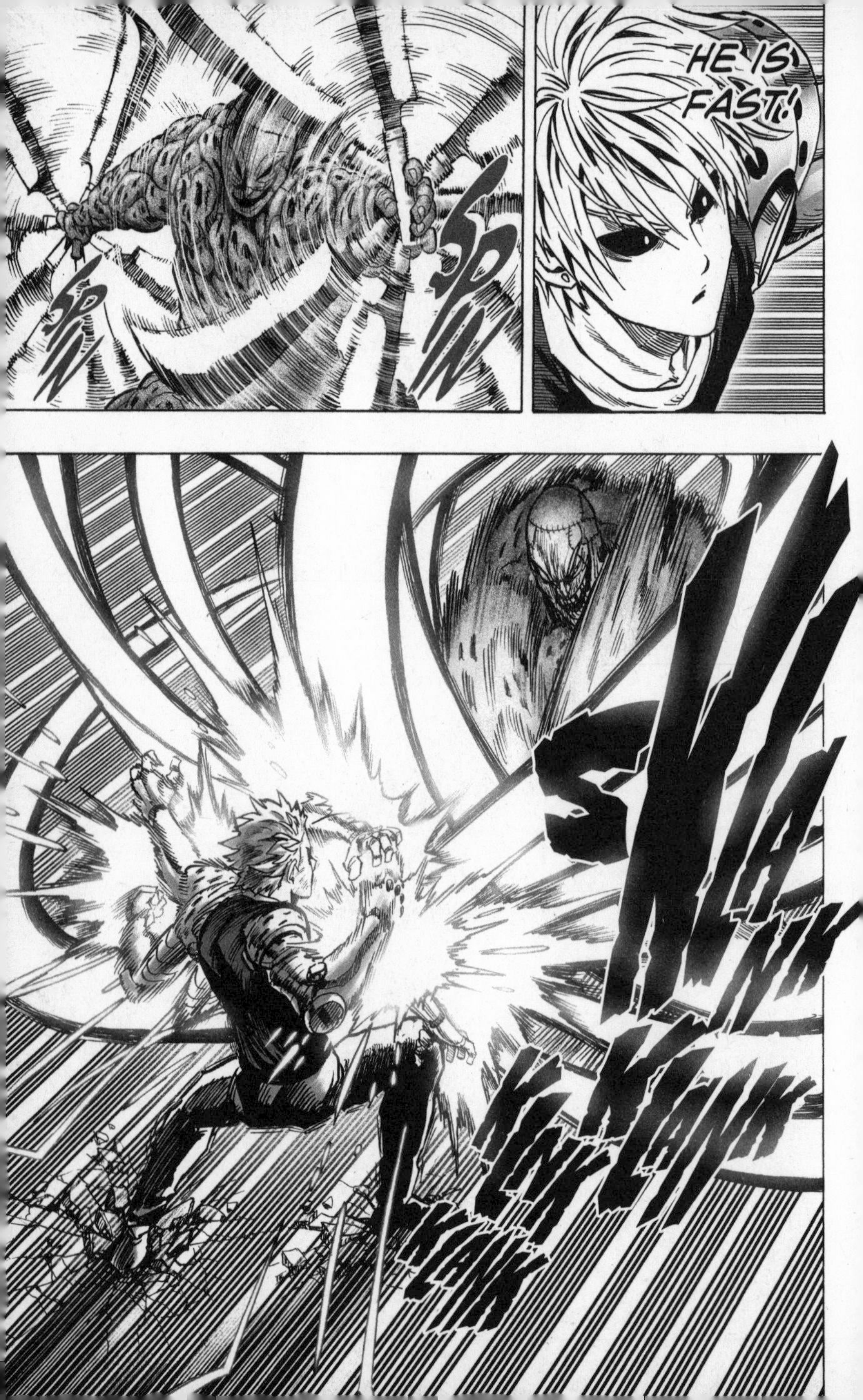
HE IS FAST!

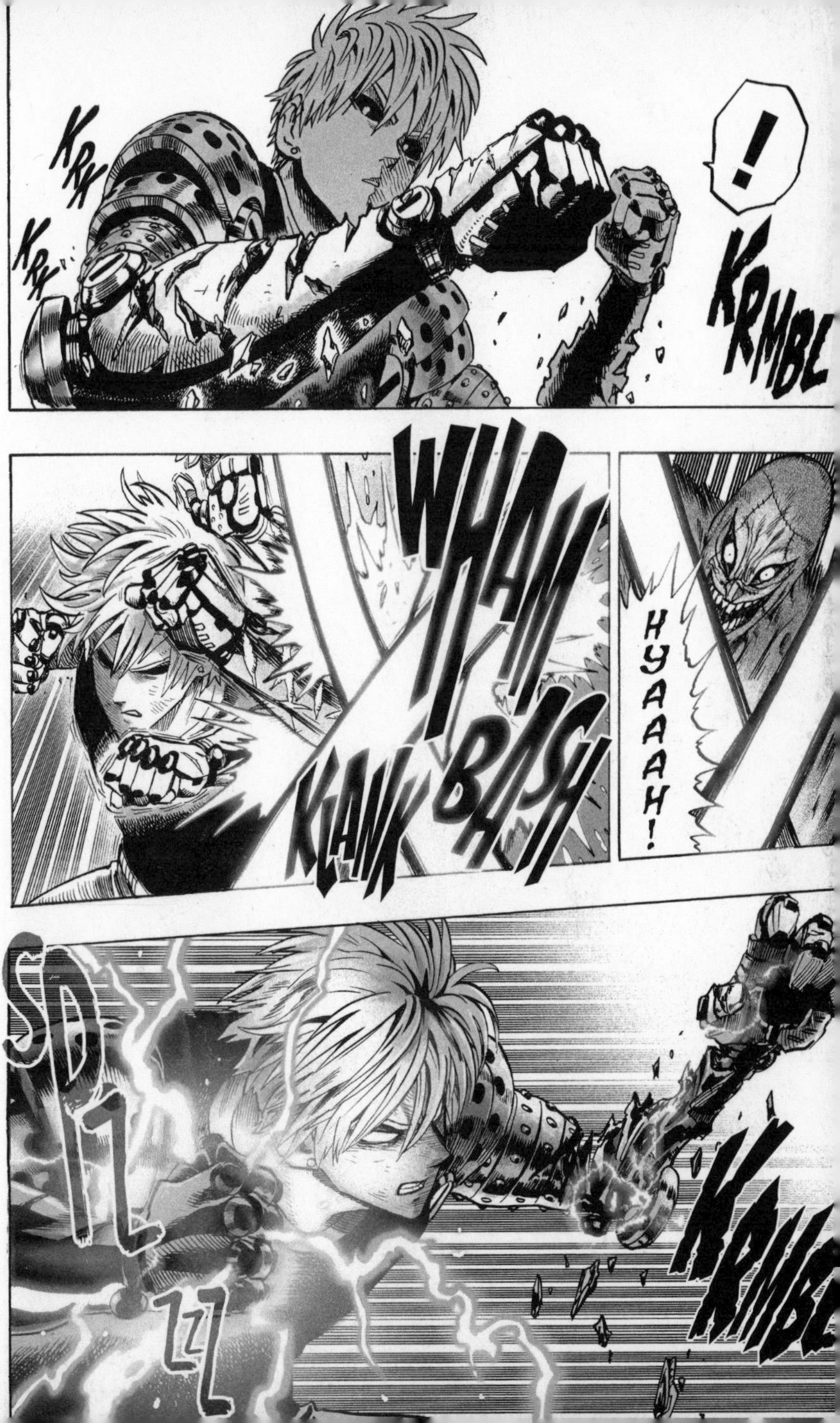

!
KRMBL
KRK
KRK
HYAAAAH!
WHAM
BASH
KLANK
KRMBL
SDZZ
ZZ

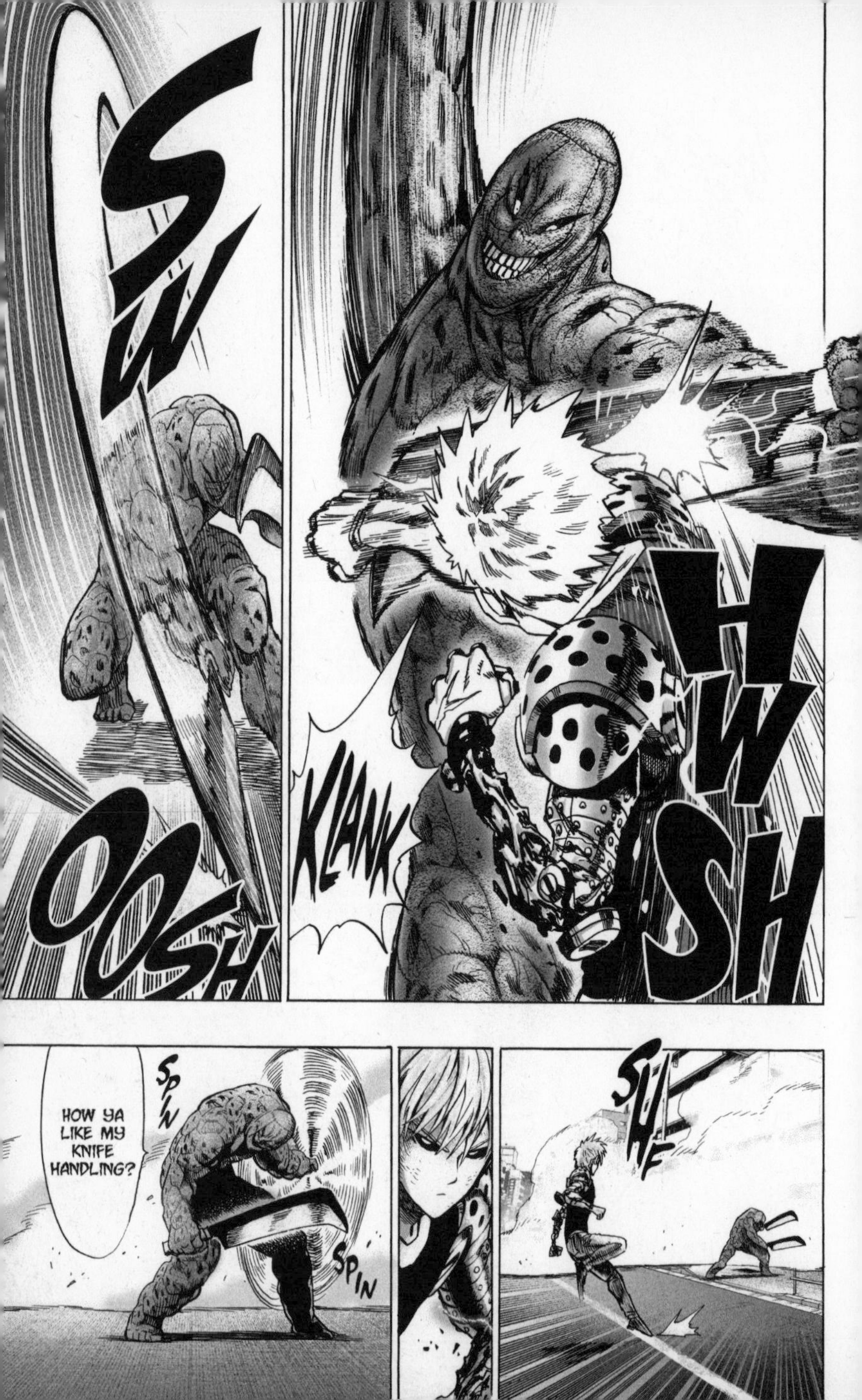
HWSH
KLANK
SWOOSH
SHF
SPIN
HOW YA LIKE MY KNIFE HANDLING?
SPIN

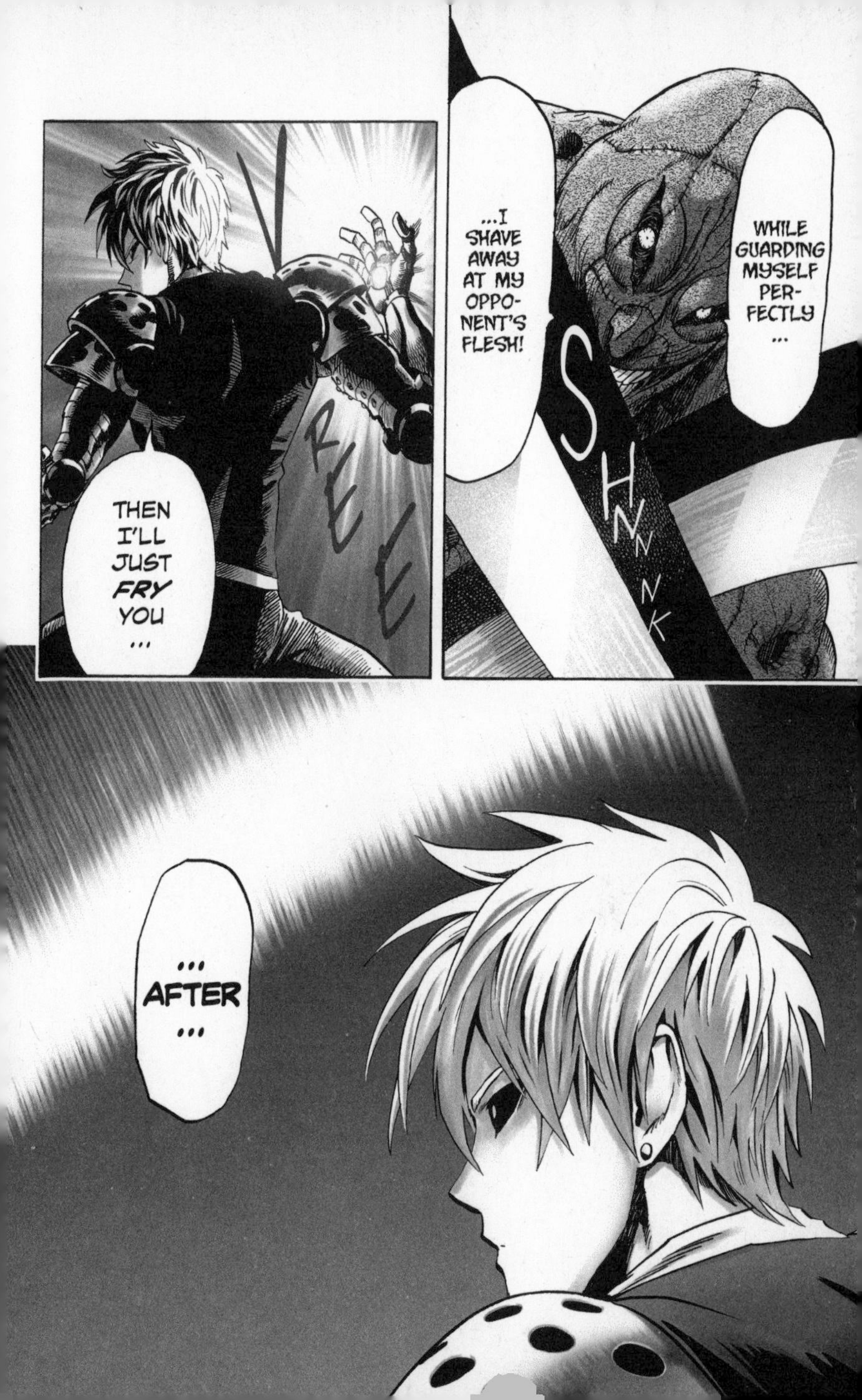
WHILE GUARDING MYSELF PER- FECTLY ...
...I SHAVE AWAY AT MY OPPO- NENT'S FLESH!
SHHNNNK
THEN I'LL JUST FRY YOU ...
REEE
... AFTER ...

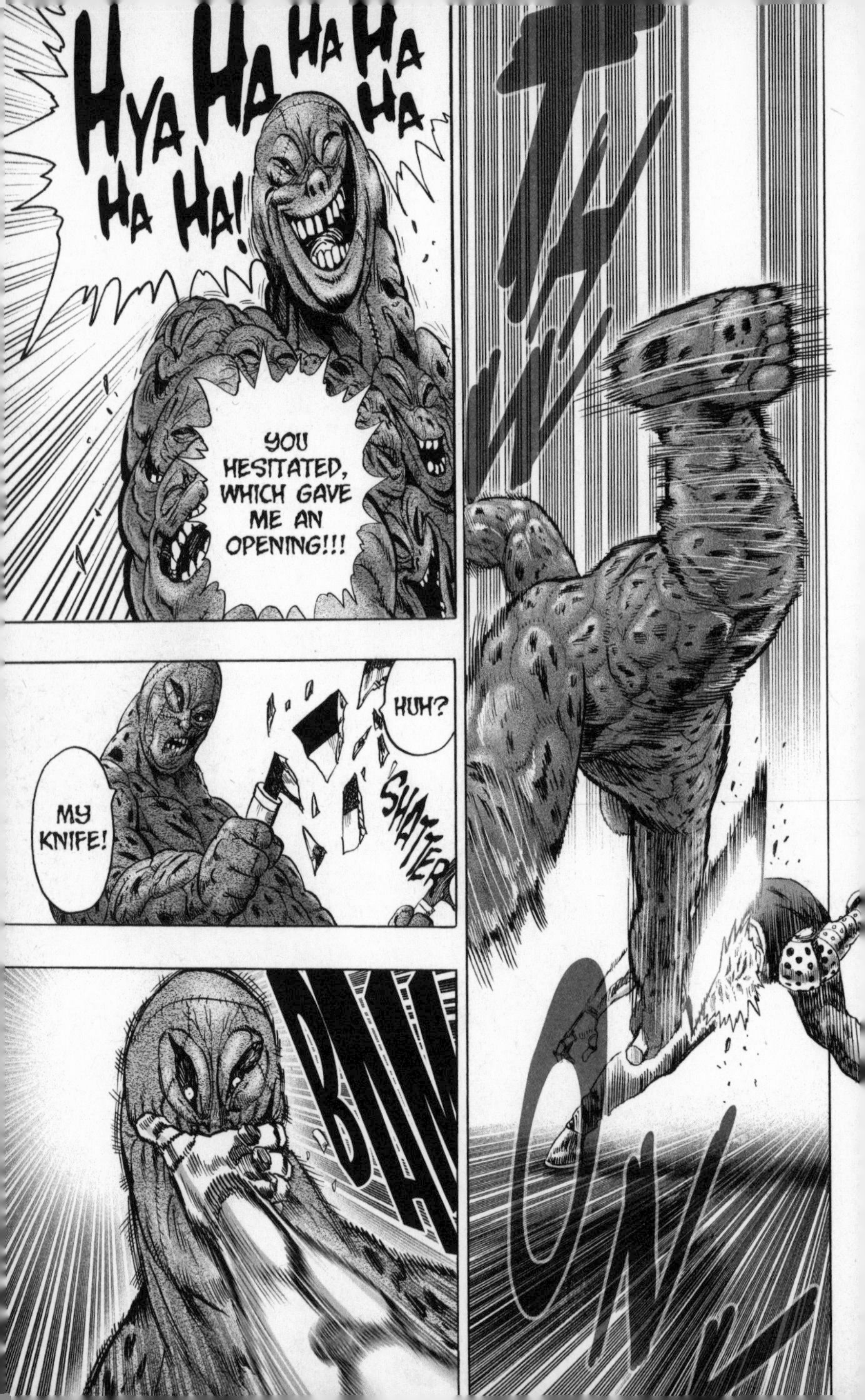
HYA HA HA HA HA HA HA HA HA!
YOU HESITATED, WHICH GAVE ME AN OPENING!!!
HUH?
SHATTER
MY KNIFE!

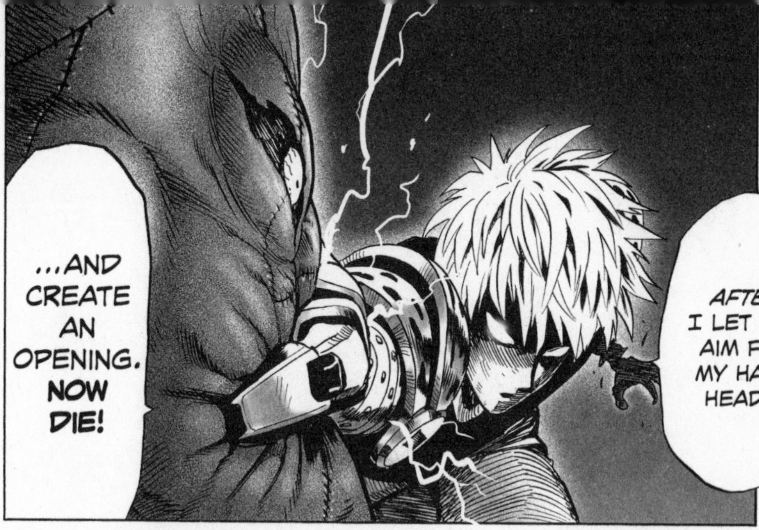
AFTER I LET YOU AIM FOR MY HARD HEAD...
...AND CREATE AN OPENING. NOW DIE!

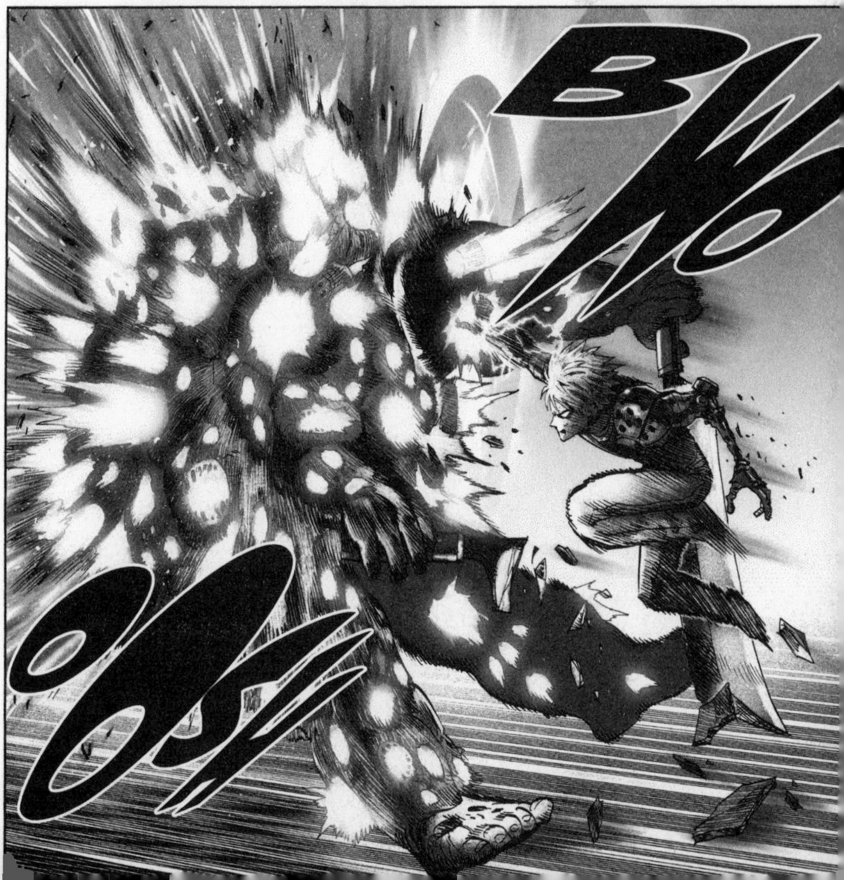

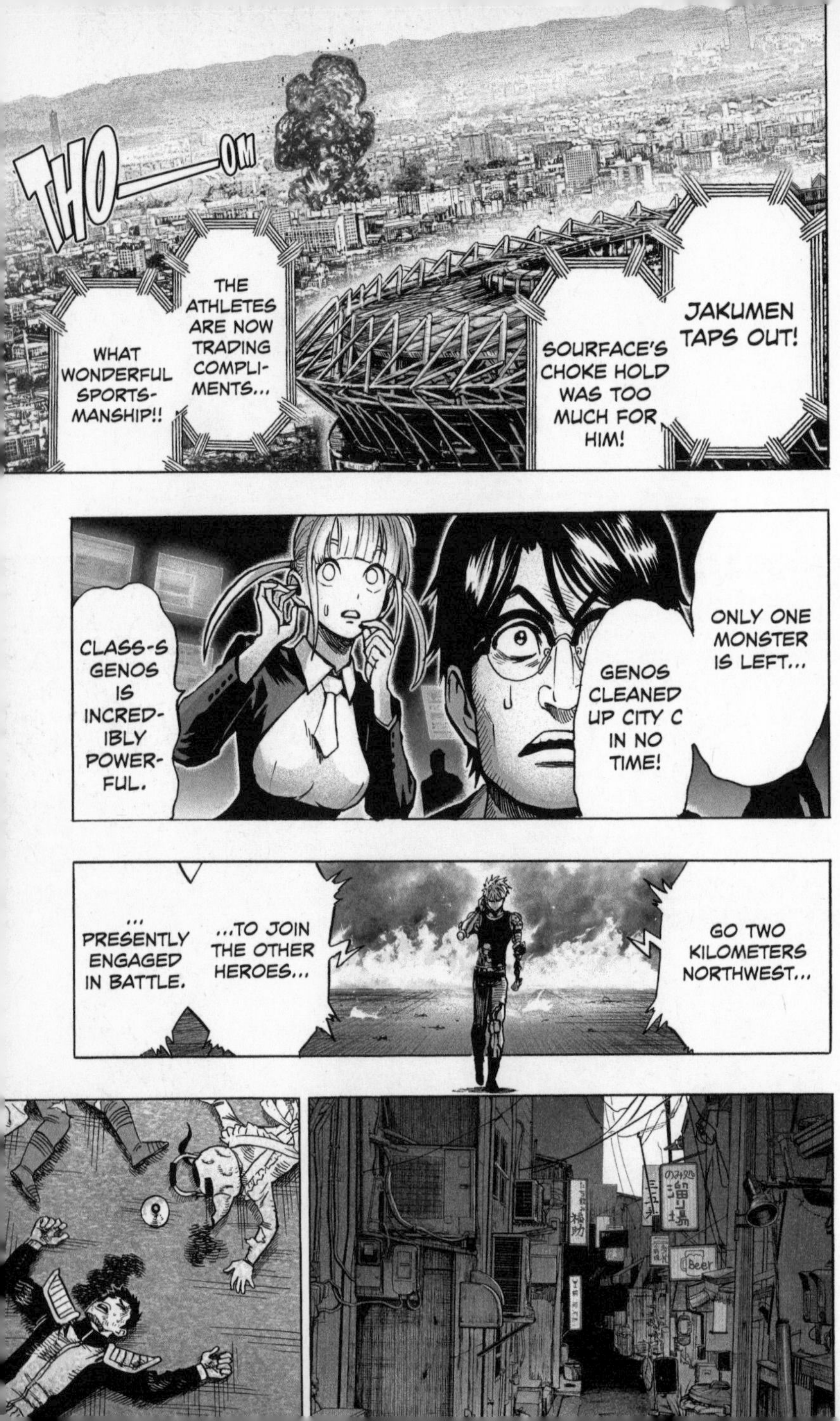
JAKUMEN TAPS OUT!
SOURFACE'S CHOKE HOLD WAS TOO MUCH FOR HIM!
THE ATHLETES ARE NOW TRADING COMPLIMENTS...
WHAT WONDERFUL SPORTSMANSHIP!!
THO——OM
ONLY ONE MONSTER IS LEFT...
GENOS CLEANED UP CITY C IN NO TIME!
CLASS-S GENOS IS INCREDIBLY POWERFUL.
GO TWO KILOMETERS NORTHWEST...
...TO JOIN THE OTHER HEROES...
... PRESENTLY ENGAGED IN BATTLE.
のみ処
溜り場
Beer

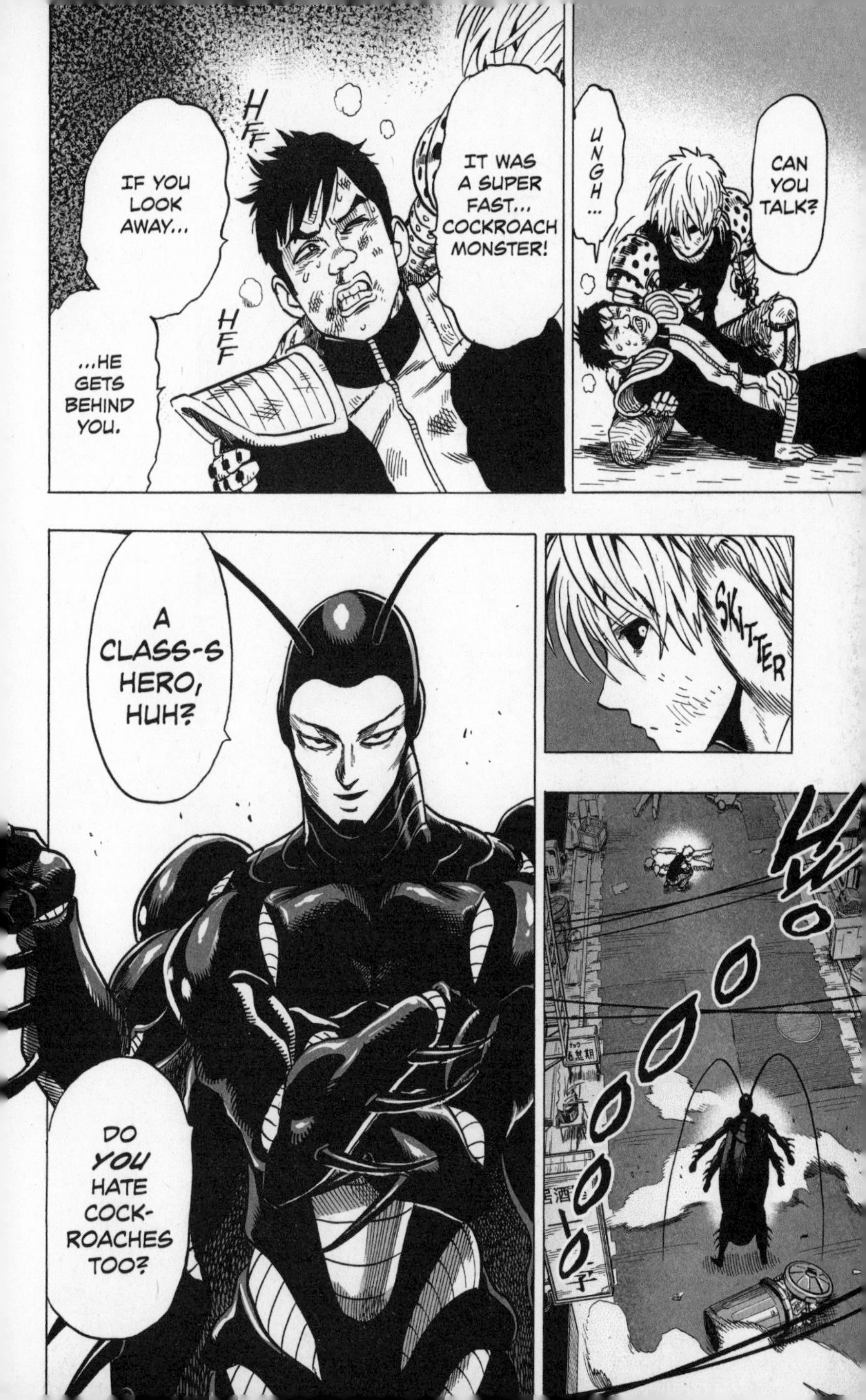
CAN YOU TALK?
UNGH...
IT WAS A SUPER FAST... COCKROACH MONSTER!
HFF
IF YOU LOOK AWAY...
HFF
...HE GETS BEHIND YOU.
SKITTER
A CLASS-S HERO, HUH?
DO *YOU* HATE COCK-ROACHES TOO?

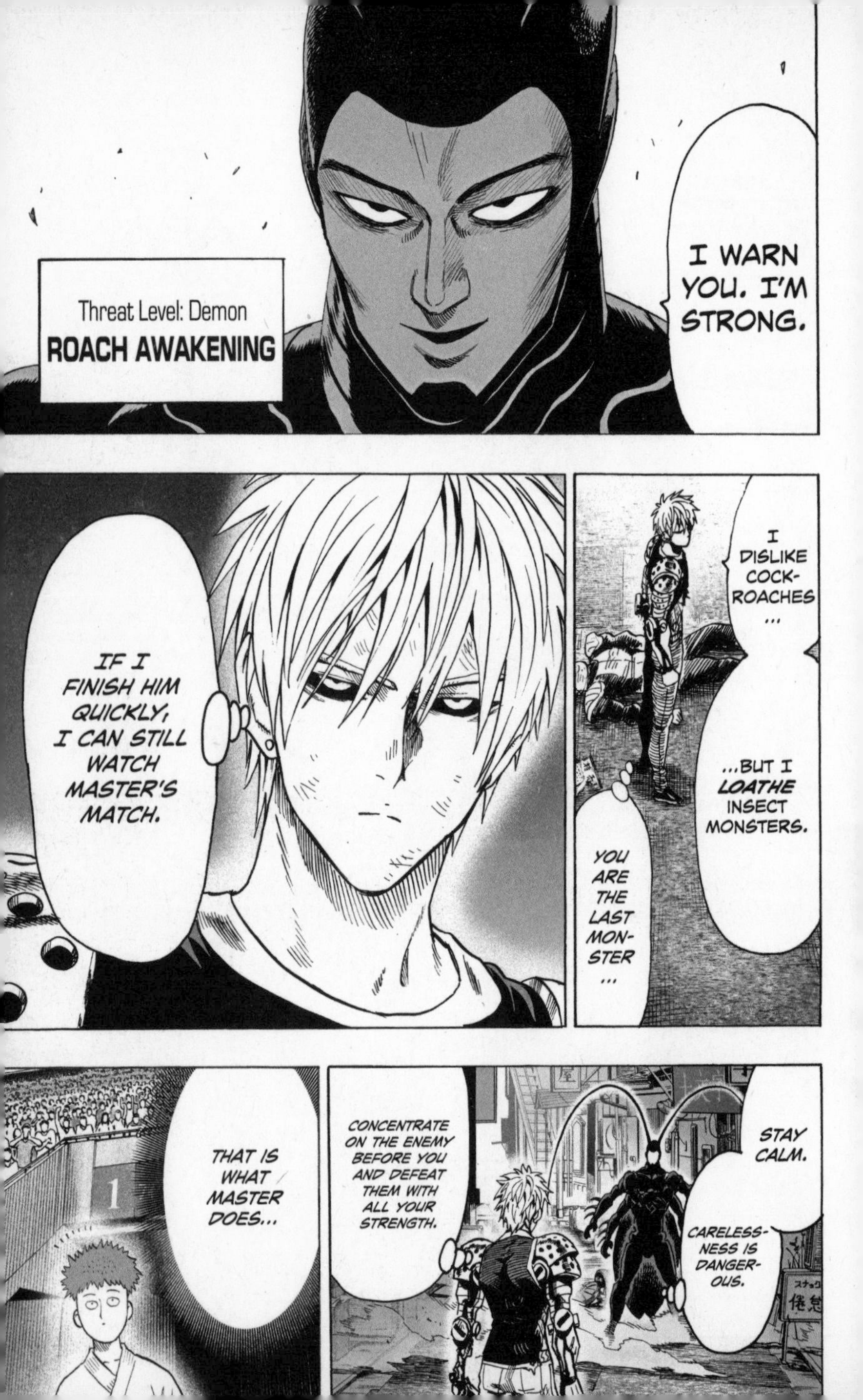
I WARN YOU. I'M STRONG.
Threat Level: Demon
ROACH AWAKENING
I DISLIKE COCK-ROACHES ...
...BUT I LOATHE INSECT MONSTERS.
YOU ARE THE LAST MON-STER ...
IF I FINISH HIM QUICKLY, I CAN STILL WATCH MASTER'S MATCH.
STAY CALM.
CARELESS-NESS IS DANGER-OUS.
CONCENTRATE ON THE ENEMY BEFORE YOU AND DEFEAT THEM WITH ALL YOUR STRENGTH.
THAT IS WHAT MASTER DOES...

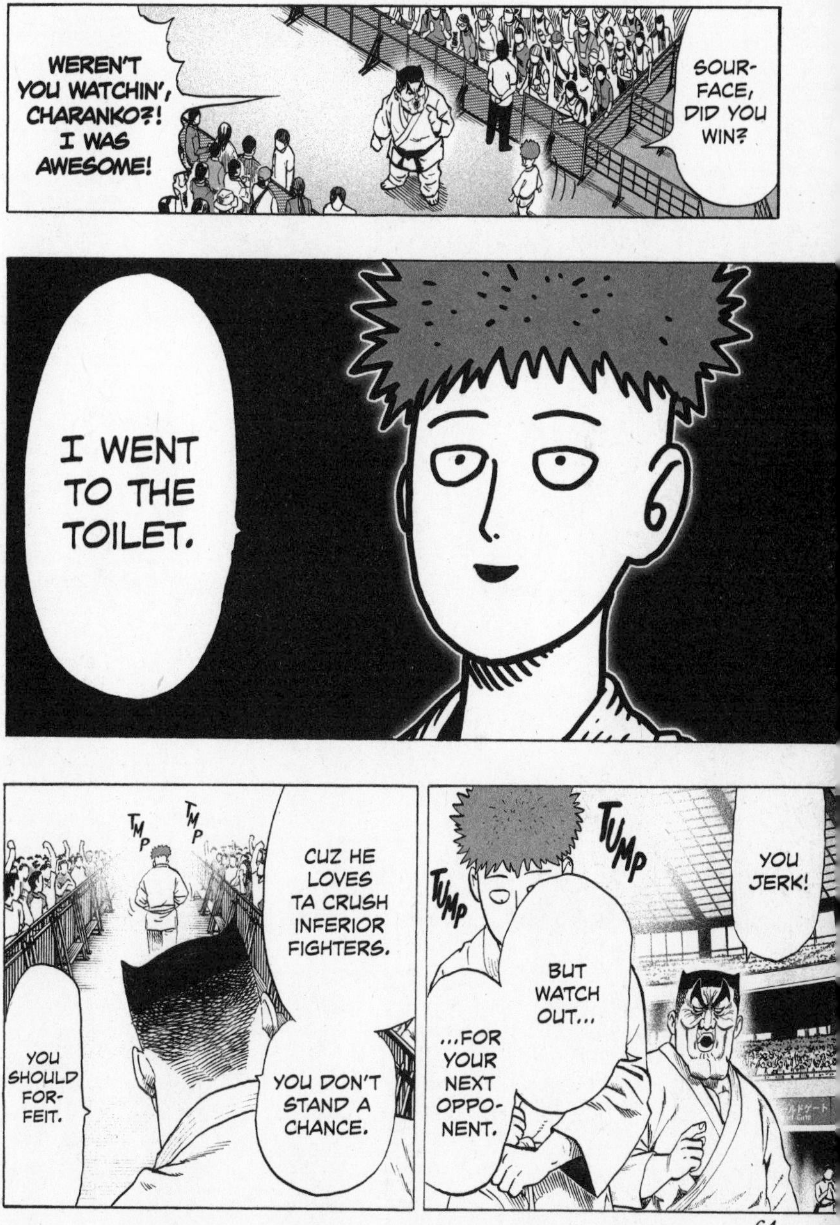
SOUR-FACE, DID YOU WIN?
WEREN'T YOU WATCHIN', CHARANKO?! I WAS AWESOME!
I WENT TO THE TOILET.
TUMP
TUMP
YOU JERK!
BUT WATCH OUT...
...FOR YOUR NEXT OPPO-NENT.
TMP
TMP
CUZ HE LOVES TA CRUSH INFERIOR FIGHTERS.
YOU DON'T STAND A CHANCE.
YOU SHOULD FOR-FEIT.

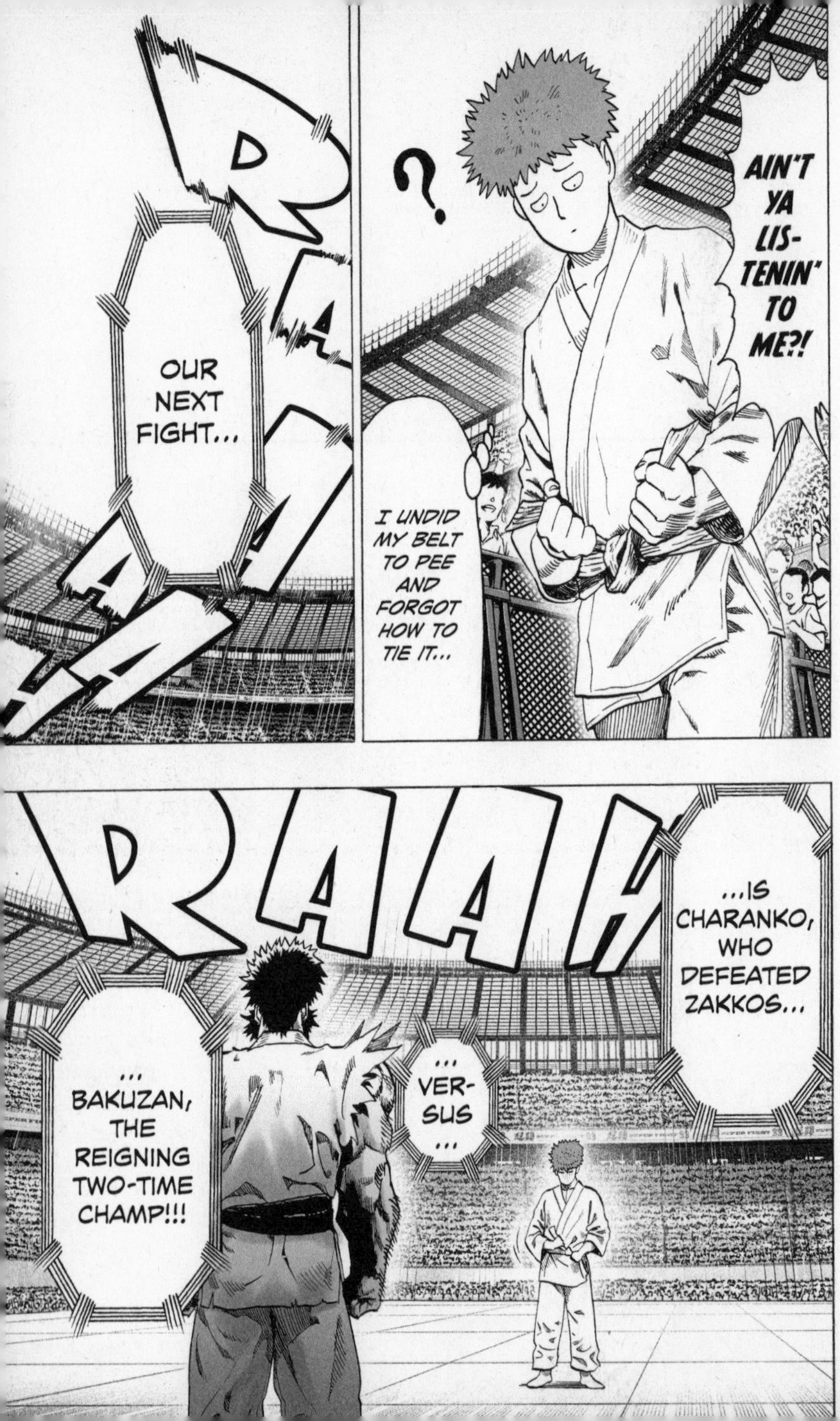
AIN'T YA LIS-TENIN' TO ME?!
?
I UNDID MY BELT TO PEE AND FORGOT HOW TO TIE IT...
OUR NEXT FIGHT...
RAAH
...IS CHARANKO, WHO DEFEATED ZAKKOS...
...VERSUS...
...BAKUZAN, THE REIGNING TWO-TIME CHAMP!!!

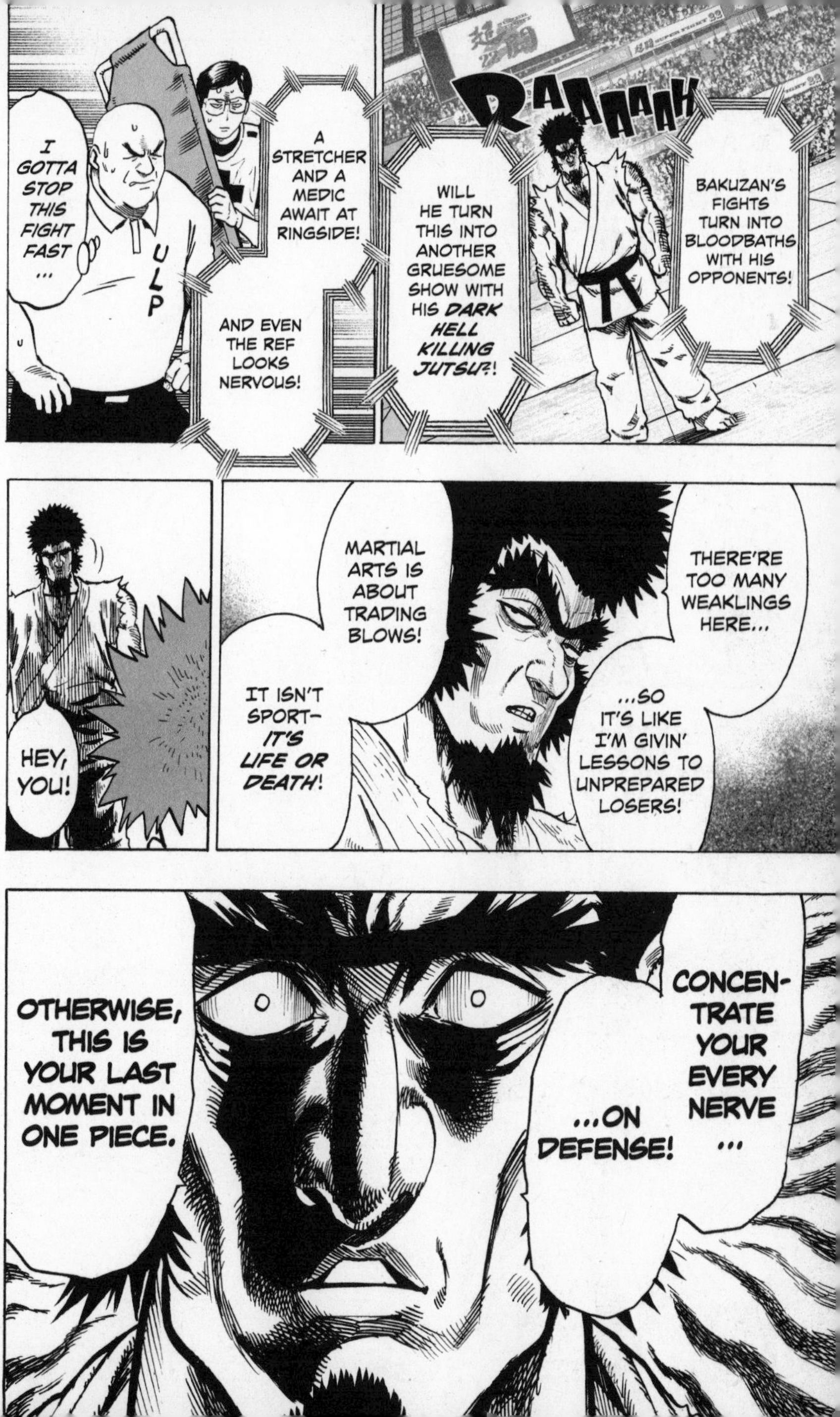
RAAAAAH
BAKUZAN'S FIGHTS TURN INTO BLOODBATHS WITH HIS OPPONENTS!
WILL HE TURN THIS INTO ANOTHER GRUESOME SHOW WITH HIS *DARK HELL KILLING JUTSU*?!
A STRETCHER AND A MEDIC AWAIT AT RINGSIDE!
AND EVEN THE REF LOOKS NERVOUS!
ULP
I GOTTA STOP THIS FIGHT FAST...
THERE'RE TOO MANY WEAKLINGS HERE...
...SO IT'S LIKE I'M GIVIN' LESSONS TO UNPREPARED LOSERS!
MARTIAL ARTS IS ABOUT TRADING BLOWS!
IT ISN'T SPORT—*IT'S LIFE OR DEATH*!
HEY, YOU!
CONCENTRATE YOUR EVERY NERVE...
...ON DEFENSE!
OTHERWISE, THIS IS YOUR LAST MOMENT IN ONE PIECE.

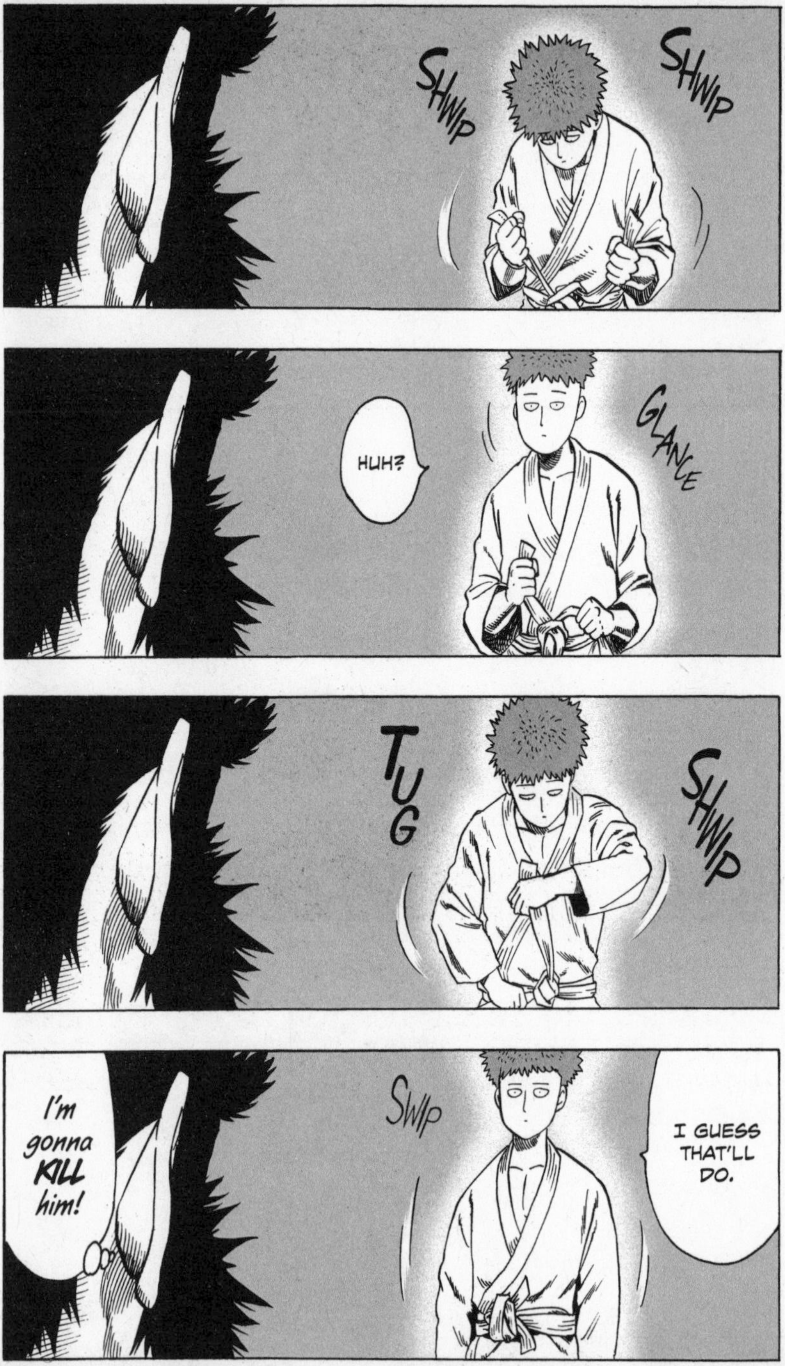
SHWIP
SHWIP
GLANCE
HUH?
SHWIP
TUG
I GUESS THAT'LL DO.
SWIP
I'm gonna **KILL** him!

Class-C Hero
Shoulderpads

PUNCH 64: LIMIT

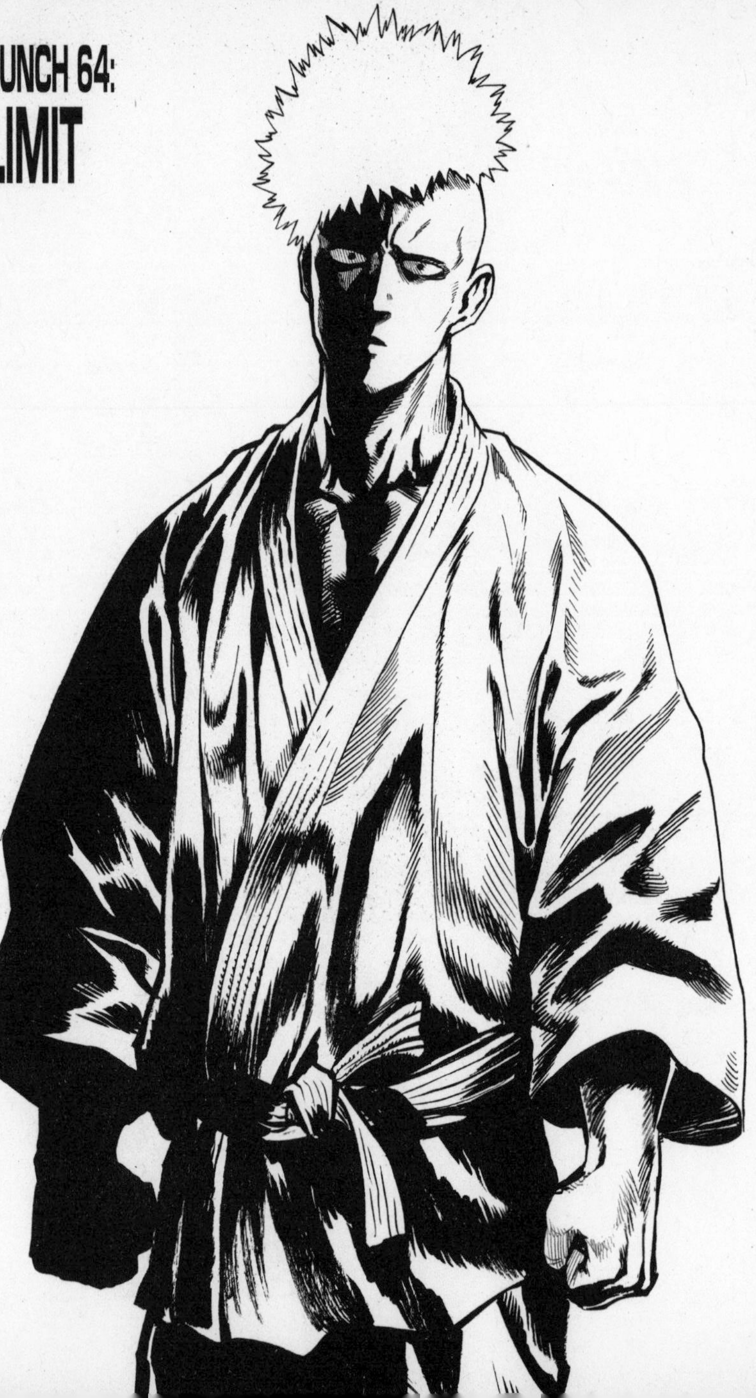

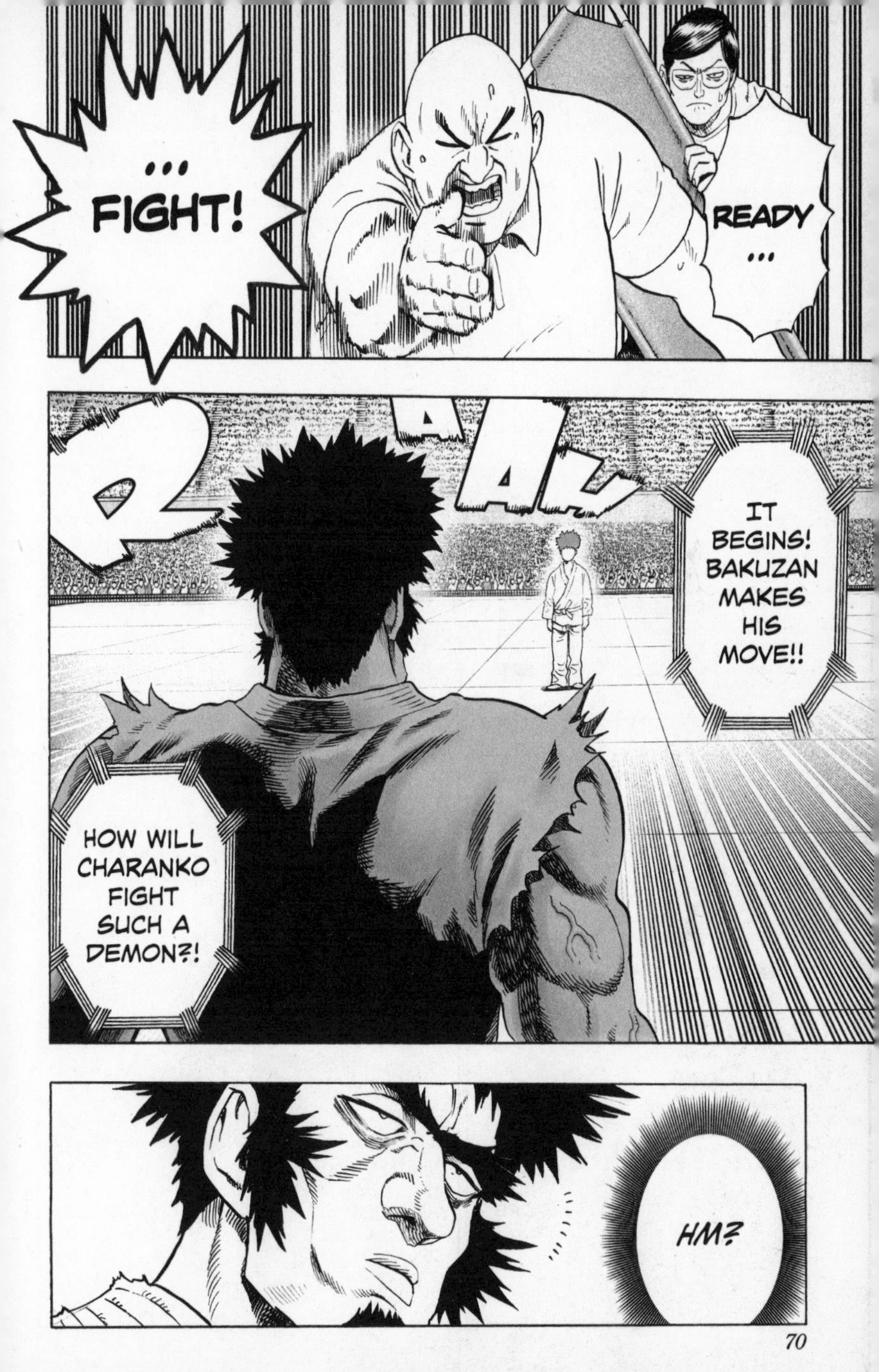
READY ...
... FIGHT!
IT BEGINS! BAKUZAN MAKES HIS MOVE!!
HOW WILL CHARANKO FIGHT SUCH A DEMON?!
HM?

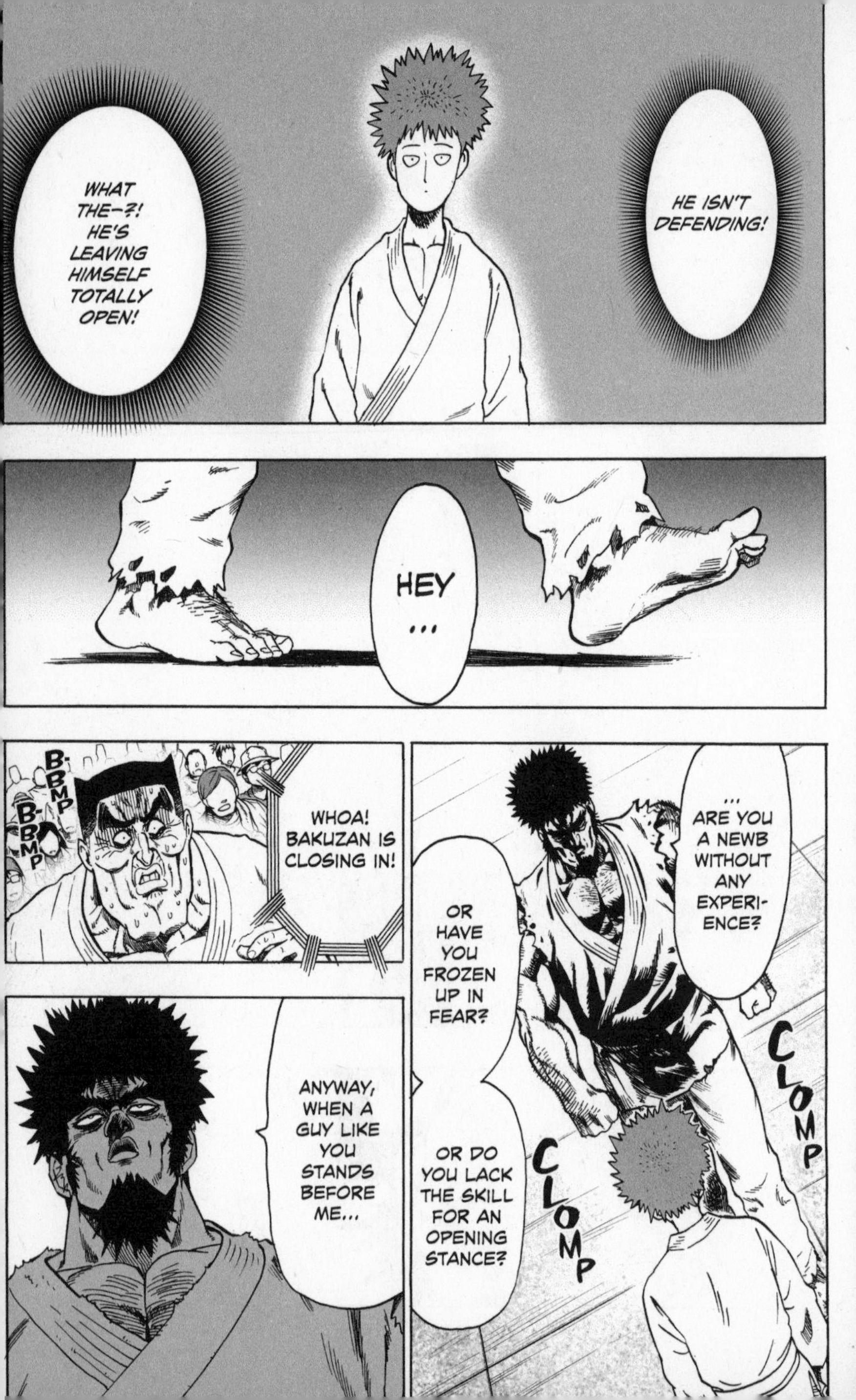
HE ISN'T DEFENDING!
WHAT THE—?! HE'S LEAVING HIMSELF TOTALLY OPEN!
HEY ...
... ARE YOU A NEWB WITHOUT ANY EXPERIENCE?
OR HAVE YOU FROZEN UP IN FEAR?
OR DO YOU LACK THE SKILL FOR AN OPENING STANCE?
CLOMP
CLOMP
B-BBMP
B-BBMP
WHOA! BAKUZAN IS CLOSING IN!
ANYWAY, WHEN A GUY LIKE YOU STANDS BEFORE ME...

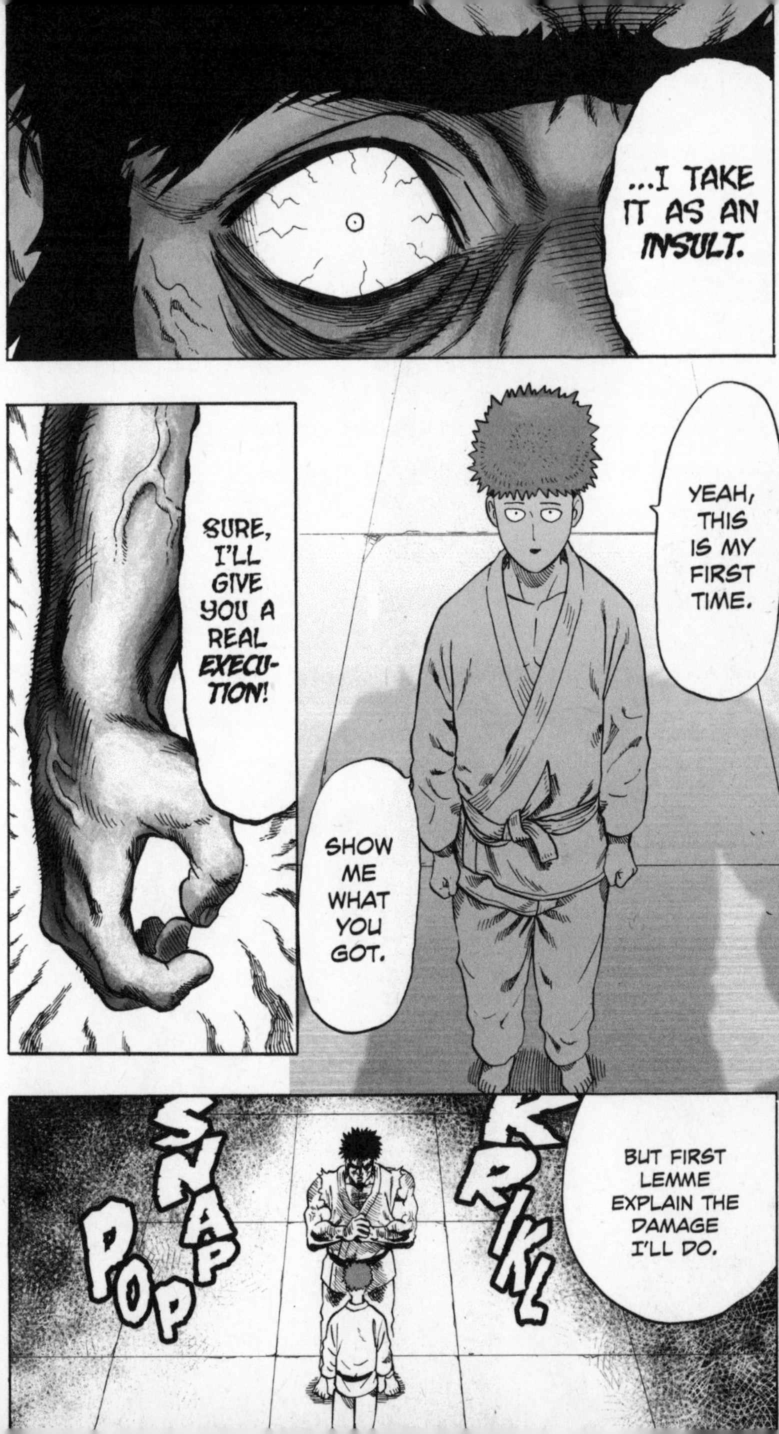
...I TAKE IT AS AN INSULT.
YEAH, THIS IS MY FIRST TIME.
SHOW ME WHAT YOU GOT.
SURE, I'LL GIVE YOU A REAL EXECUTION!
BUT FIRST LEMME EXPLAIN THE DAMAGE I'LL DO.
KRIKL
SNAP
POP

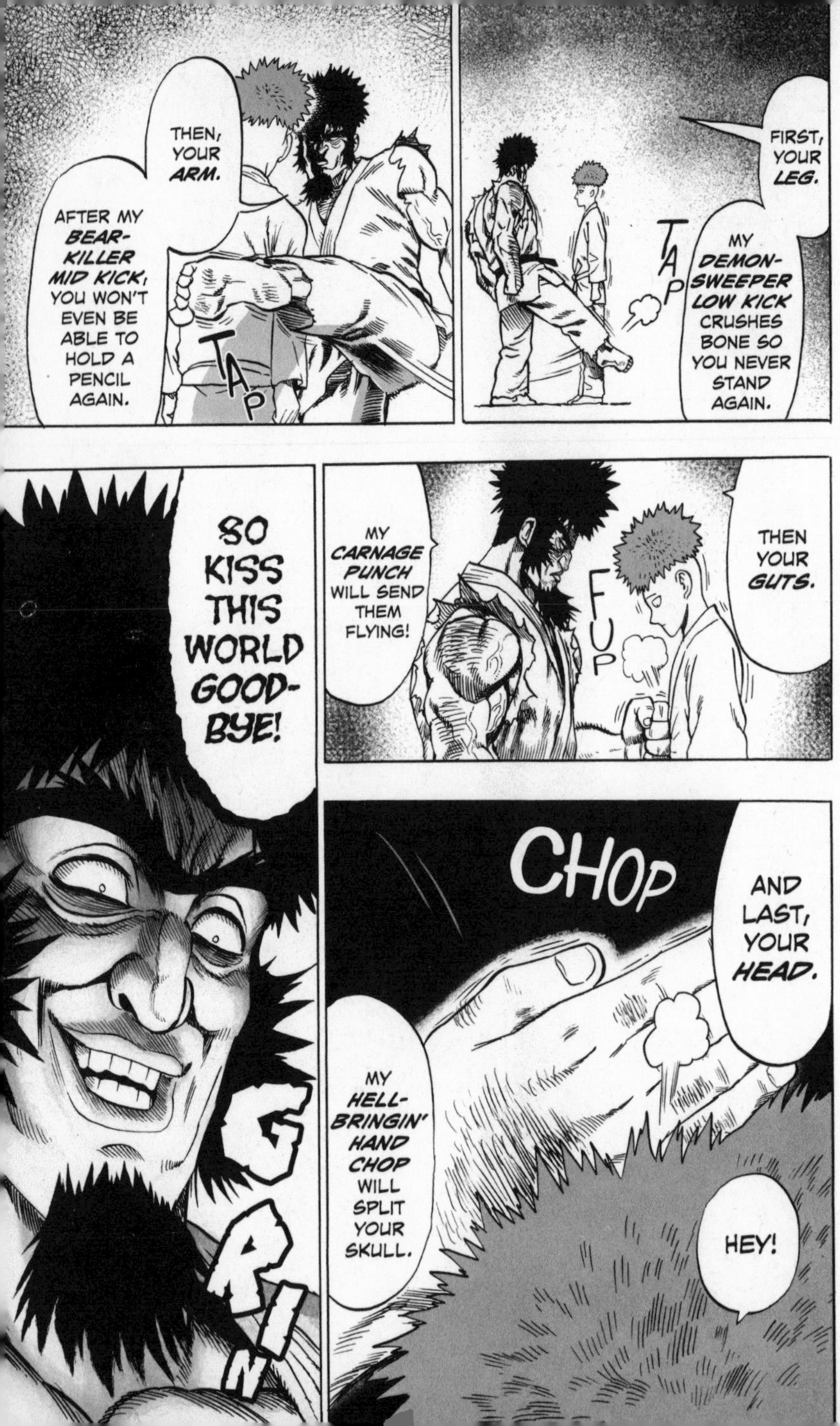
FIRST, YOUR LEG.
TAP
MY DEMON-SWEEPER LOW KICK CRUSHES BONE SO YOU NEVER STAND AGAIN.
THEN, YOUR ARM.
AFTER MY BEAR-KILLER MID KICK, YOU WON'T EVEN BE ABLE TO HOLD A PENCIL AGAIN.
TAP
THEN YOUR GUTS.
FUP
MY CARNAGE PUNCH WILL SEND THEM FLYING!
CHOP
AND LAST, YOUR HEAD.
MY HELL-BRINGIN' HAND CHOP WILL SPLIT YOUR SKULL.
HEY!
SO KISS THIS WORLD GOOD-BYE!
GRIN

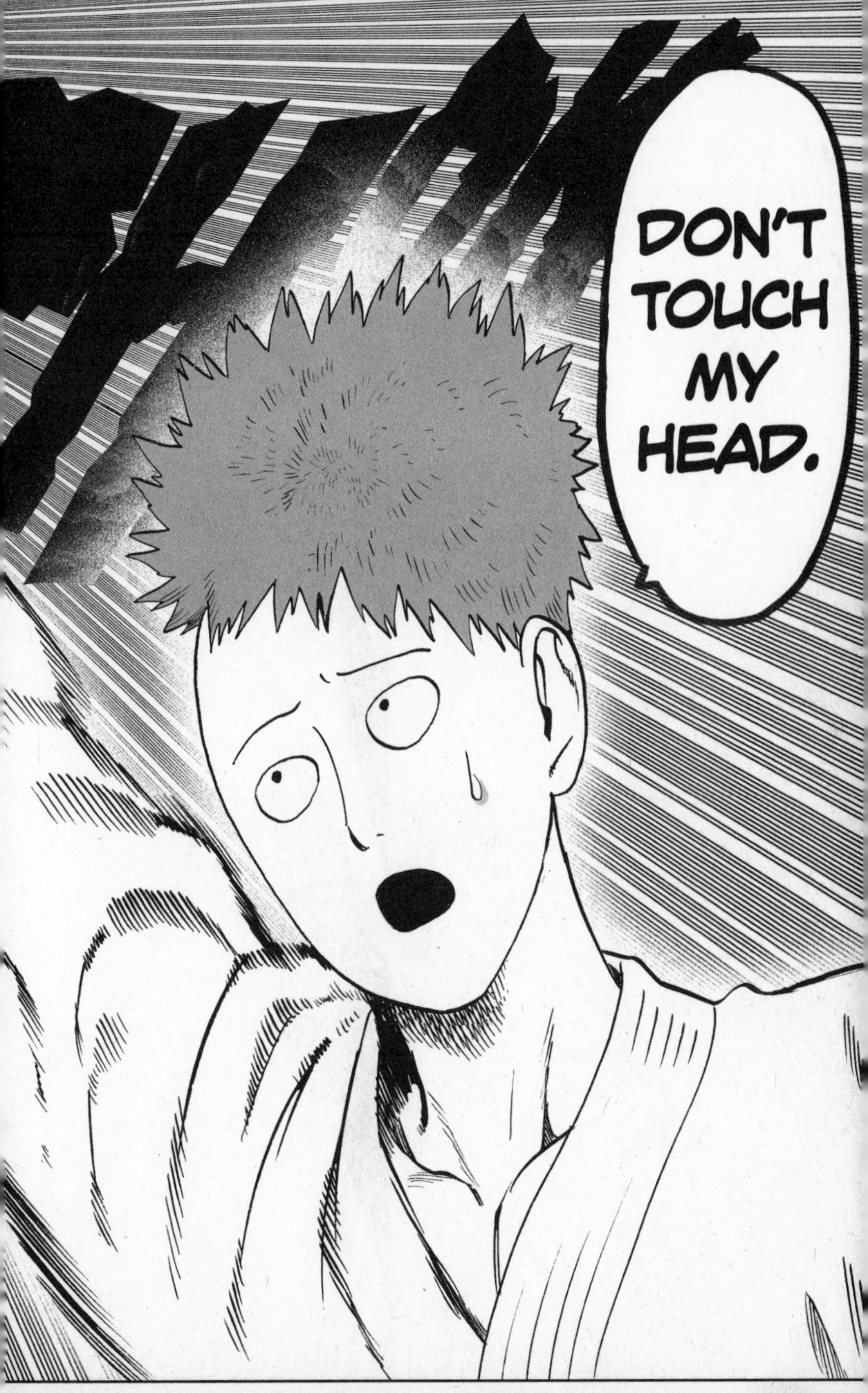
DON'T TOUCH MY HEAD.

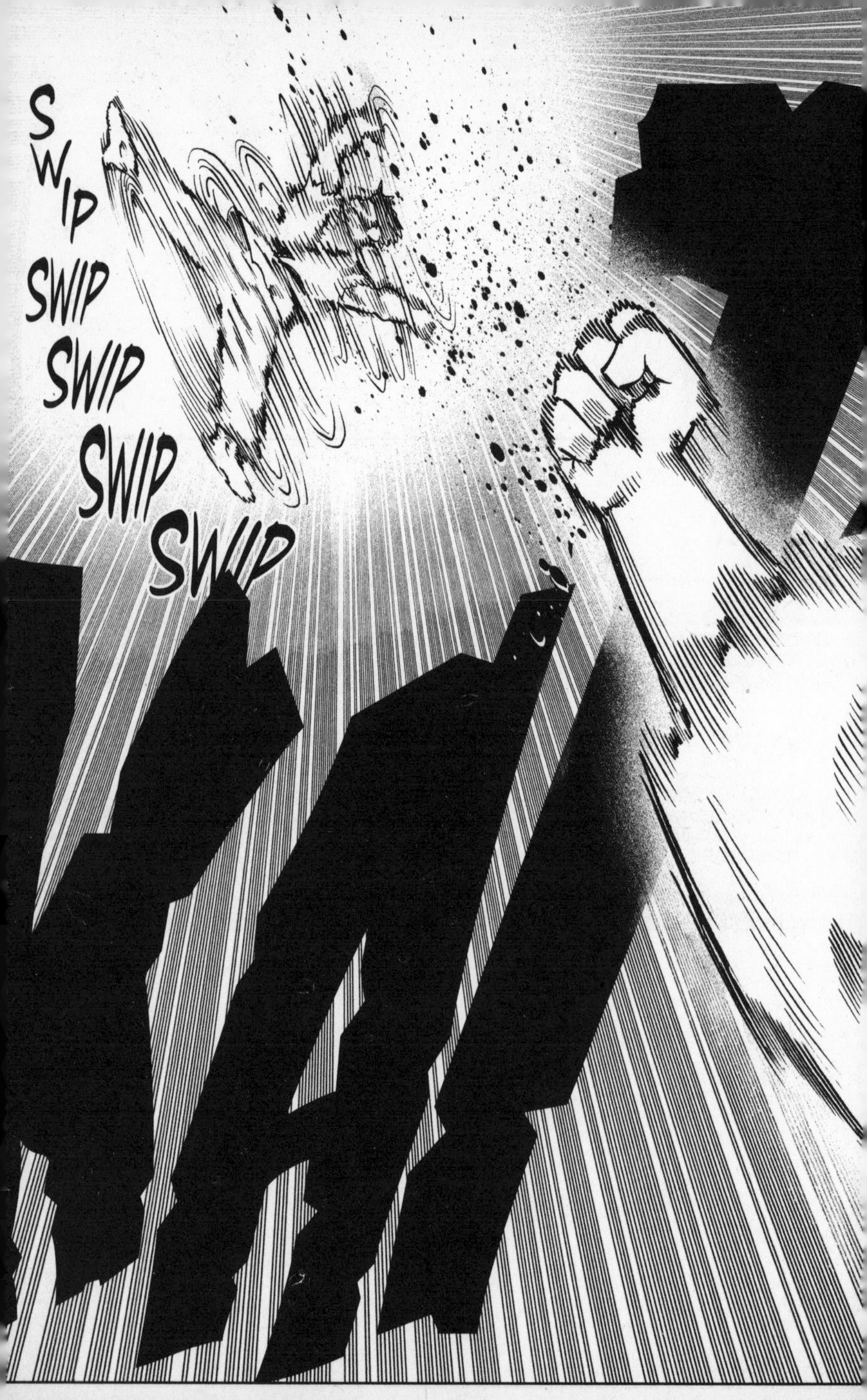
SWIP
SWIP
SWIP
SWIP
SWIP

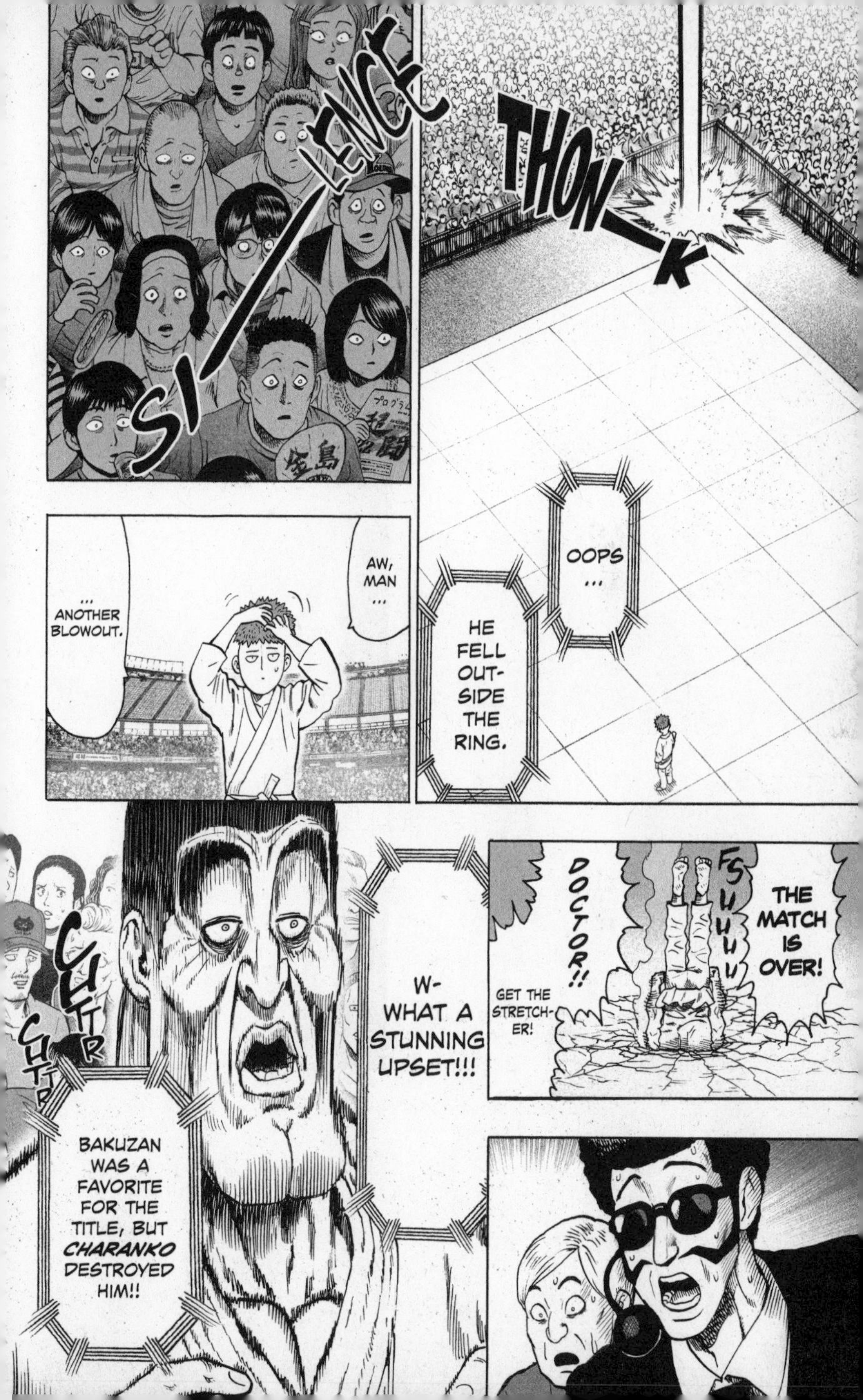
THON—K
SI—LENCE
OOPS...
HE FELL OUTSIDE THE RING.
AW, MAN...
...ANOTHER BLOWOUT.
THE MATCH IS OVER!
FSHUUU
DOCTOR!!
GET THE STRETCHER!
W-WHAT A STUNNING UPSET!!!
CHTTR CHTTR
BAKUZAN WAS A FAVORITE FOR THE TITLE, BUT *CHARANKO* DESTROYED HIM!!

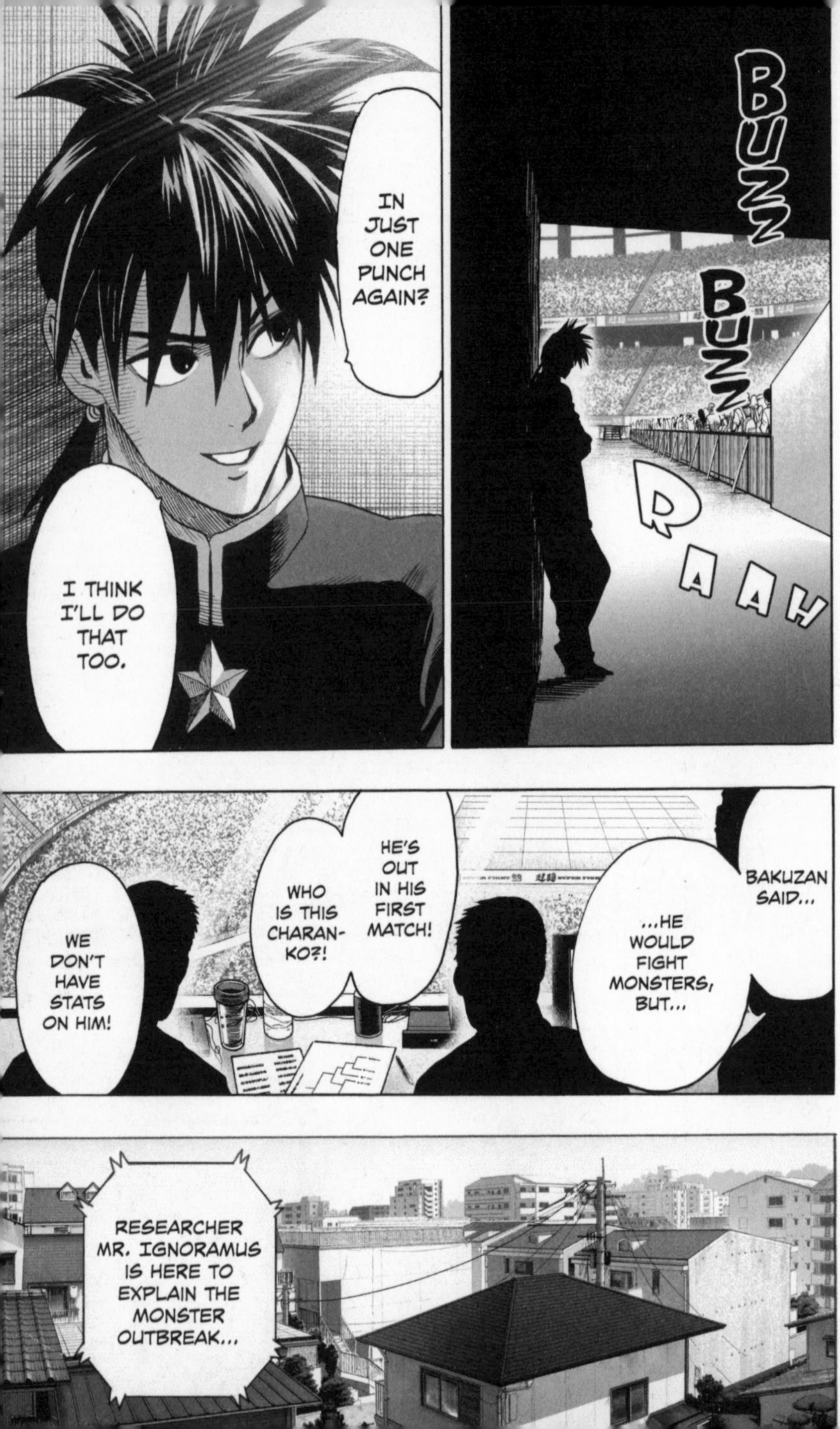
BUZZ
BUZZ
RAAAH
IN JUST ONE PUNCH AGAIN?
I THINK I'LL DO THAT TOO.
BAKUZAN SAID...
...HE WOULD FIGHT MONSTERS, BUT...
HE'S OUT IN HIS FIRST MATCH!
WHO IS THIS CHARAN-KO?!
WE DON'T HAVE STATS ON HIM!
RESEARCHER MR. IGNORAMUS IS HERE TO EXPLAIN THE MONSTER OUTBREAK...

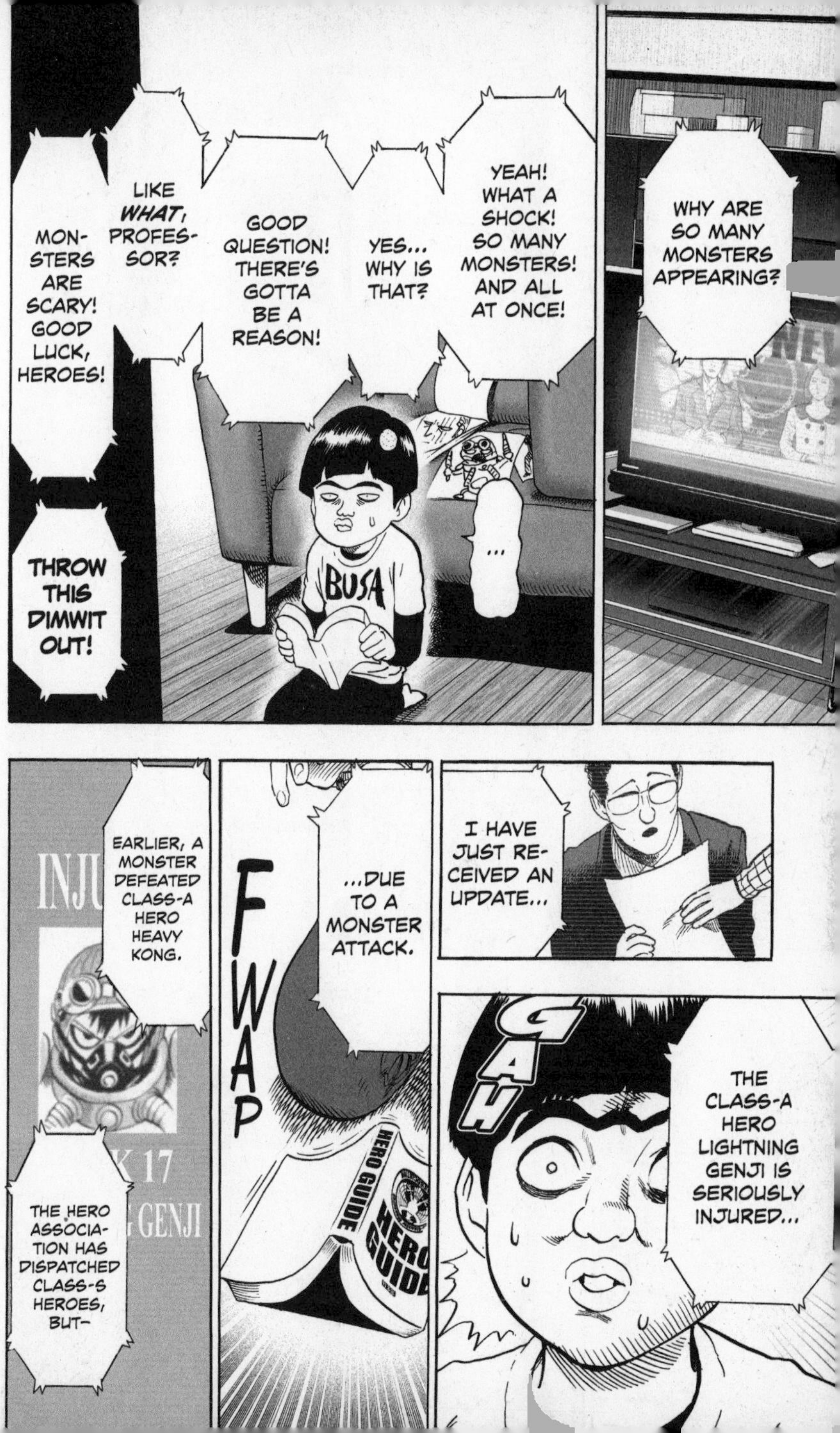
WHY ARE SO MANY MONSTERS APPEARING?
YEAH! WHAT A SHOCK! SO MANY MONSTERS! AND ALL AT ONCE!
YES... WHY IS THAT?
GOOD QUESTION! THERE'S GOTTA BE A REASON!
LIKE WHAT, PROFESSOR?
MONSTERS ARE SCARY! GOOD LUCK, HEROES!
...
THROW THIS DIMWIT OUT!
BUSA
I HAVE JUST RECEIVED AN UPDATE...
THE CLASS-A HERO LIGHTNING GENJI IS SERIOUSLY INJURED...
GAH
...DUE TO A MONSTER ATTACK.
FWAP
HERO GUIDE
EARLIER, A MONSTER DEFEATED CLASS-A HERO HEAVY KONG.
THE HERO ASSOCIATION HAS DISPATCHED CLASS-S HEROES, BUT-

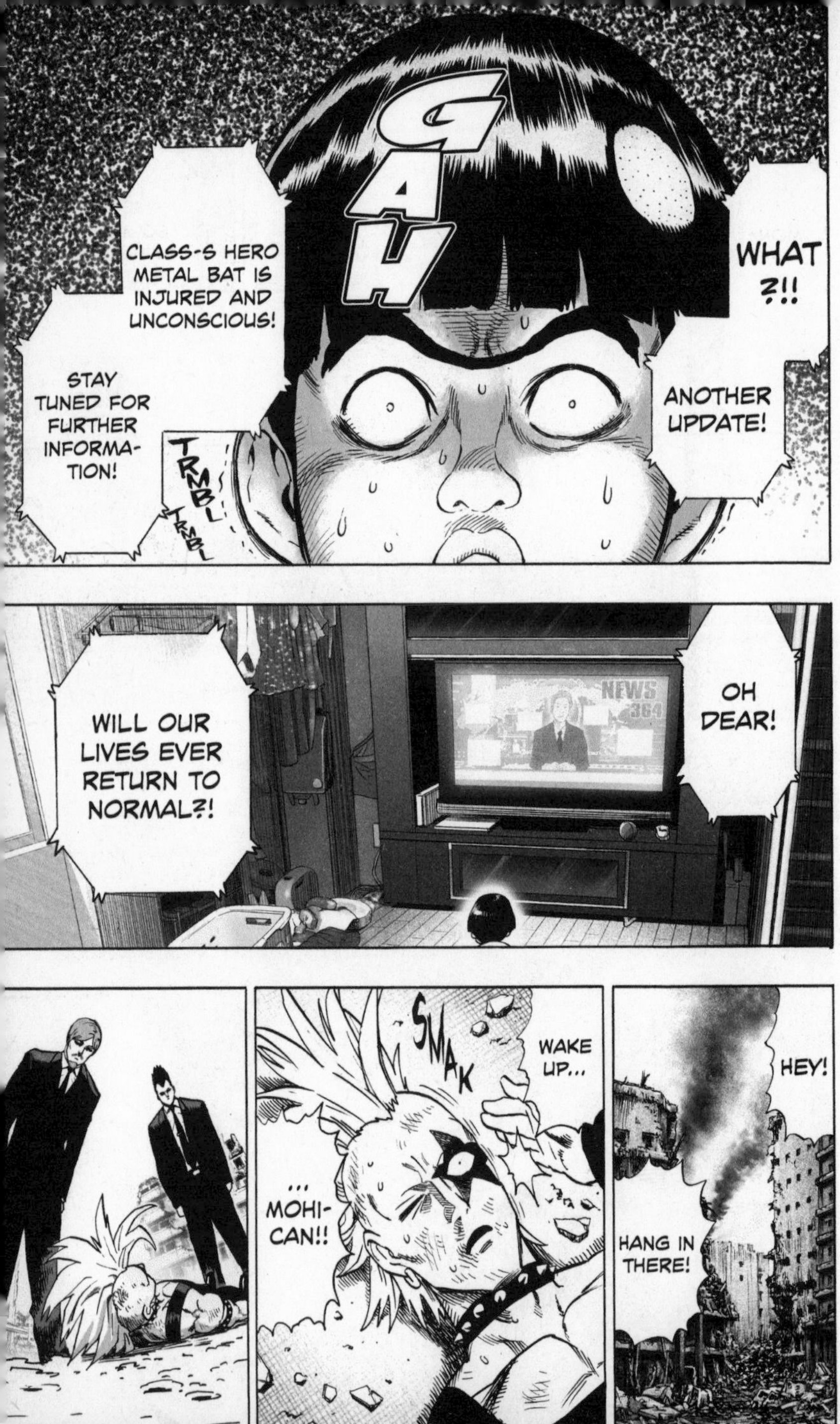
WHAT?!!
ANOTHER UPDATE!
GAH
CLASS-S HERO METAL BAT IS INJURED AND UNCONSCIOUS!
STAY TUNED FOR FURTHER INFORMATION!
TRMBL TRMBL
OH DEAR!
WILL OUR LIVES EVER RETURN TO NORMAL?!
NEWS 364
HEY!
HANG IN THERE!
WAKE UP...
SMAK
...MOHICAN!!

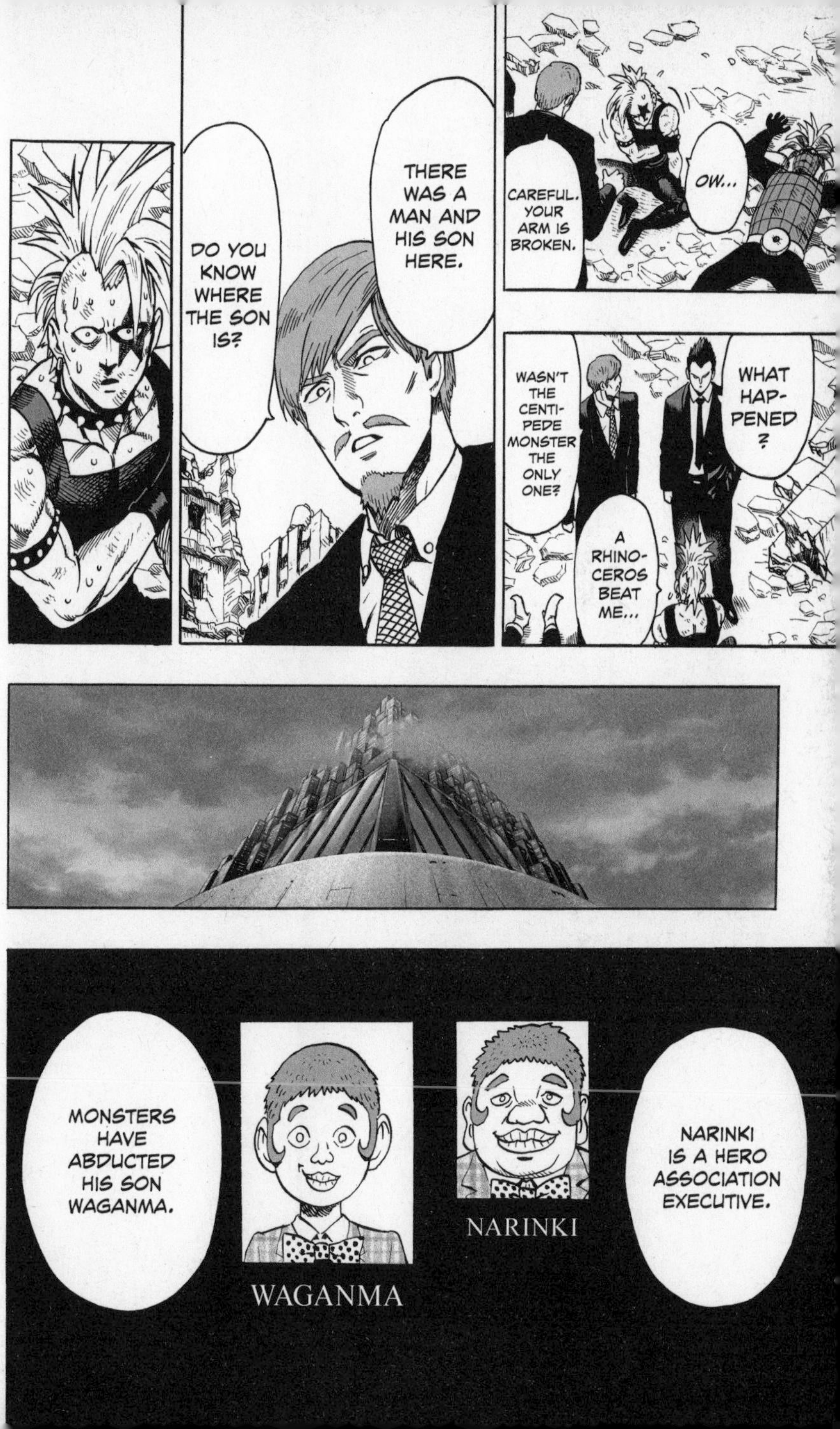
OW...
CAREFUL. YOUR ARM IS BROKEN.
WHAT HAPPENED?
WASN'T THE CENTIPEDE MONSTER THE ONLY ONE?
A RHINOCEROS BEAT ME...
THERE WAS A MAN AND HIS SON HERE.
DO YOU KNOW WHERE THE SON IS?
NARINKI IS A HERO ASSOCIATION EXECUTIVE.
NARINKI
WAGANMA
MONSTERS HAVE ABDUCTED HIS SON WAGANMA.

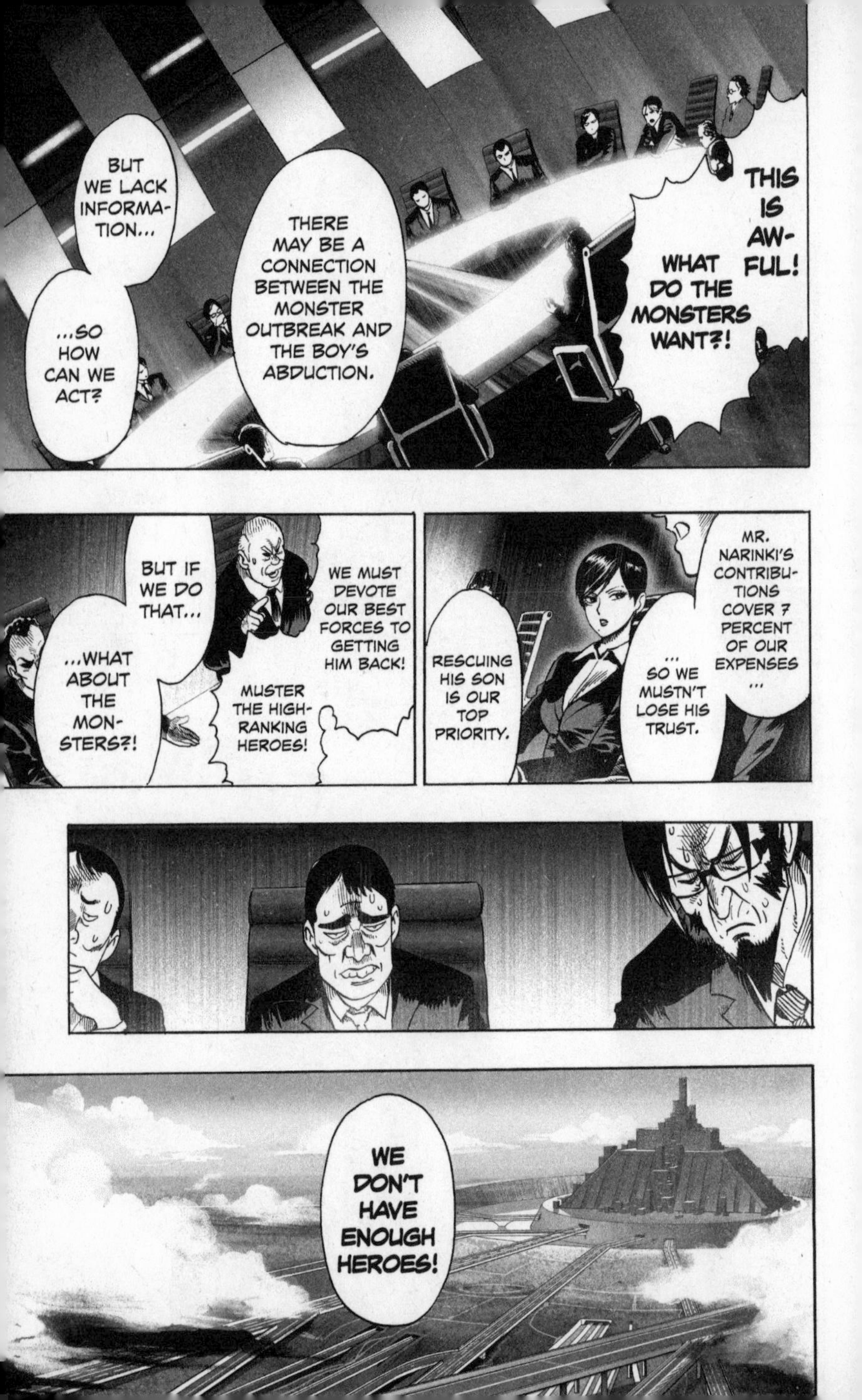
THIS IS AW-FUL!
WHAT DO THE MONSTERS WANT?!
THERE MAY BE A CONNECTION BETWEEN THE MONSTER OUTBREAK AND THE BOY'S ABDUCTION.
BUT WE LACK INFORMA-TION...
...SO HOW CAN WE ACT?
MR. NARINKI'S CONTRIBU-TIONS COVER 7 PERCENT OF OUR EXPENSES...
...SO WE MUSTN'T LOSE HIS TRUST.
RESCUING HIS SON IS OUR TOP PRIORITY.
WE MUST DEVOTE OUR BEST FORCES TO GETTING HIM BACK!
MUSTER THE HIGH-RANKING HEROES!
BUT IF WE DO THAT...
...WHAT ABOUT THE MON-STERS?!
WE DON'T HAVE ENOUGH HEROES!

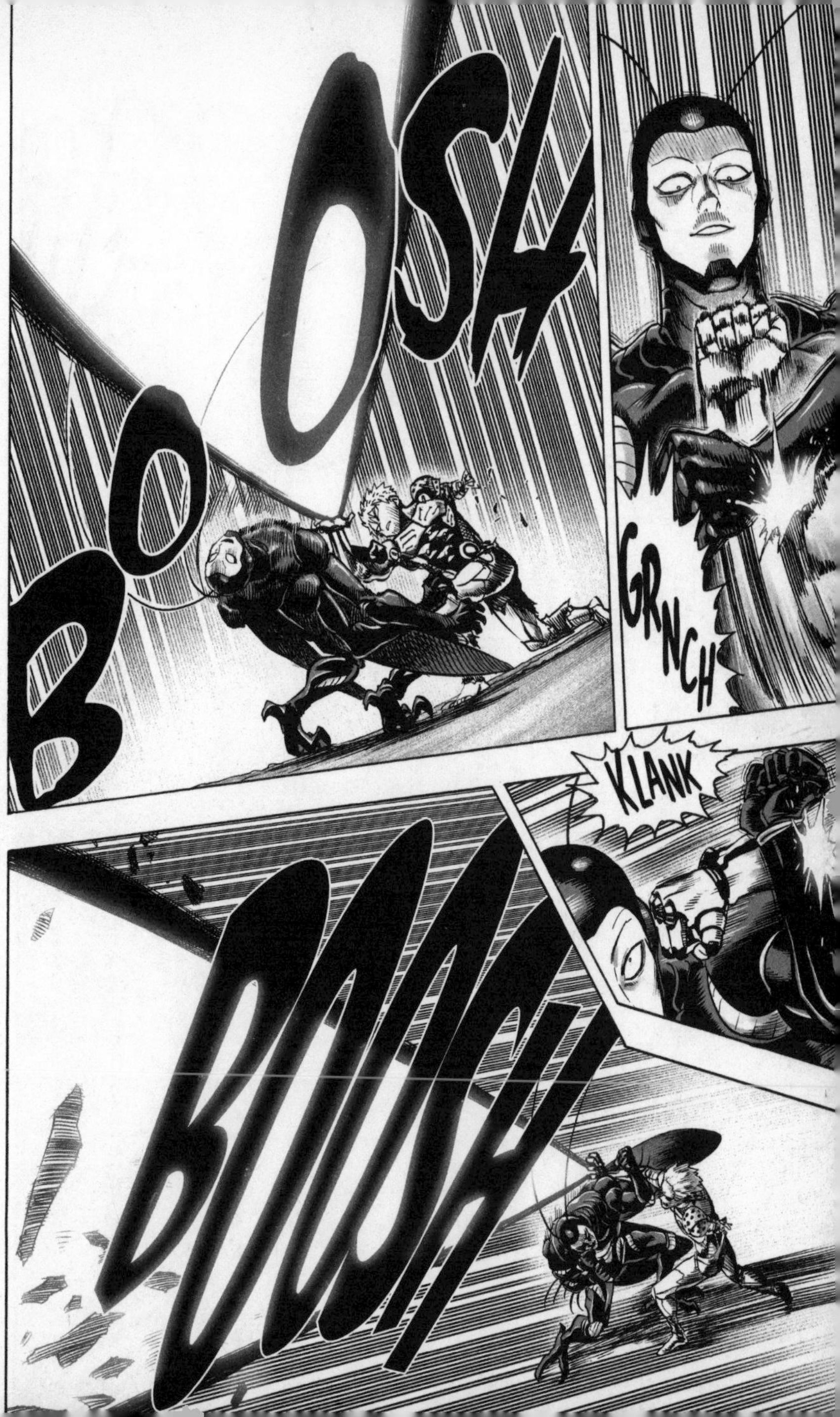
GRNCH
BOOOSH
KLANK
BOOOSH

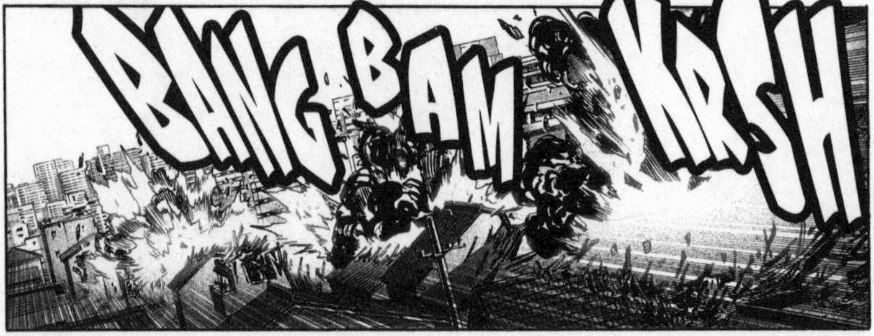
BANG BAM KRSH
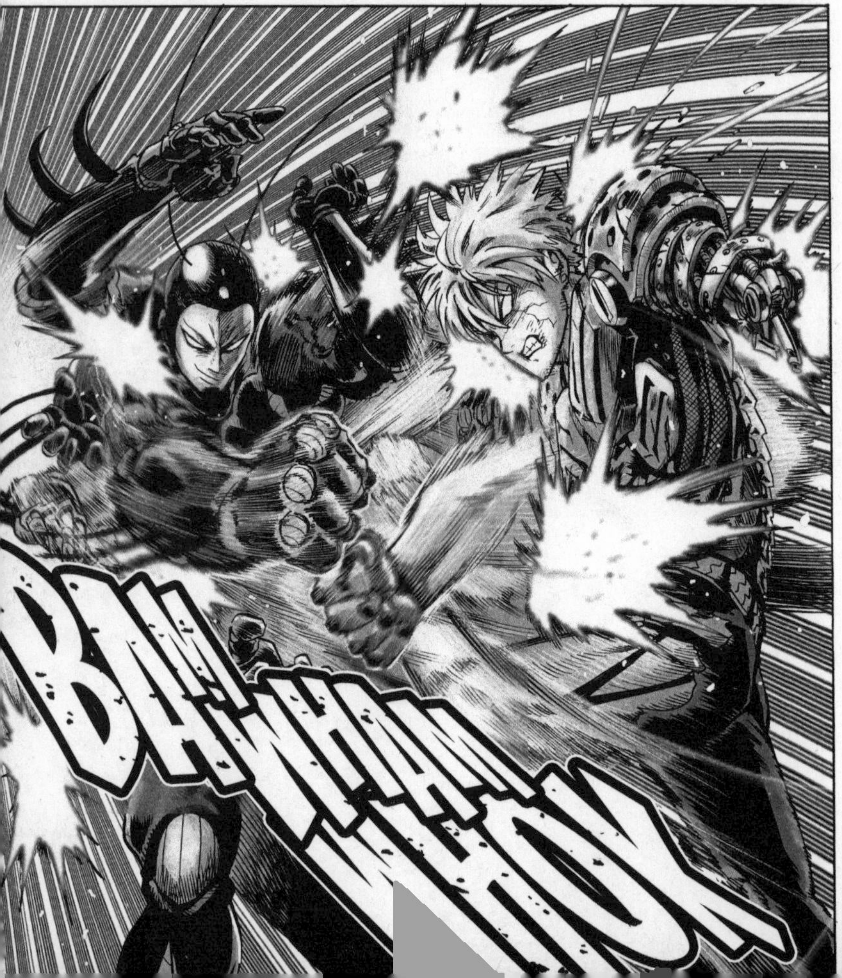
BAM WHAM

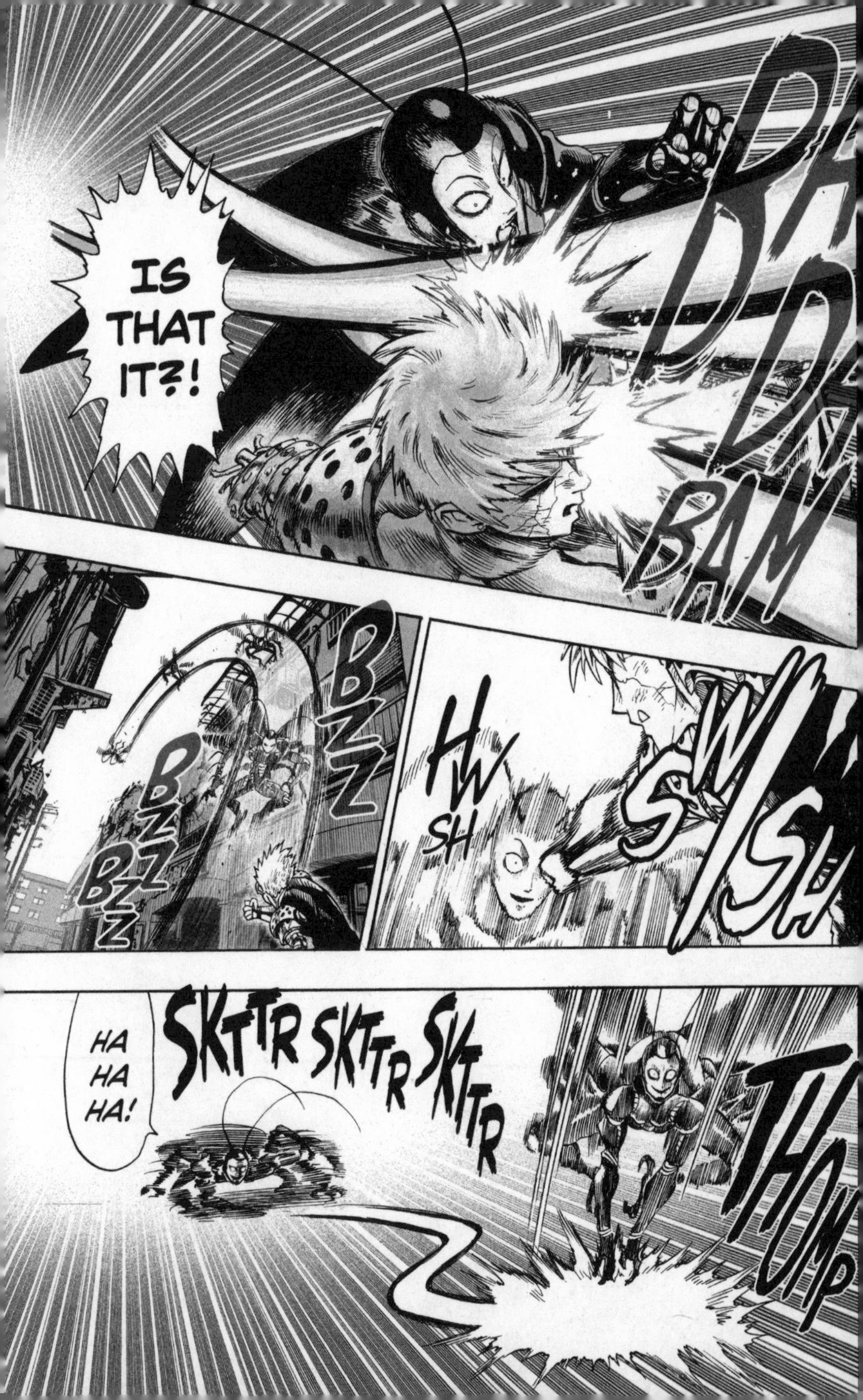

BAM
IS THAT IT?!
HWSH
BZZ
BZZ
BZZ
THUMP
SKTTR SKTTR SKTTR
HA HA HA!

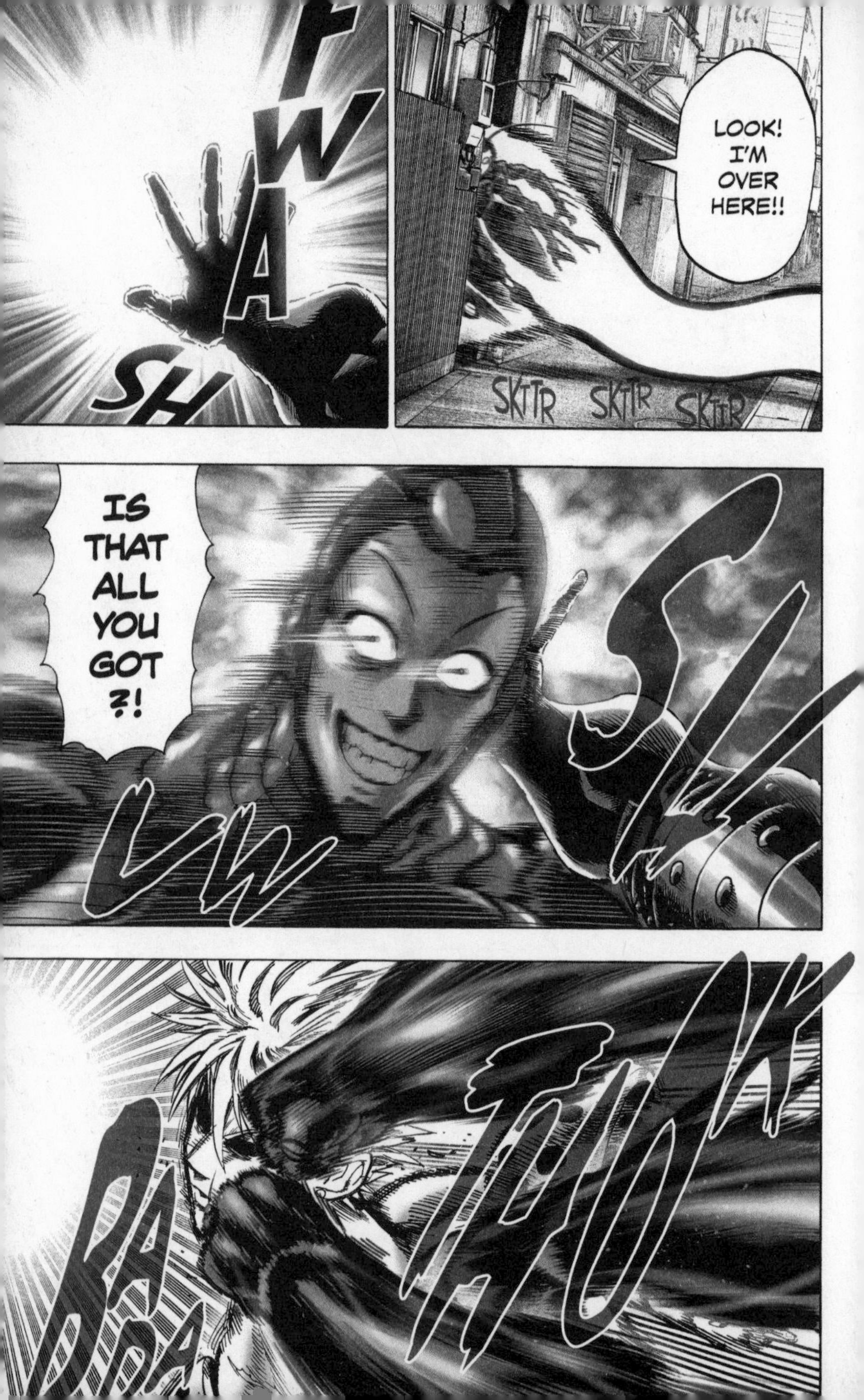
LOOK! I'M OVER HERE!!
SKTTR SKTTR SKTTR
FWASH
IS THAT ALL YOU GOT?!

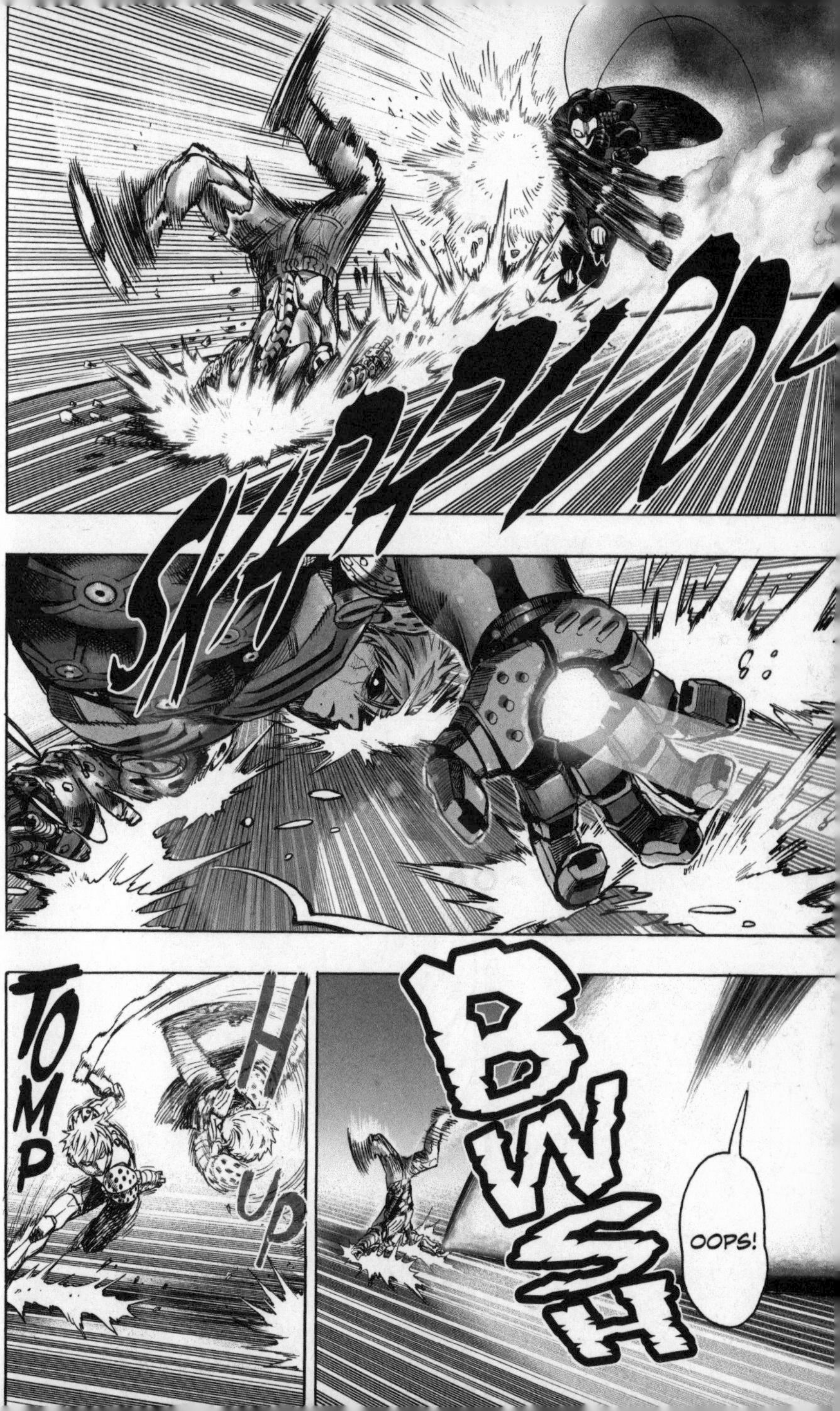
BWSH
OOPS!
HUP
TOMP

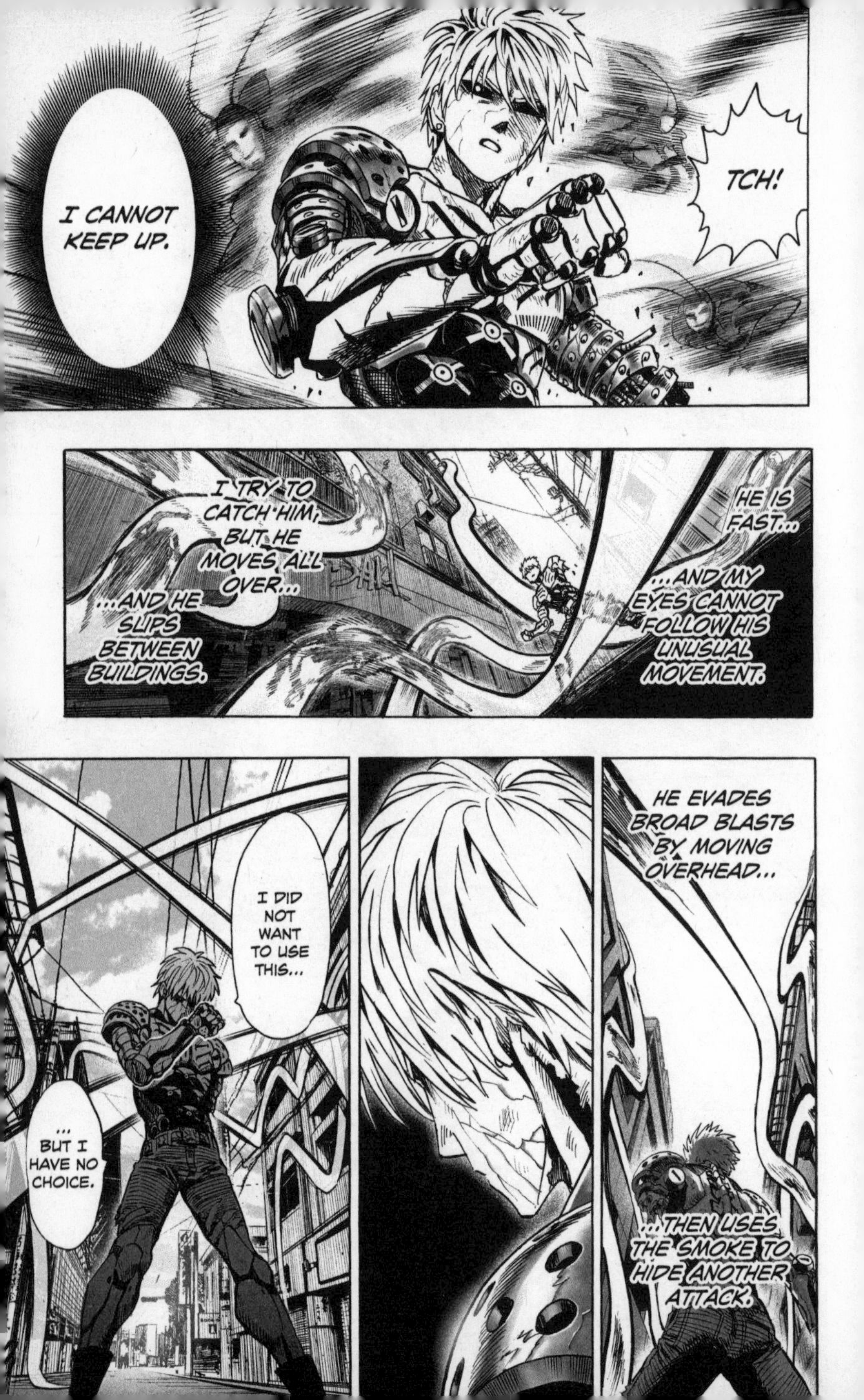
TCH!
I CANNOT KEEP UP.
HE IS FAST...
...AND MY EYES CANNOT FOLLOW HIS UNUSUAL MOVEMENT.
I TRY TO CATCH HIM, BUT HE MOVES ALL OVER...
...AND HE SLIPS BETWEEN BUILDINGS.
HE EVADES BROAD BLASTS BY MOVING OVERHEAD...
...THEN USES THE SMOKE TO HIDE ANOTHER ATTACK.
I DID NOT WANT TO USE THIS...
...BUT I HAVE NO CHOICE.

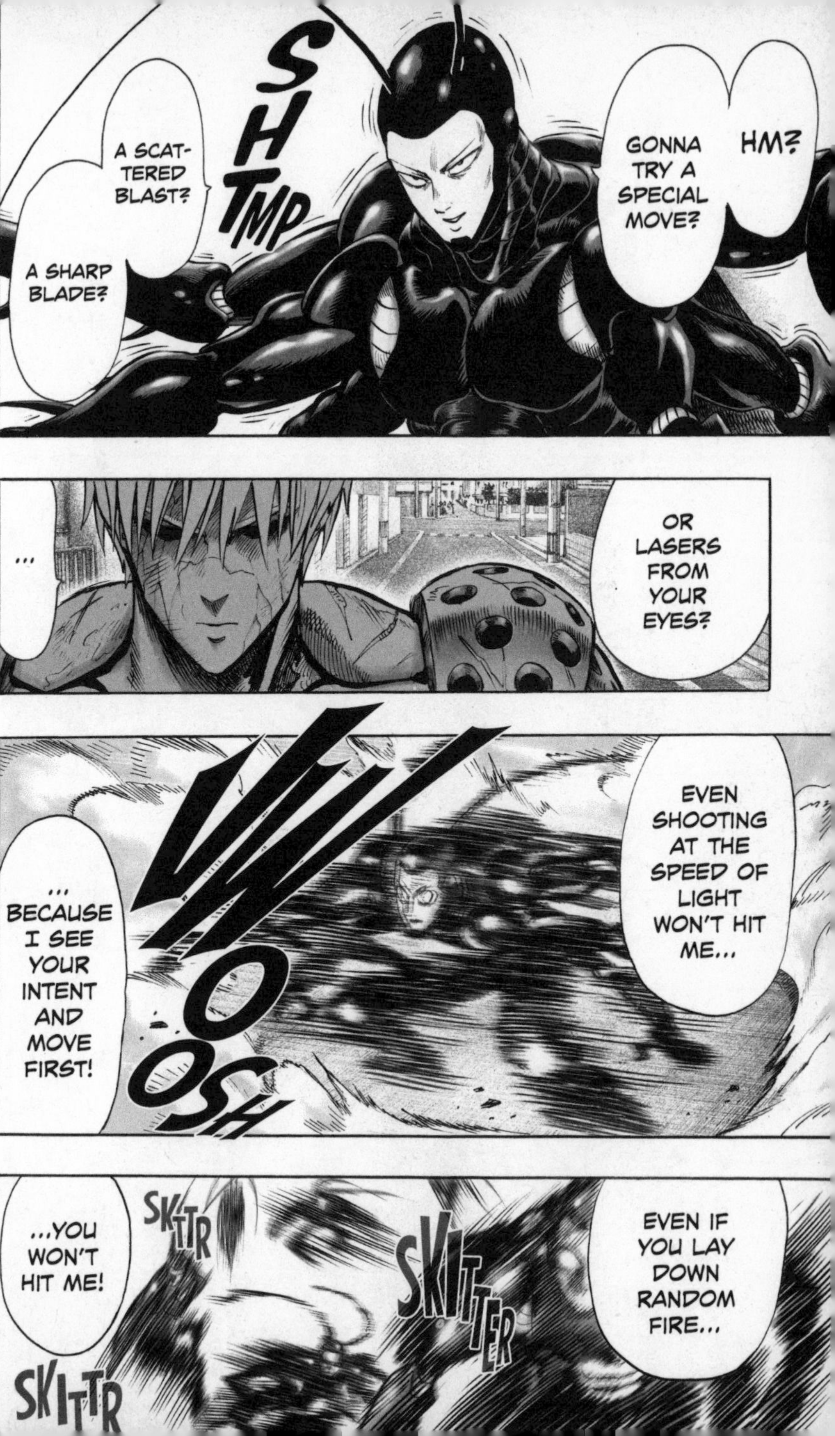
HM?
GONNA TRY A SPECIAL MOVE?
SHTMP
A SCAT-TERED BLAST?
A SHARP BLADE?
OR LASERS FROM YOUR EYES?
...
EVEN SHOOTING AT THE SPEED OF LIGHT WON'T HIT ME...
WHOOSH
... BECAUSE I SEE YOUR INTENT AND MOVE FIRST!
EVEN IF YOU LAY DOWN RANDOM FIRE...
SKITTER
SKITTR
...YOU WON'T HIT ME!
SKITTR

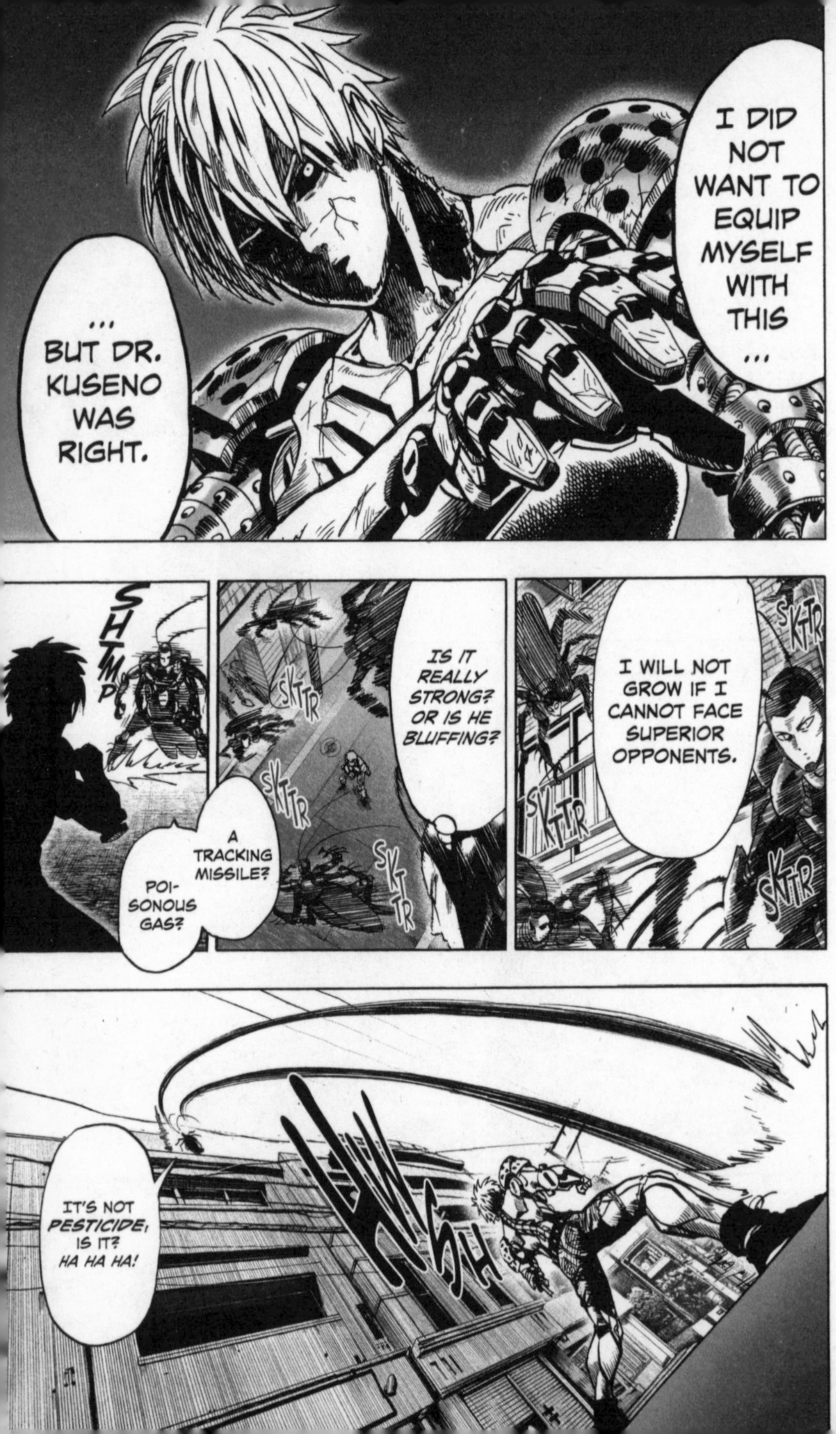
I DID NOT WANT TO EQUIP MYSELF WITH THIS ...
... BUT DR. KUSENO WAS RIGHT.
SKTTR
I WILL NOT GROW IF I CANNOT FACE SUPERIOR OPPONENTS.
SKTTR
SKTTR
IS IT REALLY STRONG? OR IS HE BLUFFING?
SKTTR
SKTTR
SKTTR
SHTMP
A TRACKING MISSILE?
POI-SONOUS GAS?
WHSH
IT'S NOT *PESTICIDE*, IS IT? HA HA HA!

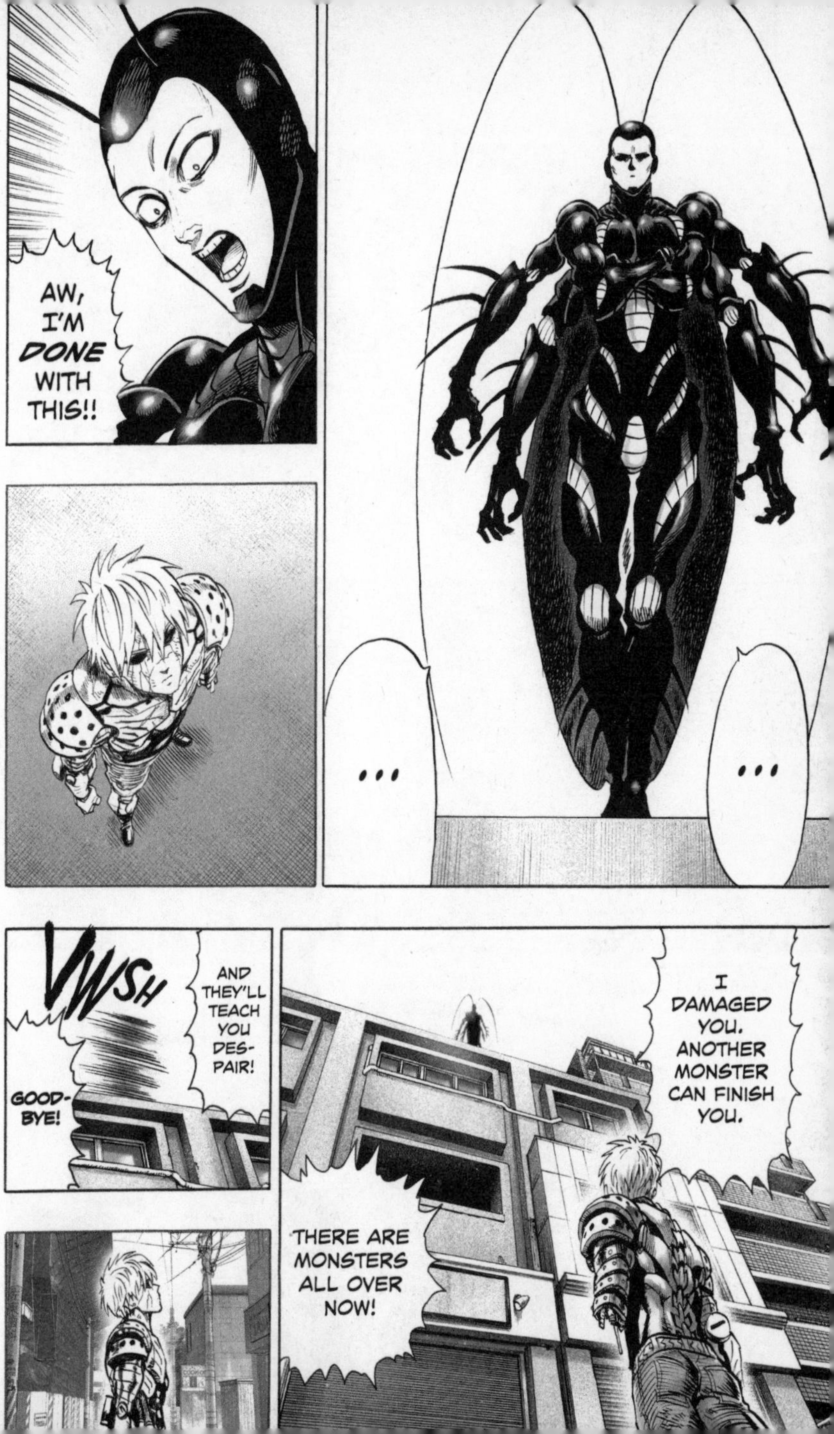
...
...
AW, I'M *DONE* WITH THIS!!
I DAMAGED YOU. ANOTHER MONSTER CAN FINISH YOU.
THERE ARE MONSTERS ALL OVER NOW!
AND THEY'LL TEACH YOU DES-PAIR!
GOOD-BYE!
VWSH

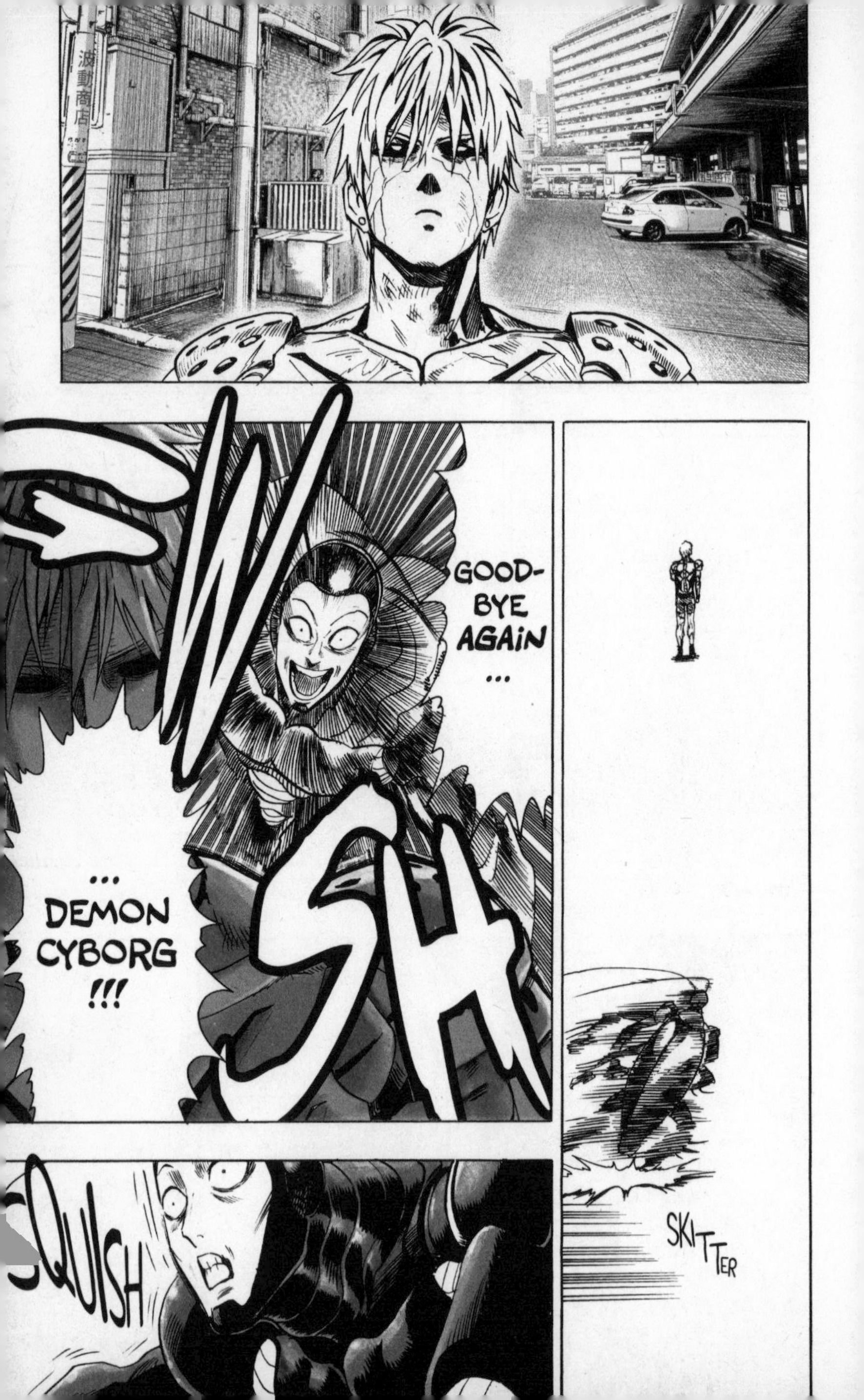

波動商店
SKITTER
GOOD-BYE AGAIN ...
WH
SH
... DEMON CYBORG !!!
SQUISH

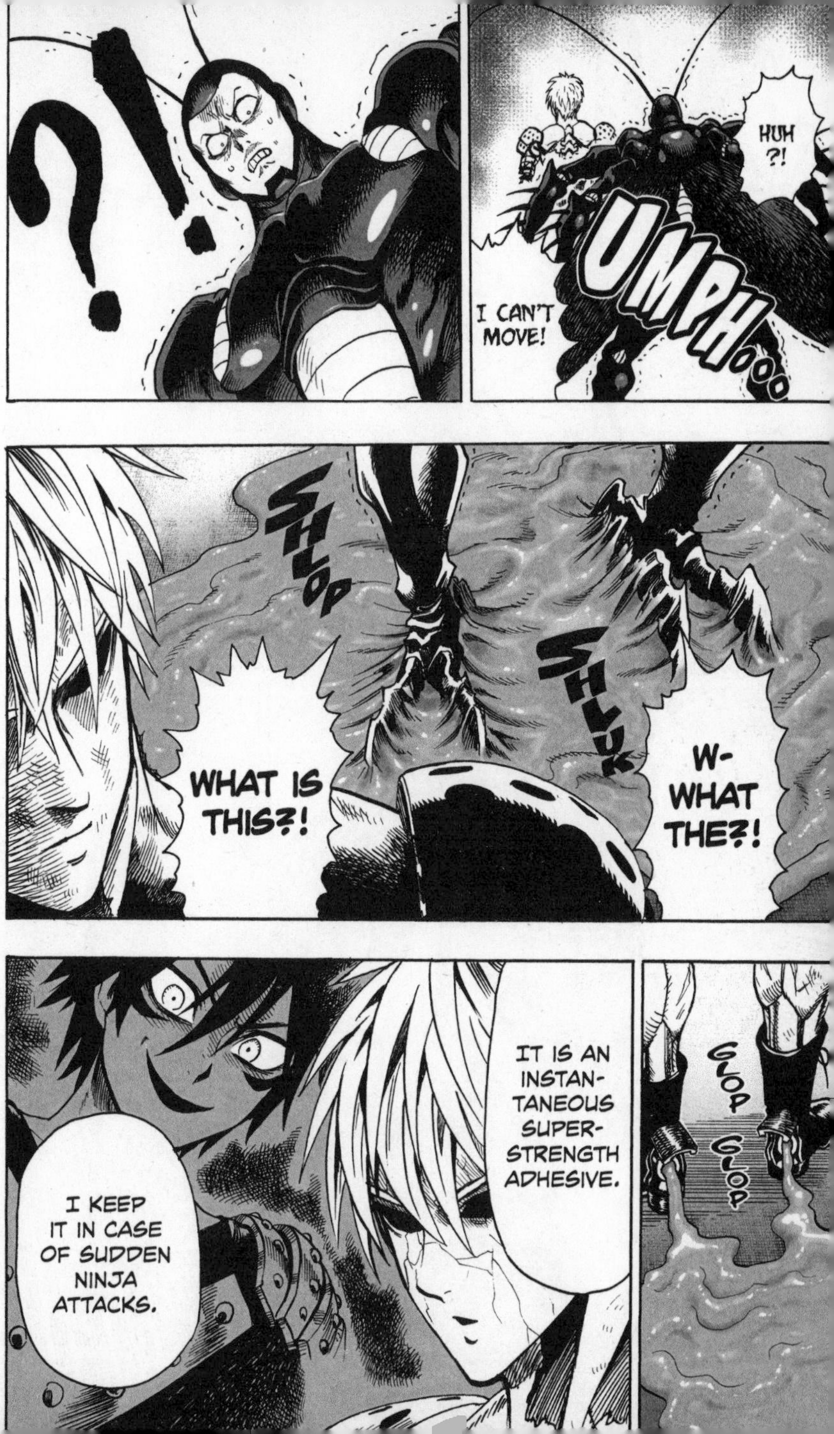
HUH ?!
UMPH...
I CAN'T MOVE!
?!
W-WHAT THE?!
SHLUK
SHLOP
WHAT IS THIS?!
GLOP GLOP
IT IS AN INSTANTANEOUS SUPER-STRENGTH ADHESIVE.
I KEEP IT IN CASE OF SUDDEN NINJA ATTACKS.

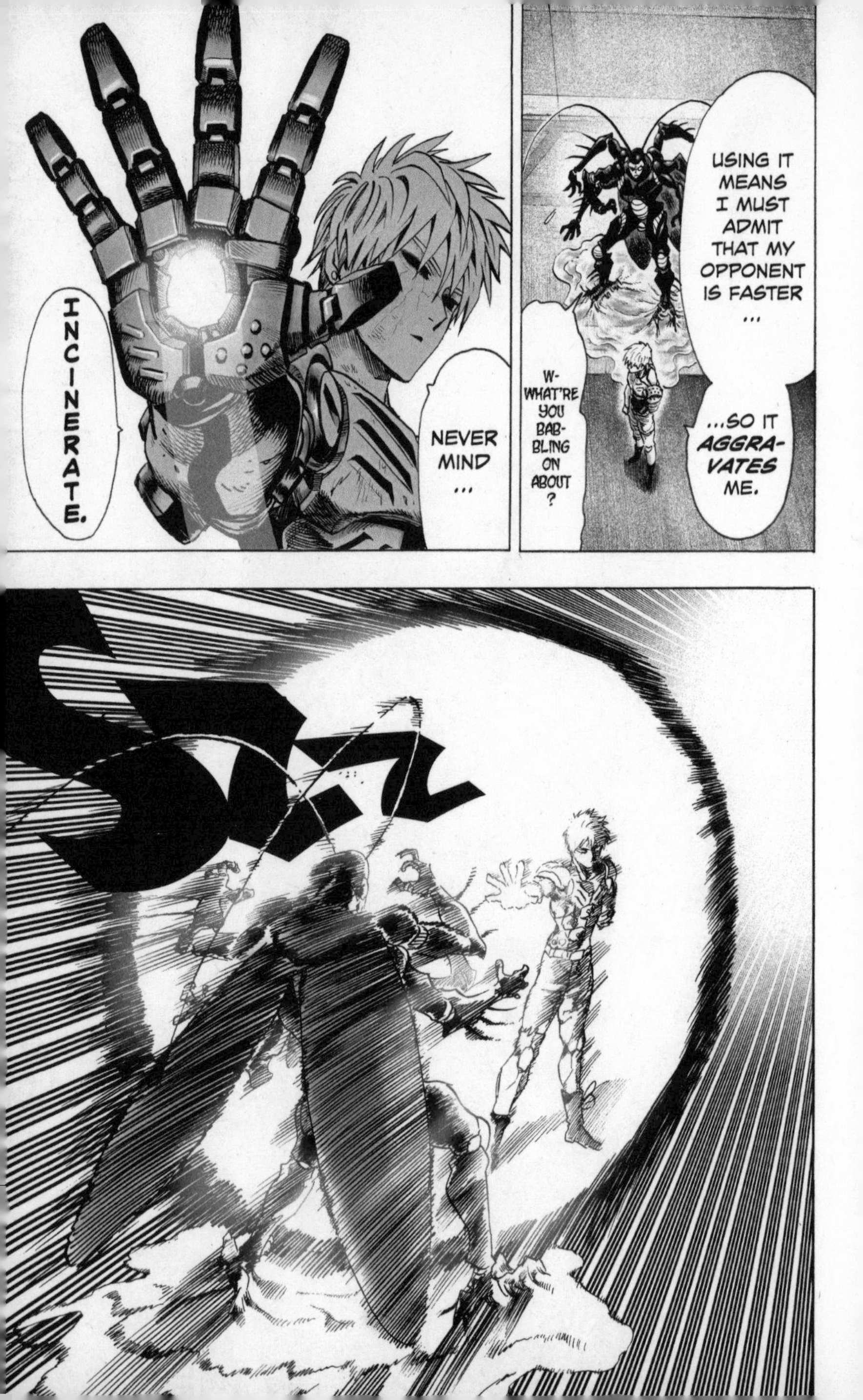
USING IT MEANS I MUST ADMIT THAT MY OPPONENT IS FASTER ...
W-WHAT'RE YOU BAB-BLING ON ABOUT ?
...SO IT AGGRA-VATES ME.
NEVER MIND ...
INCINERATE.

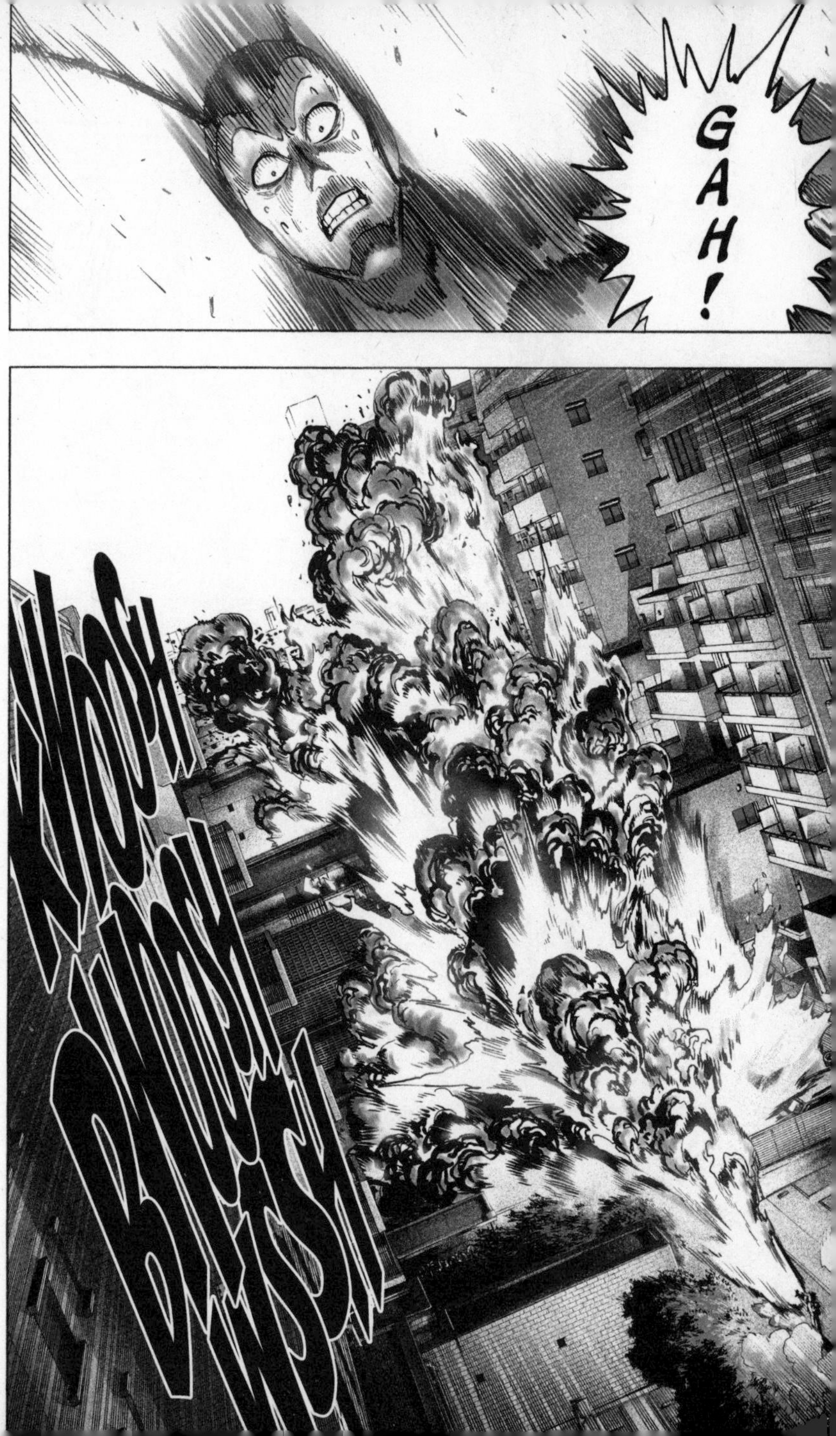
GAH!
WHOOSH
WHOOSH

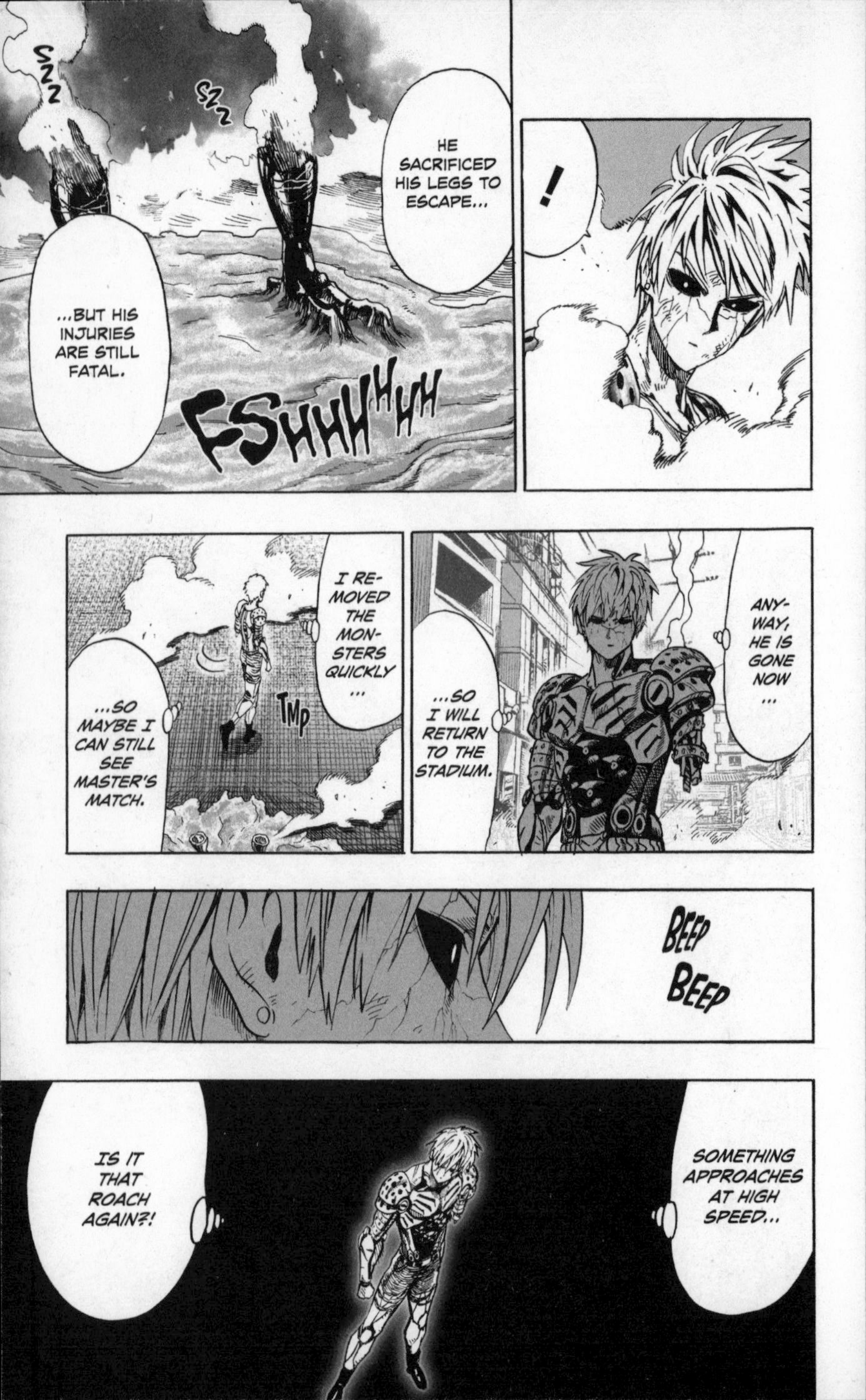
!
HE SACRIFICED HIS LEGS TO ESCAPE...
SZZ
SZZ
...BUT HIS INJURIES ARE STILL FATAL.
FSHHHHHH
ANYWAY, HE IS GONE NOW...
...SO I WILL RETURN TO THE STADIUM.
I REMOVED THE MONSTERS QUICKLY...
TMP
...SO MAYBE I CAN STILL SEE MASTER'S MATCH.
BEEP
BEEP
SOMETHING APPROACHES AT HIGH SPEED...
IS IT THAT ROACH AGAIN?!

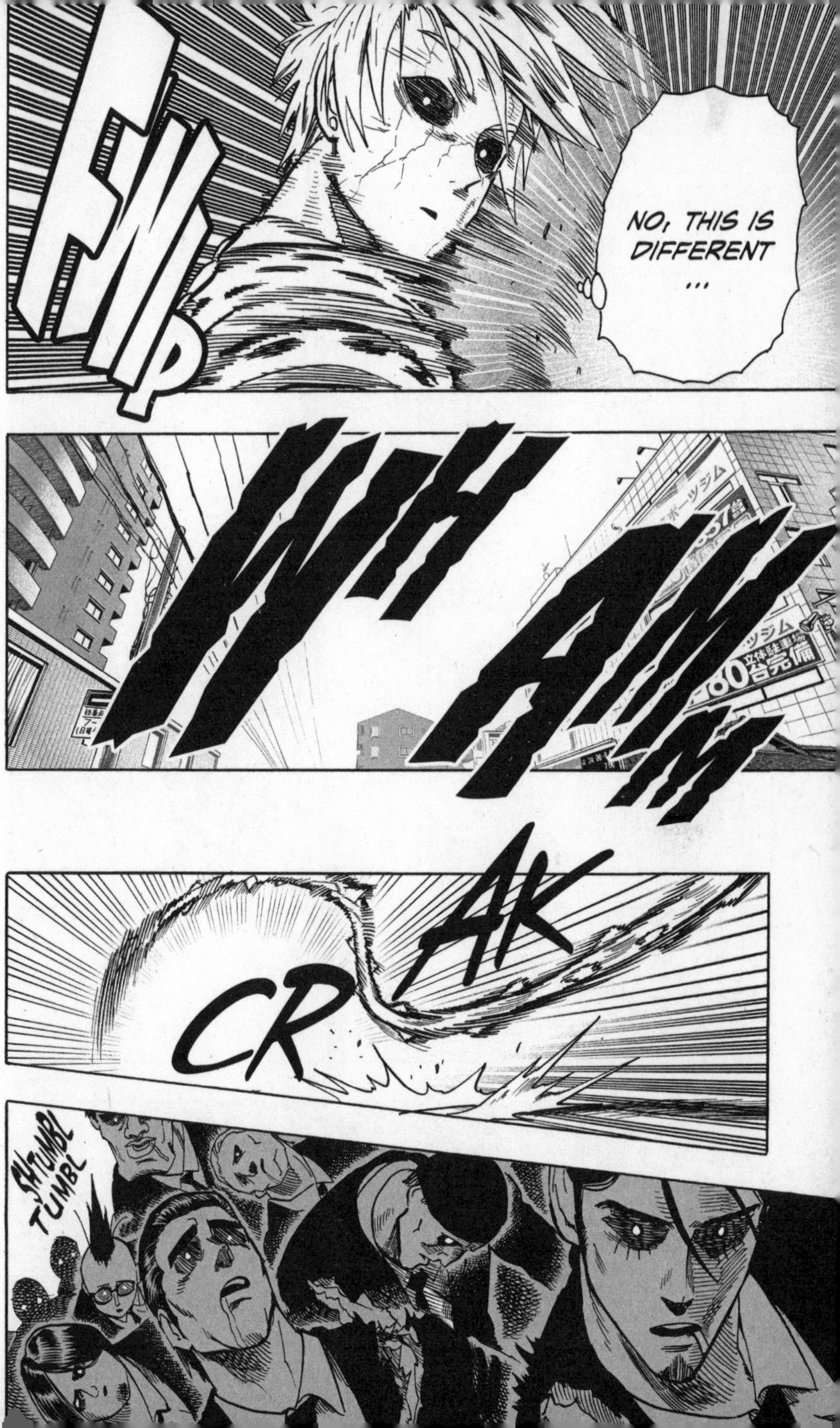
NO, THIS IS DIFFERENT ...
FWIP
WHAMM
CRAK
STUMBL
TUMBL

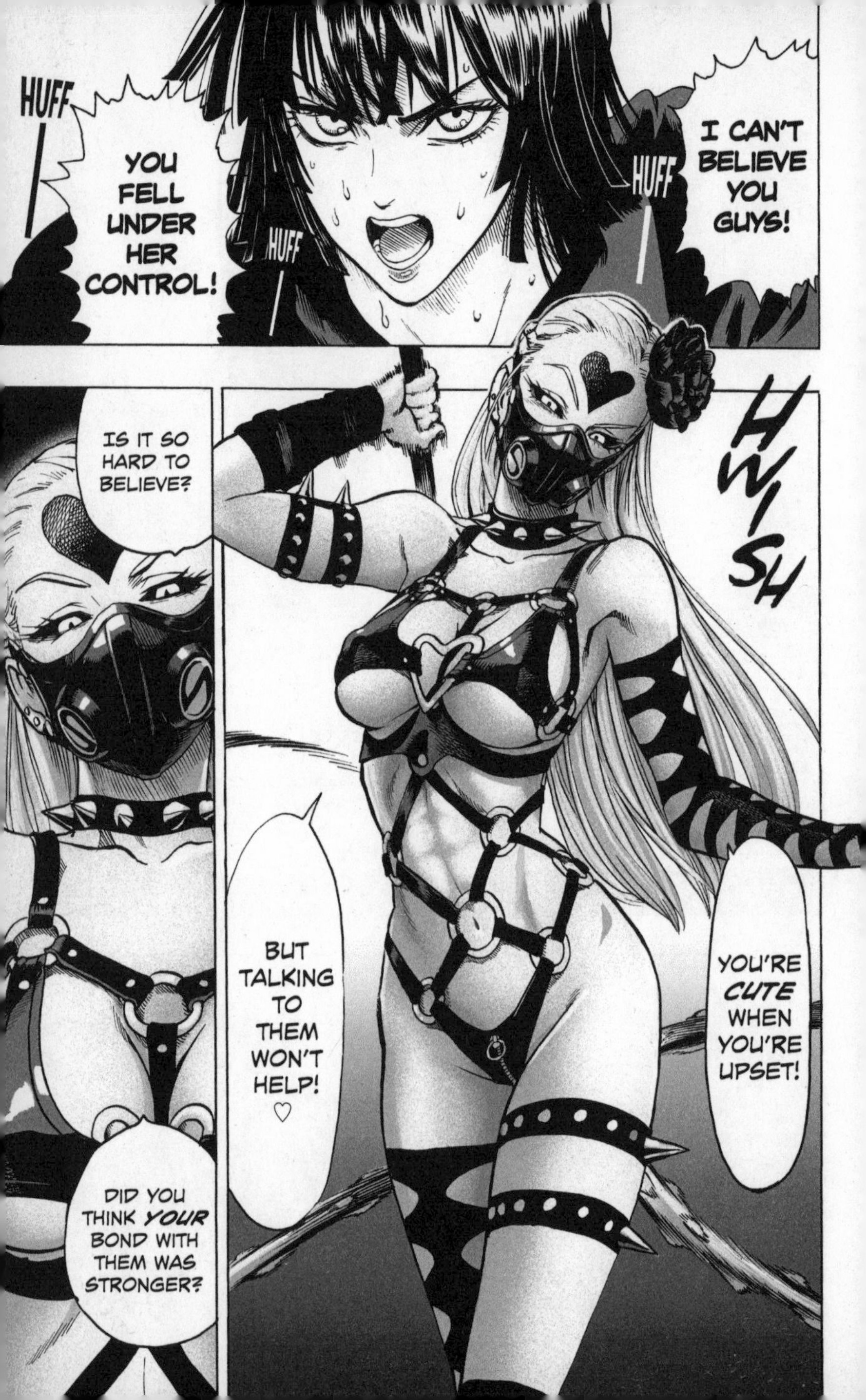
I CAN'T BELIEVE YOU GUYS!
HUFF
HUFF
YOU FELL UNDER HER CONTROL!
HUFF
HWISH
YOU'RE *CUTE* WHEN YOU'RE UPSET!
BUT TALKING TO THEM WON'T HELP! ♡
IS IT SO HARD TO BELIEVE?
DID YOU THINK *YOUR* BOND WITH THEM WAS STRONGER?

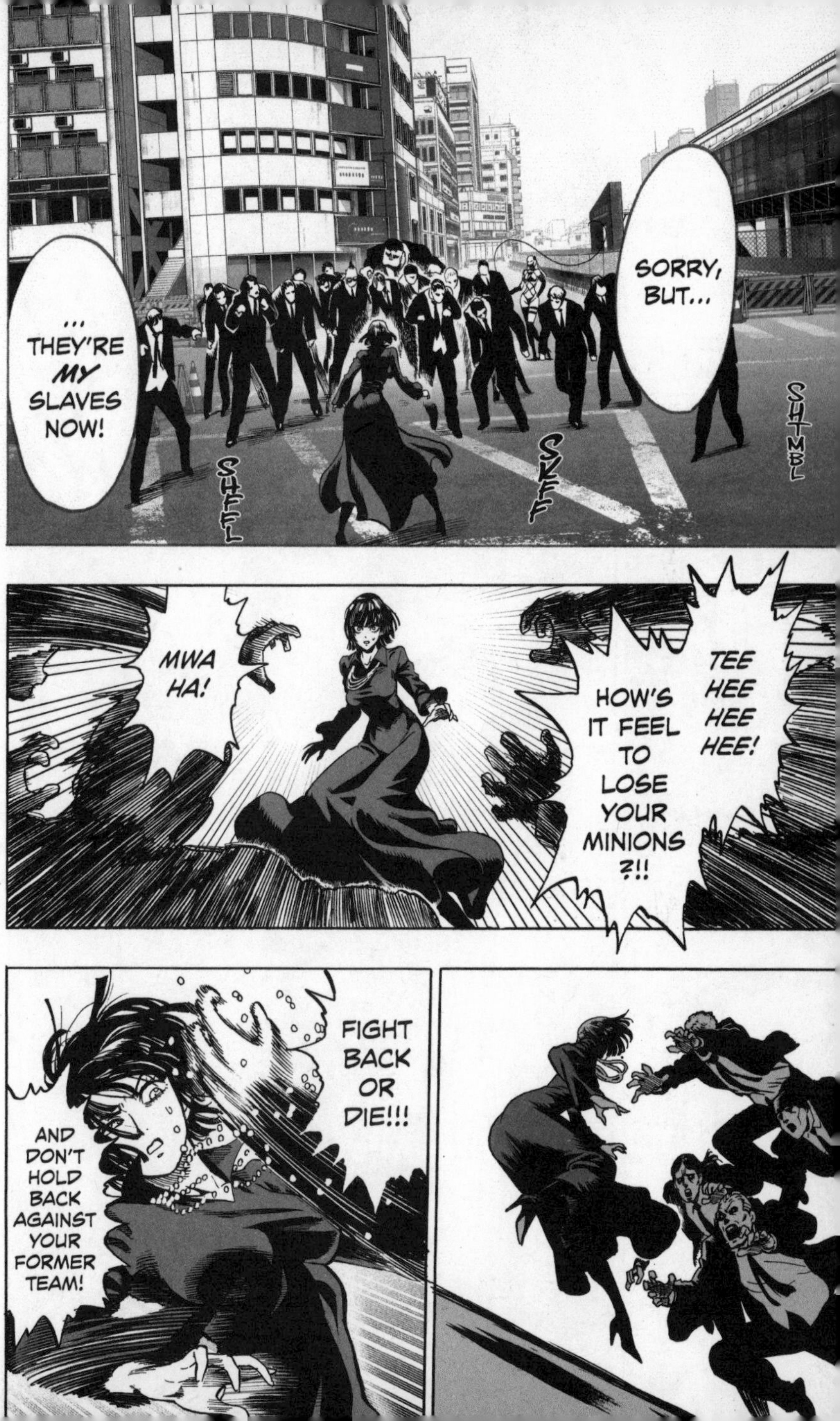
SORRY, BUT...
SHTMBL
SKFF
... THEY'RE MY SLAVES NOW!
SHFFL
TEE HEE HEE HEE!
HOW'S IT FEEL TO LOSE YOUR MINIONS ?!!
MWA HA!
FIGHT BACK OR DIE!!!
AND DON'T HOLD BACK AGAINST YOUR FORMER TEAM!

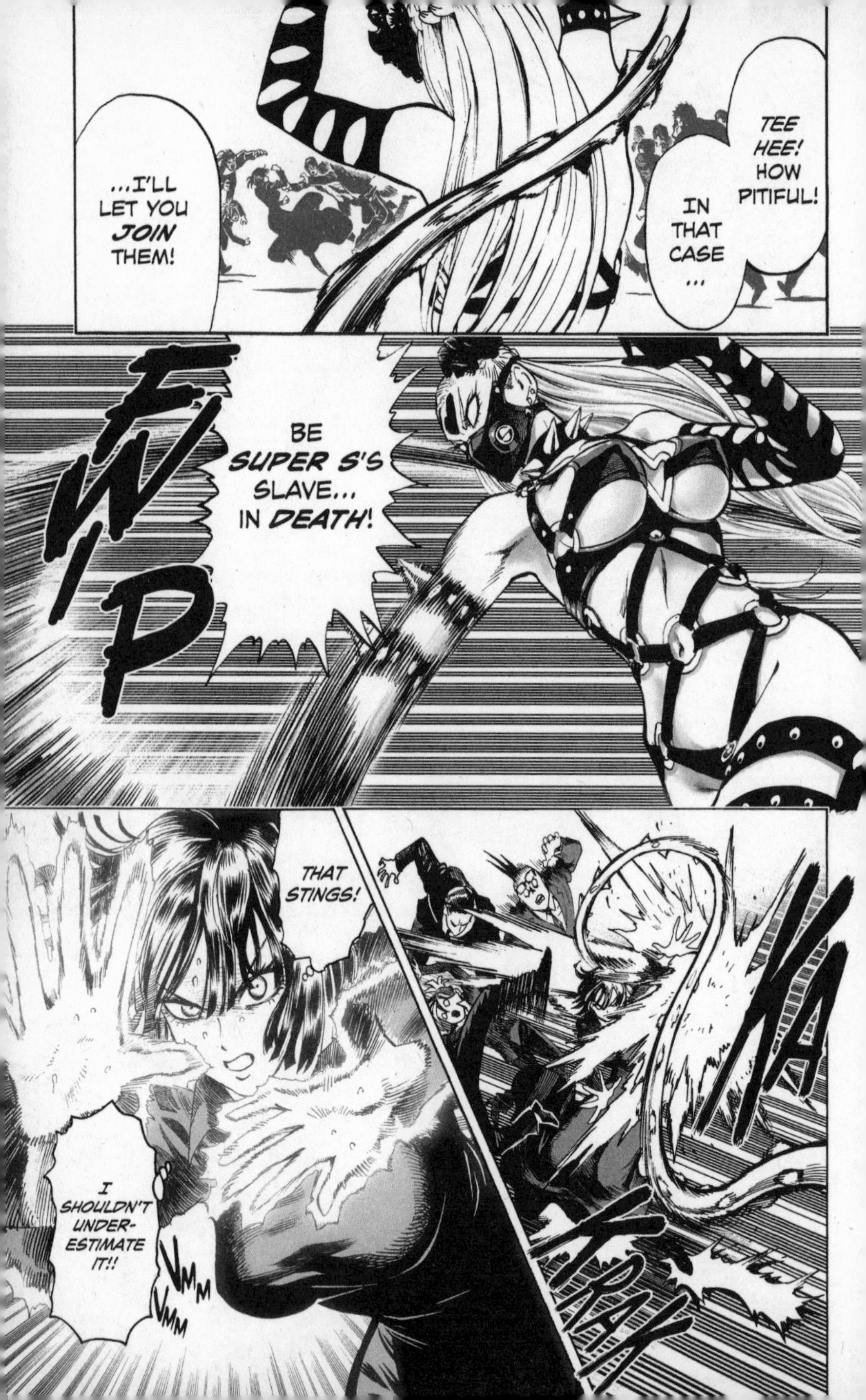
TEE HEE! HOW PITIFUL!
IN THAT CASE...
...I'LL LET YOU JOIN THEM!
FWIP
BE SUPER S'S SLAVE... IN DEATH!
KA
KRAK
THAT STINGS!
I SHOULDN'T UNDER-ESTIMATE IT!!
VMM VMM

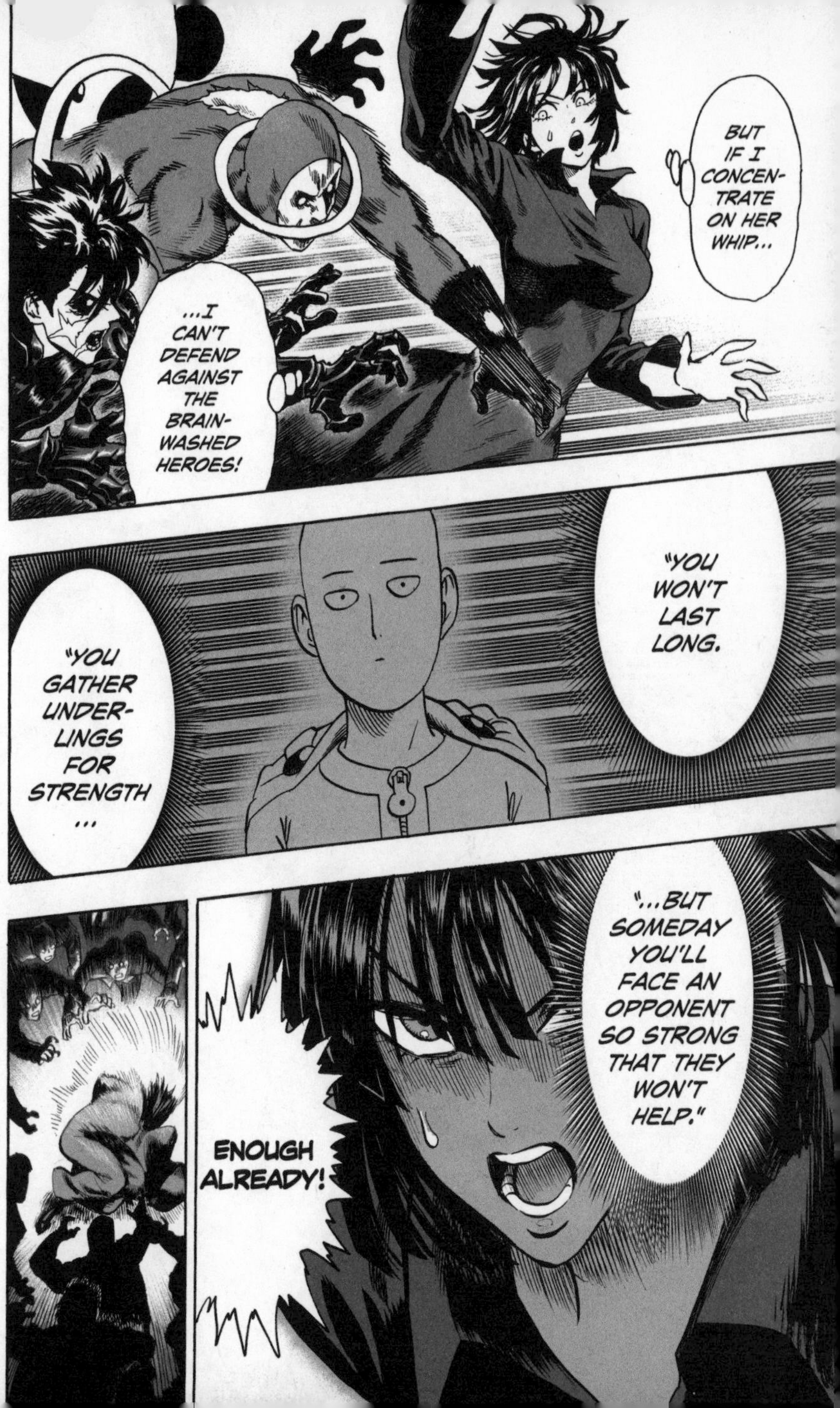
BUT IF I CONCENTRATE ON HER WHIP...
...I CAN'T DEFEND AGAINST THE BRAIN-WASHED HEROES!
"YOU WON'T LAST LONG.
"YOU GATHER UNDERLINGS FOR STRENGTH...
"...BUT SOMEDAY YOU'LL FACE AN OPPONENT SO STRONG THAT THEY WON'T HELP."
ENOUGH ALREADY!

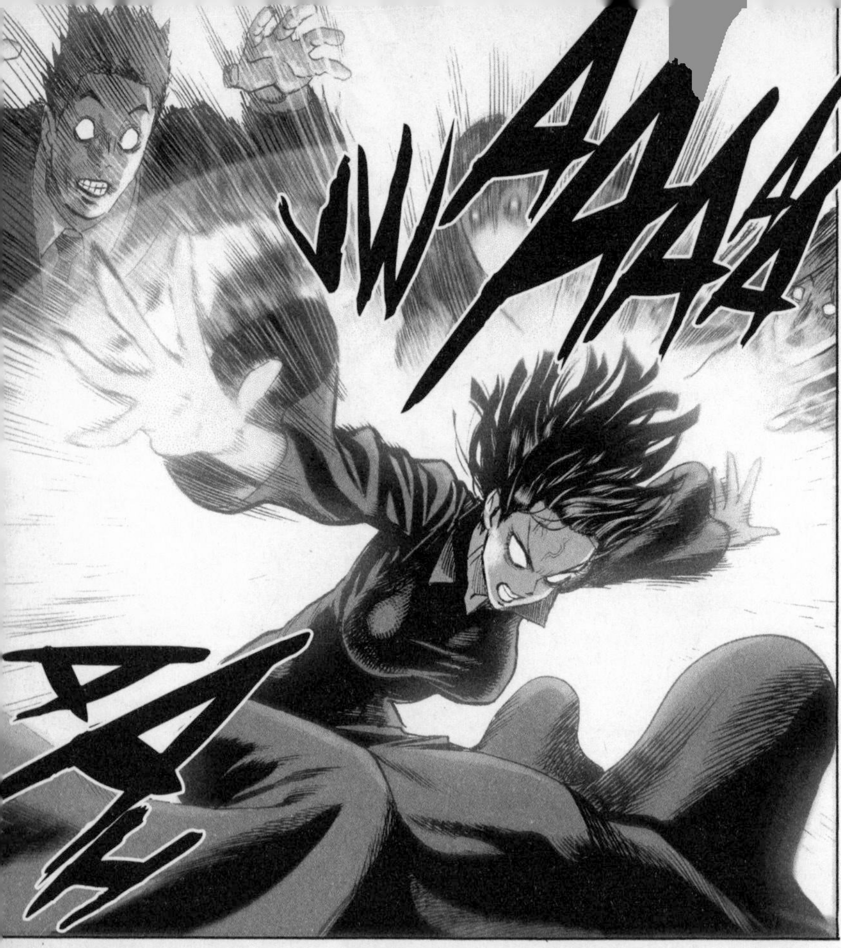
WAAAAA
AAH
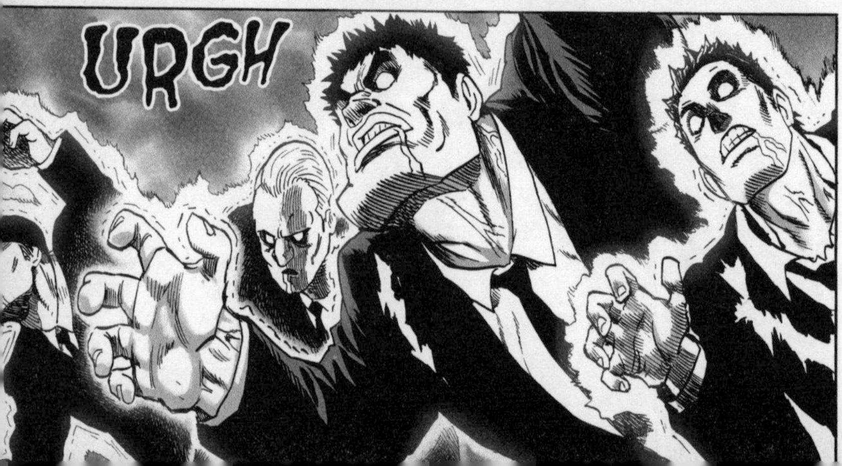
URGH

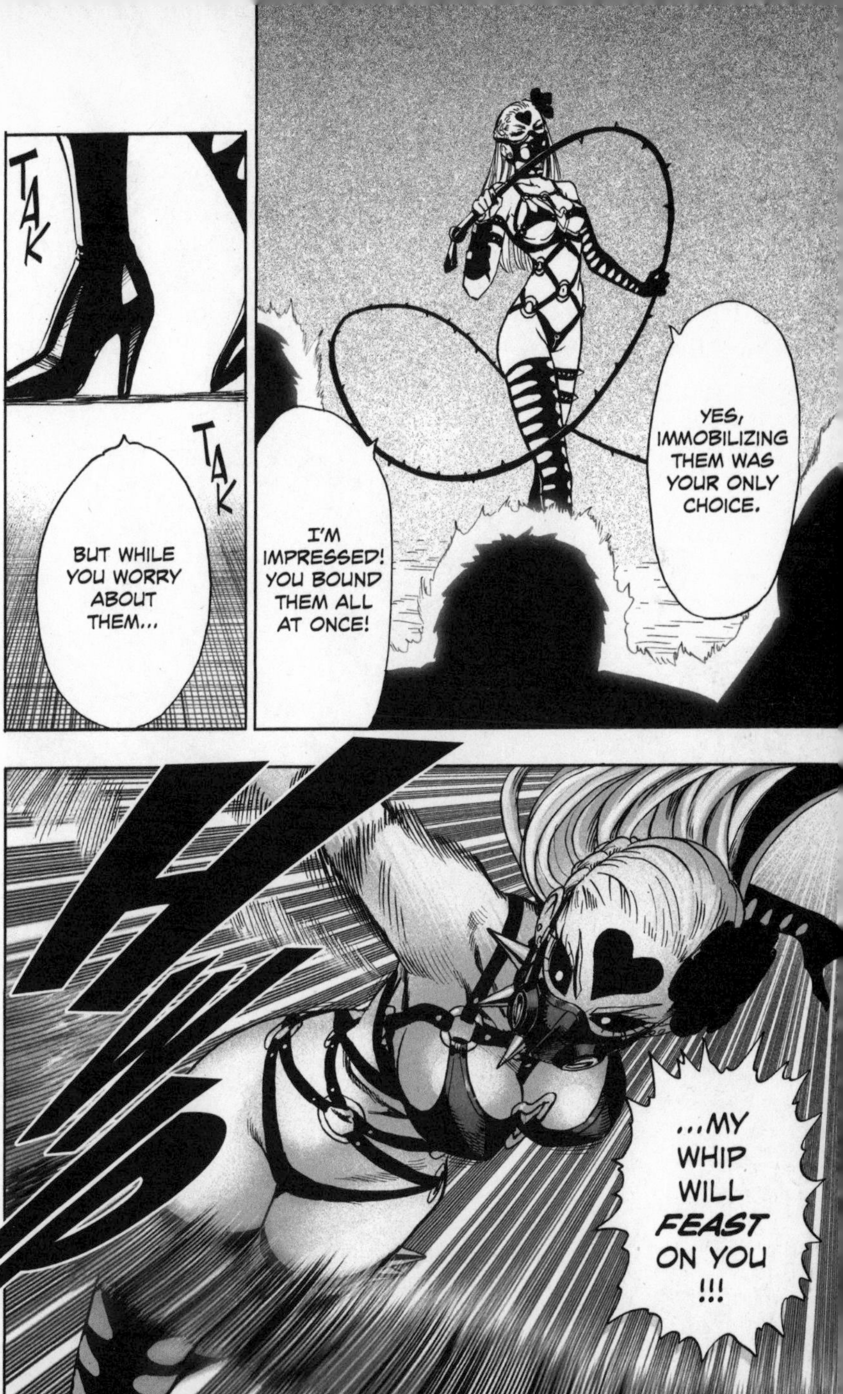
YES, IMMOBILIZING THEM WAS YOUR ONLY CHOICE.
I'M IMPRESSED! YOU BOUND THEM ALL AT ONCE!
TAK
TAK
BUT WHILE YOU WORRY ABOUT THEM...
...MY WHIP WILL *FEAST* ON YOU !!!

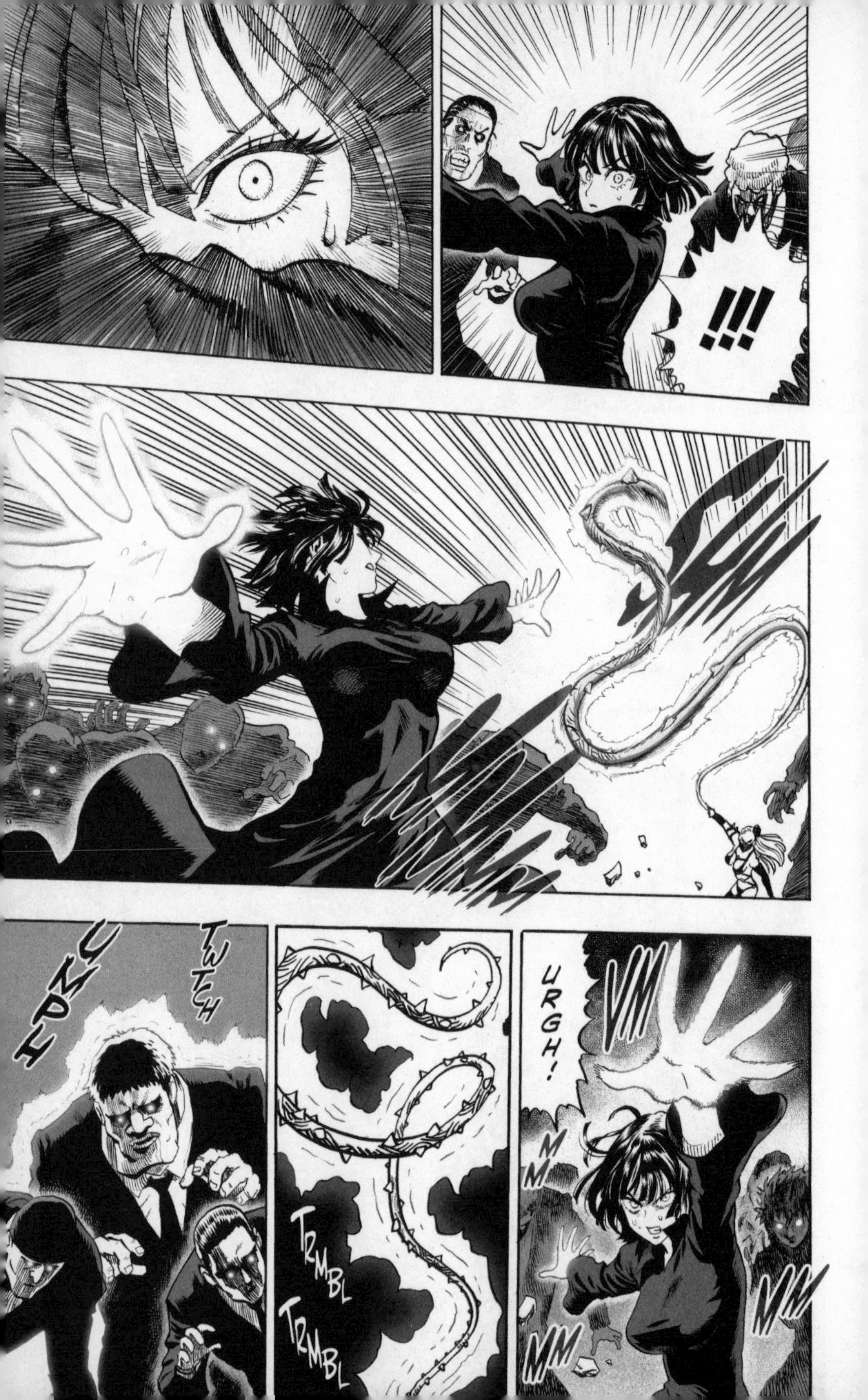
!!!
URGH!
MMM
VVV
TRMBL
TRMBL
TWTCH
UMPH

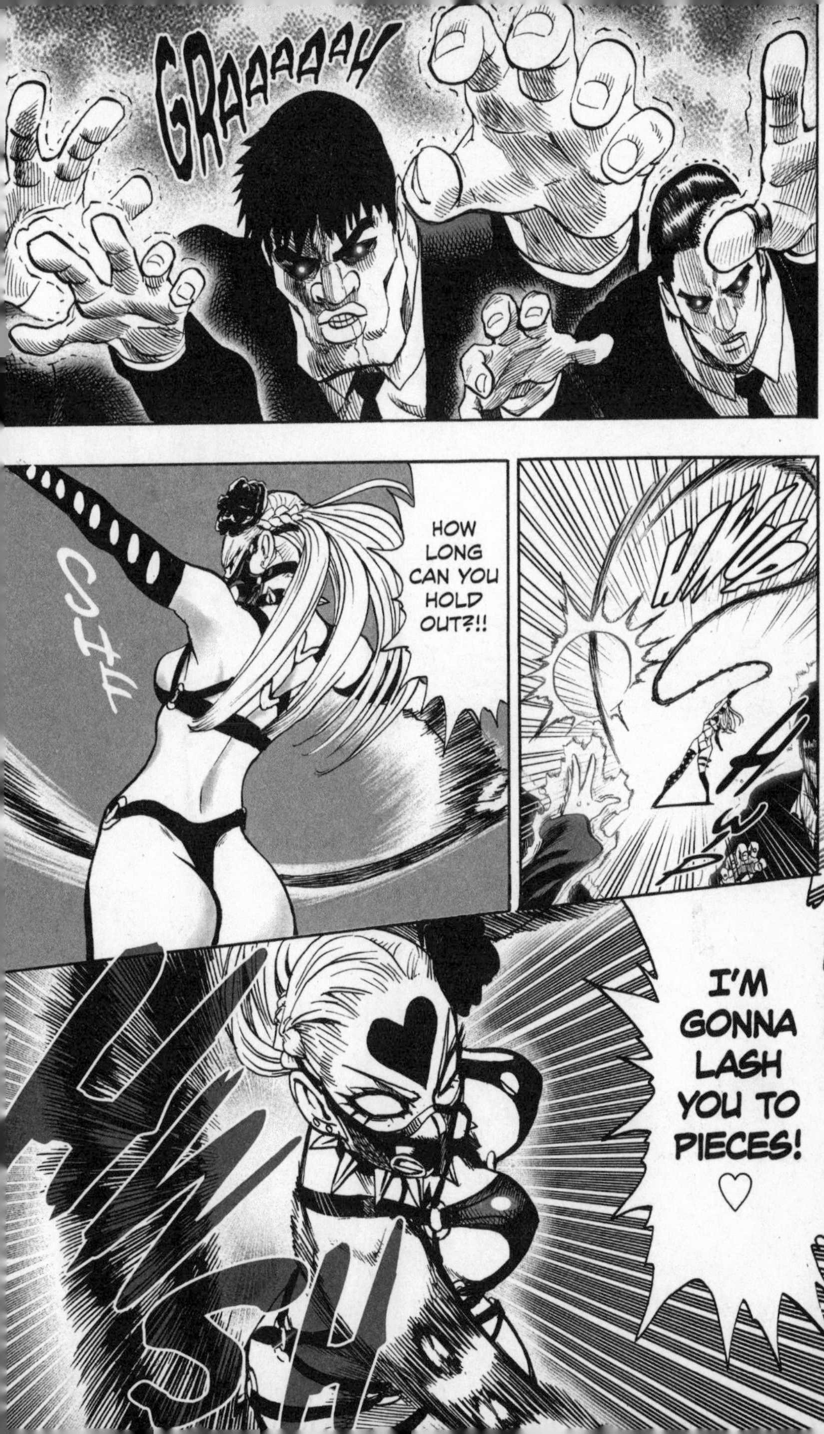
GRAAAAAH
HOW LONG CAN YOU HOLD OUT?!!
I'M GONNA LASH YOU TO PIECES! ♥

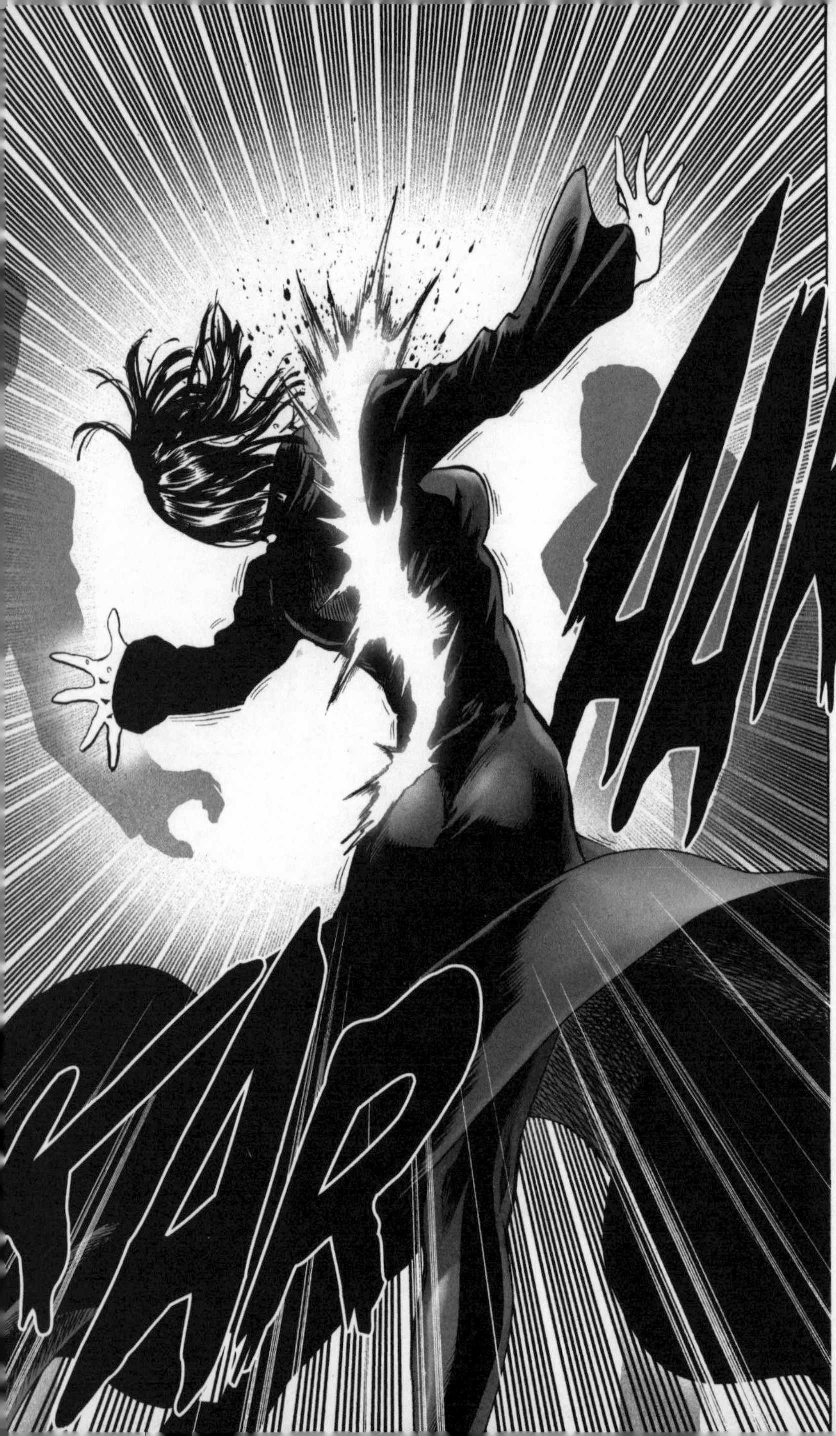

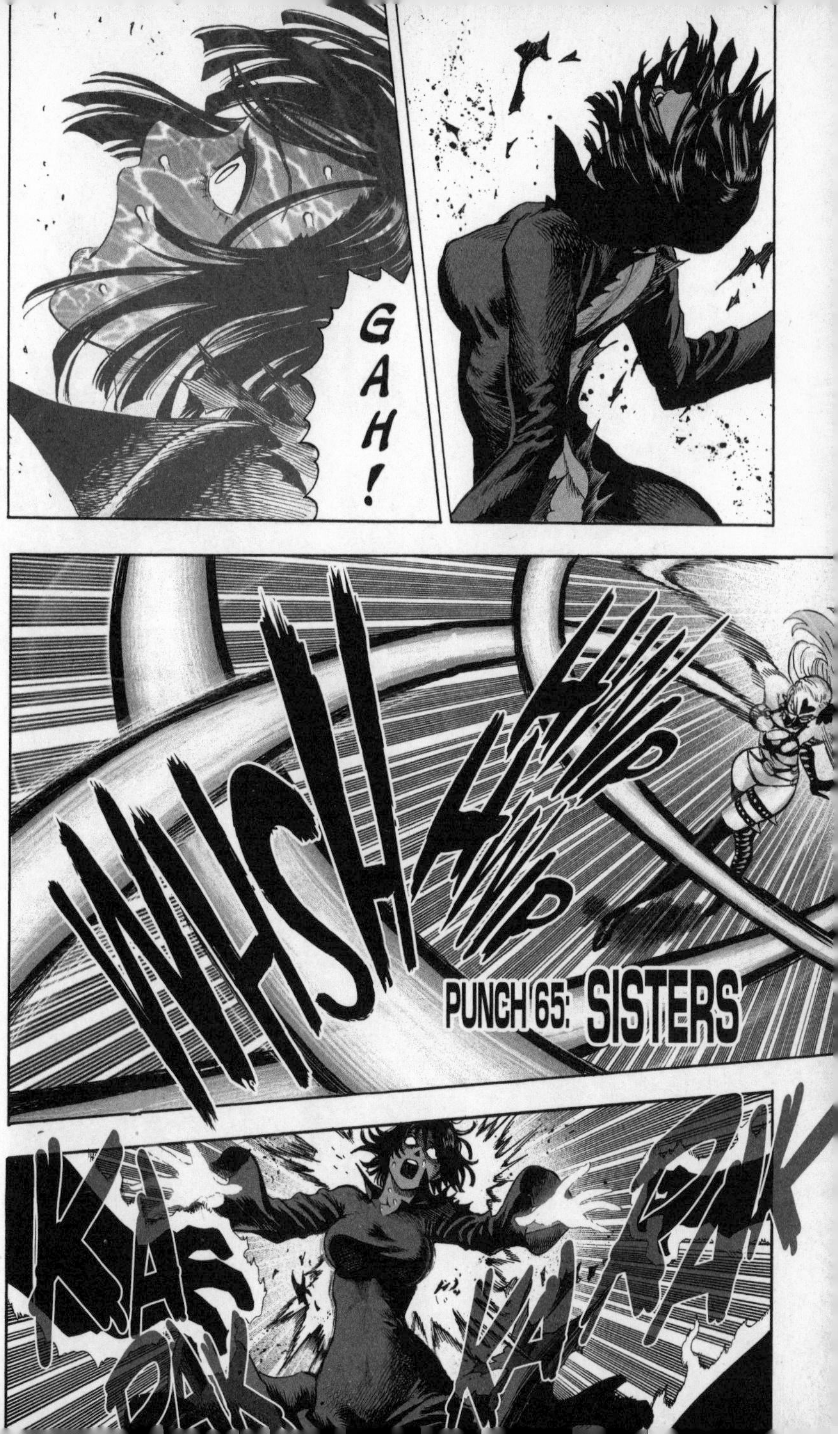
GAH!
FWUMP
FWUMP
WHSH
PUNCH 65: SISTERS
KA-
DAK
KA-
DAK
KA-
DAK

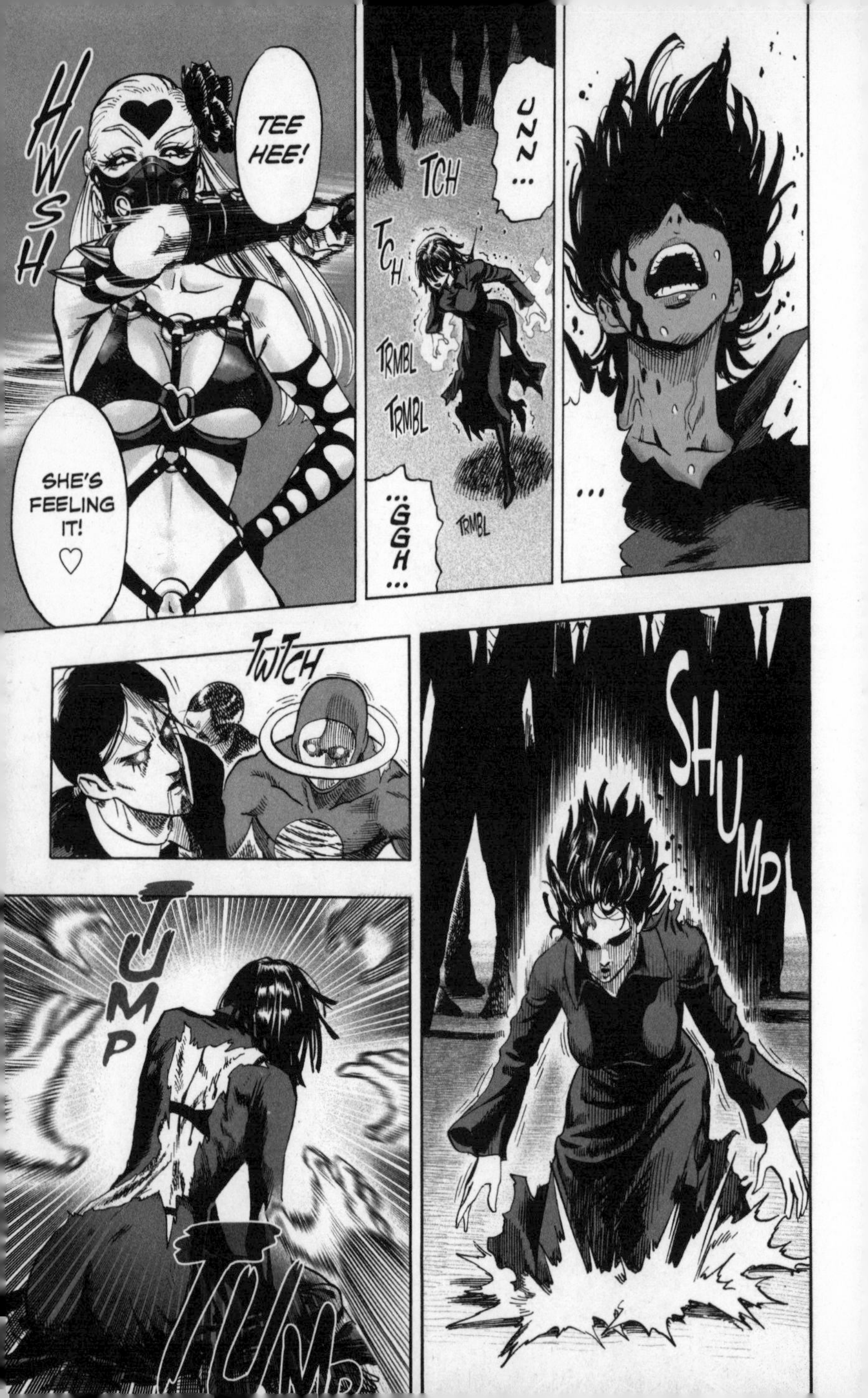
...
UNN...
TCH
TCH
TRMBL
TRMBL
...GGH...
TRMBL
HWSH
TEE HEE!
SHE'S FEELING IT! ♡
SHUMP
TWITCH
JUMP
THUMP

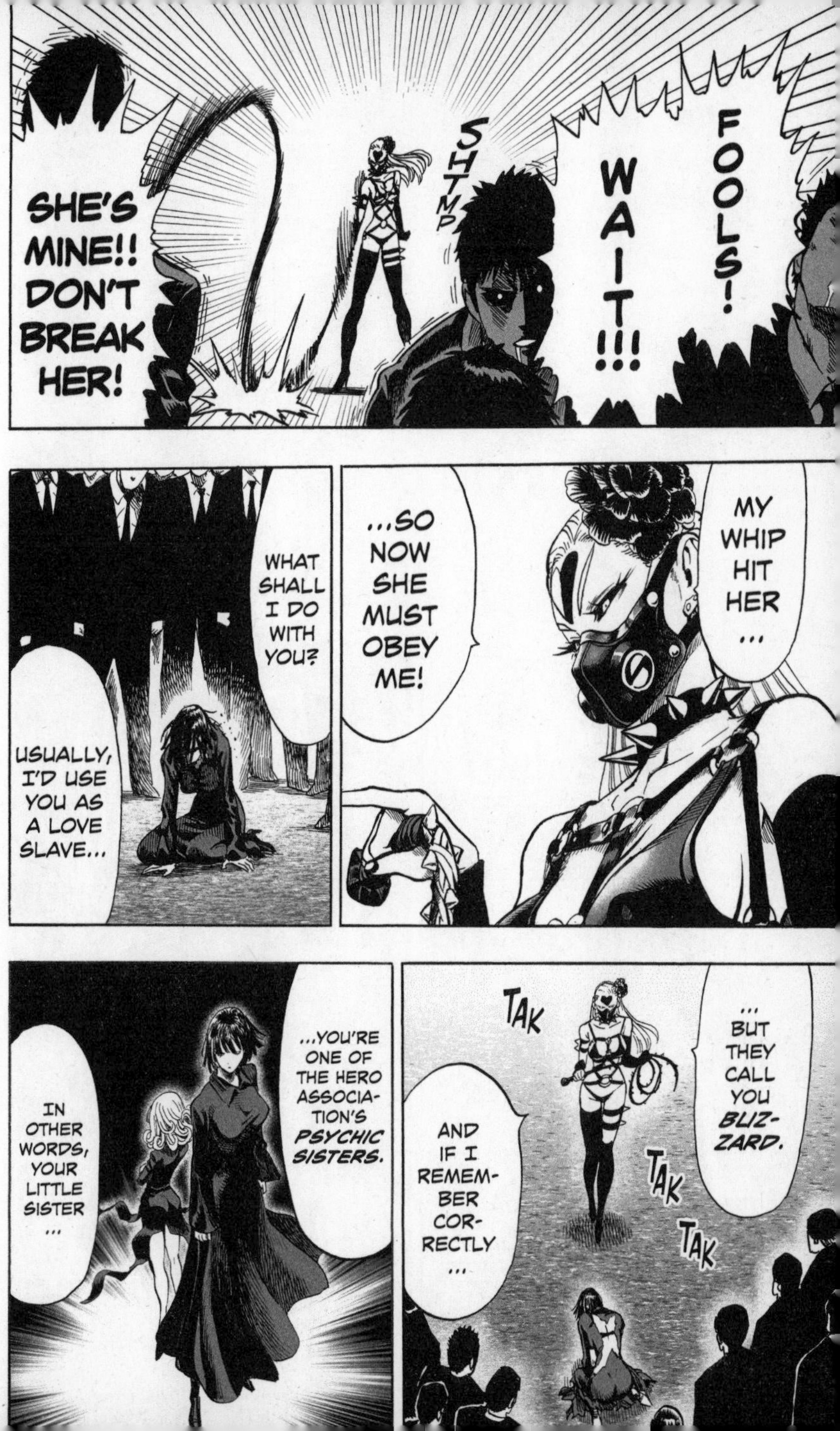
FOOLS!
WAIT!!!
SHTMP
SHE'S MINE!! DON'T BREAK HER!
MY WHIP HIT HER...
...SO NOW SHE MUST OBEY ME!
WHAT SHALL I DO WITH YOU?
USUALLY, I'D USE YOU AS A LOVE SLAVE...
...BUT THEY CALL YOU *BLIZZARD*.
TAK
TAK
TAK
AND IF I REMEMBER CORRECTLY...
...YOU'RE ONE OF THE HERO ASSOCIATION'S *PSYCHIC SISTERS*.
IN OTHER WORDS, YOUR LITTLE SISTER...

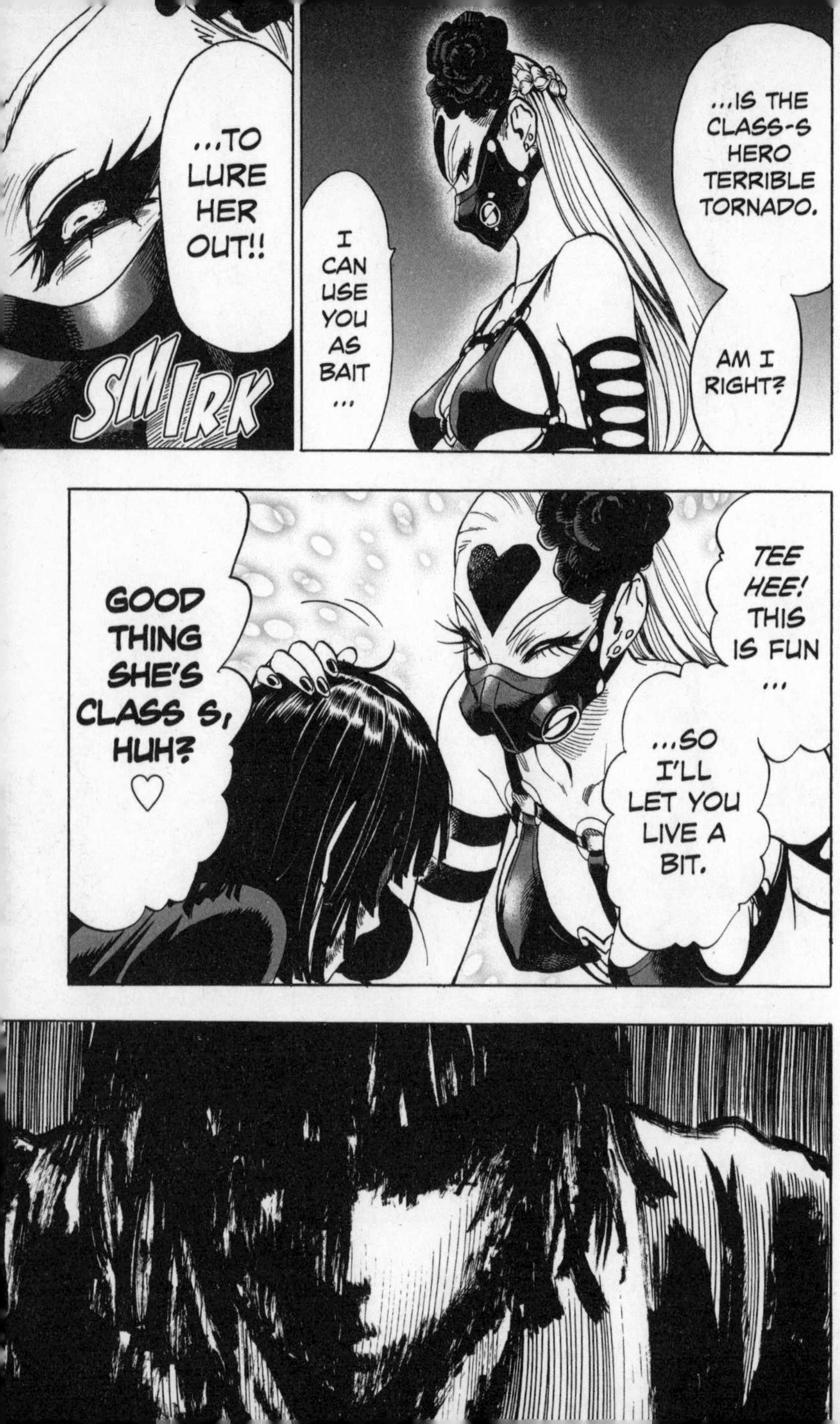
...IS THE CLASS-S HERO TERRIBLE TORNADO.
AM I RIGHT?
I CAN USE YOU AS BAIT...
...TO LURE HER OUT!!
SMIRK
TEE HEE! THIS IS FUN...
...SO I'LL LET YOU LIVE A BIT.
GOOD THING SHE'S CLASS S, HUH? ♡

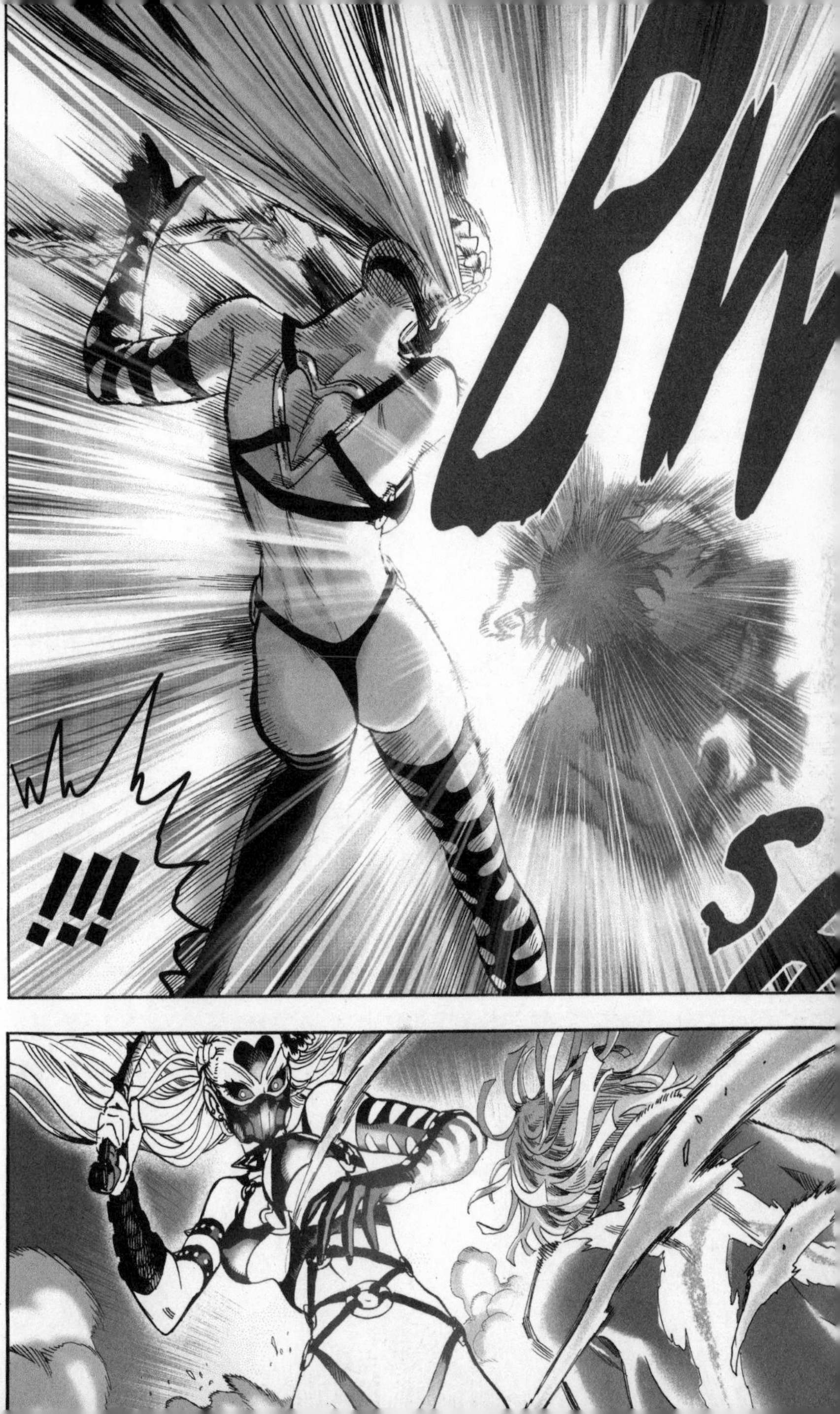
!!!

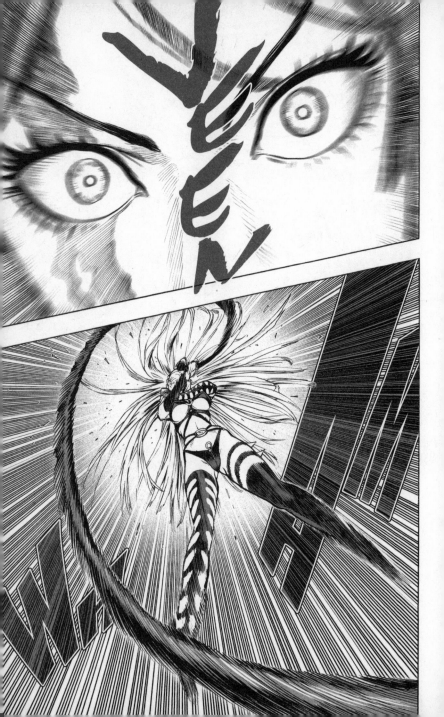

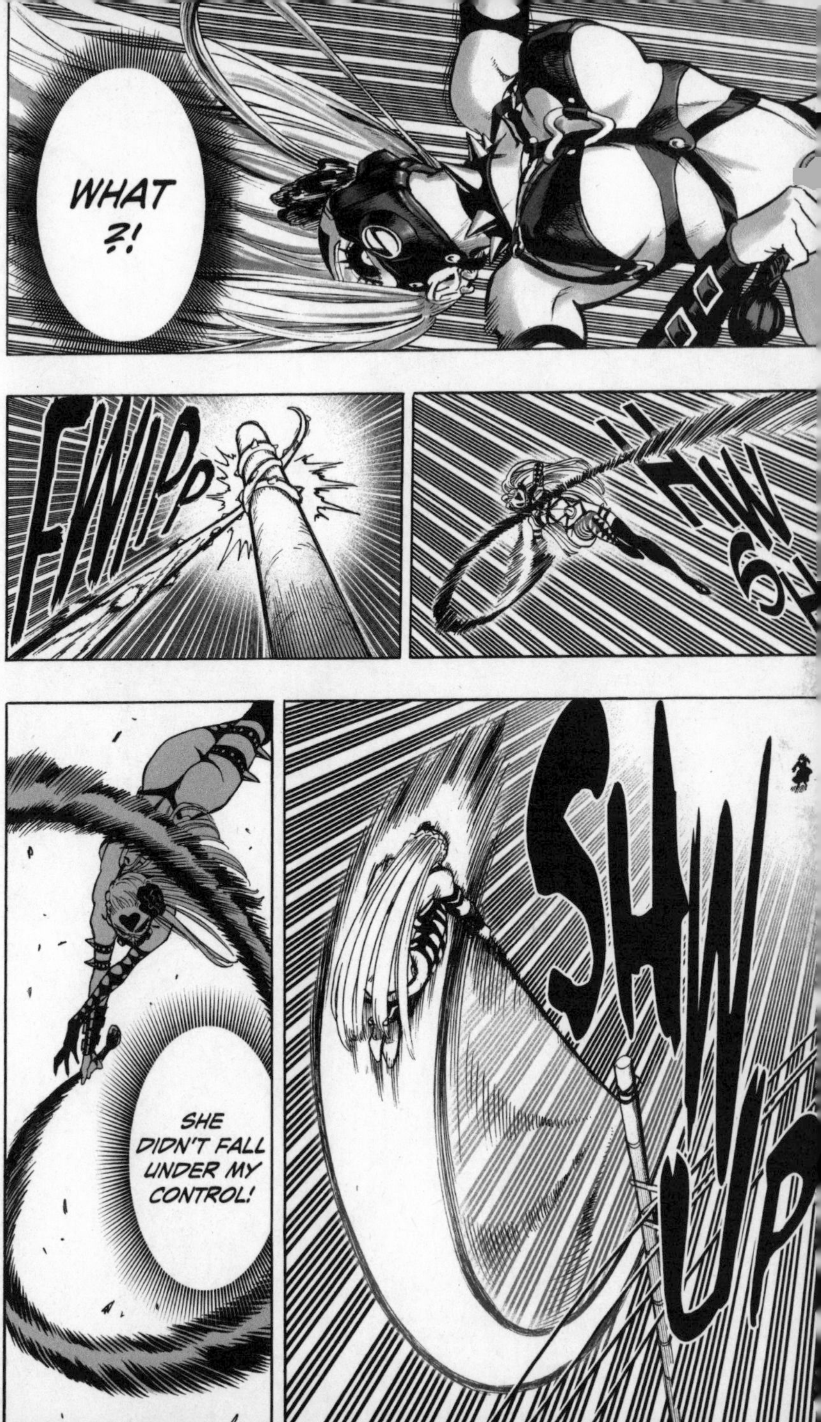
WHAT ?!
FWIPP
SHE DIDN'T FALL UNDER MY CONTROL!

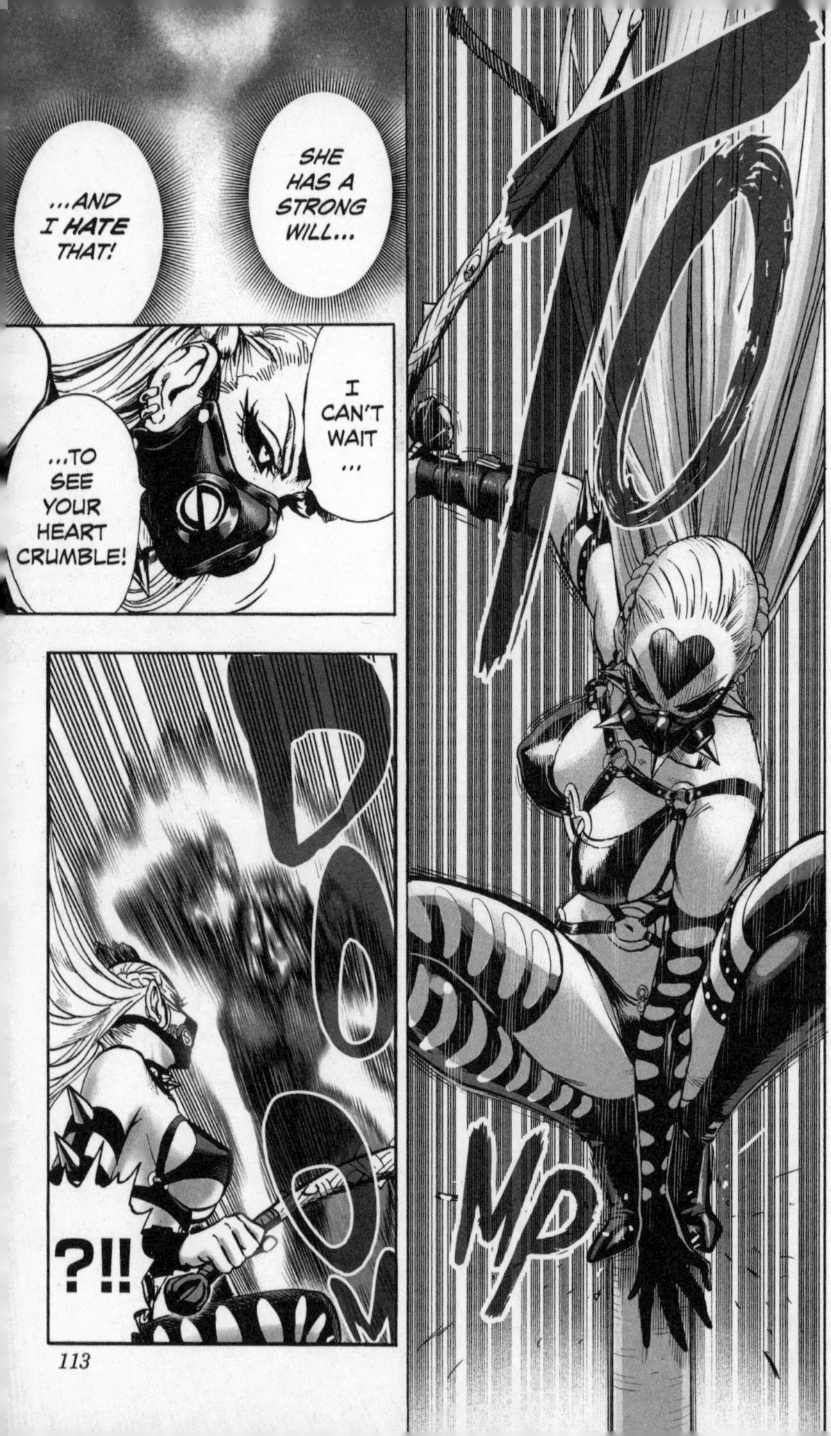
SHE HAS A STRONG WILL...
...AND I HATE THAT!
I CAN'T WAIT...
...TO SEE YOUR HEART CRUMBLE!
?!!

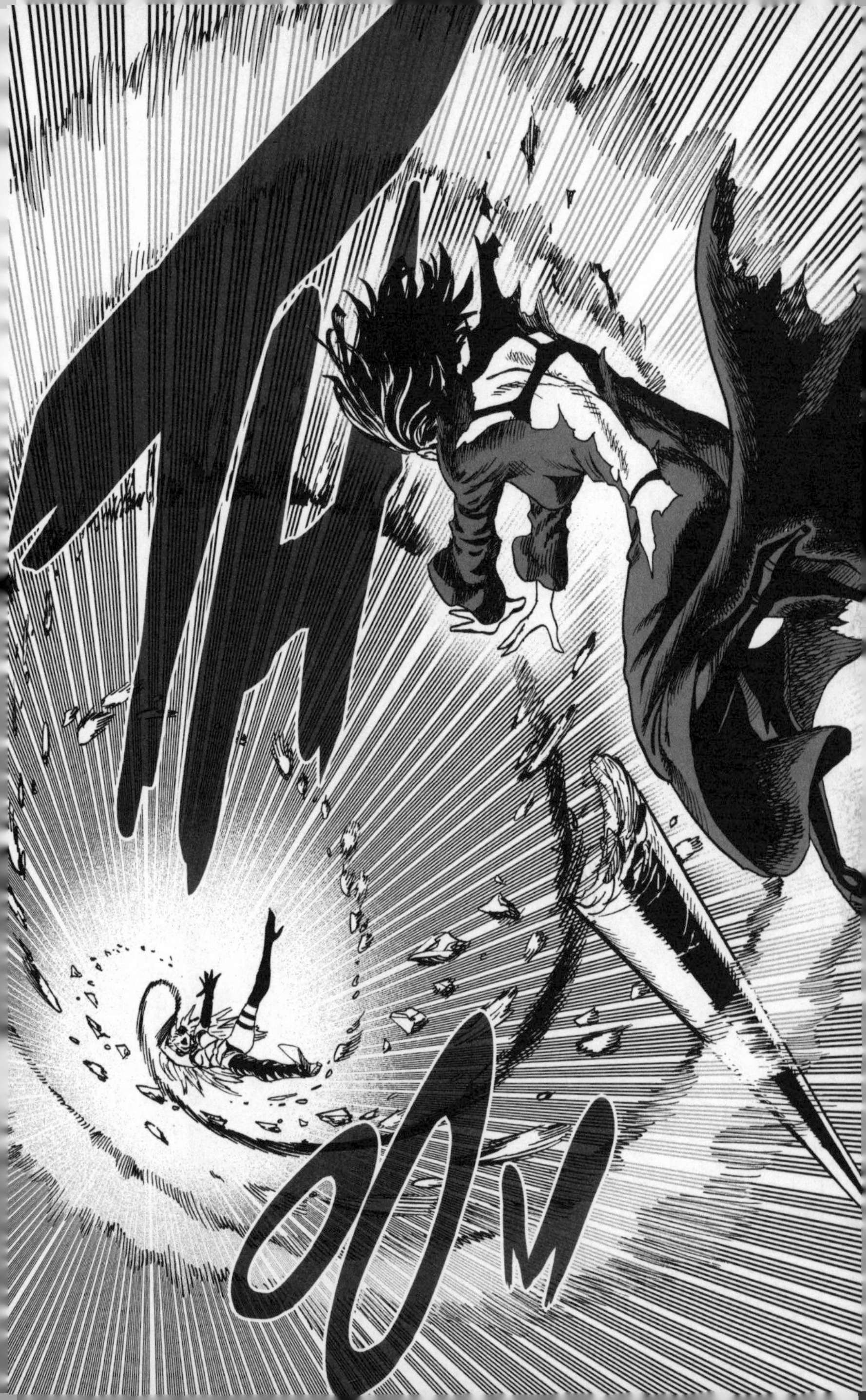

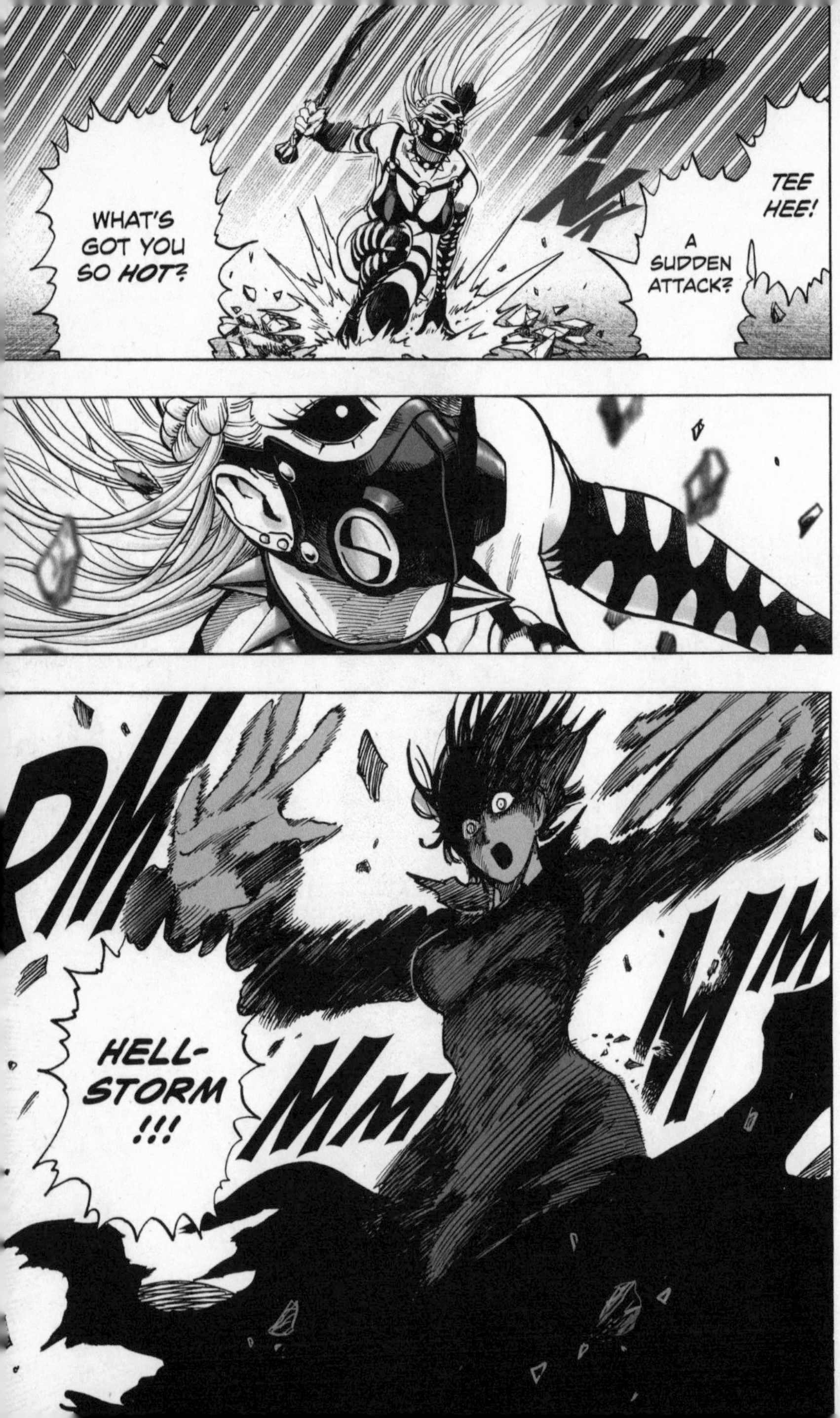
TEE HEE!
A SUDDEN ATTACK?
WHAT'S GOT YOU SO HOT?
HELL-STORM !!!

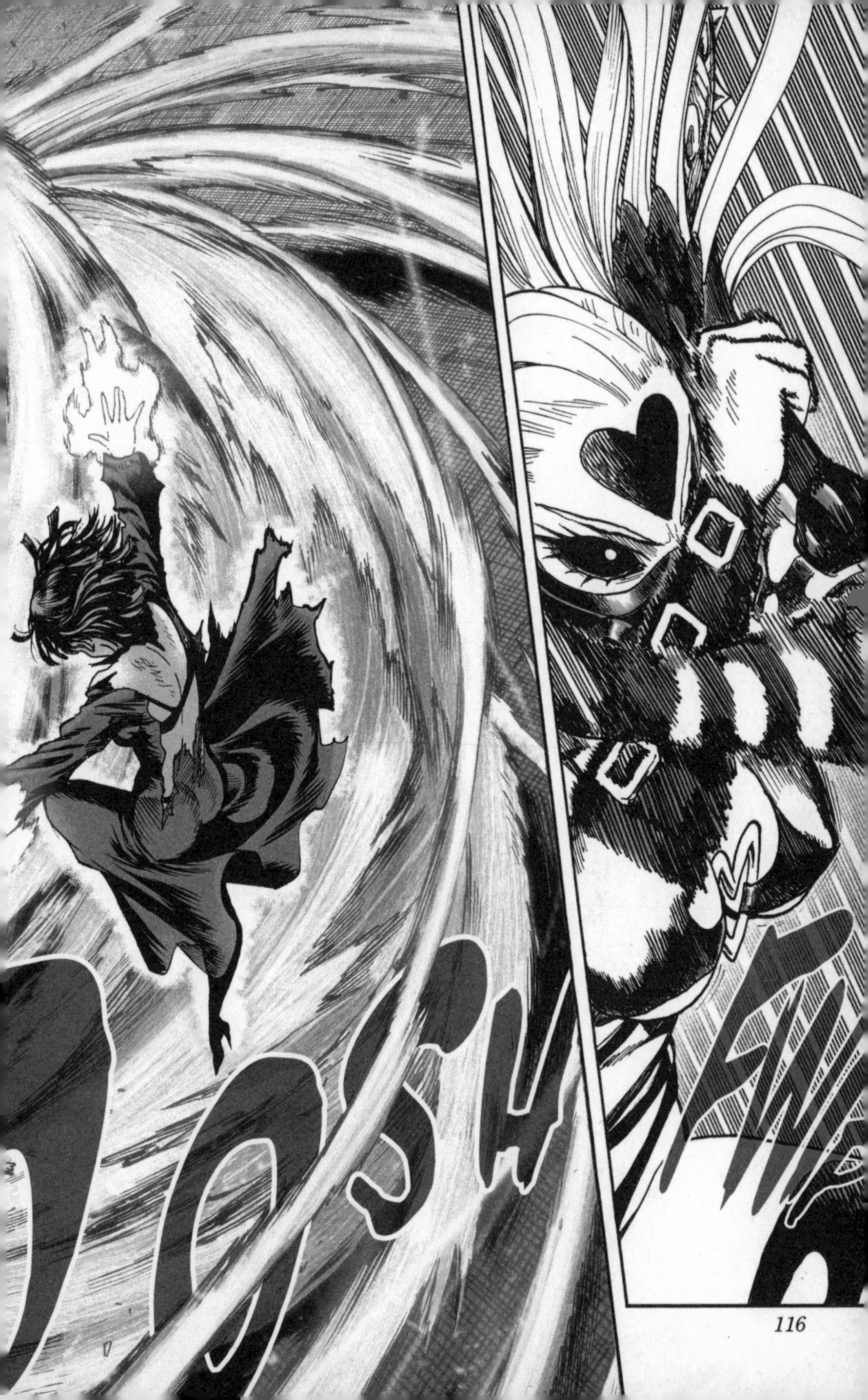

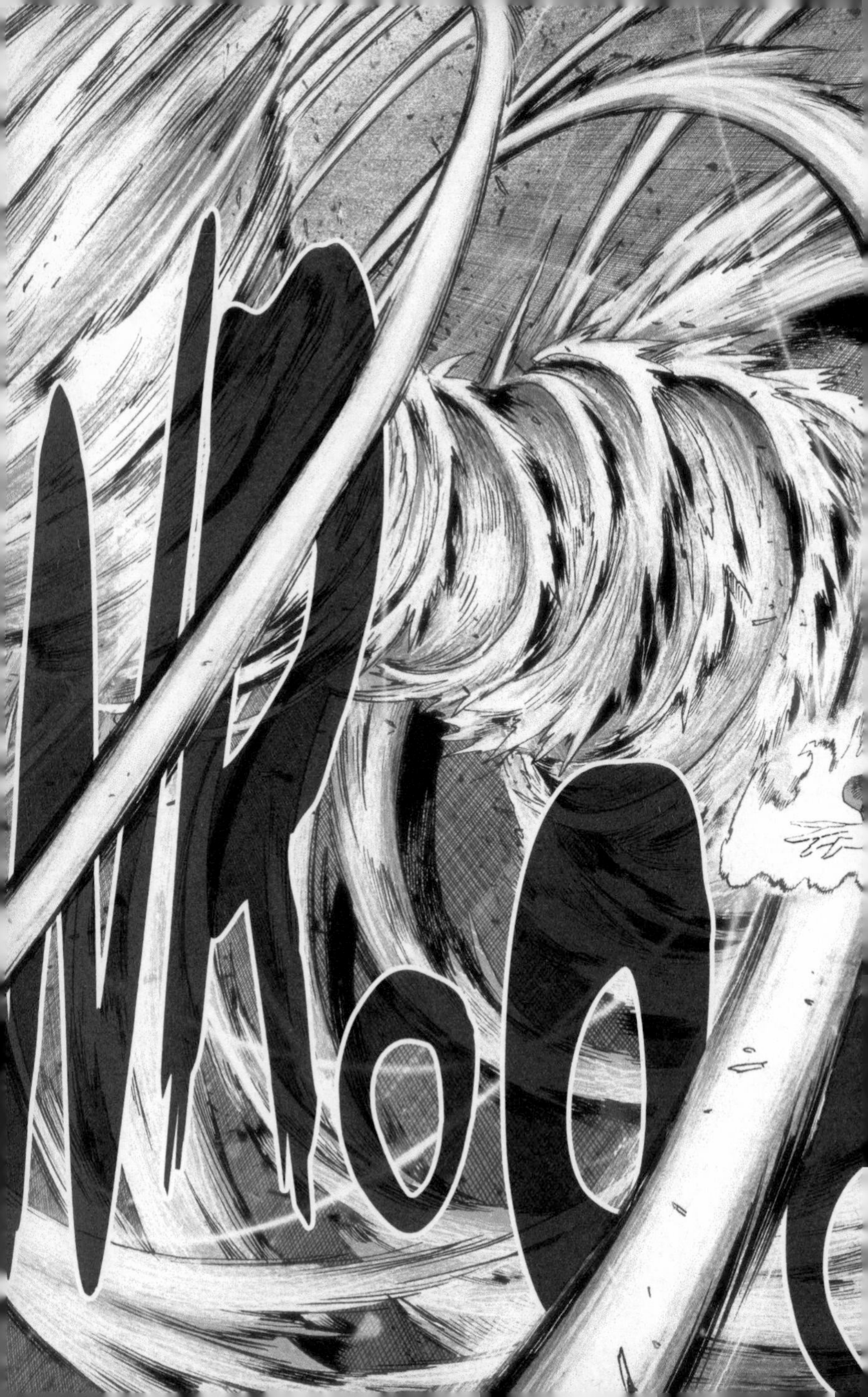
WHOO

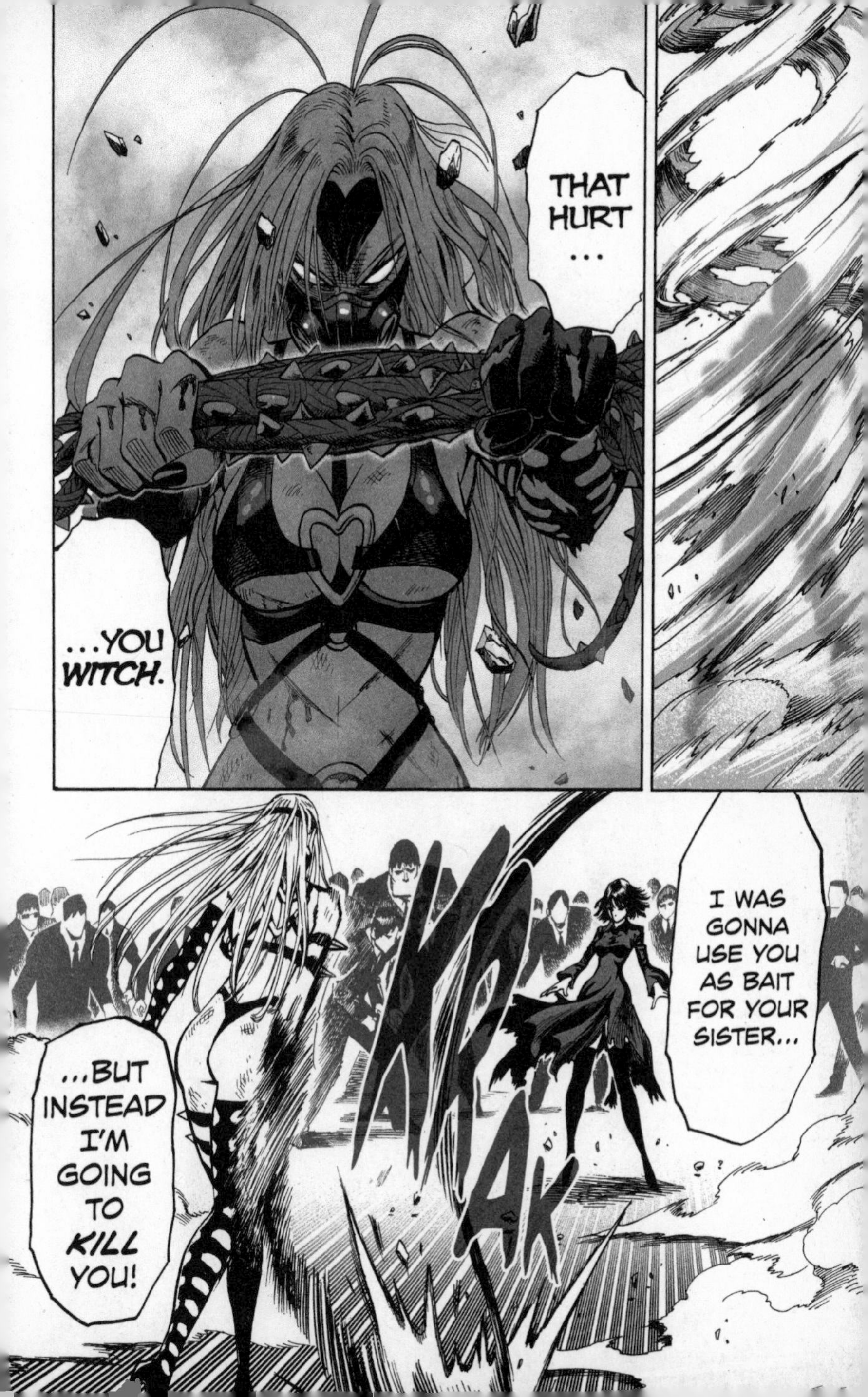
THAT HURT...
...YOU *WITCH*.
I WAS GONNA USE YOU AS BAIT FOR YOUR SISTER...
...BUT INSTEAD I'M GOING TO *KILL* YOU!
KRAK

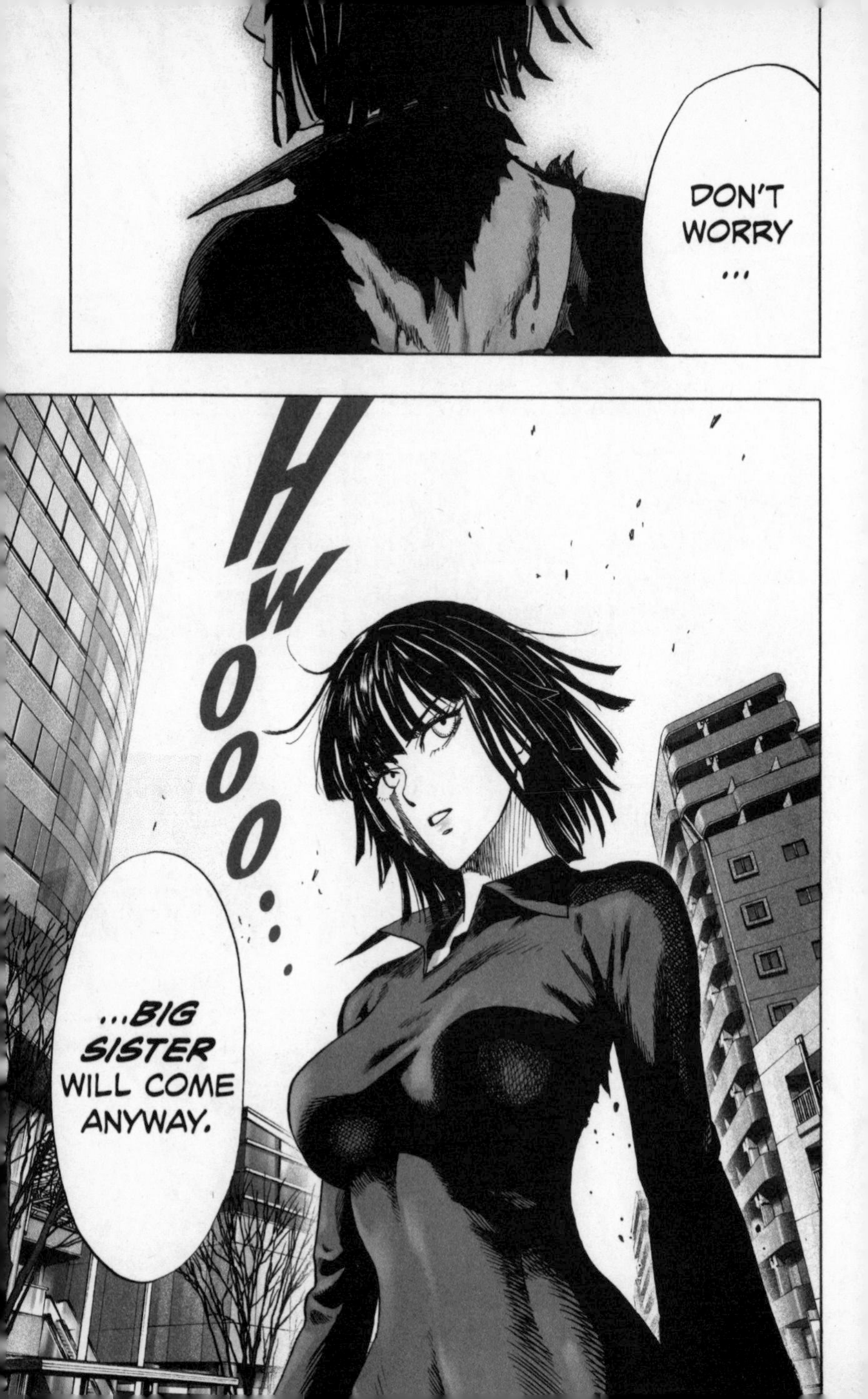
DON'T WORRY ...
HWOOO...
...BIG SISTER WILL COME ANYWAY.

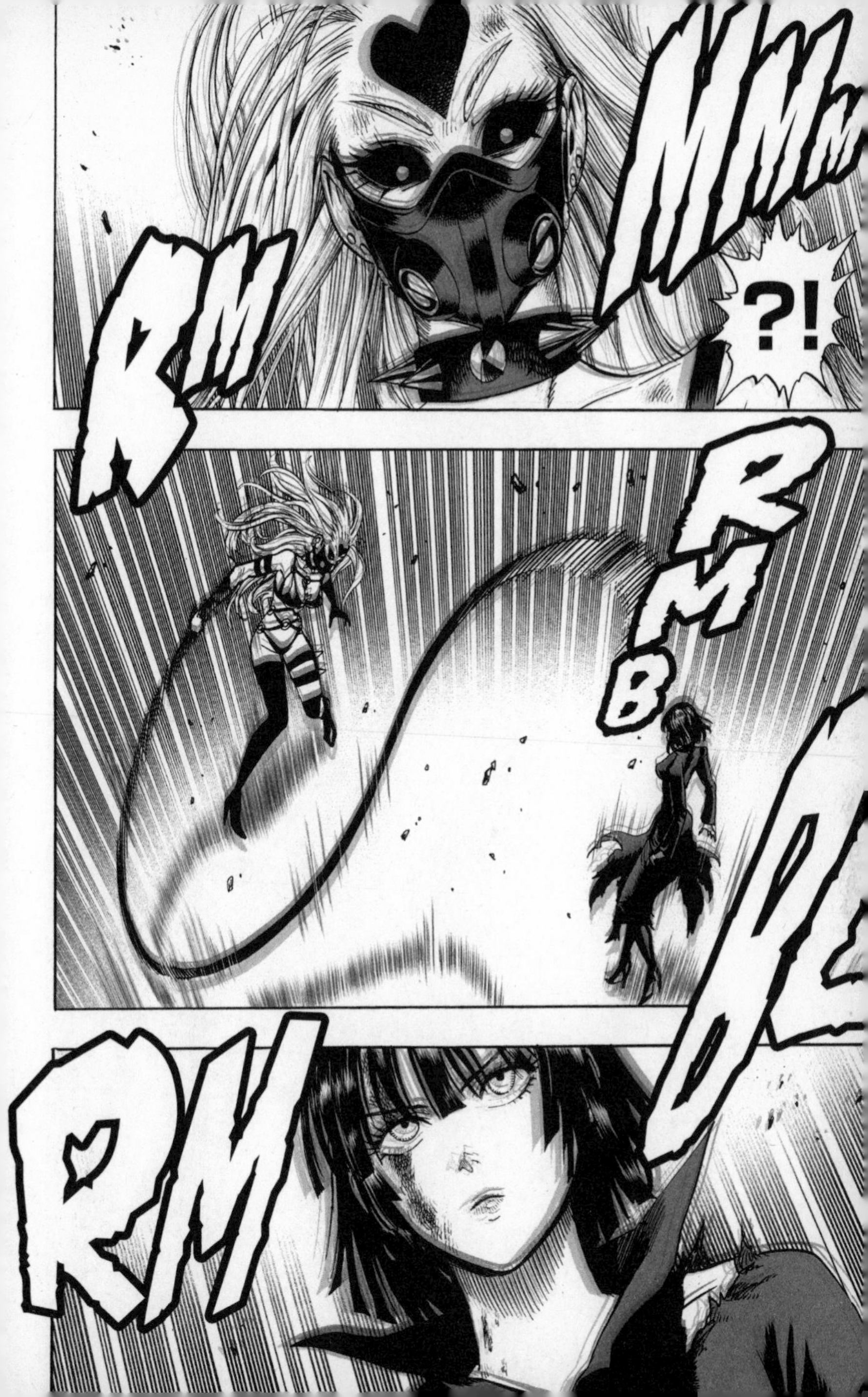
MM
?!
RM
RMB
RM

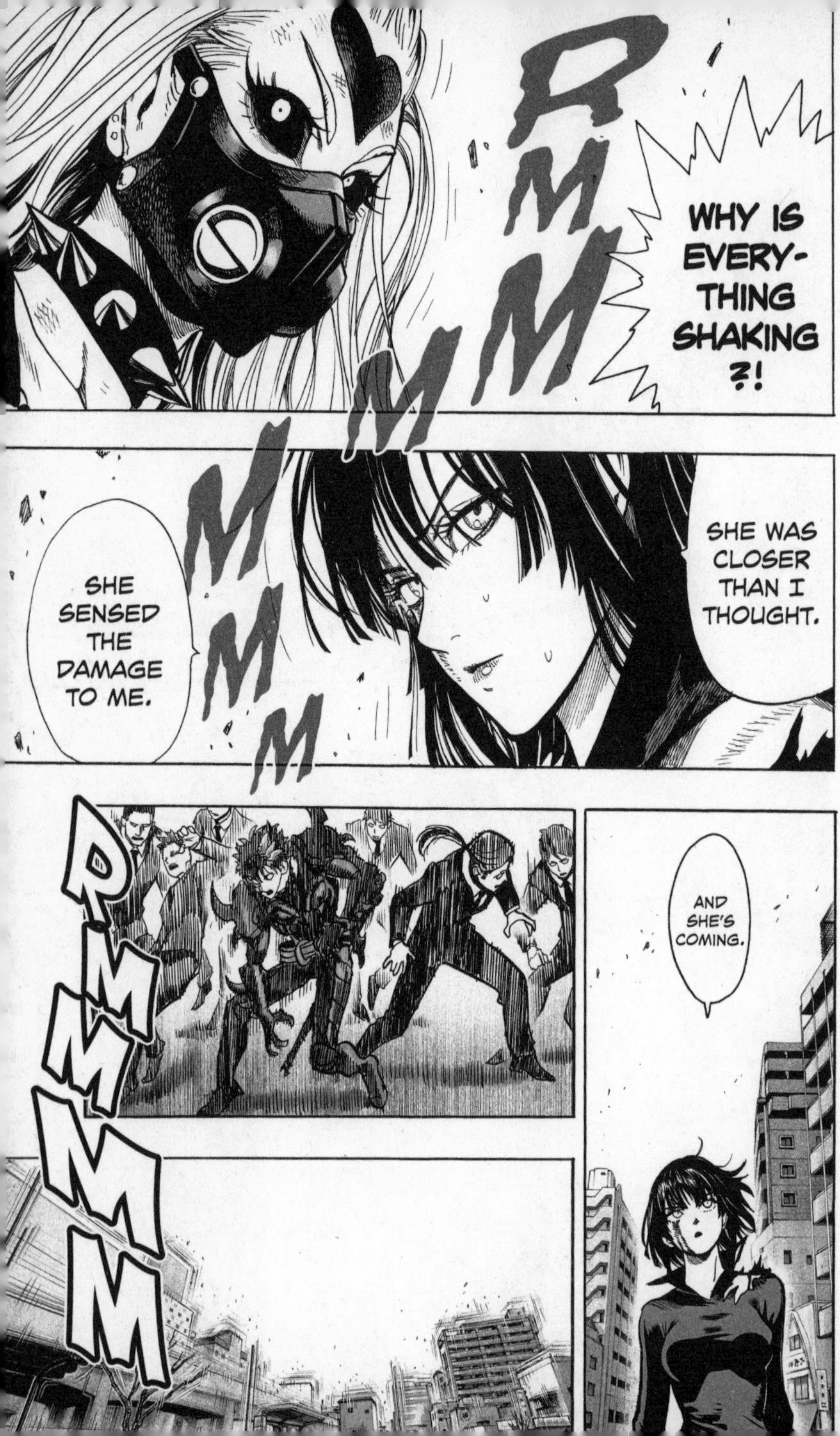
RMMM
WHY IS EVERYTHING SHAKING?!
SHE WAS CLOSER THAN I THOUGHT.
SHE SENSED THE DAMAGE TO ME.
MMMMM
AND SHE'S COMING.
RMMMMM

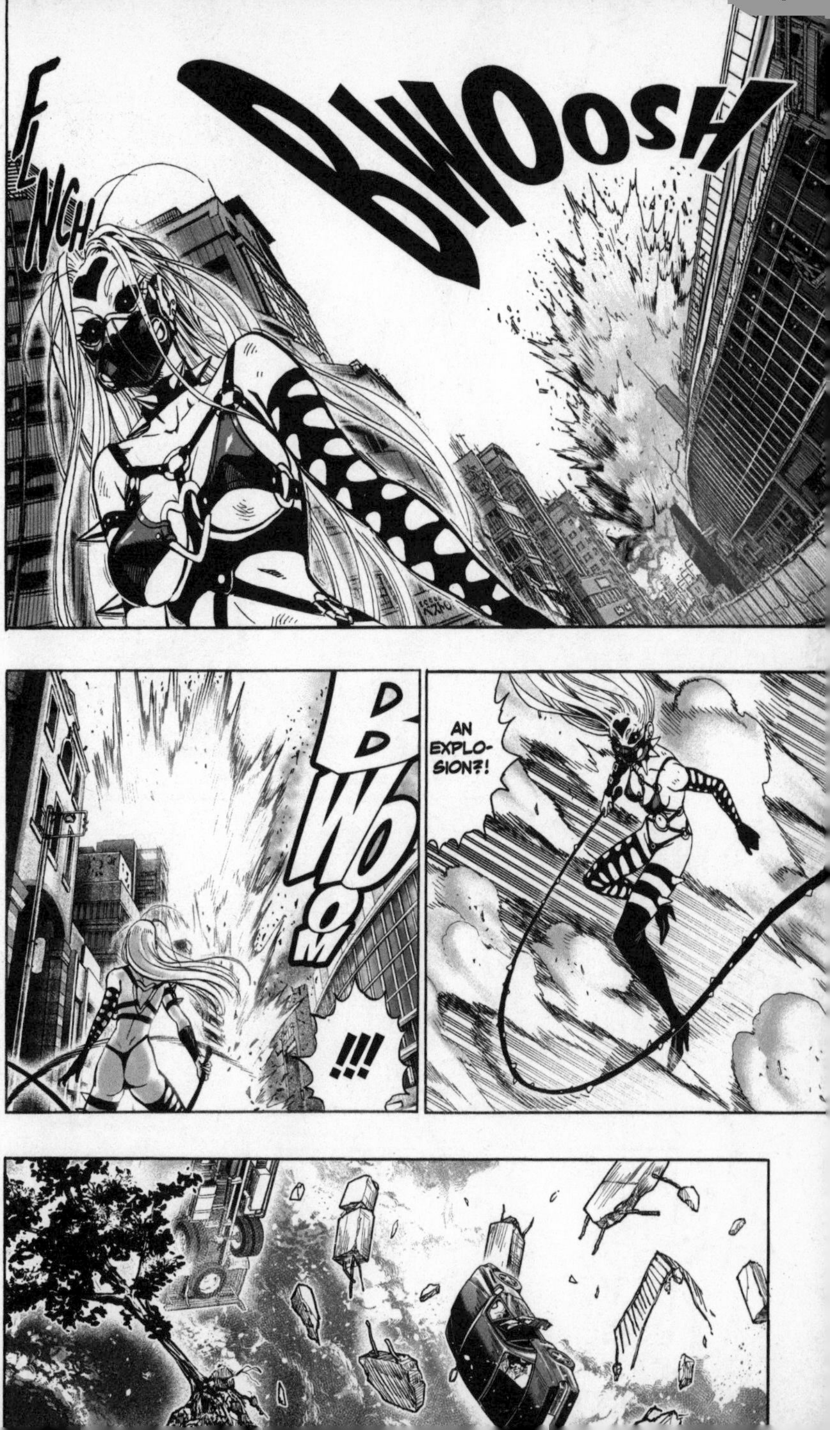
FLINCH
BWOOSH
AN EXPLOSION?!
DDBWOOM
!!!

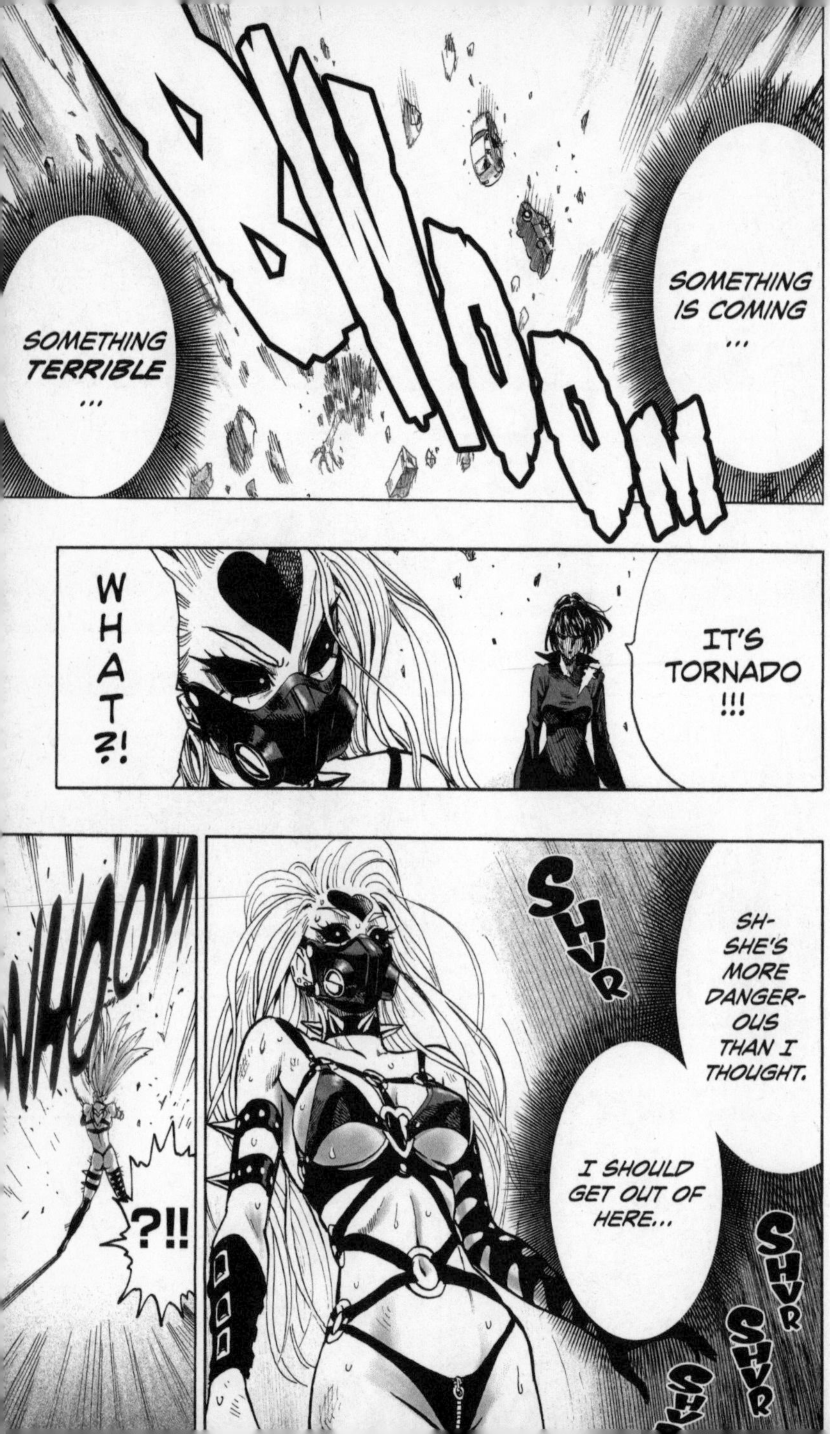
SOMETHING IS COMING ...
SOMETHING TERRIBLE ...
IT'S TORNADO !!!
WHAT?!
SHVR
SH- SHE'S MORE DANGER- OUS THAN I THOUGHT.
I SHOULD GET OUT OF HERE...
SHVR
SHVR
WHOOM
?!!

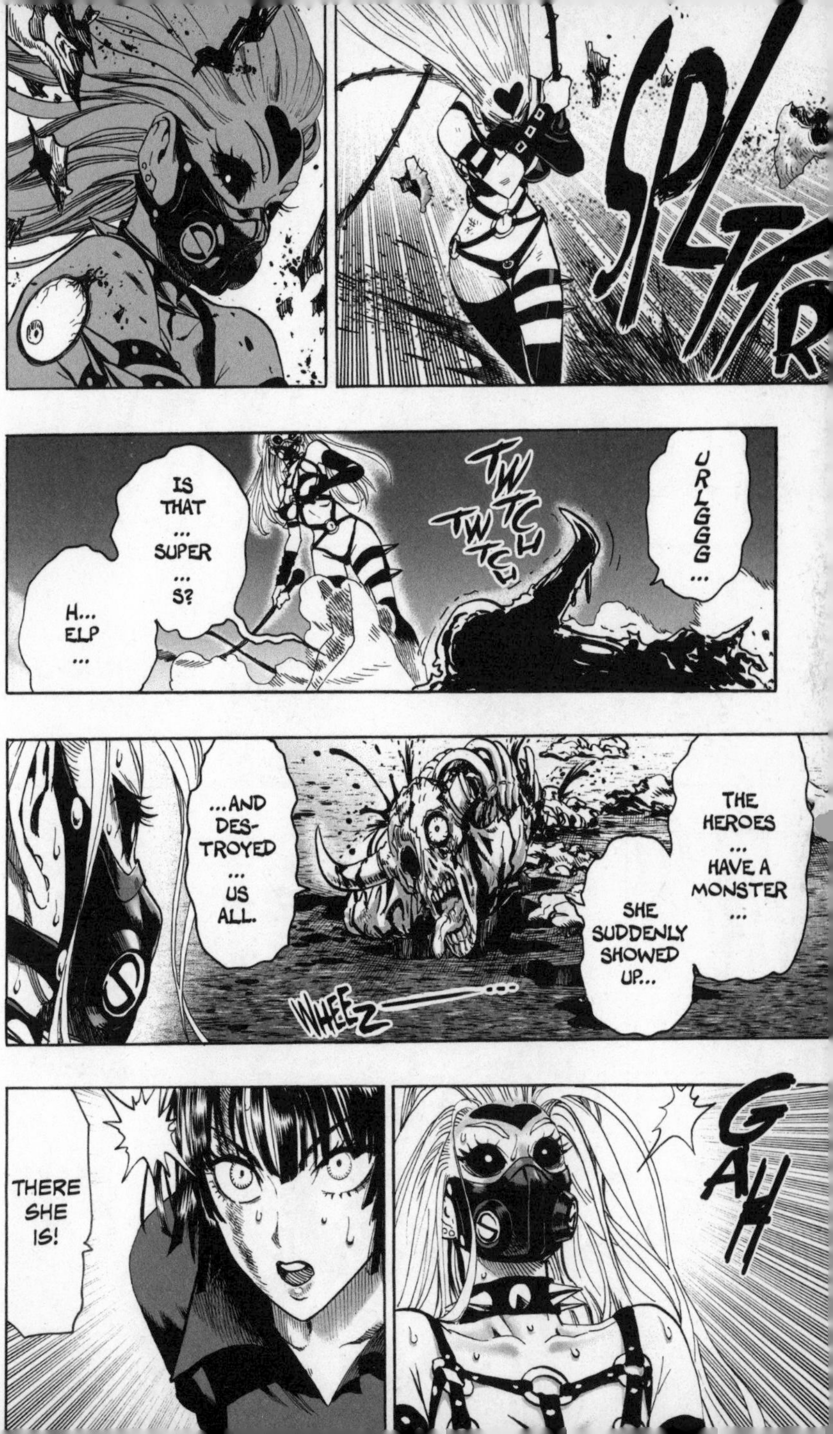
SPLTTR
URLGGG ...
TWITCH TWITCH
IS THAT ... SUPER ... S?
H... ELP ...
THE HEROES ... HAVE A MONSTER ...
SHE SUDDENLY SHOWED UP...
...AND DES-TROYED ... US ALL.
WHEEZ
GAH
THERE SHE IS!

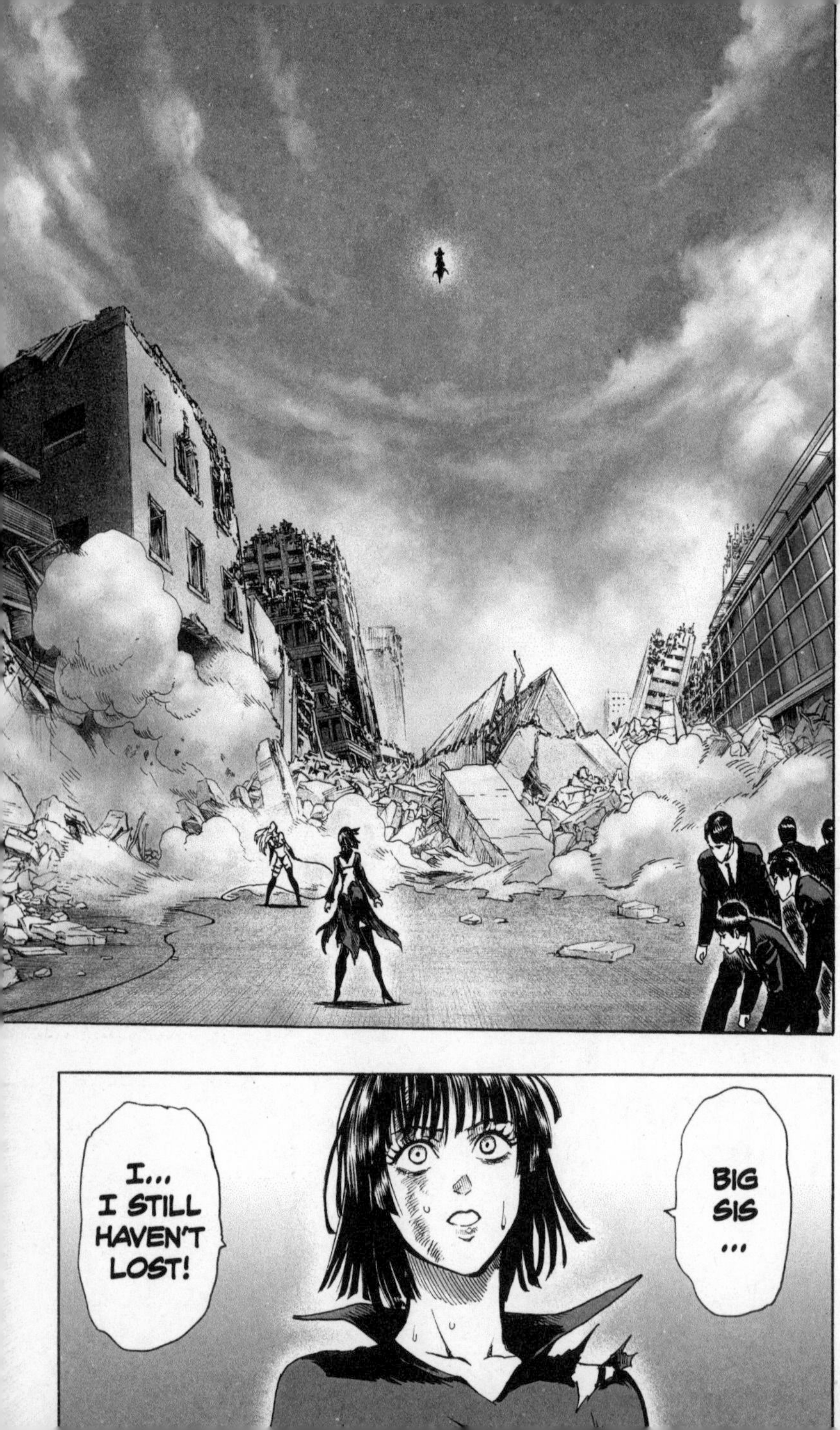
BIG SIS ...
I... I STILL HAVEN'T LOST!

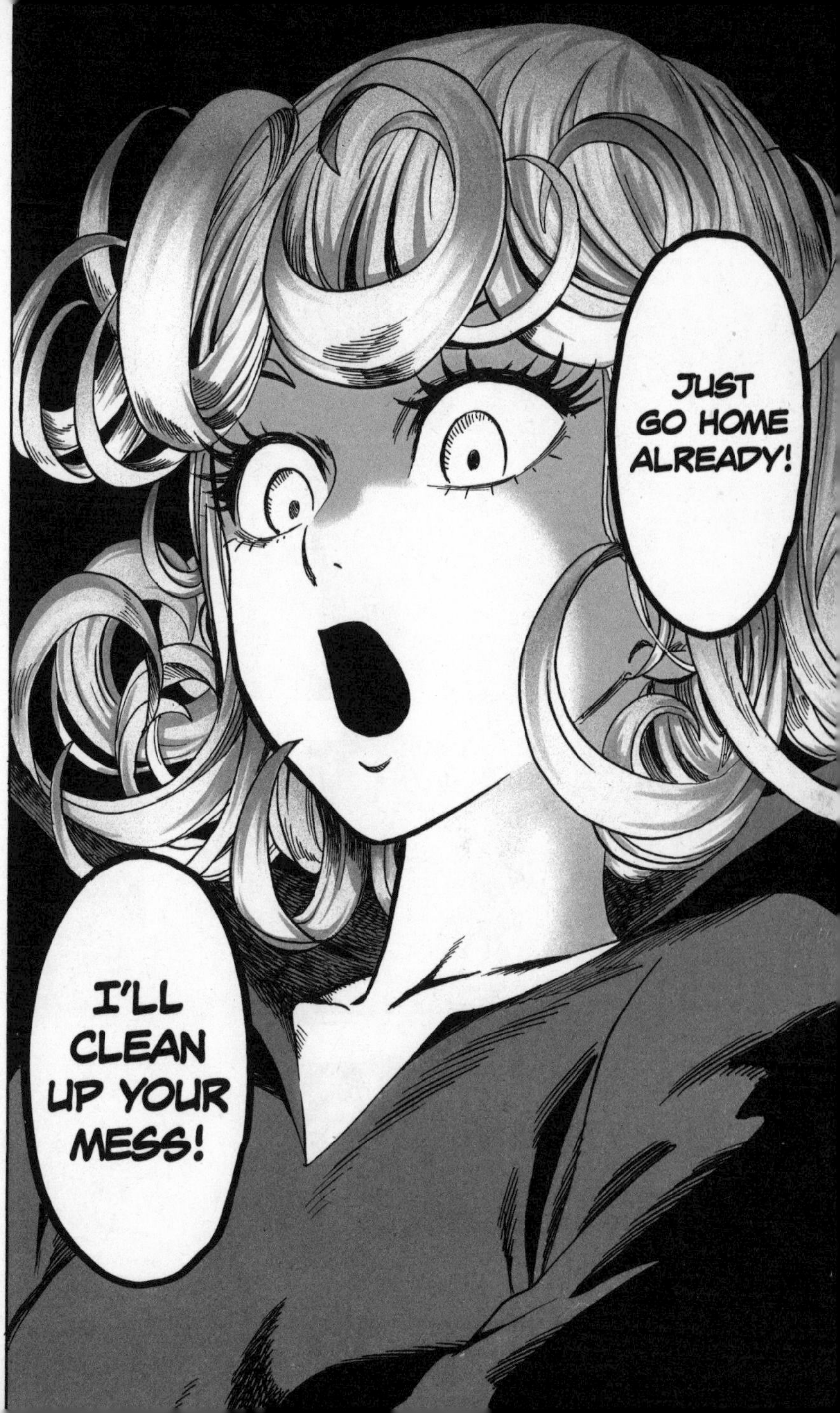
JUST GO HOME ALREADY!
I'LL CLEAN UP YOUR MESS!

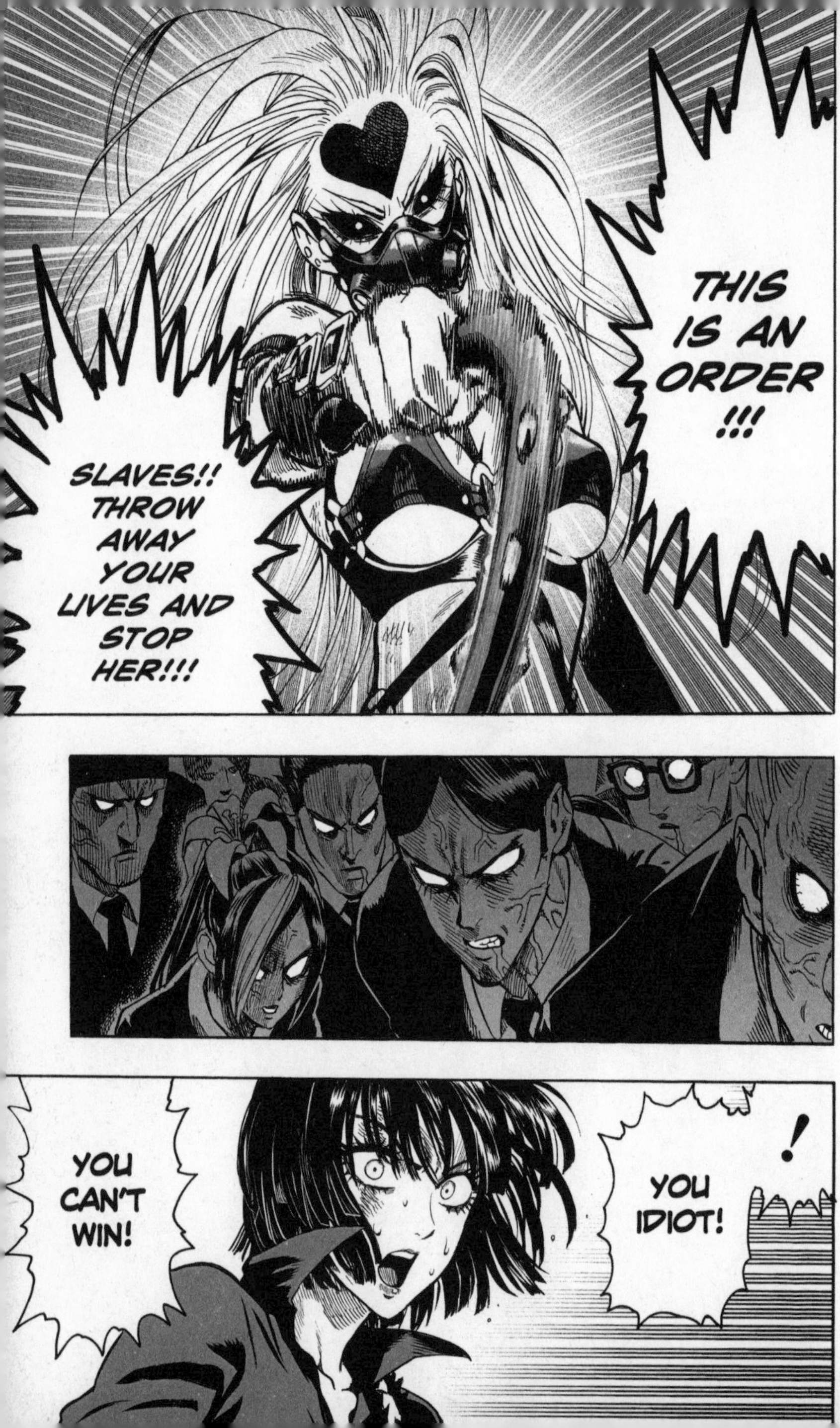
THIS IS AN ORDER!!!
SLAVES!! THROW AWAY YOUR LIVES AND STOP HER!!!
!
YOU IDIOT!
YOU CAN'T WIN!

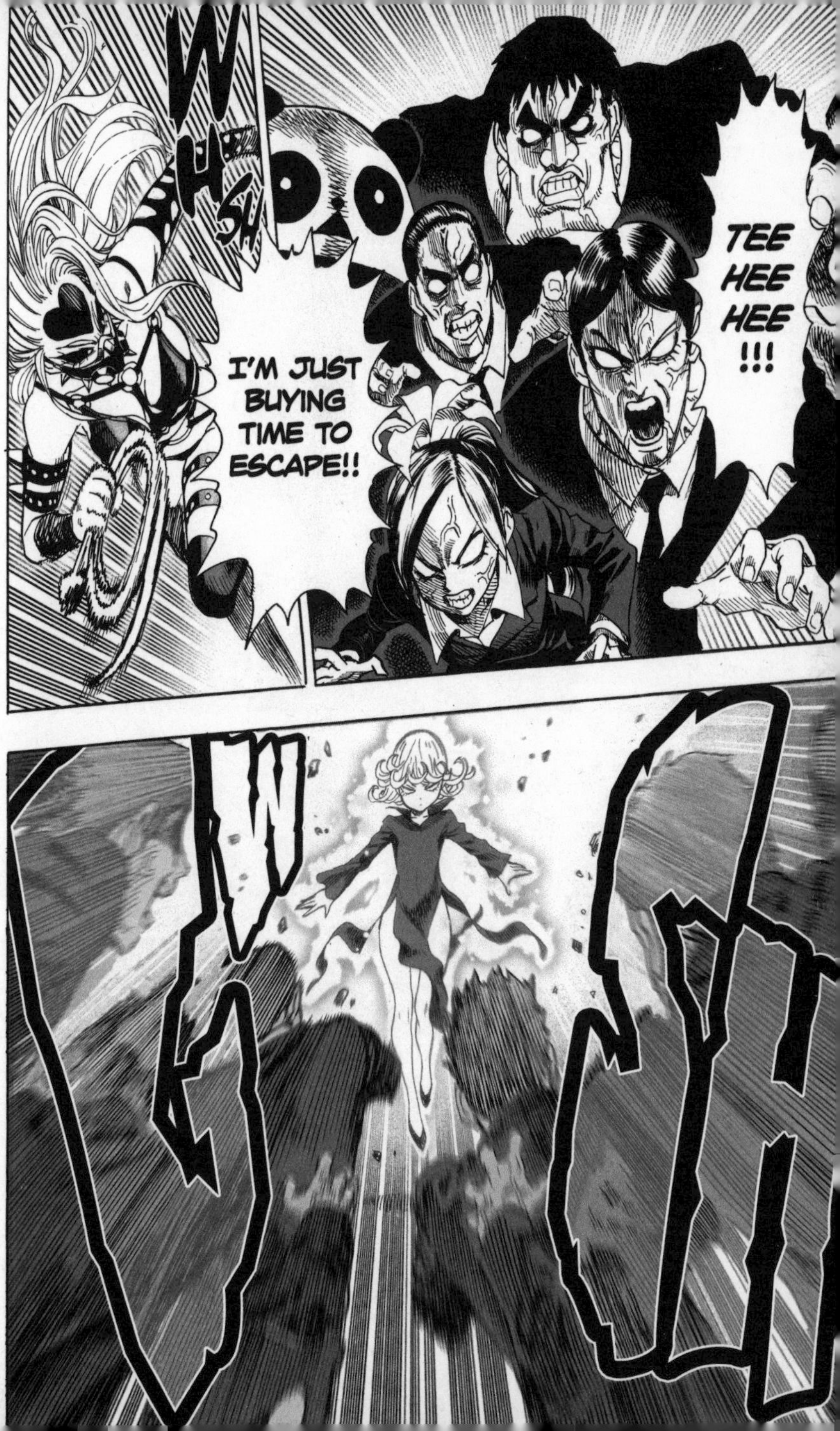
TEE HEE HEE!!!
I'M JUST BUYING TIME TO ESCAPE!!
WHSH

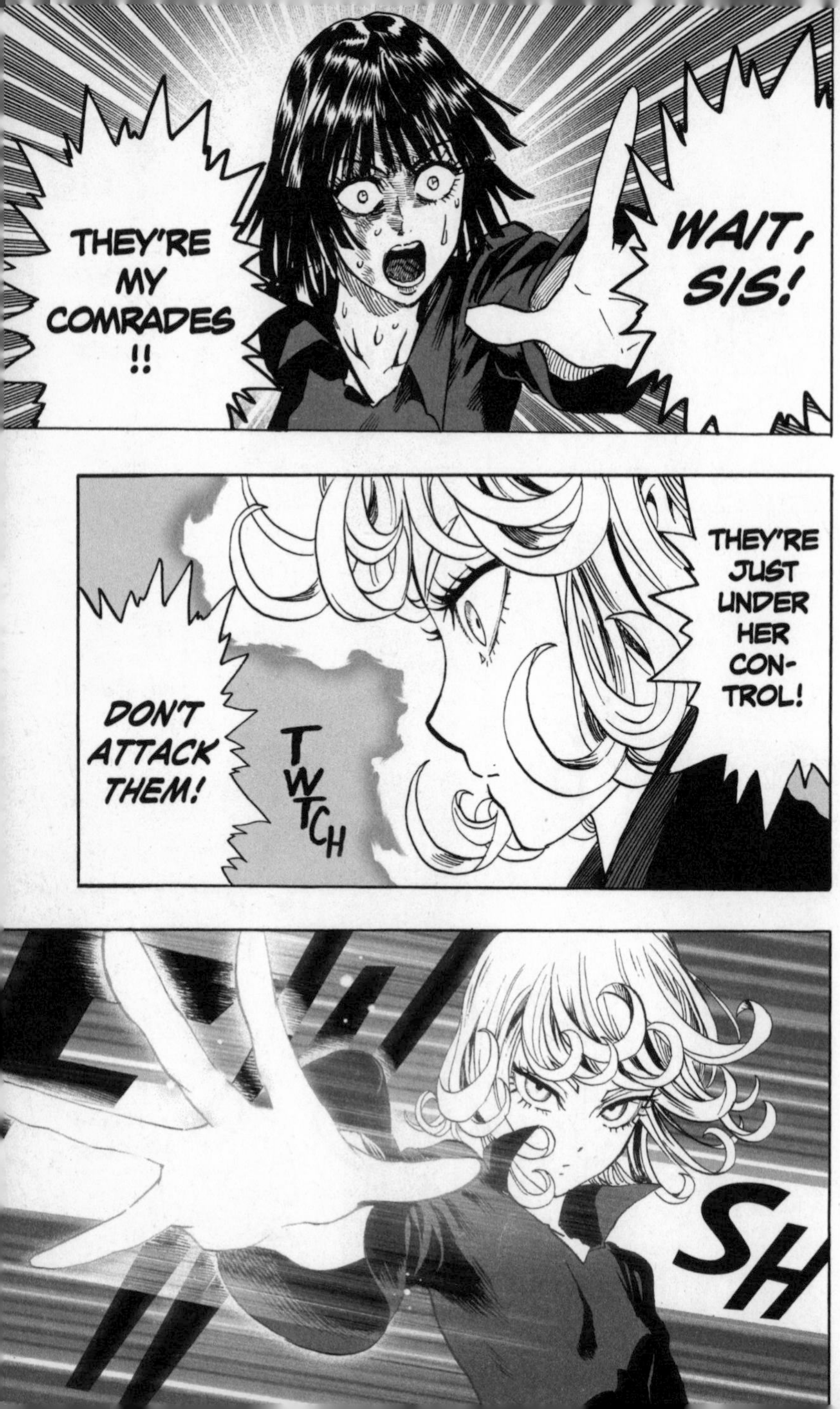
WAIT, SIS!
THEY'RE MY COMRADES!!
THEY'RE JUST UNDER HER CON-TROL!
TWTCH
DON'T ATTACK THEM!
SH

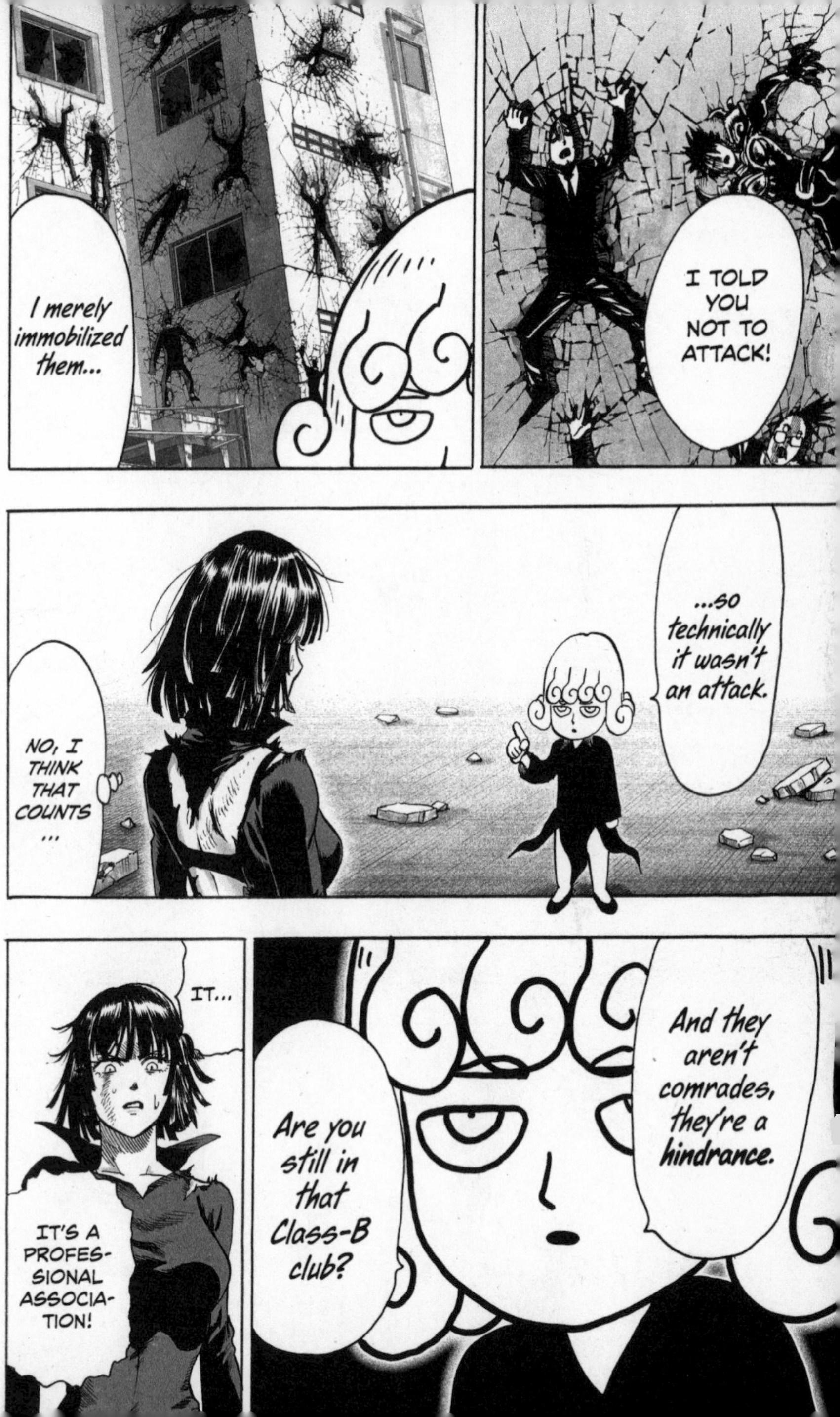
I TOLD YOU NOT TO ATTACK!
I merely immobilized them...
...so technically it wasn't an attack.
NO, I THINK THAT COUNTS...
And they aren't comrades, they're a hindrance.
Are you still in that Class-B club?
IT...
IT'S A PROFESSIONAL ASSOCIATION!

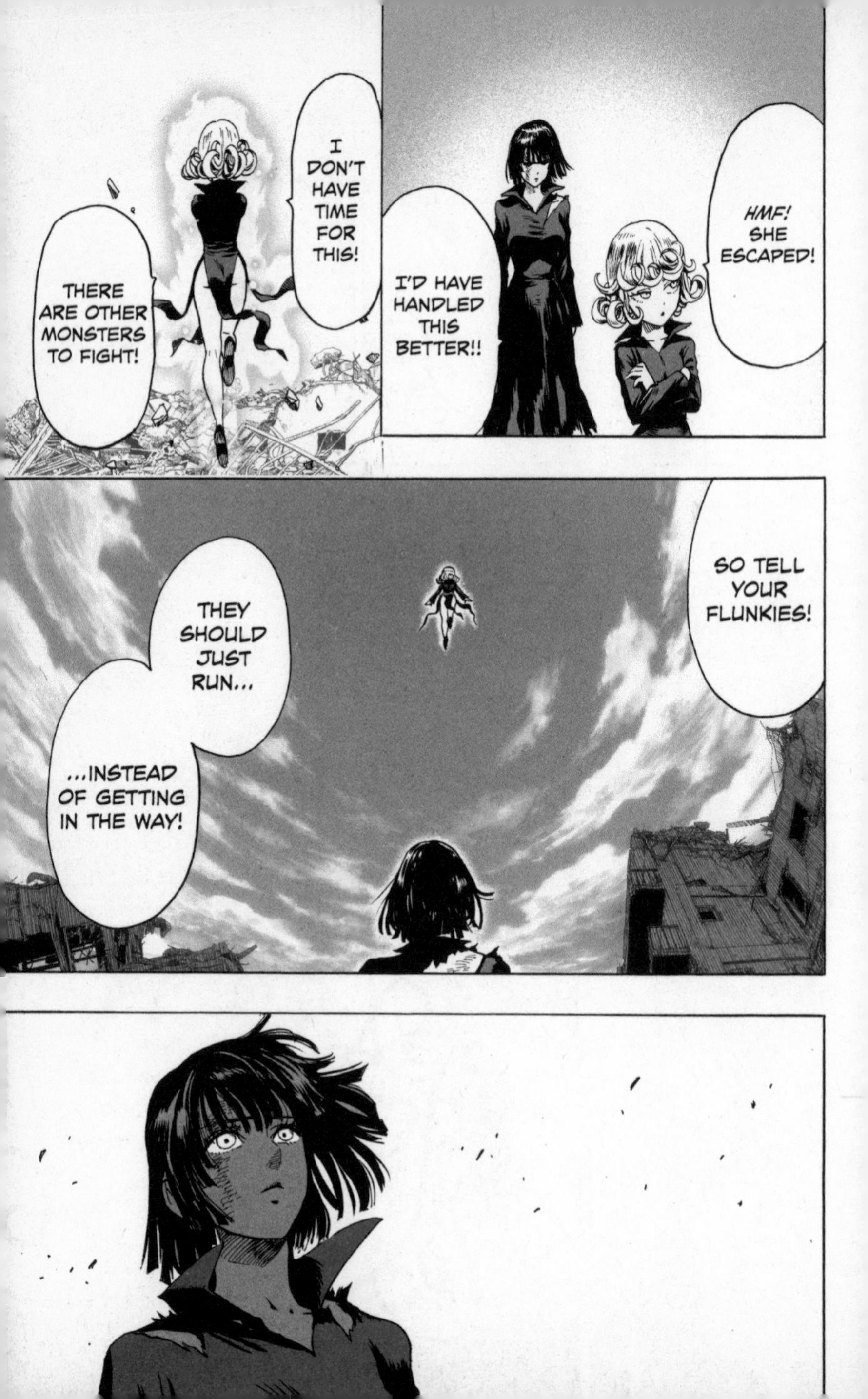
HMF! SHE ESCAPED!
I'D HAVE HANDLED THIS BETTER!!
I DON'T HAVE TIME FOR THIS!
THERE ARE OTHER MONSTERS TO FIGHT!
SO TELL YOUR FLUNKIES!
THEY SHOULD JUST RUN...
...INSTEAD OF GETTING IN THE WAY!

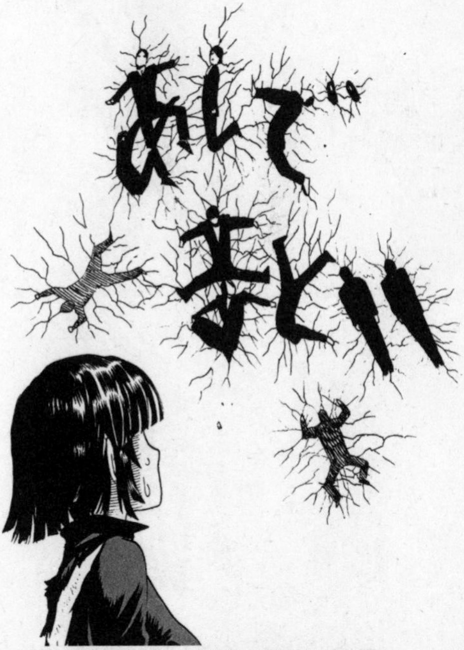
あしで
まとい

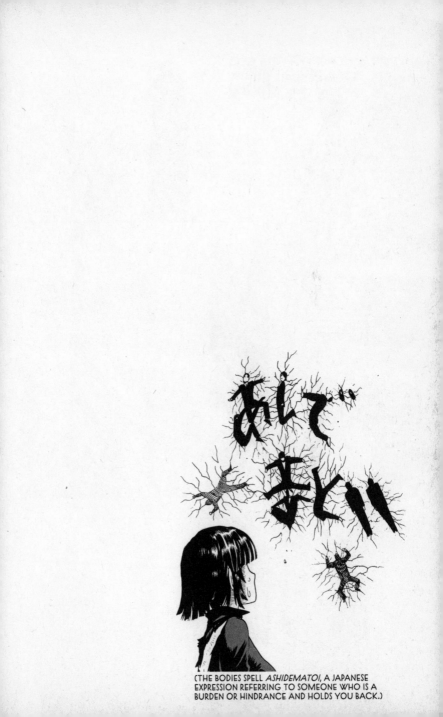

(THE BODIES SPELL *ASHIDEMATOI*, A JAPANESE EXPRESSION REFERRING TO SOMEONE WHO IS A BURDEN OR HINDRANCE AND HOLDS YOU BACK.)

PUNCH 66: THE STRONG ONES

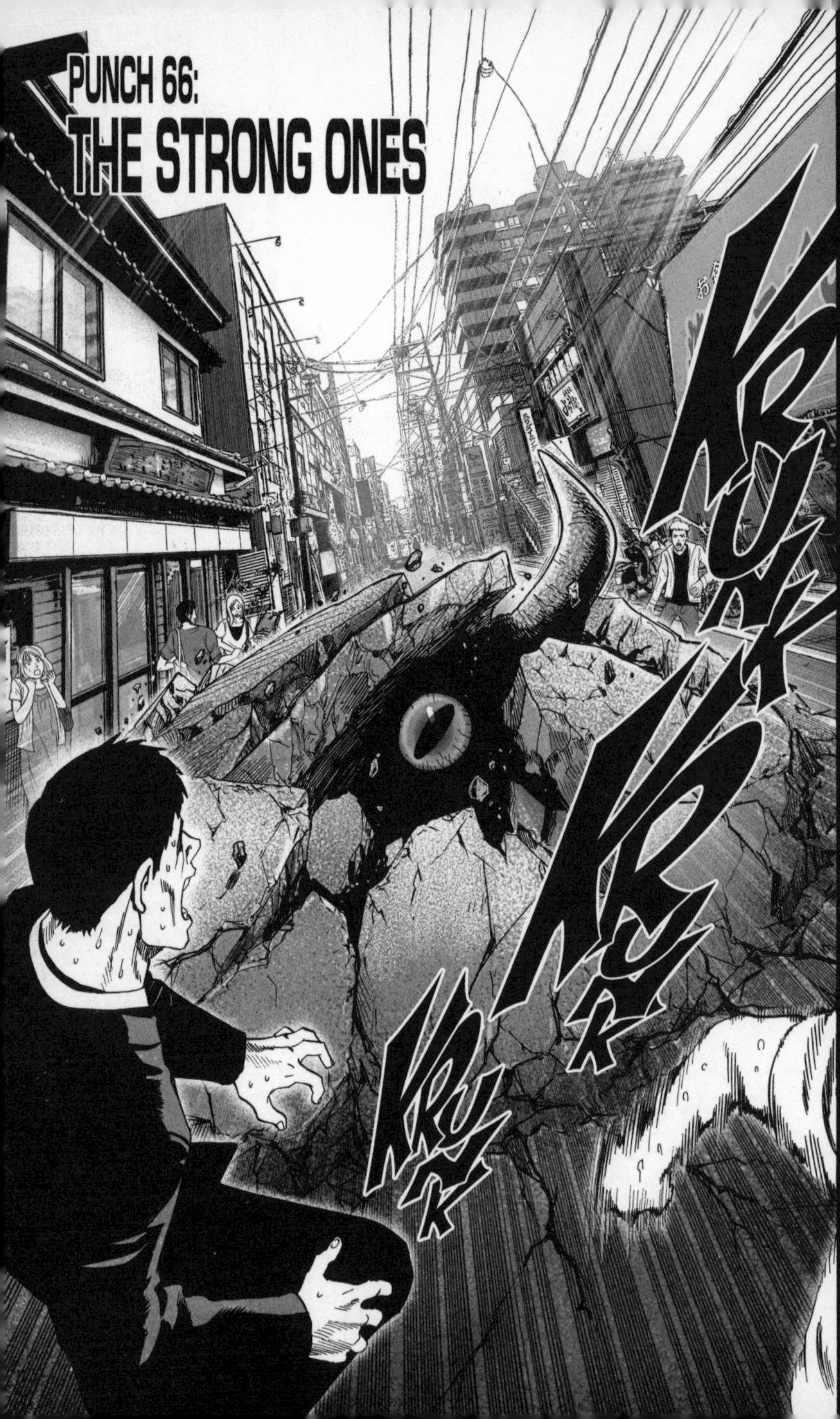
KRUNK
KRUNK
KRUNK

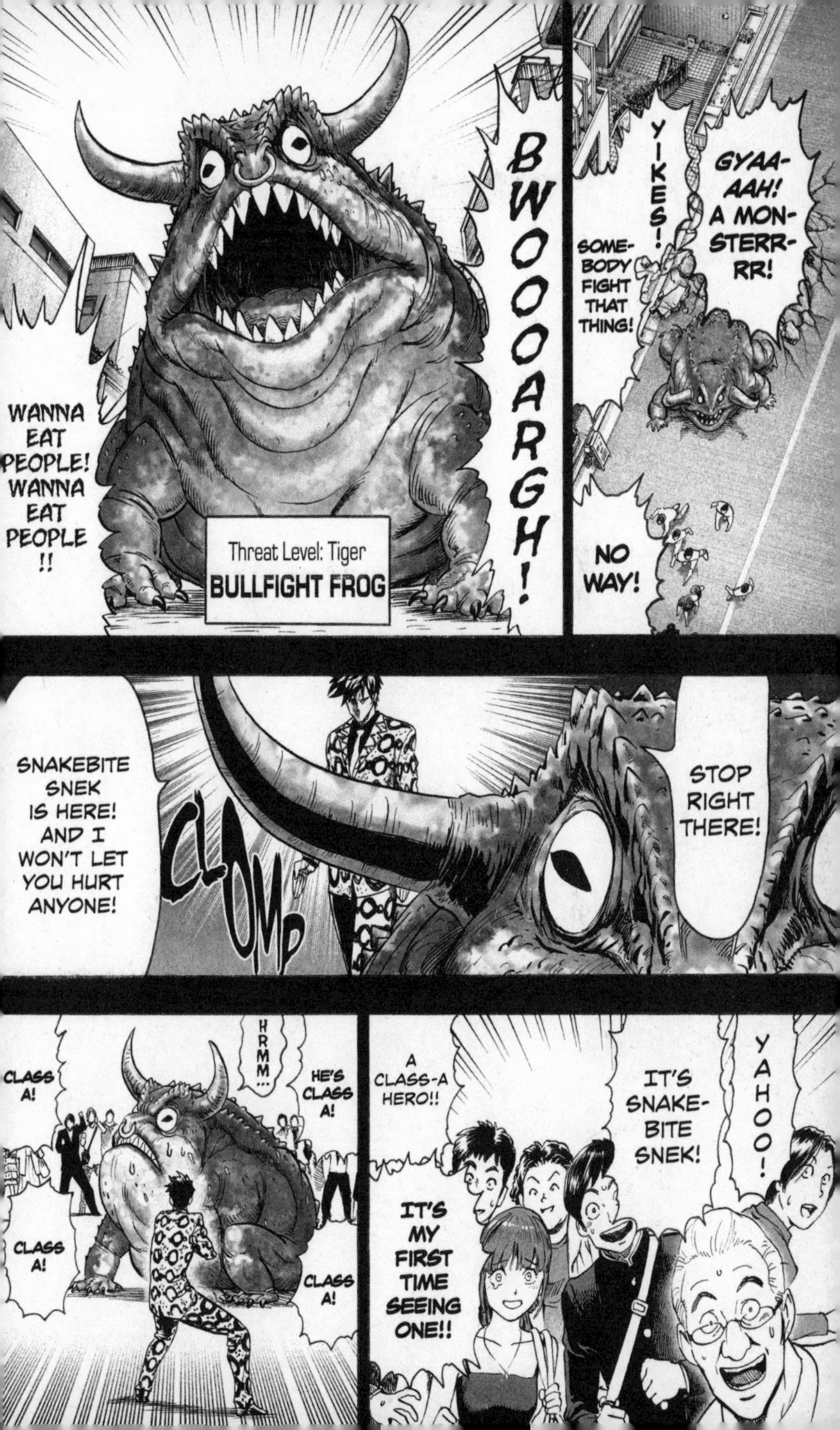
GYAAAAH! A MONSTERRR!
YIKES!
SOMEBODY FIGHT THAT THING!
NO WAY!
BWOOOARGH!
Threat Level: Tiger
BULLFIGHT FROG
WANNA EAT PEOPLE! WANNA EAT PEOPLE!!
STOP RIGHT THERE!
CLOMP
SNAKEBITE SNEK IS HERE! AND I WON'T LET YOU HURT ANYONE!
YAHOO!
IT'S SNAKEBITE SNEK!
A CLASS-A HERO!!
IT'S MY FIRST TIME SEEING ONE!!
HE'S CLASS A!
HRMM...
CLASS A!
CLASS A!
CLASS A!

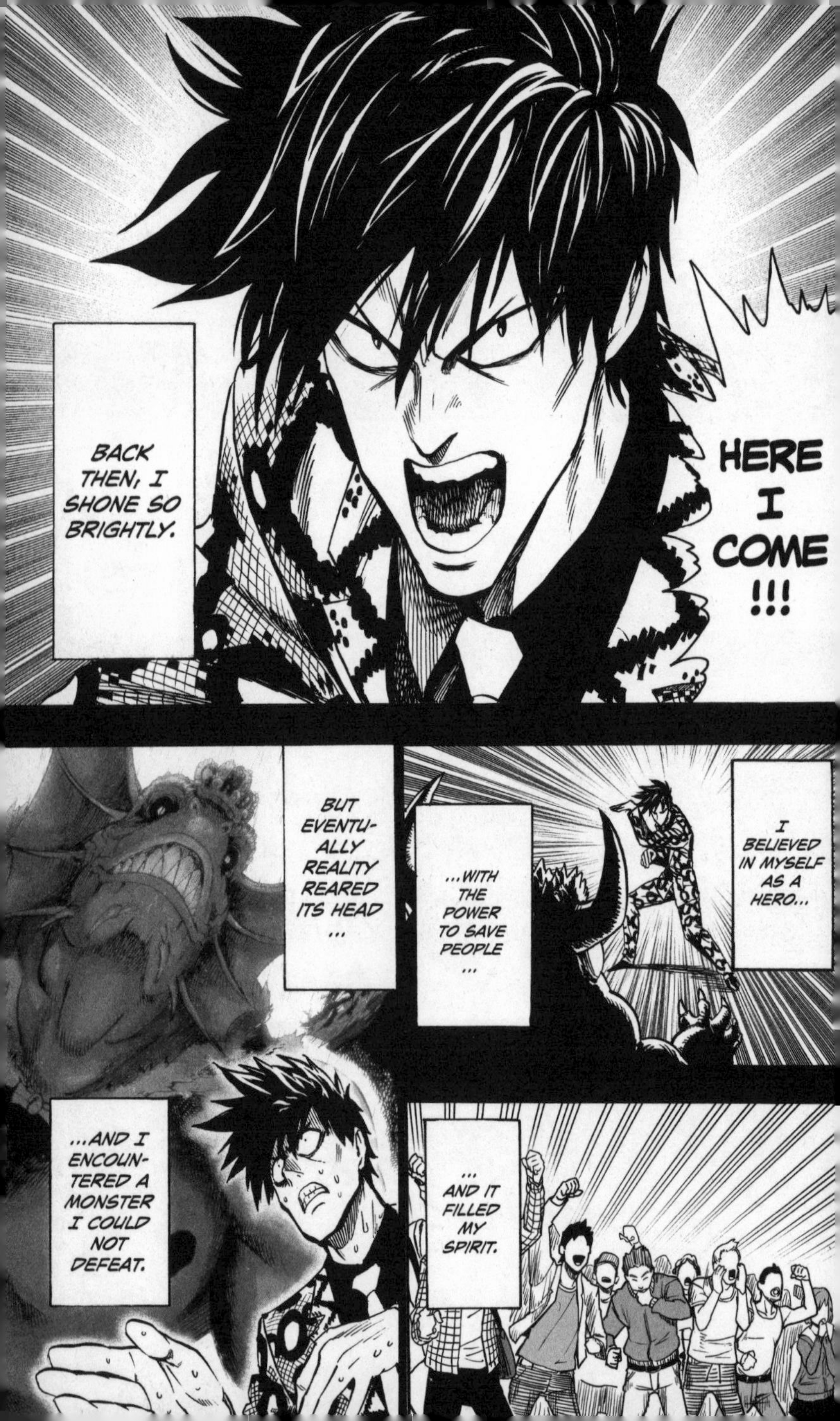
HERE I COME!!!
BACK THEN, I SHONE SO BRIGHTLY.
I BELIEVED IN MYSELF AS A HERO...
...WITH THE POWER TO SAVE PEOPLE...
BUT EVENTUALLY REALITY REARED ITS HEAD...
... AND IT FILLED MY SPIRIT.
...AND I ENCOUNTERED A MONSTER I COULD NOT DEFEAT.

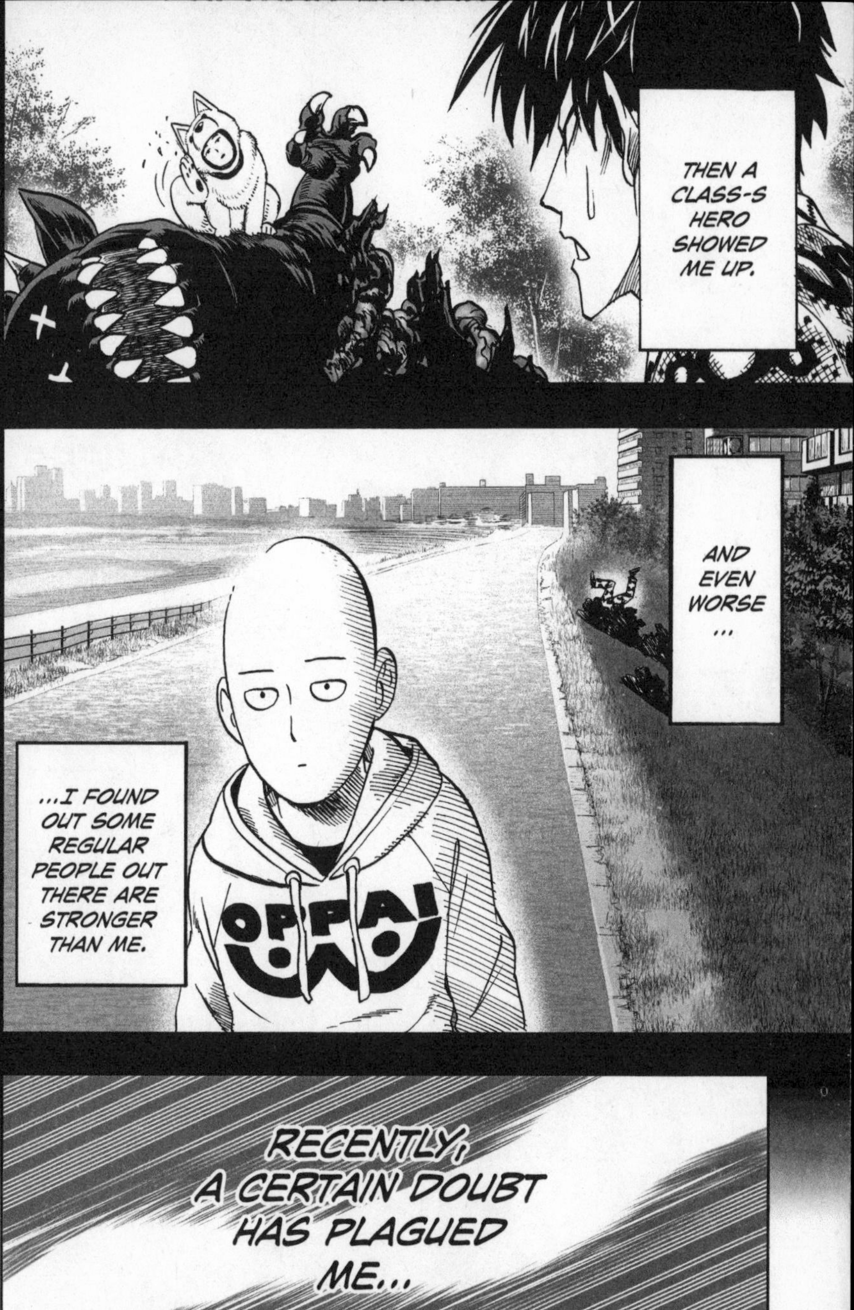
THEN A CLASS-S HERO SHOWED ME UP.
AND EVEN WORSE...
...I FOUND OUT SOME REGULAR PEOPLE OUT THERE ARE STRONGER THAN ME.
OPPAI
RECENTLY, A CERTAIN DOUBT HAS PLAGUED ME...

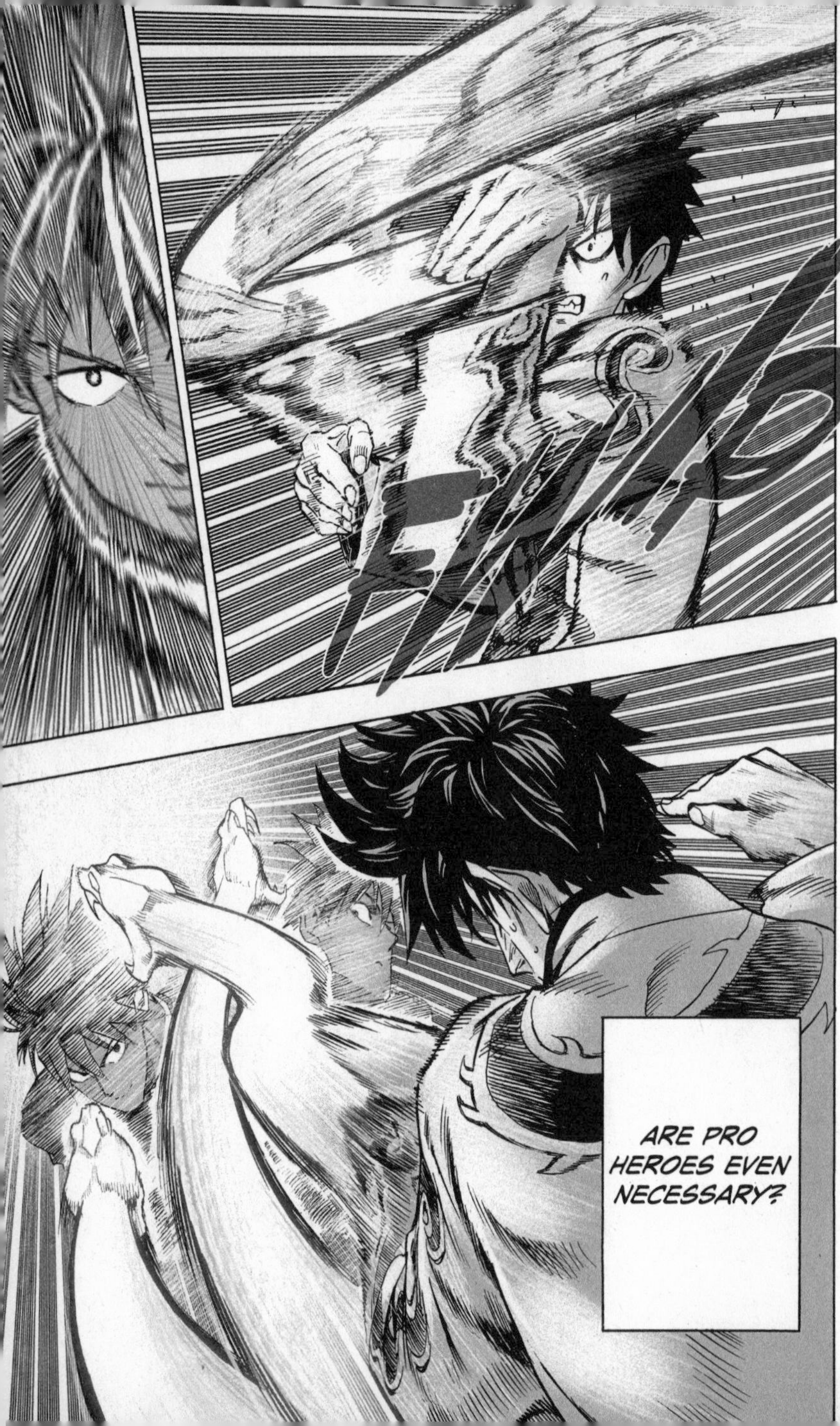
ARE PRO HEROES EVEN NECESSARY?

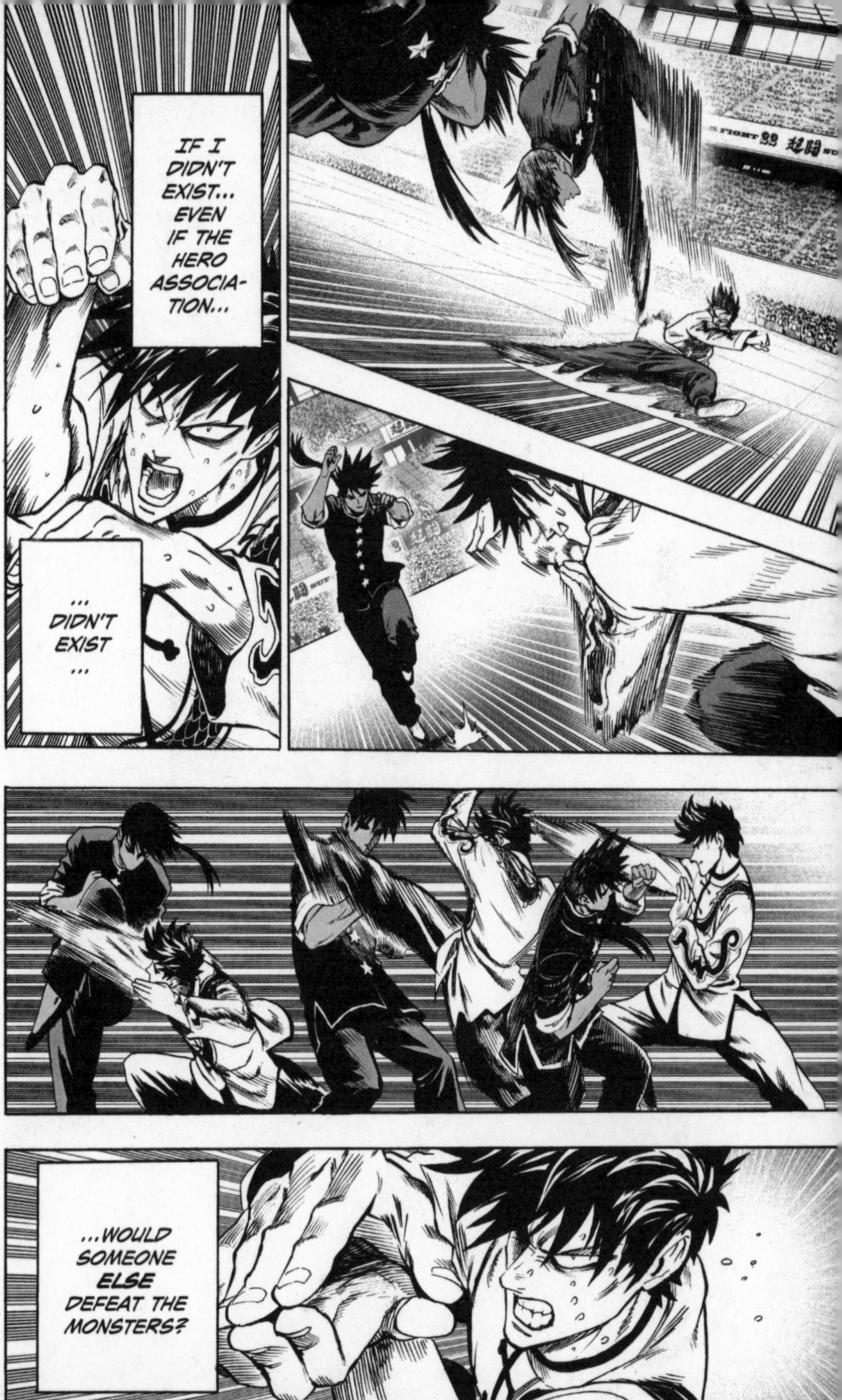
IF I DIDN'T EXIST... EVEN IF THE HERO ASSOCIATION...
...DIDN'T EXIST...
...WOULD SOMEONE ELSE DEFEAT THE MONSTERS?

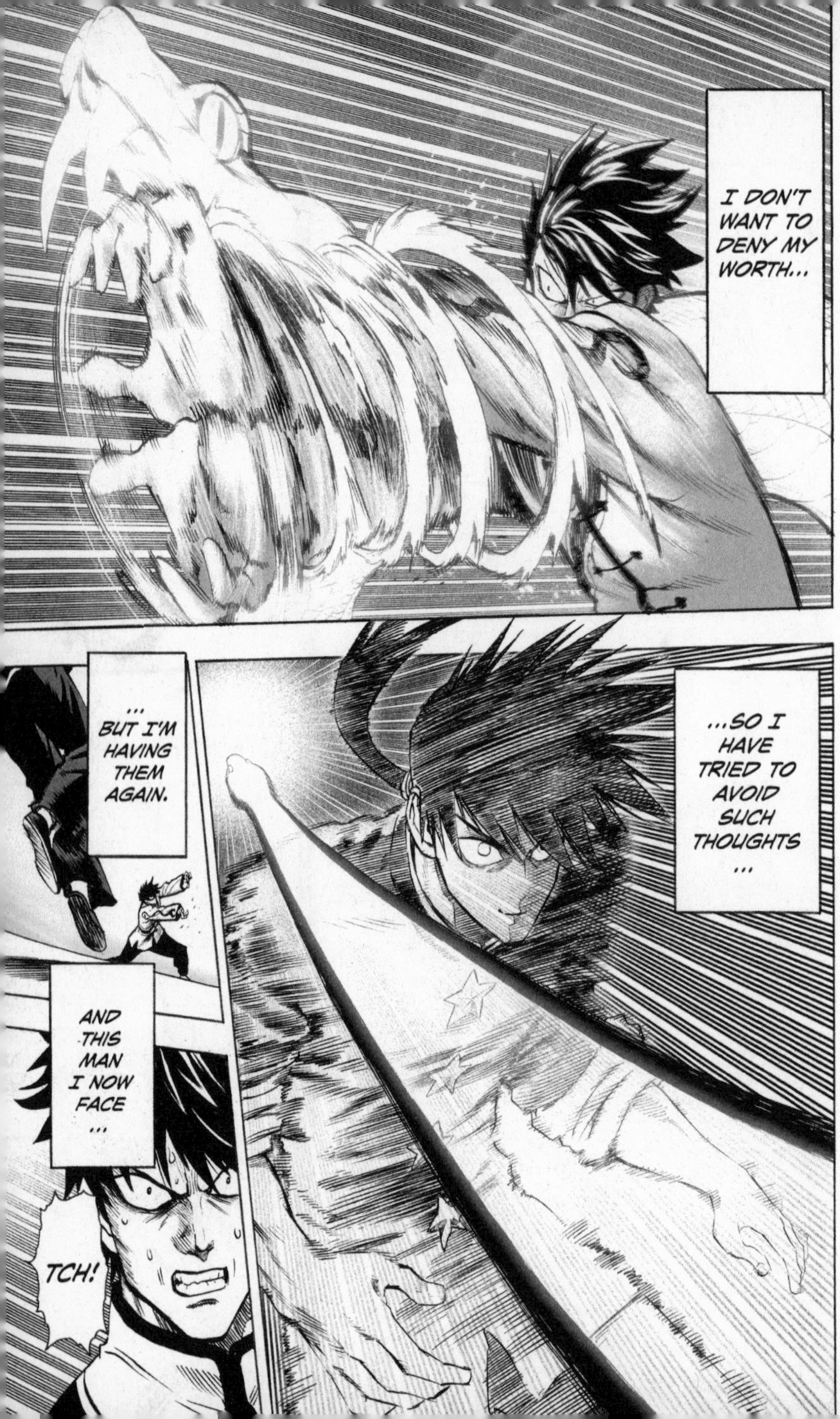
I DON'T WANT TO DENY MY WORTH...
...SO I HAVE TRIED TO AVOID SUCH THOUGHTS ...
... BUT I'M HAVING THEM AGAIN.
AND THIS MAN I NOW FACE ...
TCH!

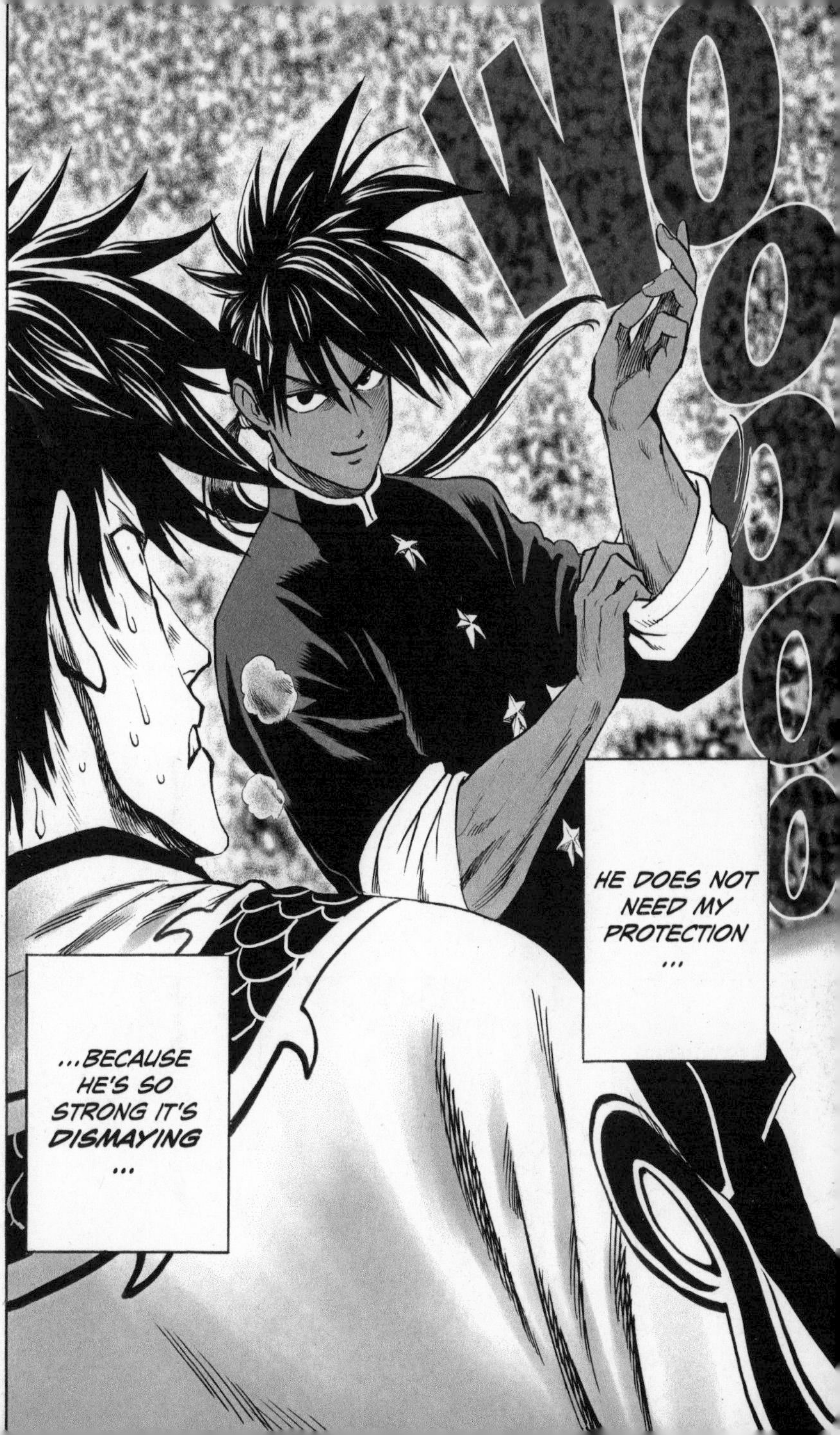
WOOOOO
HE DOES NOT NEED MY PROTECTION ...
...BECAUSE HE'S SO STRONG IT'S DISMAYING ...

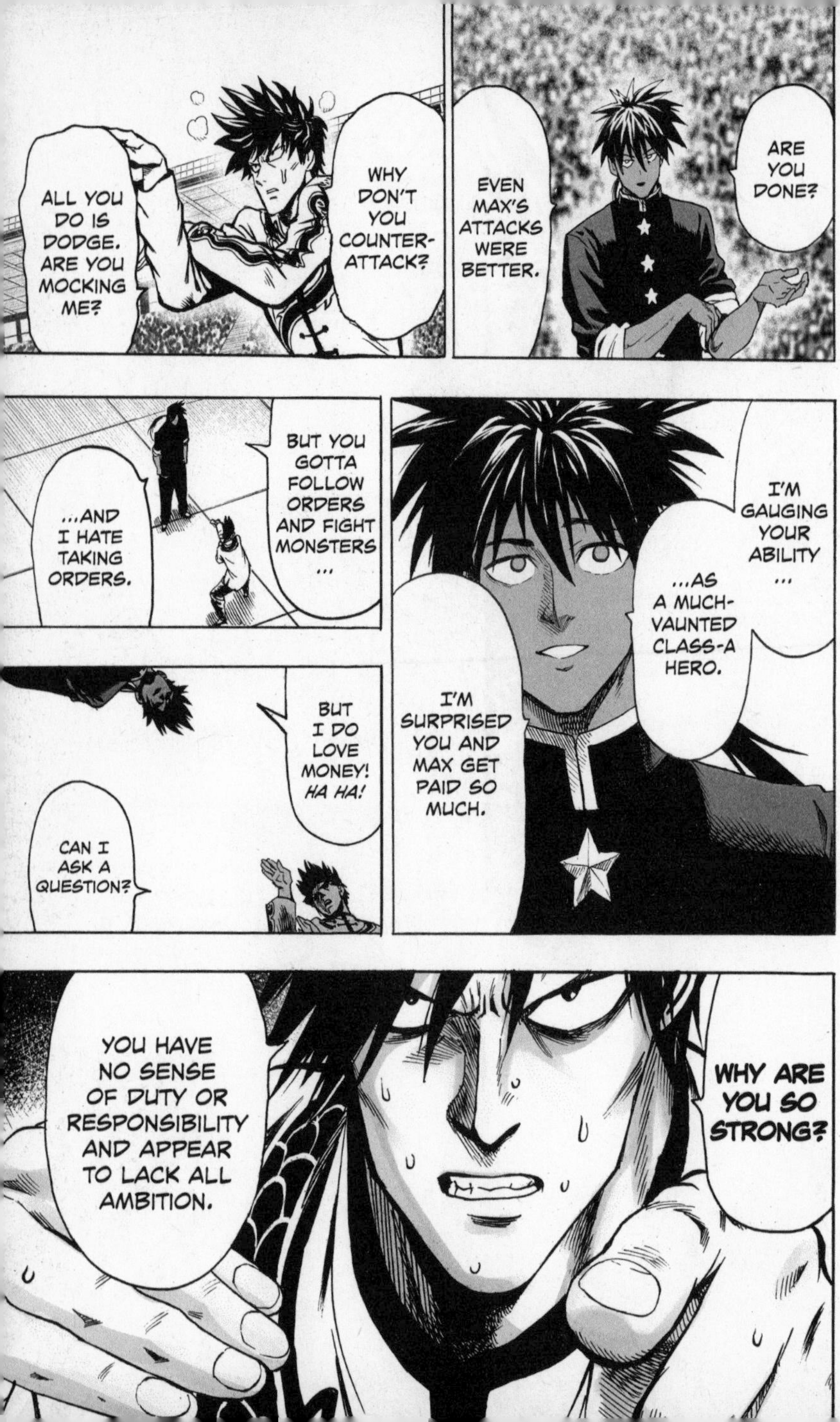
ARE YOU DONE?
EVEN MAX'S ATTACKS WERE BETTER.
WHY DON'T YOU COUNTER-ATTACK?
ALL YOU DO IS DODGE. ARE YOU MOCKING ME?
I'M GAUGING YOUR ABILITY...
...AS A MUCH-VAUNTED CLASS-A HERO.
I'M SURPRISED YOU AND MAX GET PAID SO MUCH.
BUT YOU GOTTA FOLLOW ORDERS AND FIGHT MONSTERS...
...AND I HATE TAKING ORDERS.
BUT I DO LOVE MONEY! *HA HA!*
CAN I ASK A QUESTION?
YOU HAVE NO SENSE OF DUTY OR RESPONSIBILITY AND APPEAR TO LACK ALL AMBITION.
WHY ARE YOU SO STRONG?

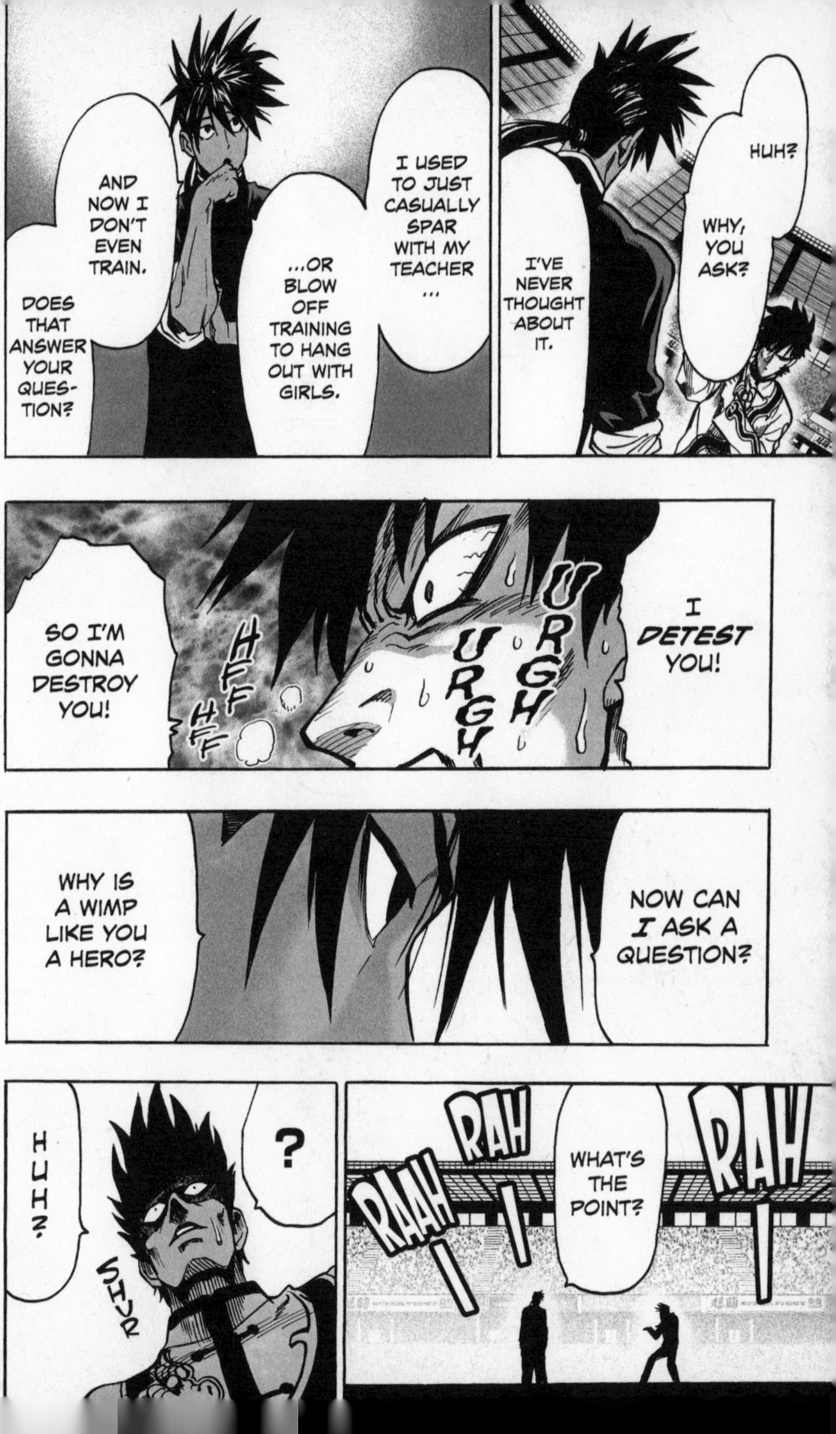
HUH?
WHY, YOU ASK?
I'VE NEVER THOUGHT ABOUT IT.
I USED TO JUST CASUALLY SPAR WITH MY TEACHER ...
...OR BLOW OFF TRAINING TO HANG OUT WITH GIRLS.
AND NOW I DON'T EVEN TRAIN.
DOES THAT ANSWER YOUR QUES-TION?
I *DETEST* YOU!
URGH
URGH
HFF
HFF
SO I'M GONNA DESTROY YOU!
NOW CAN *I* ASK A QUESTION?
WHY IS A WIMP LIKE YOU A HERO?
RAH
WHAT'S THE POINT?
RAH
RAAH
?
HUH?
SHUR

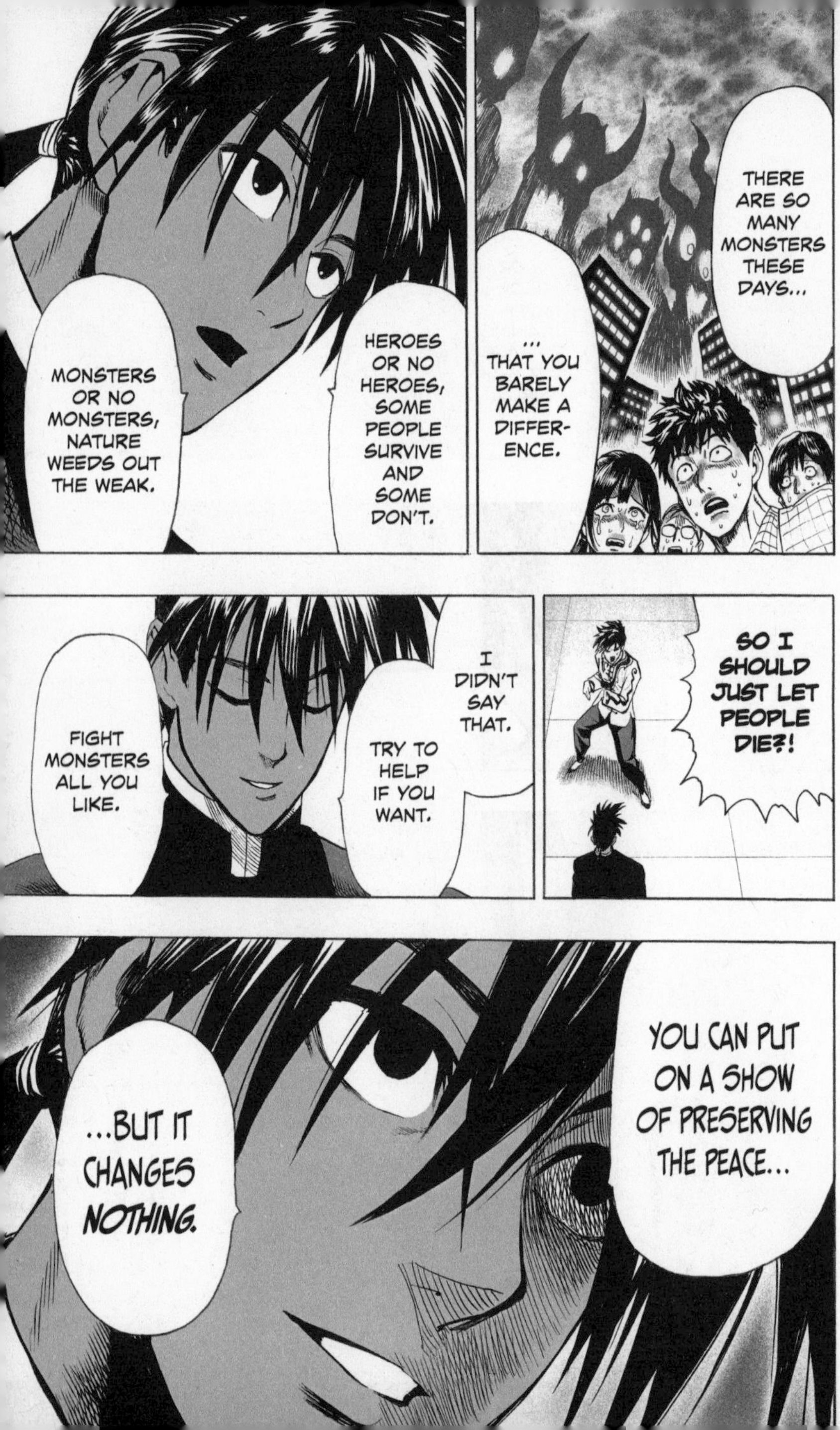
THERE ARE SO MANY MONSTERS THESE DAYS...
...THAT YOU BARELY MAKE A DIFFERENCE.
HEROES OR NO HEROES, SOME PEOPLE SURVIVE AND SOME DON'T.
MONSTERS OR NO MONSTERS, NATURE WEEDS OUT THE WEAK.
SO I SHOULD JUST LET PEOPLE DIE?!
I DIDN'T SAY THAT.
TRY TO HELP IF YOU WANT.
FIGHT MONSTERS ALL YOU LIKE.
YOU CAN PUT ON A SHOW OF PRESERVING THE PEACE...
...BUT IT CHANGES NOTHING.

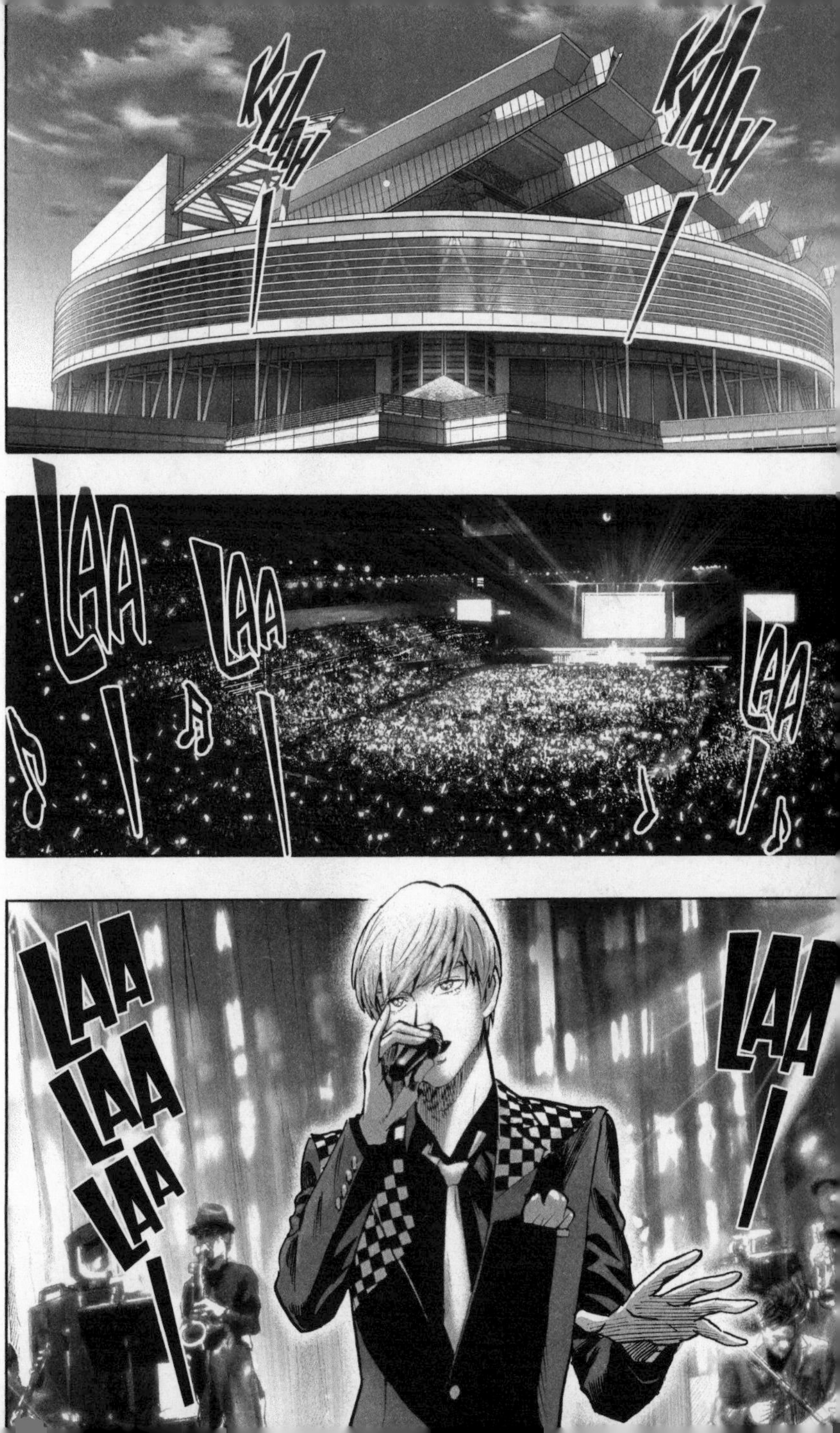
KYAAH!
KYAAH!
LAA!
LAA!
LAA!
LAA!
LAA LAA LAA LAA!

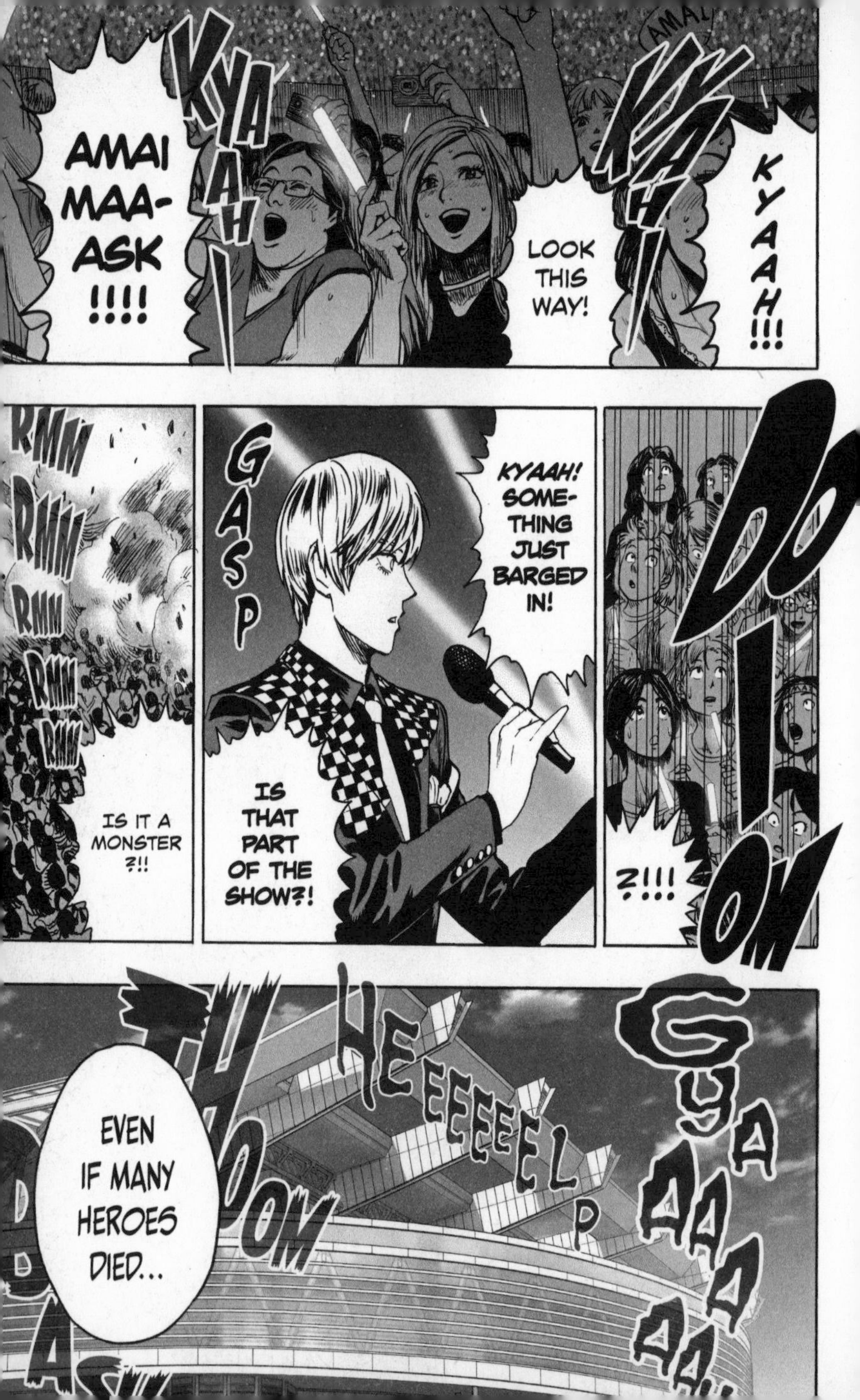

KYAAAH!!!
KYAAH
LOOK THIS WAY!
KYAAH!
AMAI MAA-ASK!!!!
DOOM
?!!!
KYAAH! SOME-THING JUST BARGED IN!
GASP
IS THAT PART OF THE SHOW?!
RMM RMM RMM RMM RMM RMM
IS IT A MONSTER?!!
GYAAAAAA...
HEEEEEELP
THOOOM
EVEN IF MANY HEROES DIED...

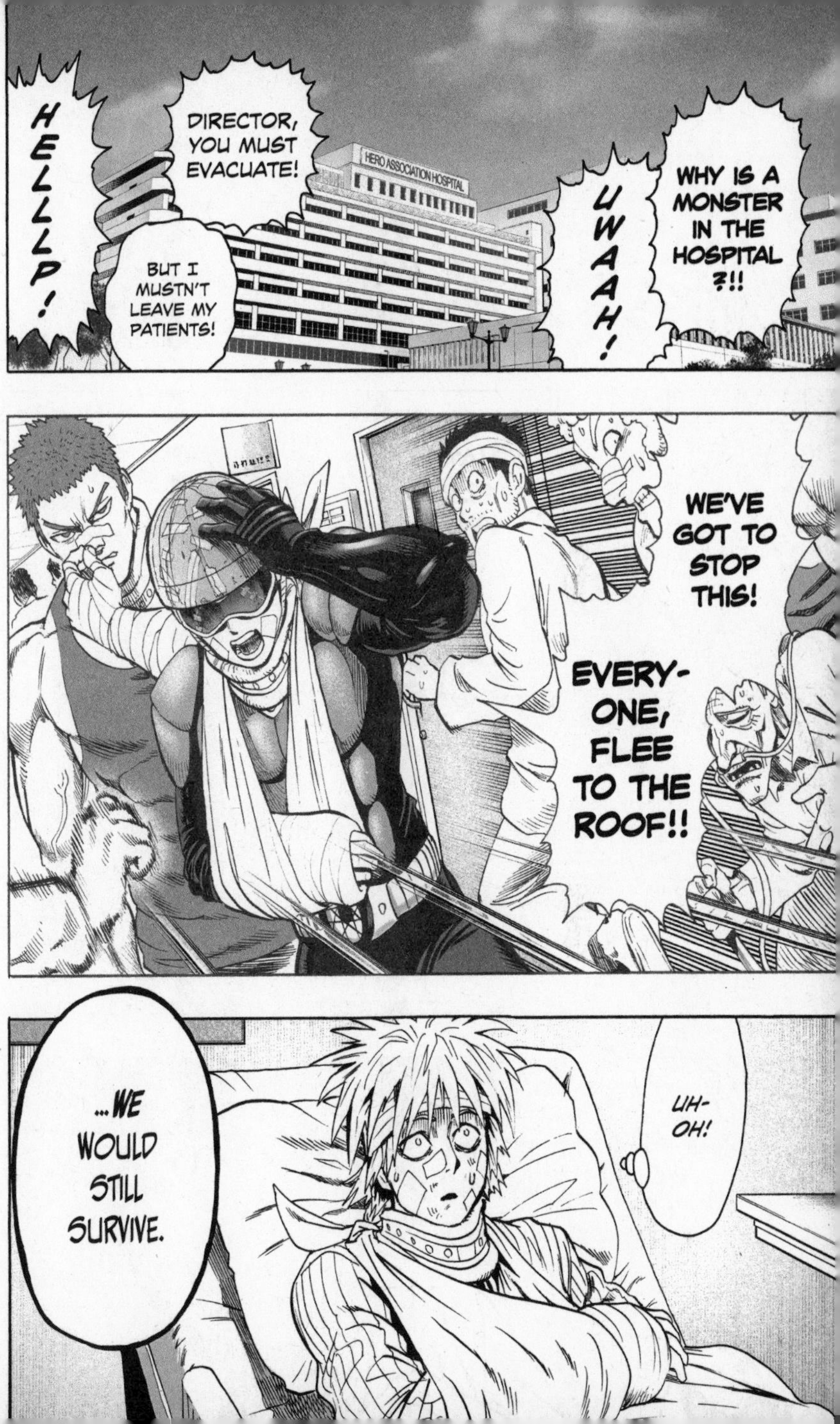
WHY IS A MONSTER IN THE HOSPITAL ?!!
UWAAH!
HERO ASSOCIATION HOSPITAL
DIRECTOR, YOU MUST EVACUATE!
BUT I MUSTN'T LEAVE MY PATIENTS!
HELLLP!
WE'VE GOT TO STOP THIS!
EVERY-ONE, FLEE TO THE ROOF!!
UH-OH!
...WE WOULD STILL SURVIVE.

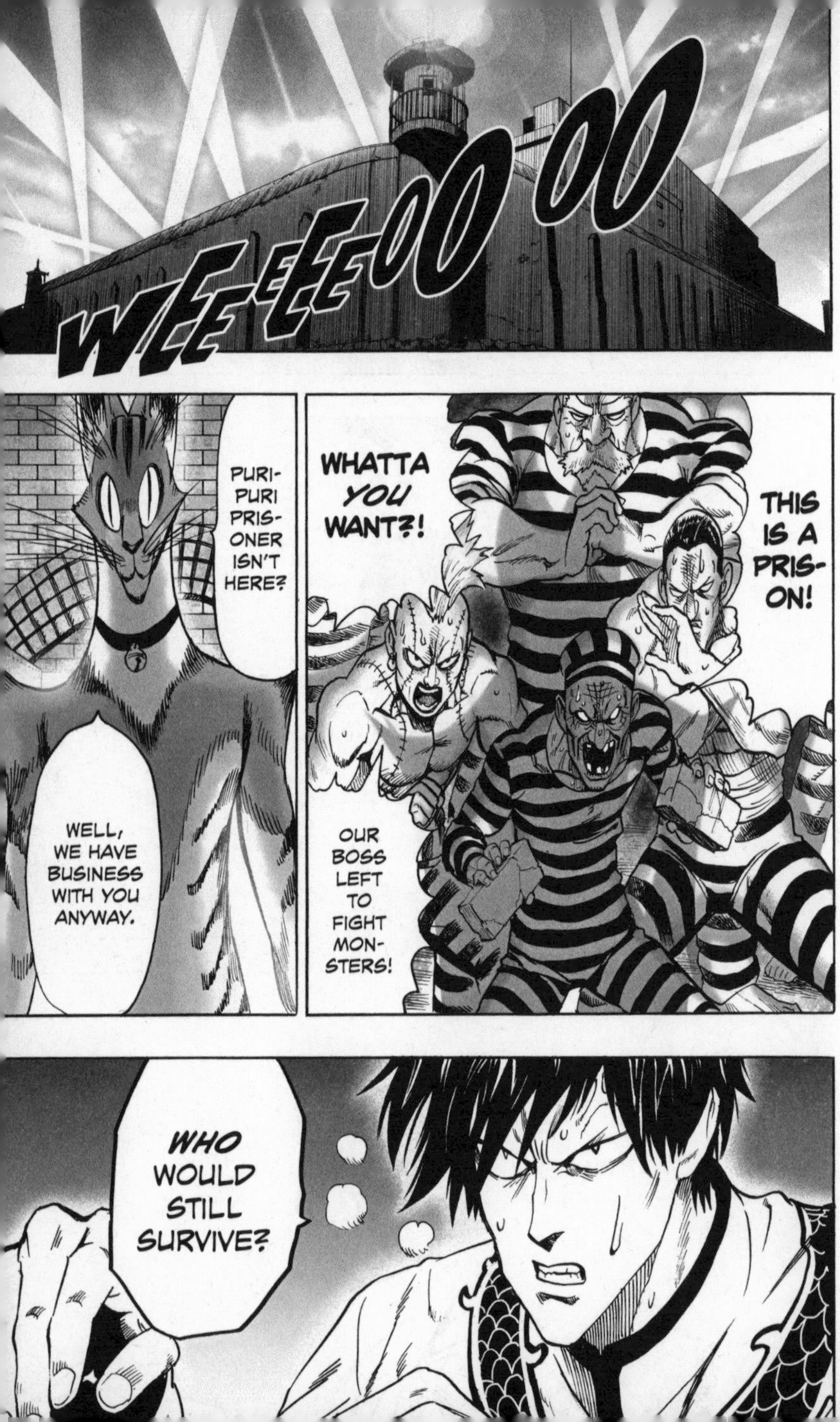
WEEEEE-OOOO
THIS IS A PRIS-ON!
WHATTA YOU WANT?!
OUR BOSS LEFT TO FIGHT MON-STERS!
PURI-PURI PRIS-ONER ISN'T HERE?
WELL, WE HAVE BUSINESS WITH YOU ANYWAY.
WHO WOULD STILL SURVIVE?

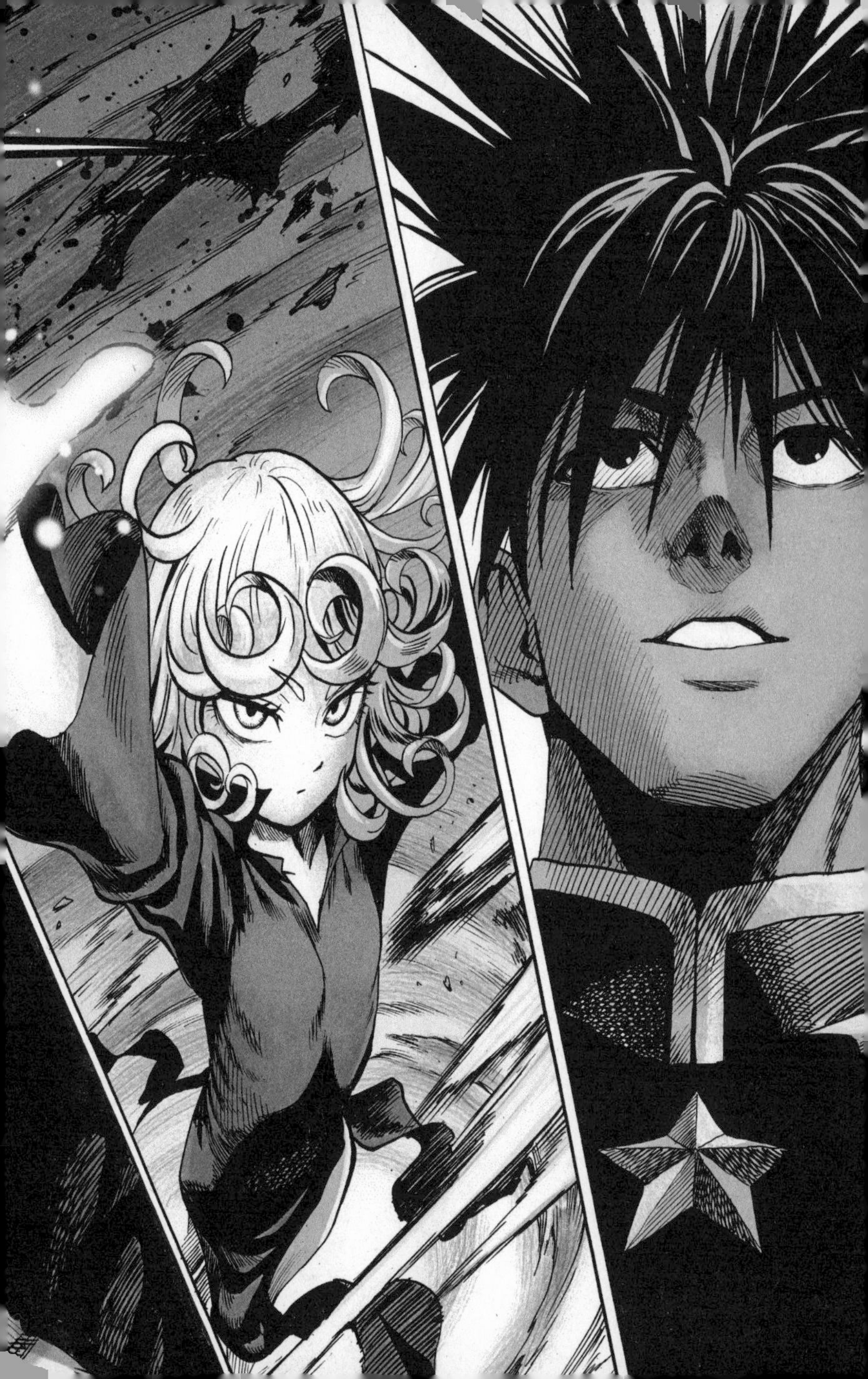

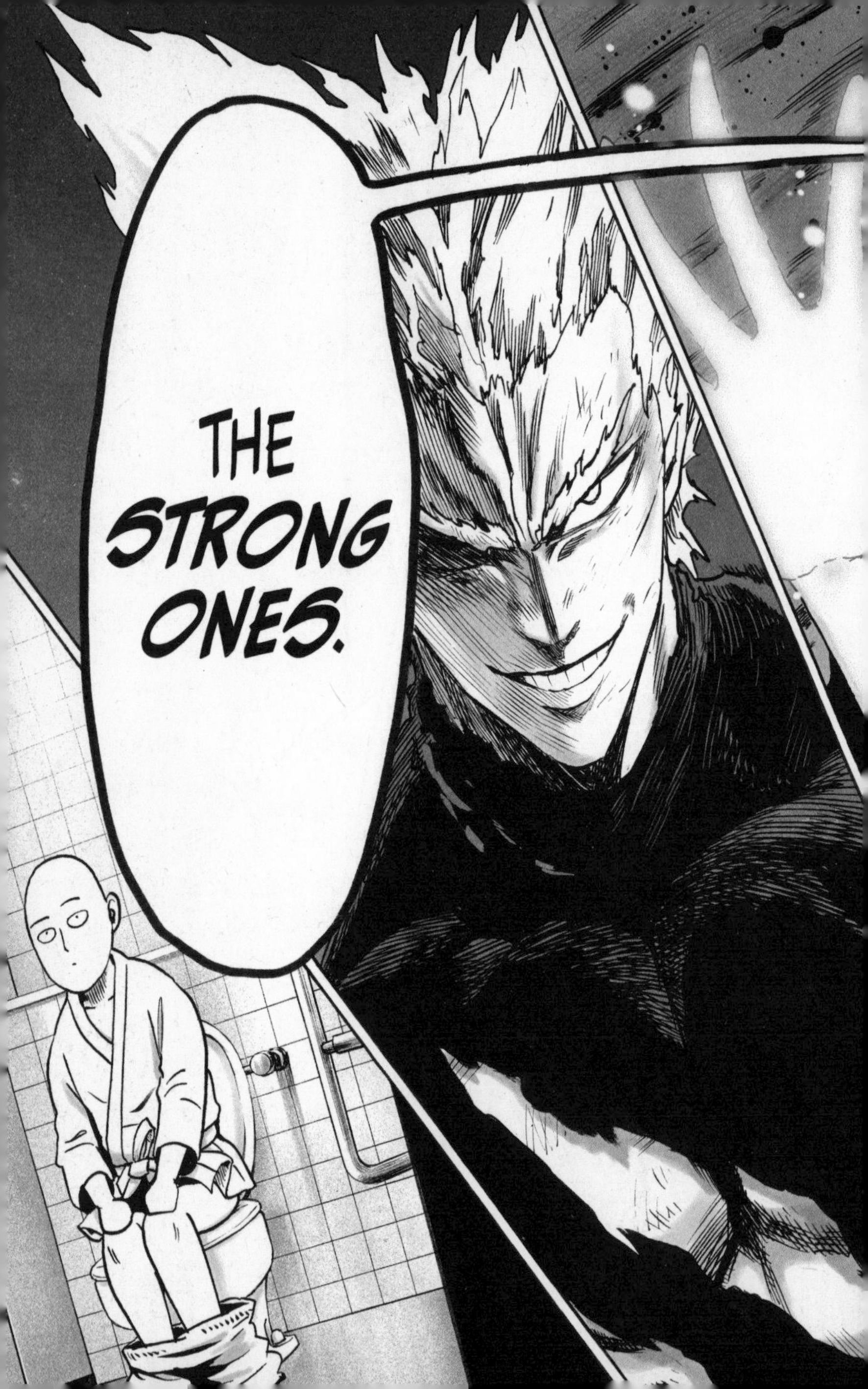
THE STRONG ONES.

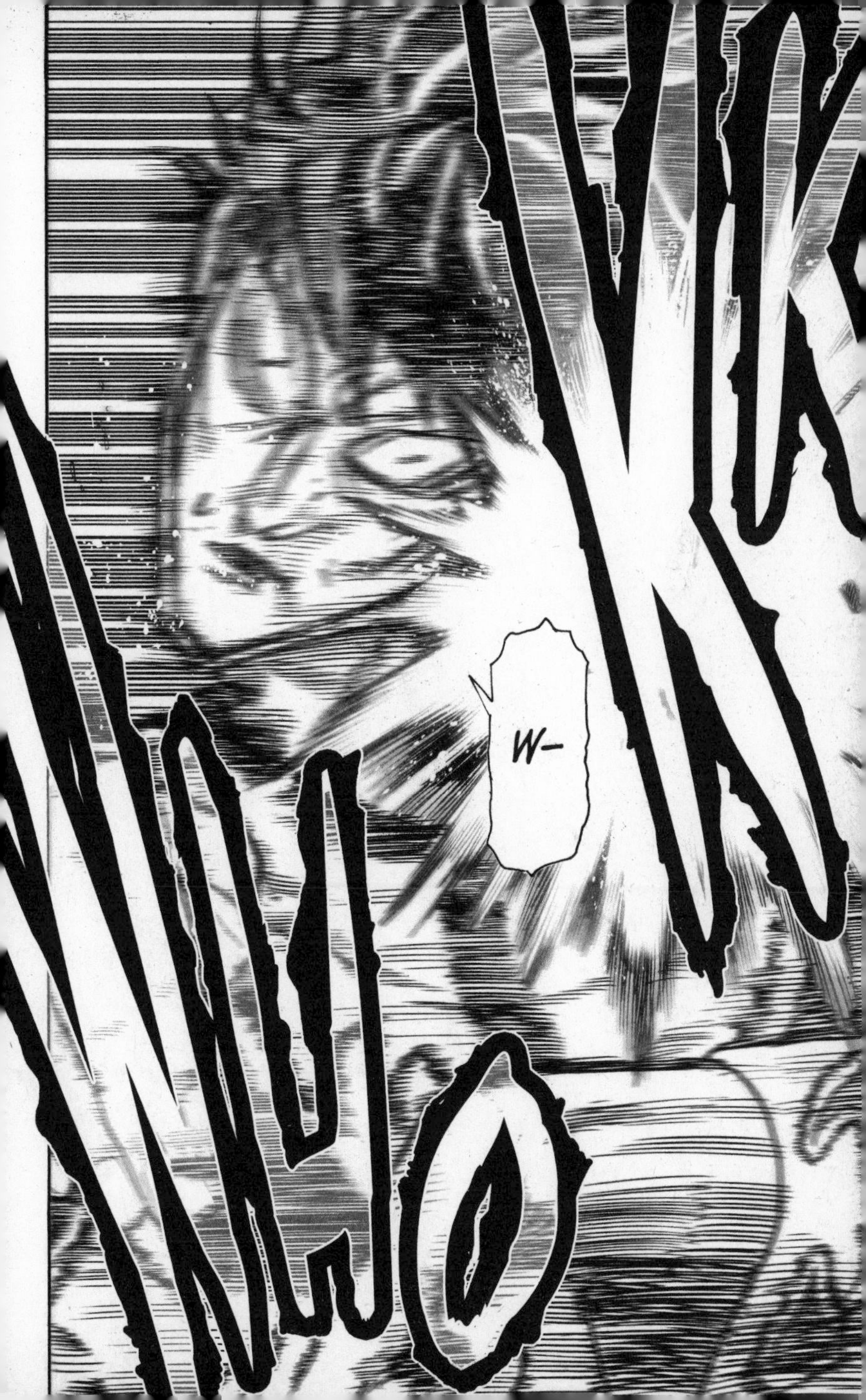
W-

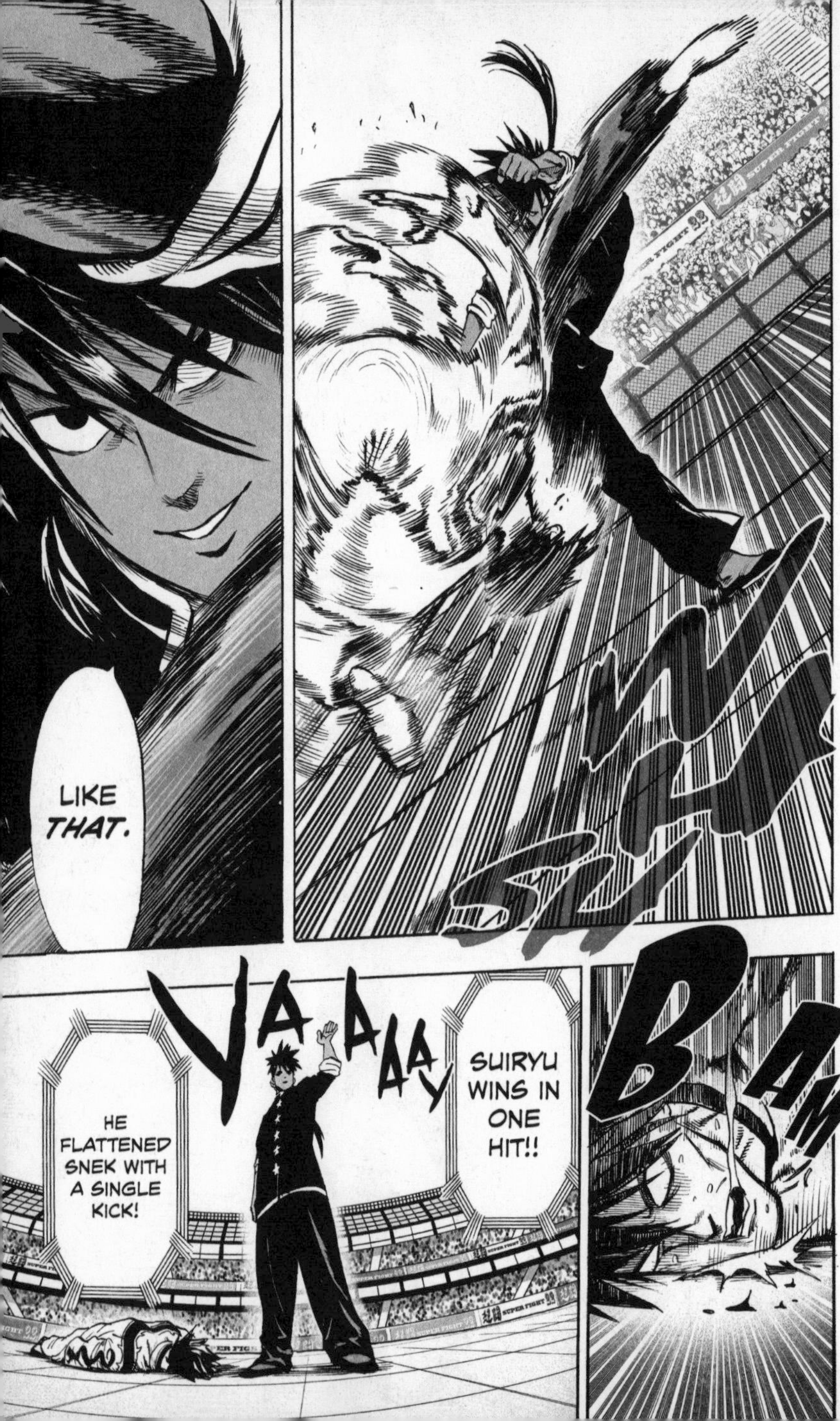
LIKE *THAT.*
BAM
SUIRYU WINS IN ONE HIT!!
YAAAAY
HE FLATTENED SNEK WITH A SINGLE KICK!

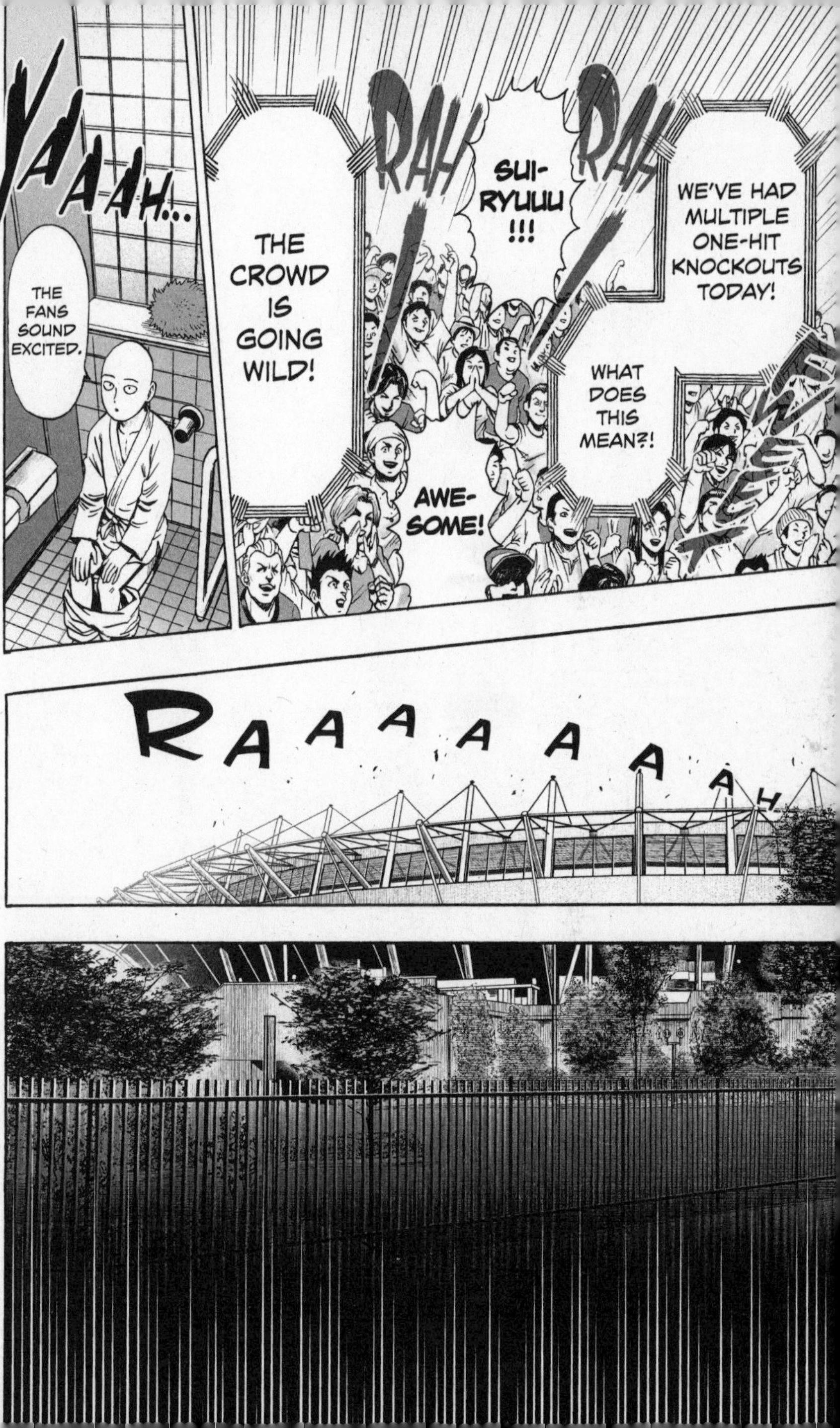
WE'VE HAD MULTIPLE ONE-HIT KNOCKOUTS TODAY!
WHAT DOES THIS MEAN?!
RAH
SUI-RYUUU!!!
RAH
THE CROWD IS GOING WILD!
AWE-SOME!
YAAAH...
THE FANS SOUND EXCITED.
RAAAAAAAH

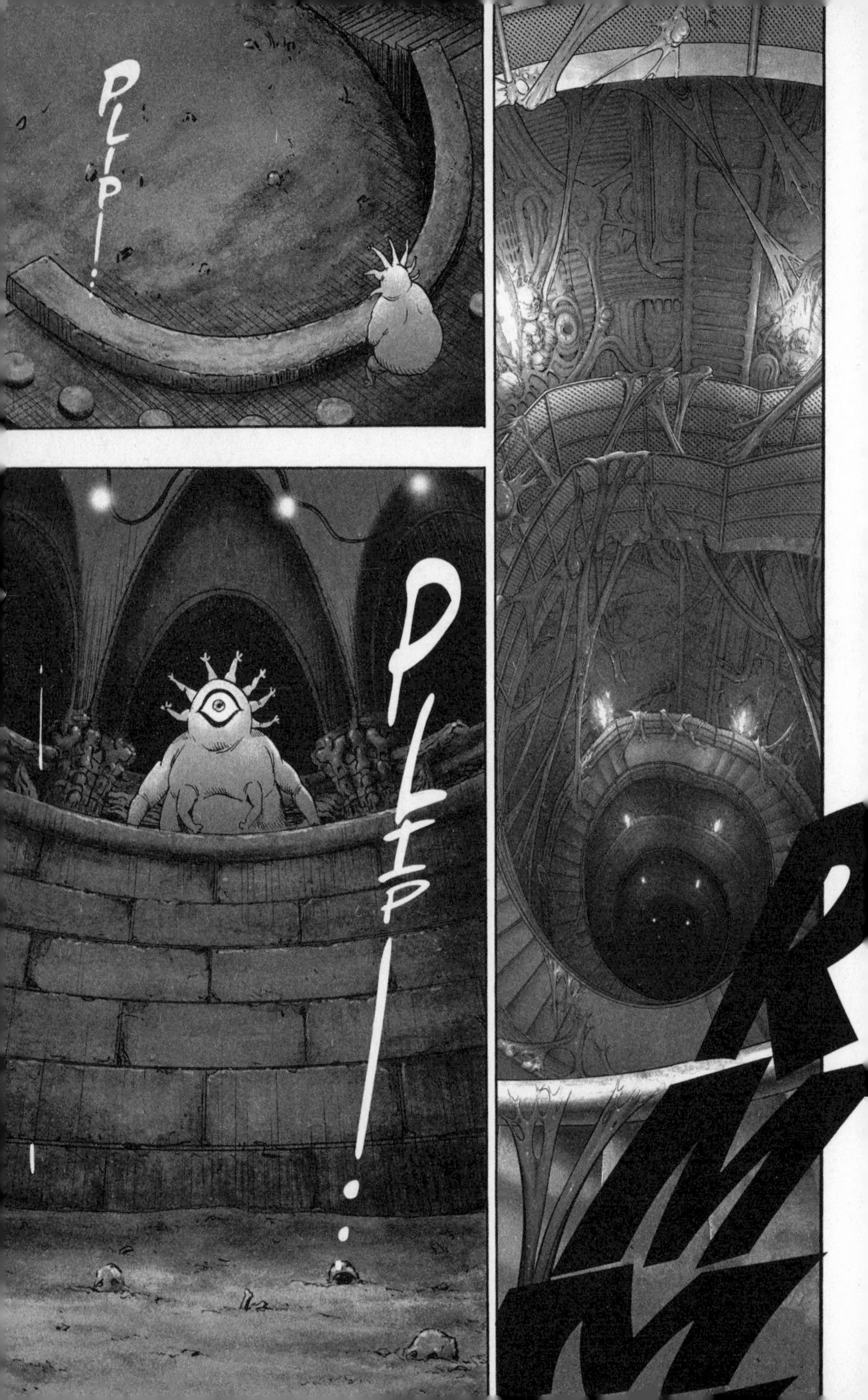
RMM
PLIP!..
PLIP!..

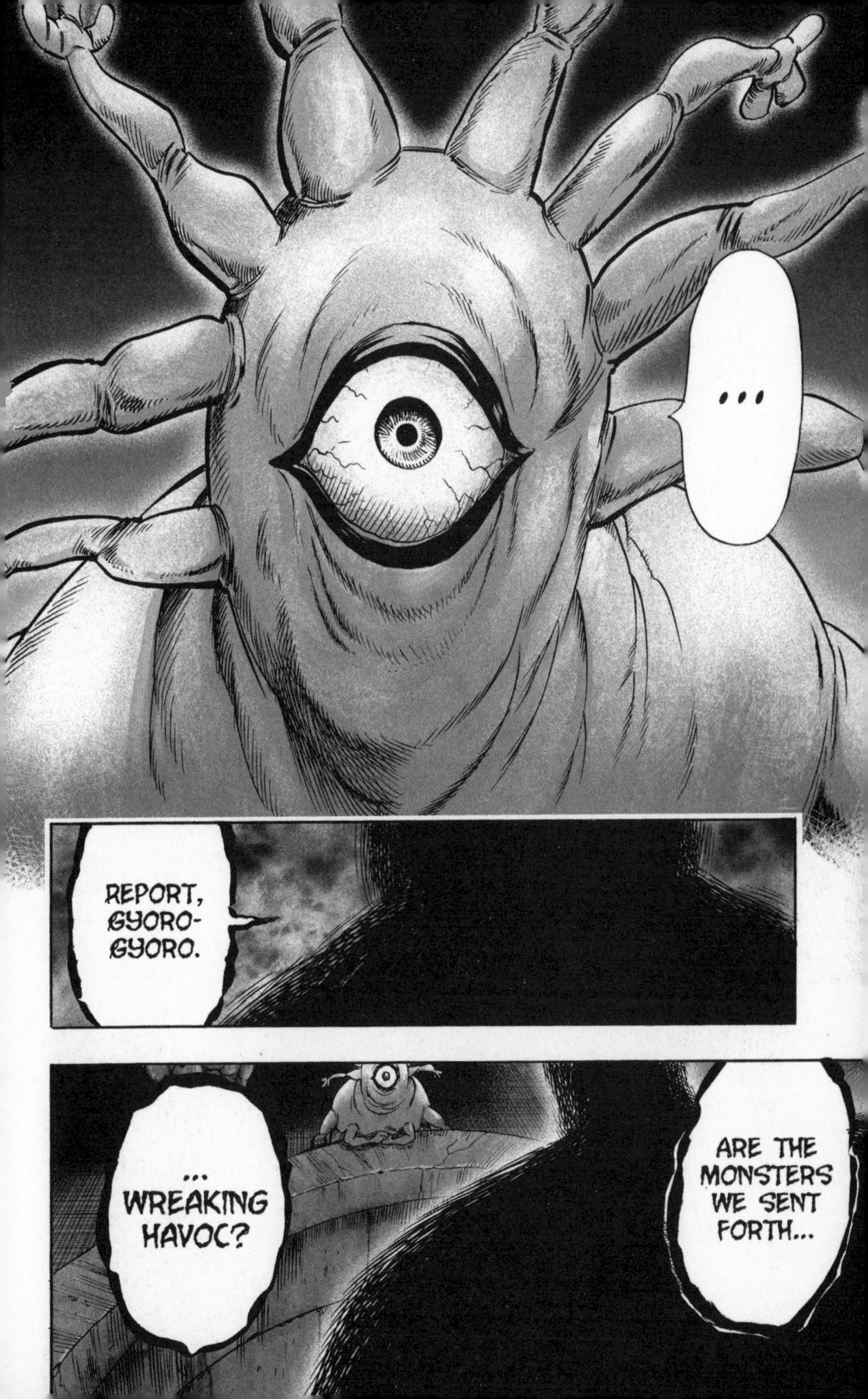
...
REPORT, GYORO-GYORO.
ARE THE MONSTERS WE SENT FORTH...
... WREAKING HAVOC?

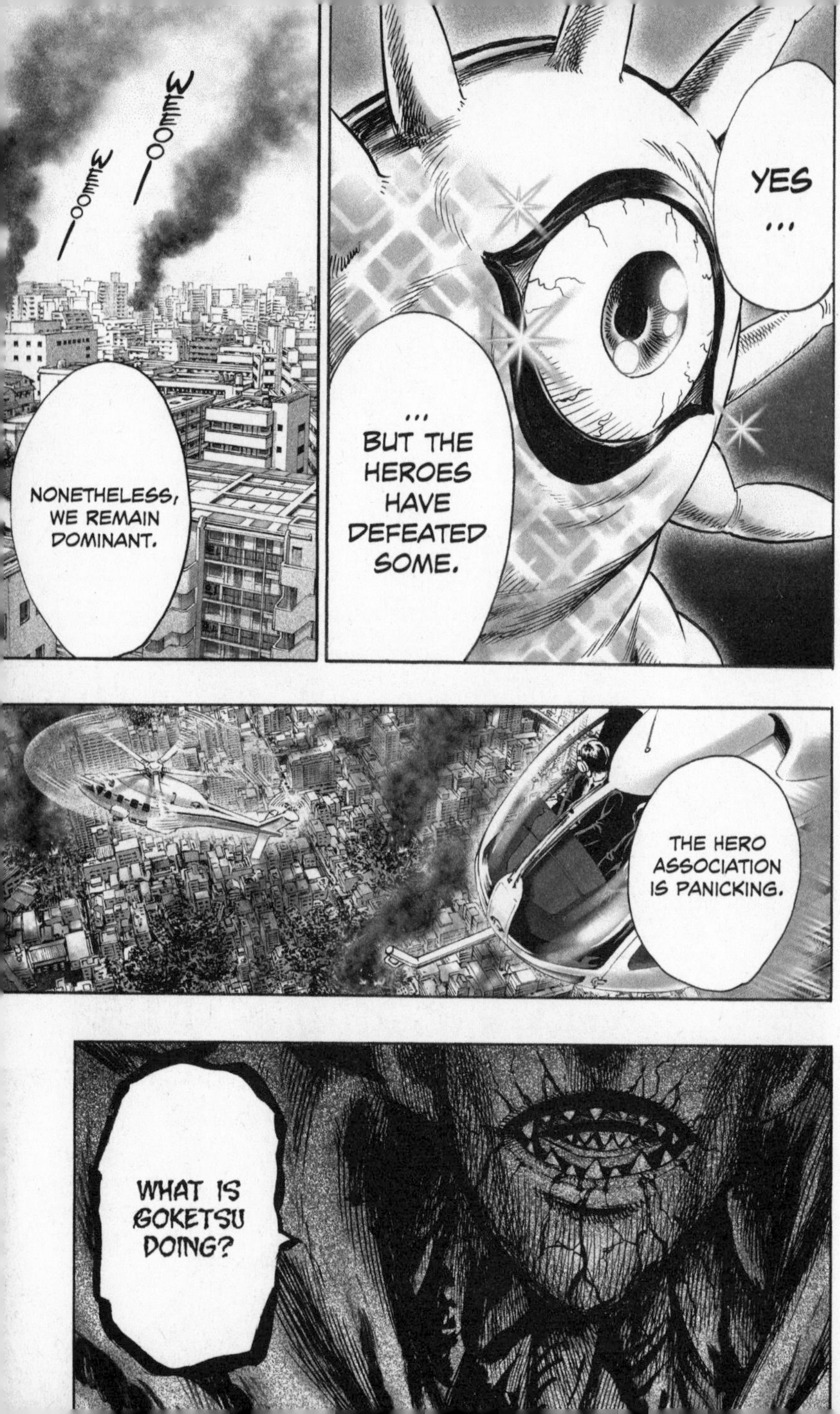
YES ...
... BUT THE HEROES HAVE DEFEATED SOME.
WEEOO—
WEEOO—
NONETHELESS, WE REMAIN DOMINANT.
THE HERO ASSOCIATION IS PANICKING.
WHAT IS GOKETSU DOING?

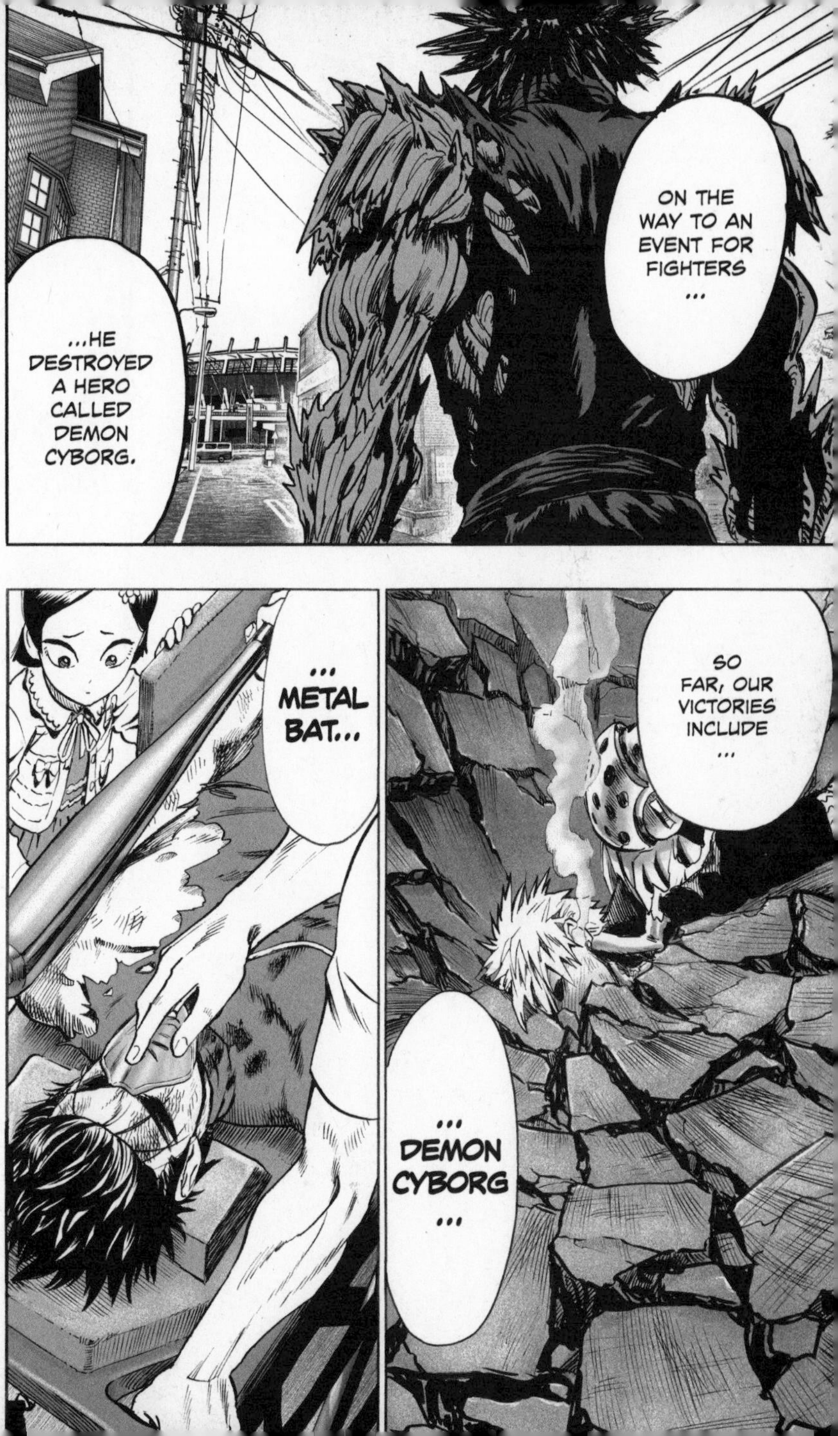
ON THE WAY TO AN EVENT FOR FIGHTERS...
...HE DESTROYED A HERO CALLED DEMON CYBORG.
SO FAR, OUR VICTORIES INCLUDE...
...DEMON CYBORG...
...METAL BAT...

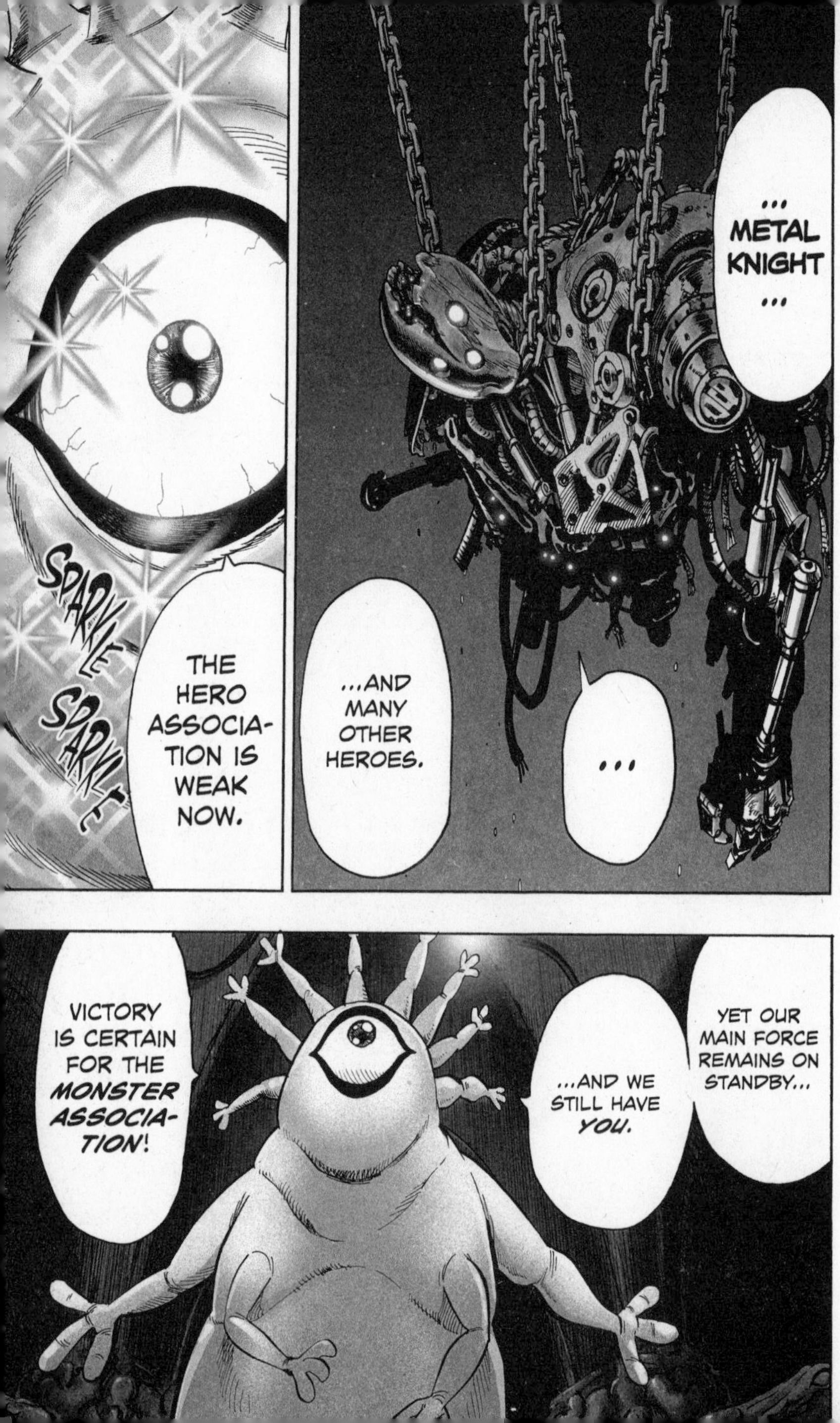

... METAL KNIGHT ...
...
...AND MANY OTHER HEROES.
SPARKLE SPARKLE
THE HERO ASSOCIA- TION IS WEAK NOW.
YET OUR MAIN FORCE REMAINS ON STANDBY...
...AND WE STILL HAVE *YOU*.
VICTORY IS CERTAIN FOR THE *MONSTER ASSOCIA- TION*!

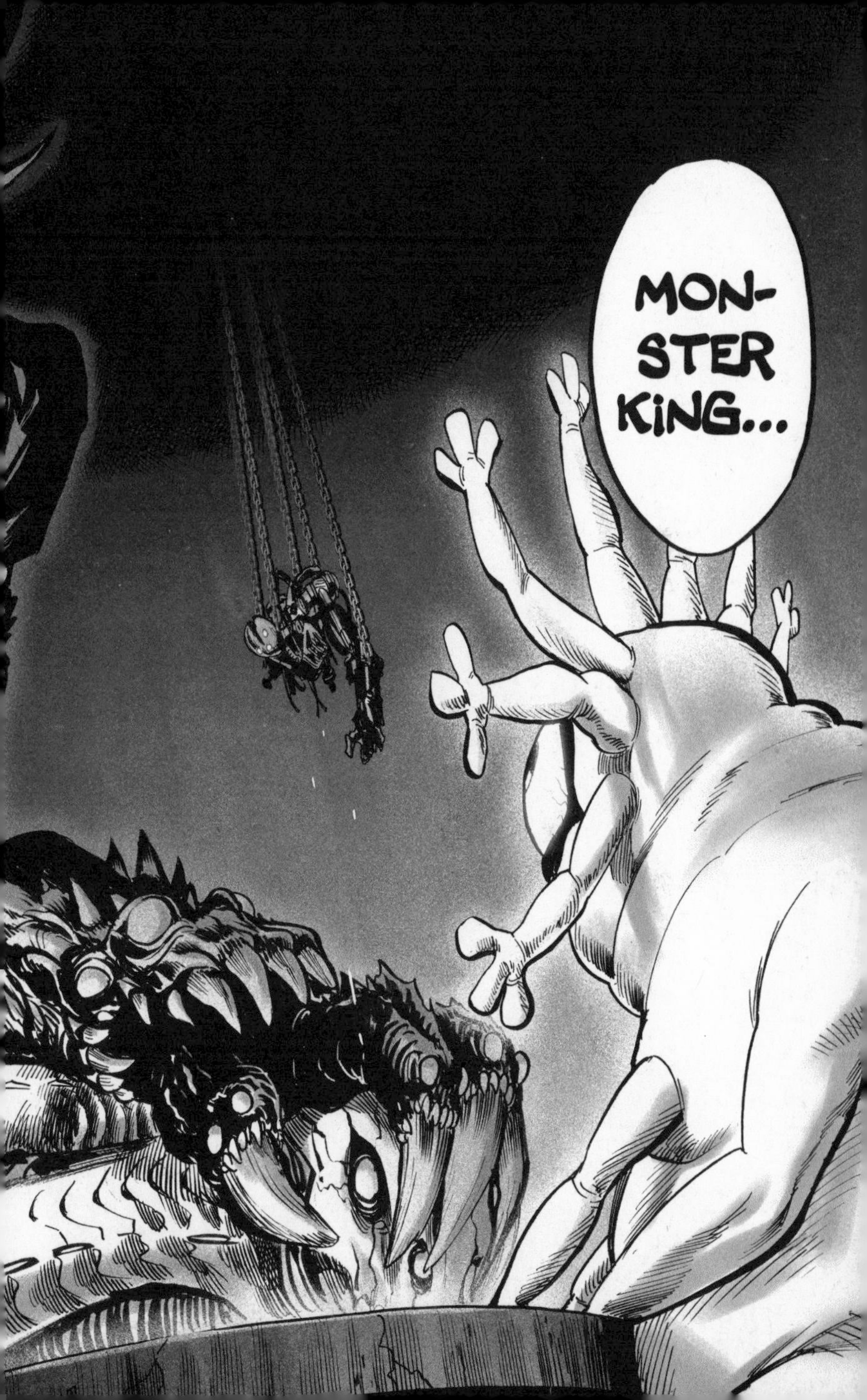
MON-
STER
KiNG...

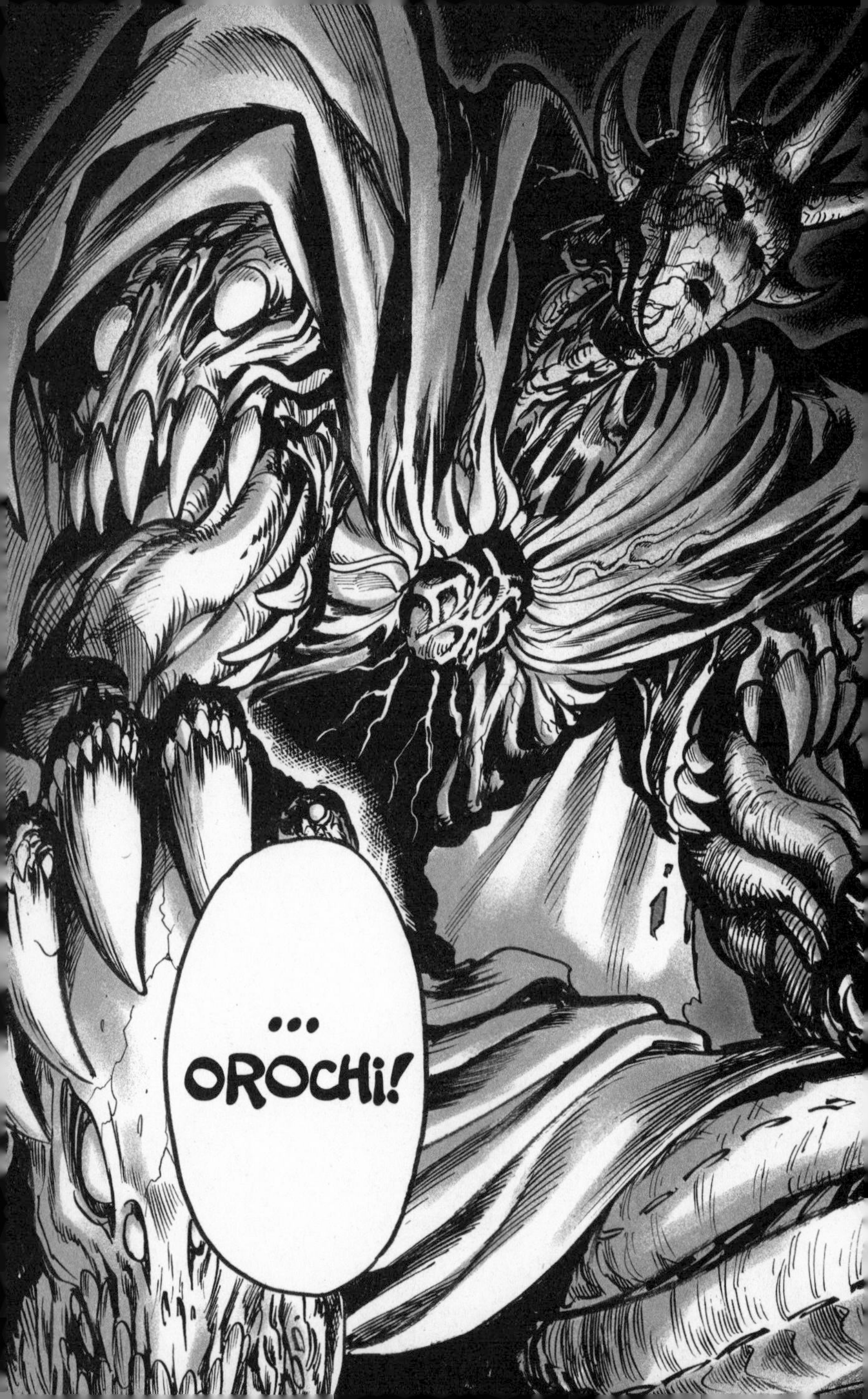
...OROCHI!

PUNCH 67: EXTRAORDINARY

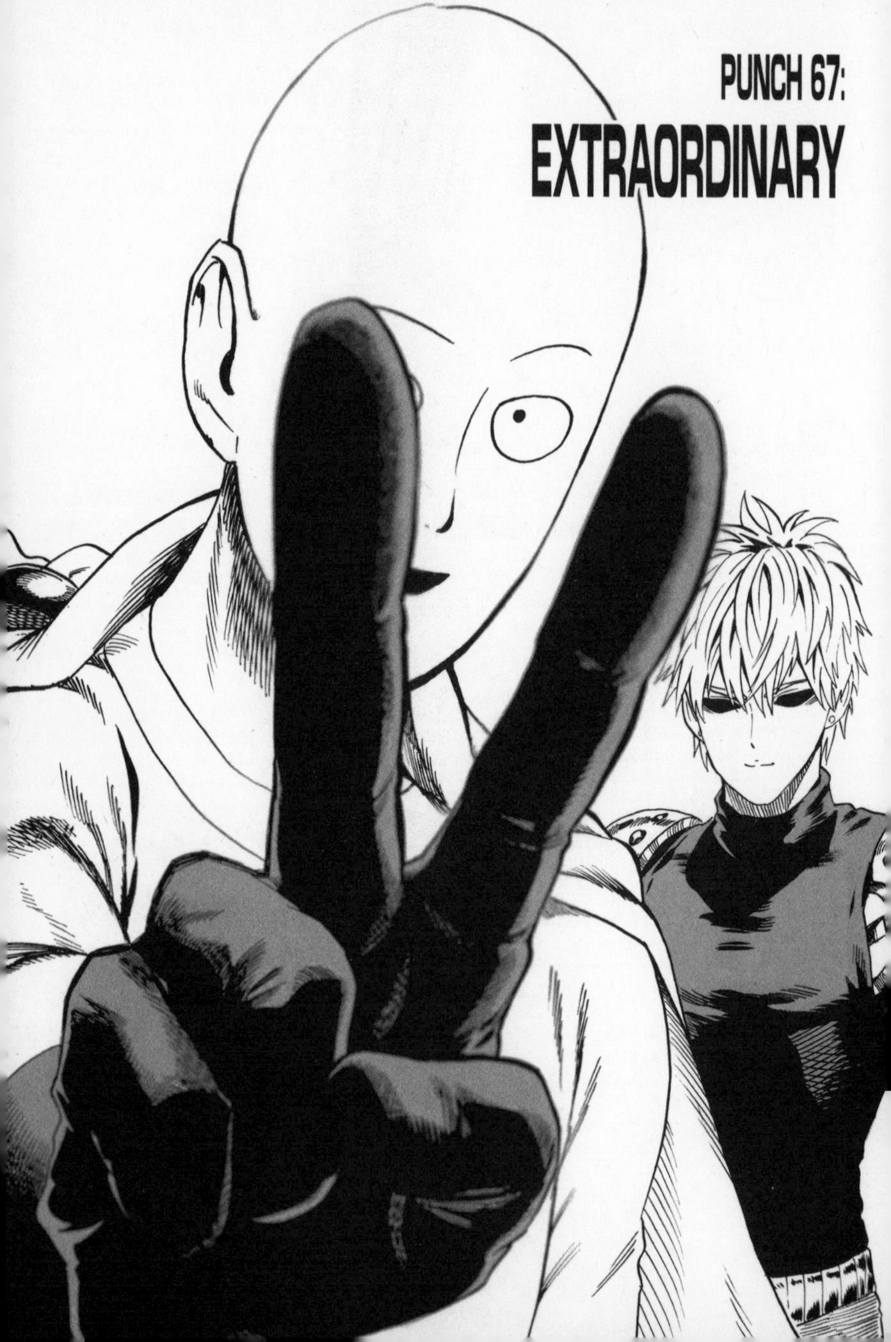

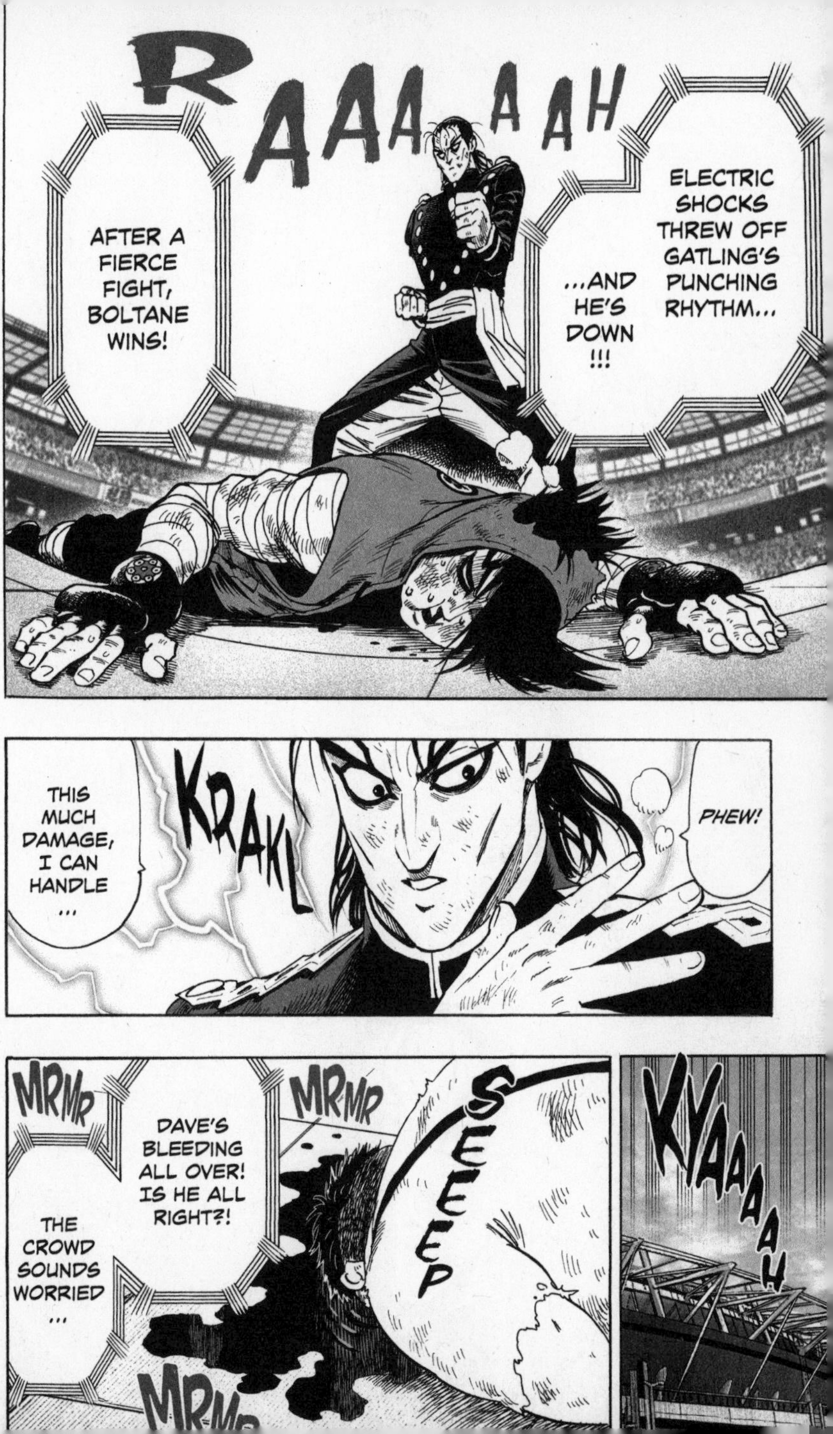
RAAAAAAH
ELECTRIC SHOCKS THREW OFF GATLING'S PUNCHING RHYTHM...
...AND HE'S DOWN !!!
AFTER A FIERCE FIGHT, BOLTANE WINS!
PHEW!
KRAKL
THIS MUCH DAMAGE, I CAN HANDLE ...
KYAAAAAH
SEEEP
MRMR
DAVE'S BLEEDING ALL OVER! IS HE ALL RIGHT?!
MRMR
THE CROWD SOUNDS WORRIED ...
MRMR

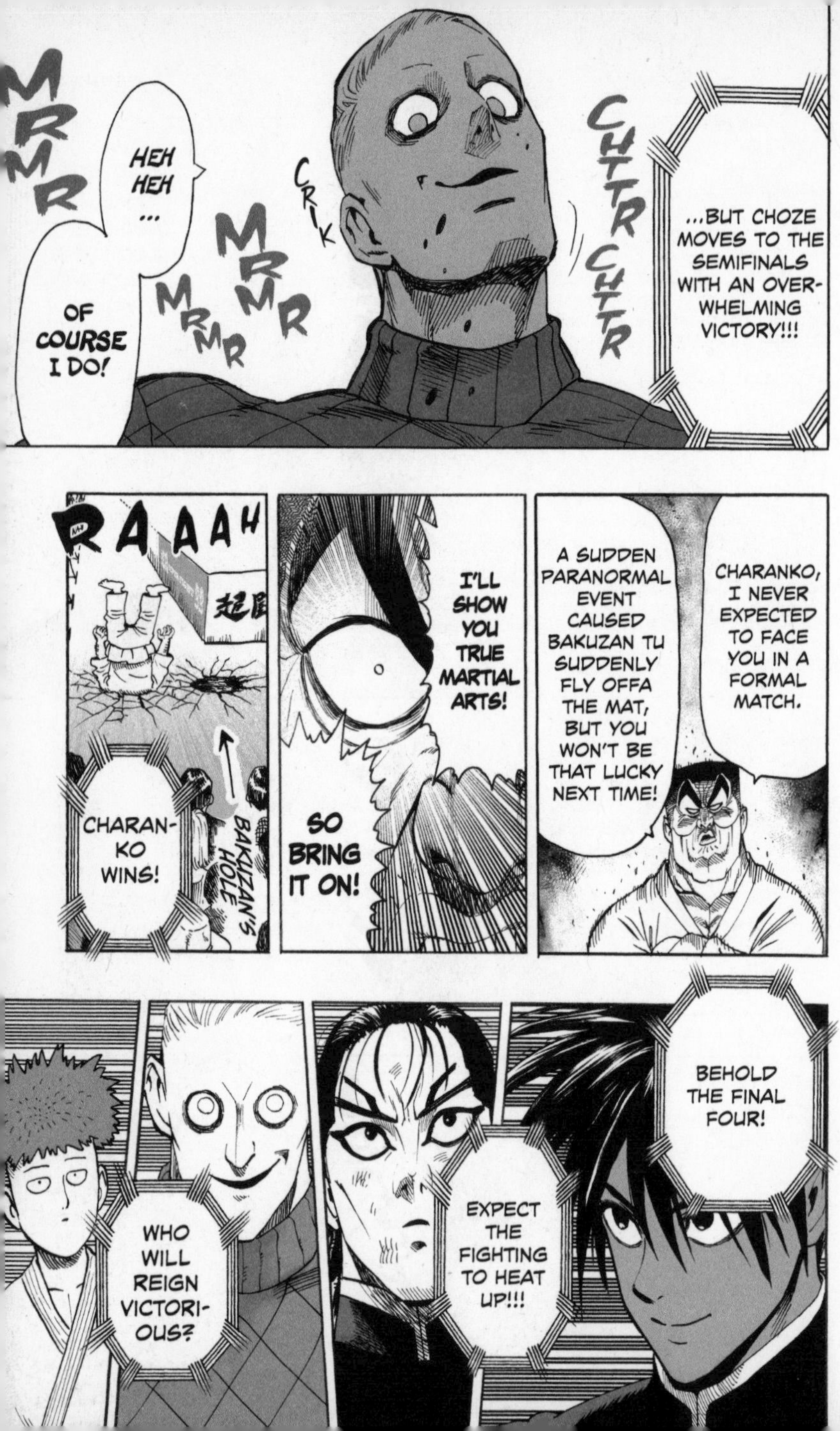
...BUT CHOZE MOVES TO THE SEMIFINALS WITH AN OVERWHELMING VICTORY!!!
CHTTR CHTTR
CRIK
MRMR MRMR
HEH HEH ...
OF COURSE I DO!
MRMR
CHARANKO, I NEVER EXPECTED TO FACE YOU IN A FORMAL MATCH.
A SUDDEN PARANORMAL EVENT CAUSED BAKUZAN TU SUDDENLY FLY OFFA THE MAT, BUT YOU WON'T BE THAT LUCKY NEXT TIME!
I'LL SHOW YOU TRUE MARTIAL ARTS!
SO BRING IT ON!
RAAAH
BAKUZAN'S HOLE
CHARANKO WINS!
BEHOLD THE FINAL FOUR!
EXPECT THE FIGHTING TO HEAT UP!!!
WHO WILL REIGN VICTORIOUS?

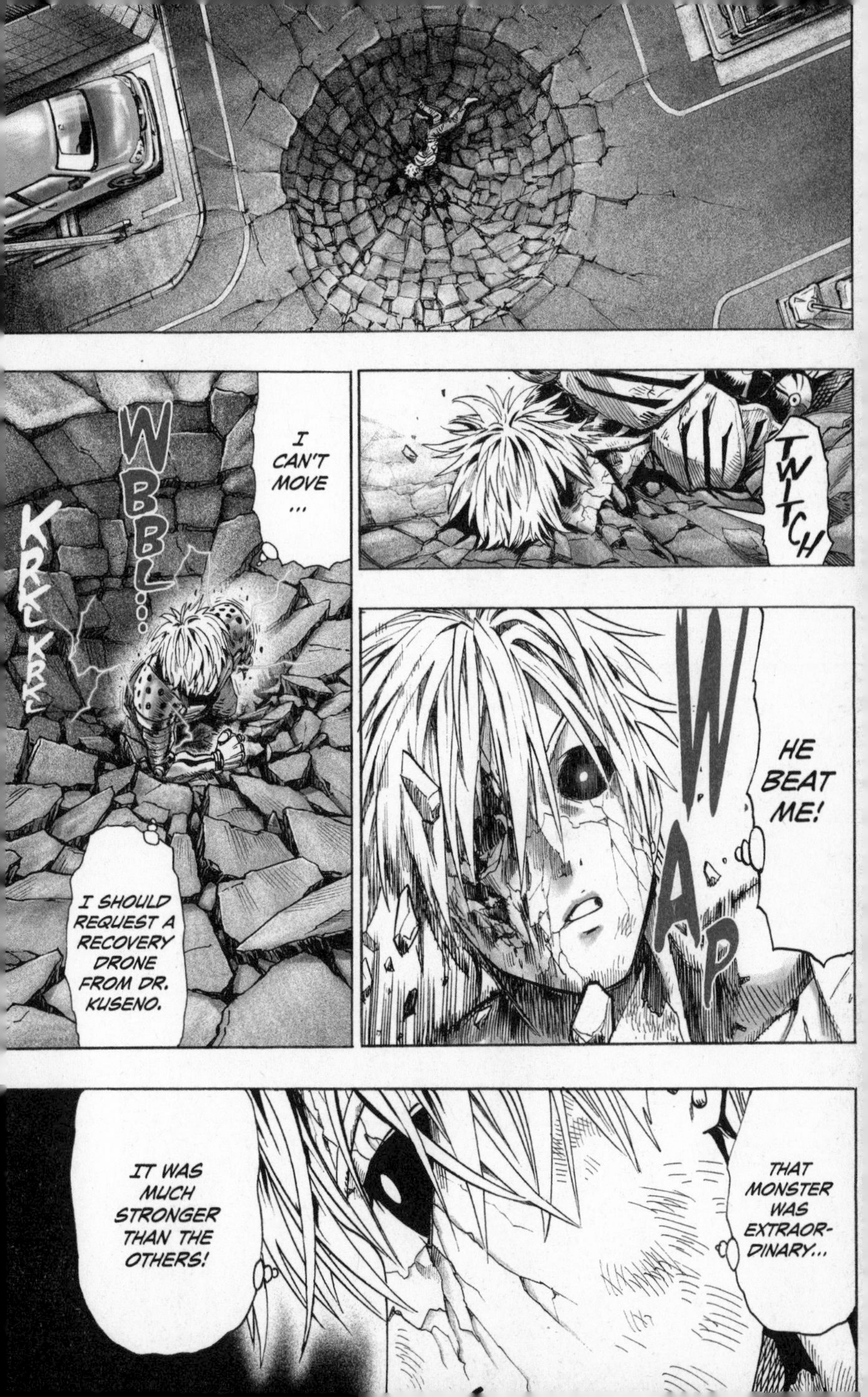
TWITCH
WAP
HE BEAT ME!
I CAN'T MOVE ...
WBBL...
KRKL KRKL
I SHOULD REQUEST A RECOVERY DRONE FROM DR. KUSENO.
THAT MONSTER WAS EXTRAOR-DINARY...
IT WAS MUCH STRONGER THAN THE OTHERS!

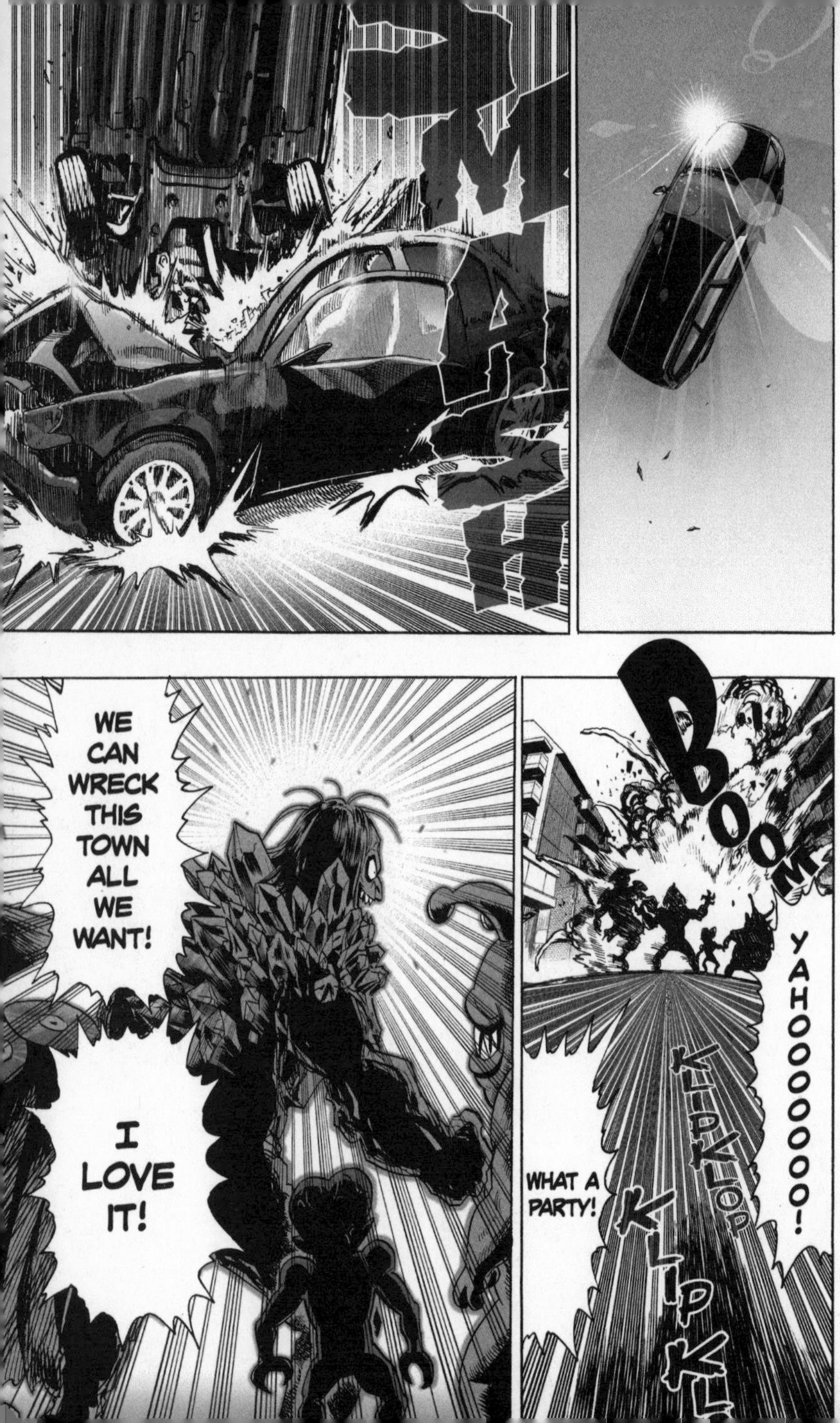
BOOM
YAHOOOOOOO!
WHAT A PARTY!
KLIPKLOP
KLIP KL
WE CAN WRECK THIS TOWN ALL WE WANT!
I LOVE IT!

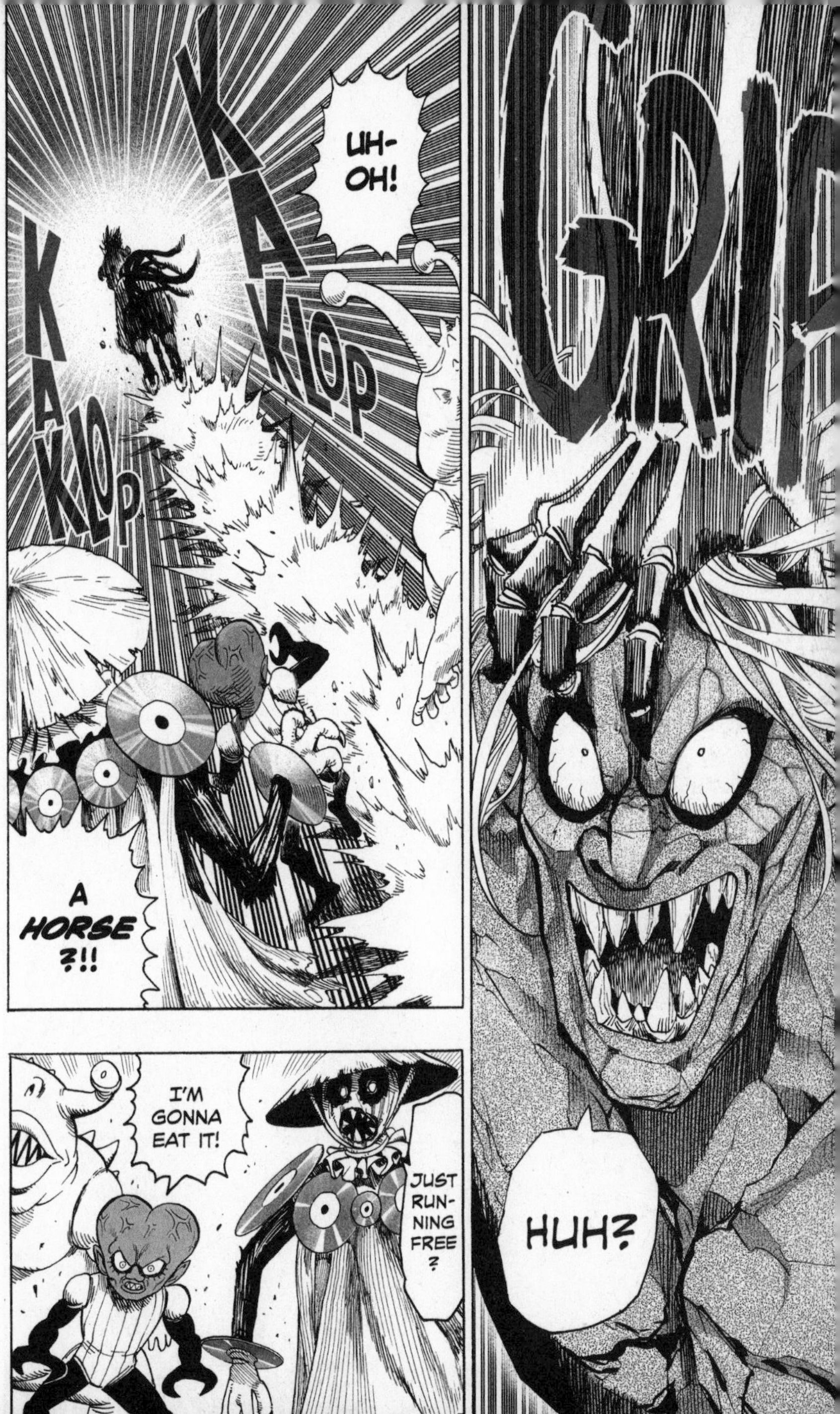
GRIP
HUH?
UH-OH!
KAKLOP
KAKLOP
A HORSE ?!!
I'M GONNA EAT IT!
JUST RUNNING FREE?

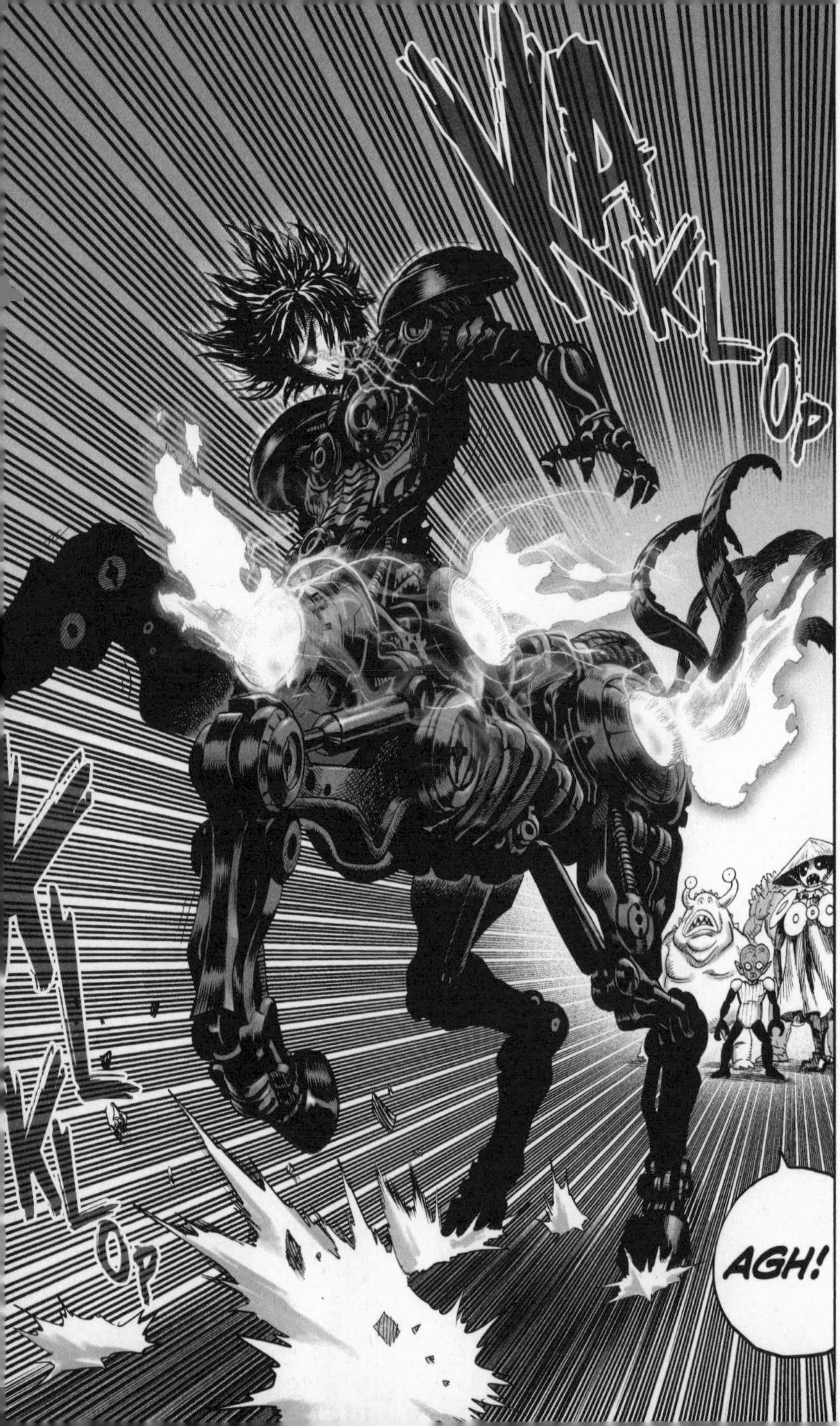
AGH!

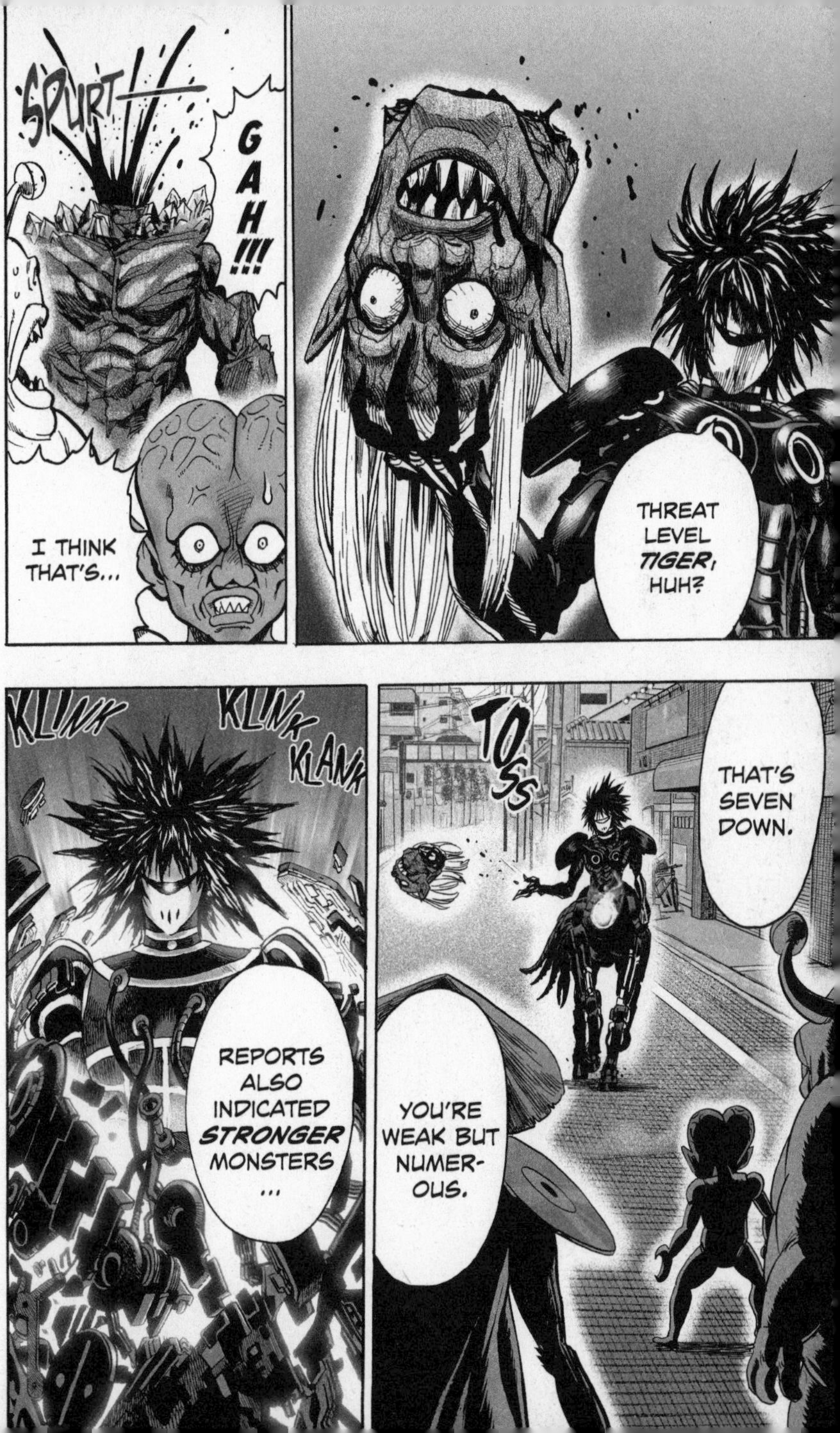
THREAT LEVEL TIGER, HUH?
SPURT
GAH!!!
I THINK THAT'S...
TOSS
THAT'S SEVEN DOWN.
YOU'RE WEAK BUT NUMEROUS.
KLINK
KLINK KLANK
REPORTS ALSO INDICATED STRONGER MONSTERS ...

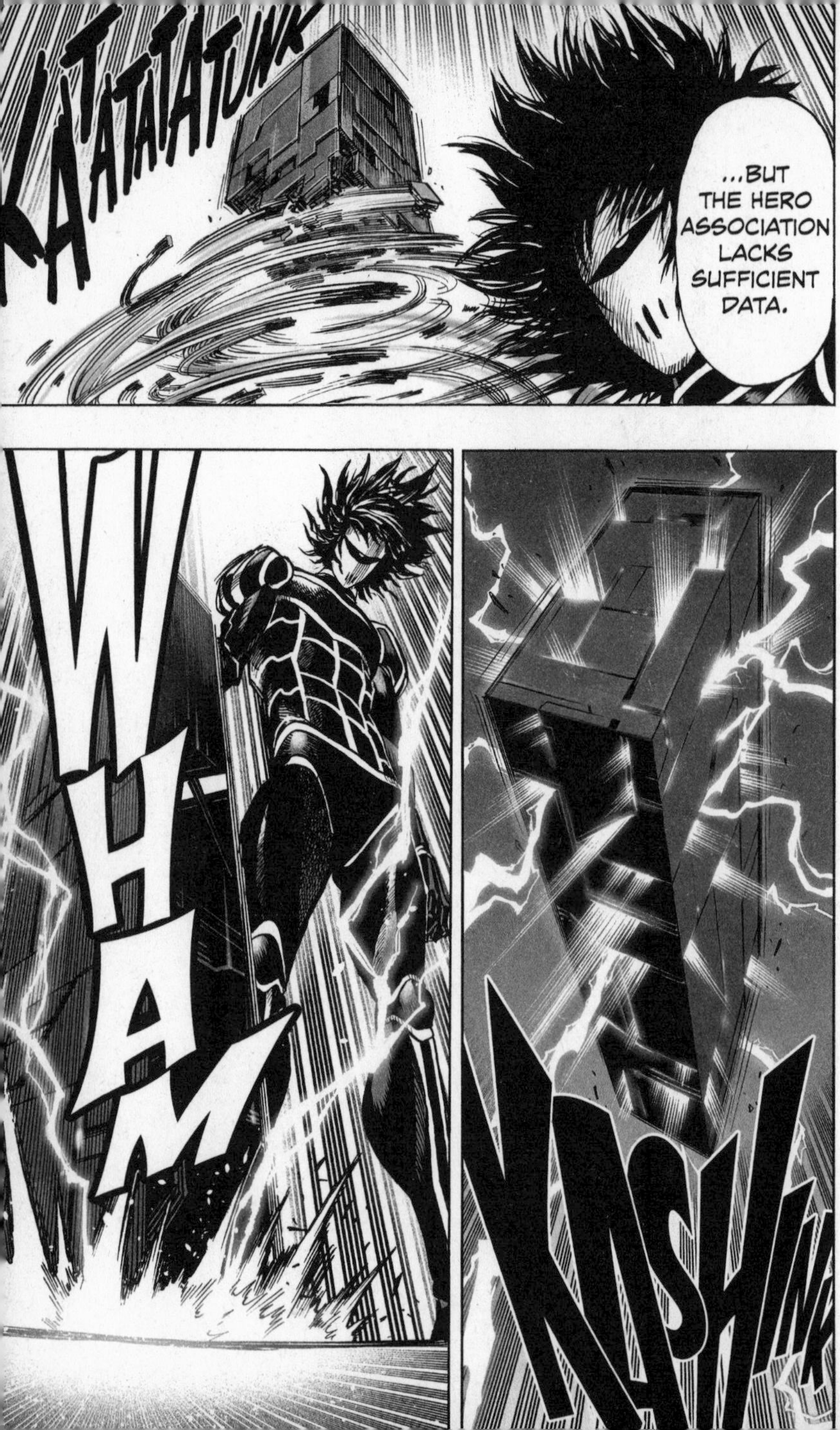
...BUT THE HERO ASSOCIATION LACKS SUFFICIENT DATA.
KATATATATUNK
KASHINK
WHAM

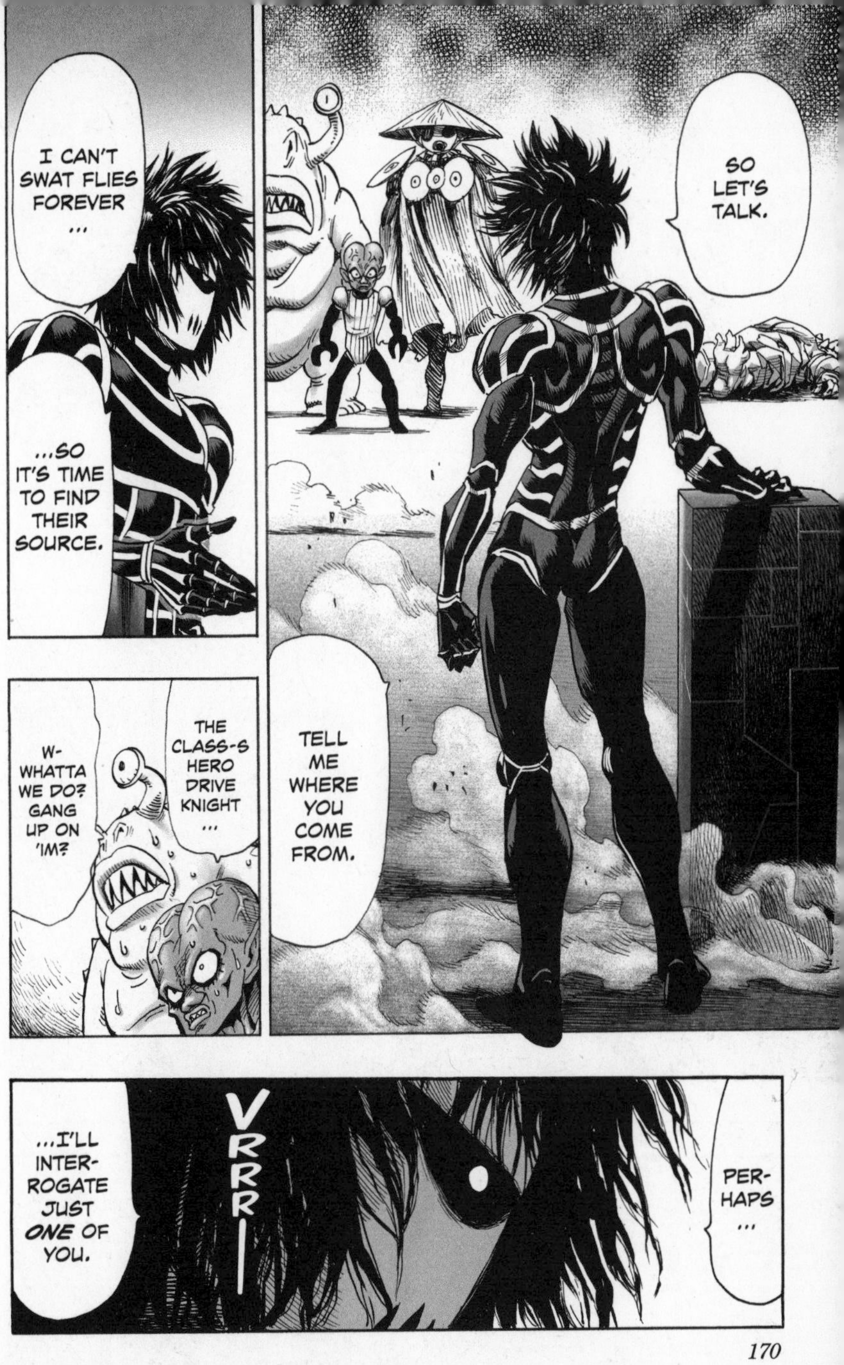
SO LET'S TALK.
TELL ME WHERE YOU COME FROM.
I CAN'T SWAT FLIES FOREVER ...
...SO IT'S TIME TO FIND THEIR SOURCE.
THE CLASS-S HERO DRIVE KNIGHT ...
W-WHATTA WE DO? GANG UP ON 'IM?
PER-HAPS ...
VRRR
...I'LL INTER-ROGATE JUST ONE OF YOU.

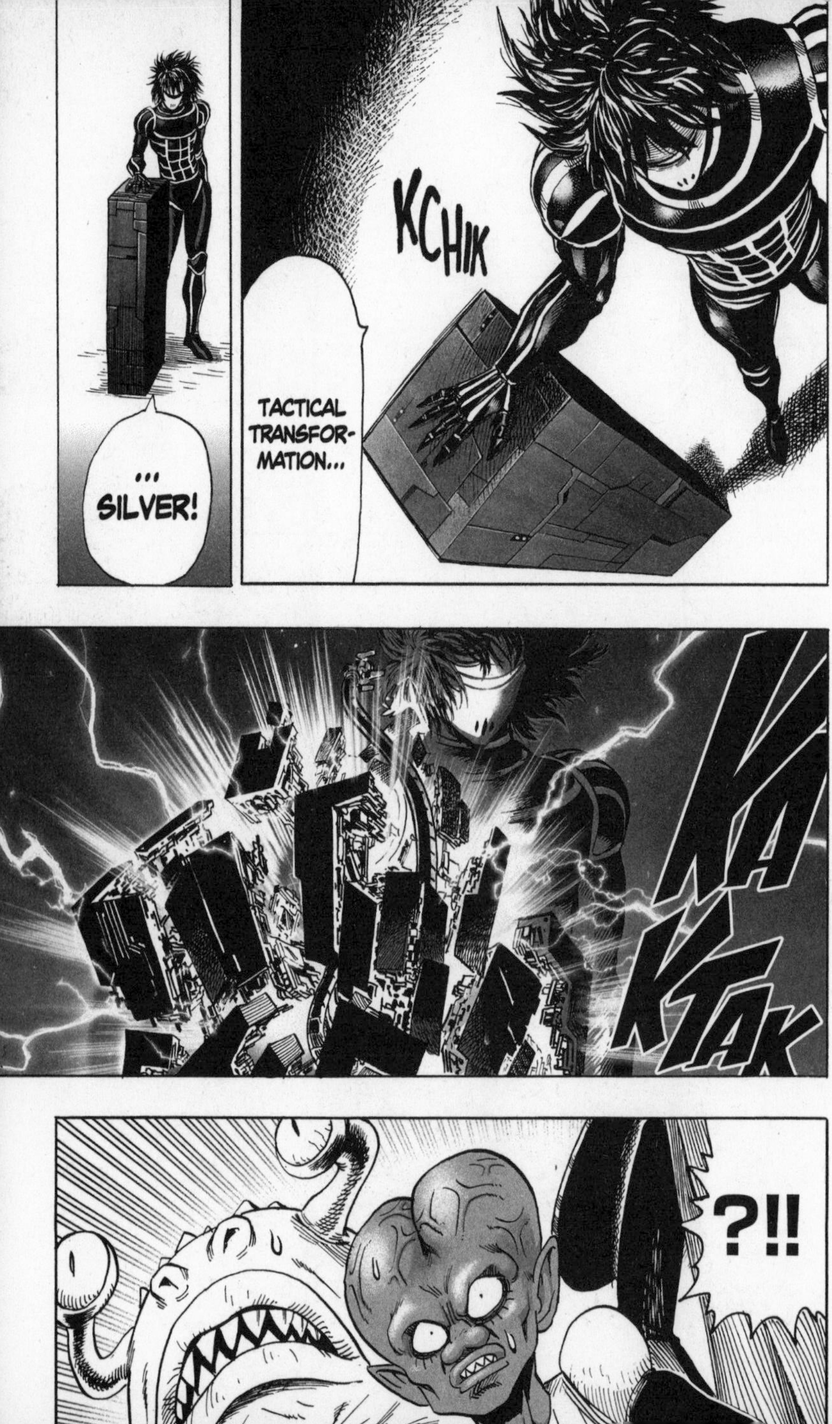
KCHIK
TACTICAL TRANSFORMATION...
... SILVER!
KA KA KTAK
?!!

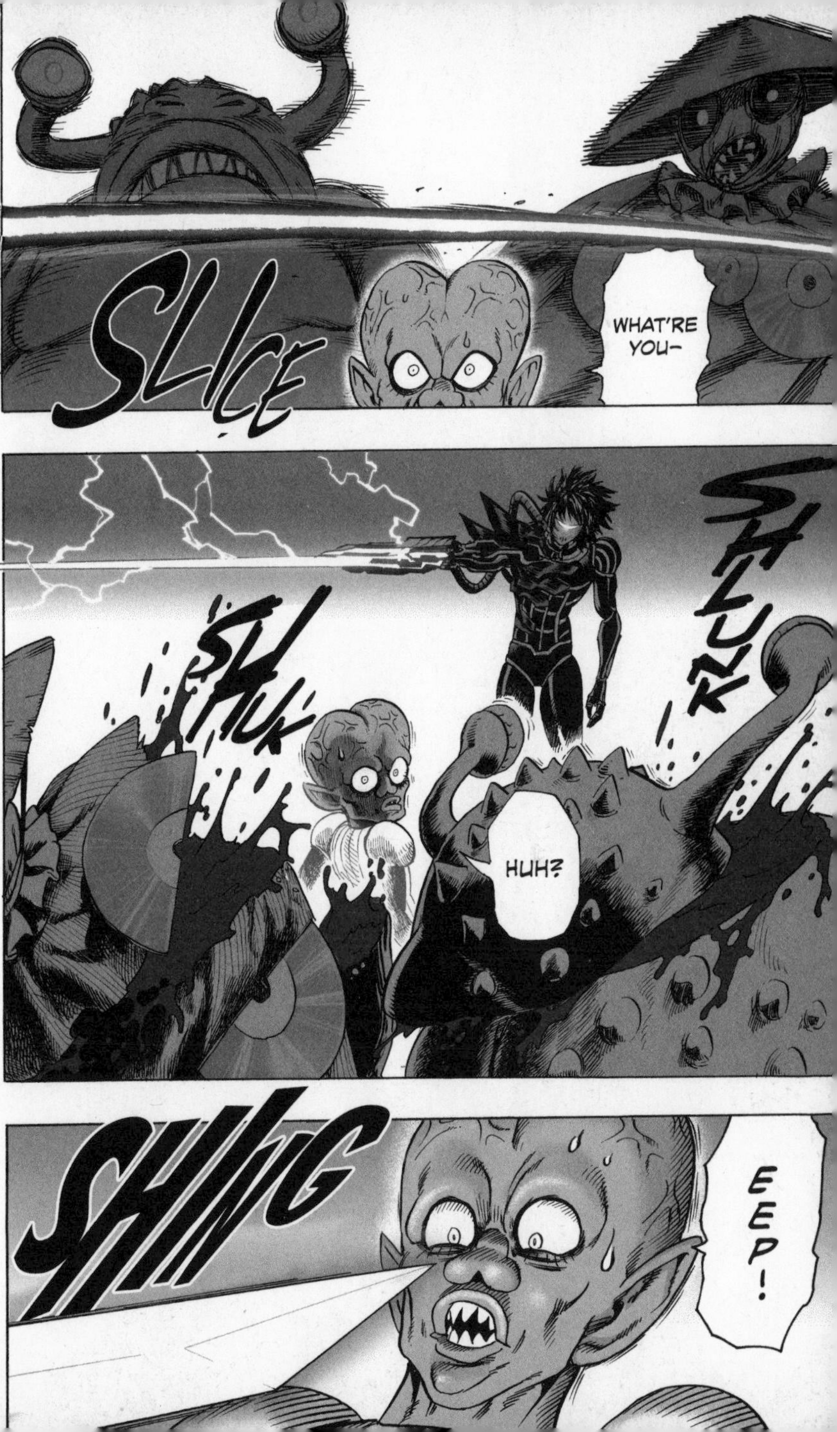
WHAT'RE YOU-
SLICE
SHLUNK!
HUH?
SHUK
EEP!
SHING

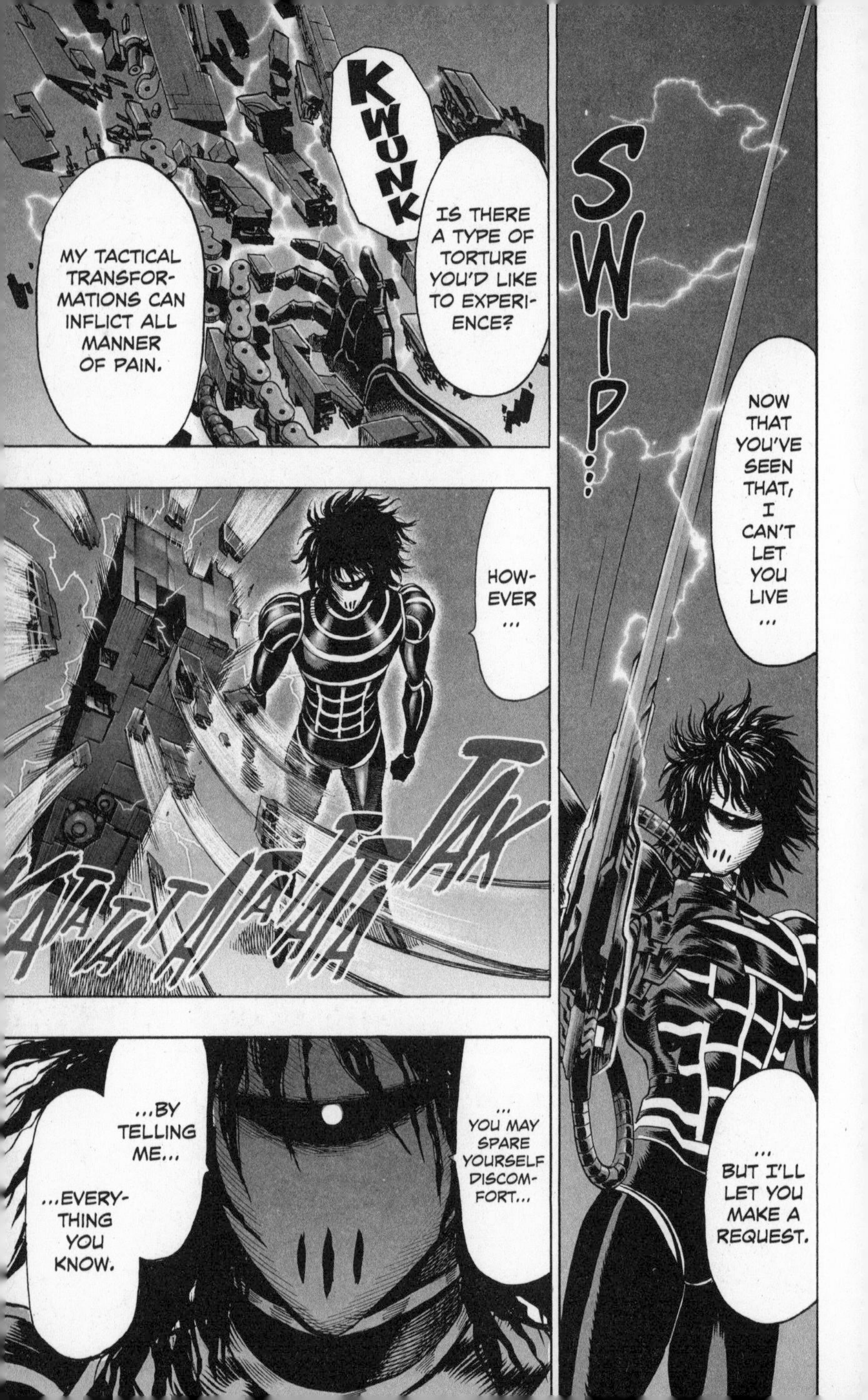
SWIP...
NOW THAT YOU'VE SEEN THAT, I CAN'T LET YOU LIVE...
...BUT I'LL LET YOU MAKE A REQUEST.
KWUNK
IS THERE A TYPE OF TORTURE YOU'D LIKE TO EXPERIENCE?
MY TACTICAL TRANSFORMATIONS CAN INFLICT ALL MANNER OF PAIN.
HOWEVER...
TAK
TAK
...YOU MAY SPARE YOURSELF DISCOMFORT...
...BY TELLING ME...
...EVERYTHING YOU KNOW.

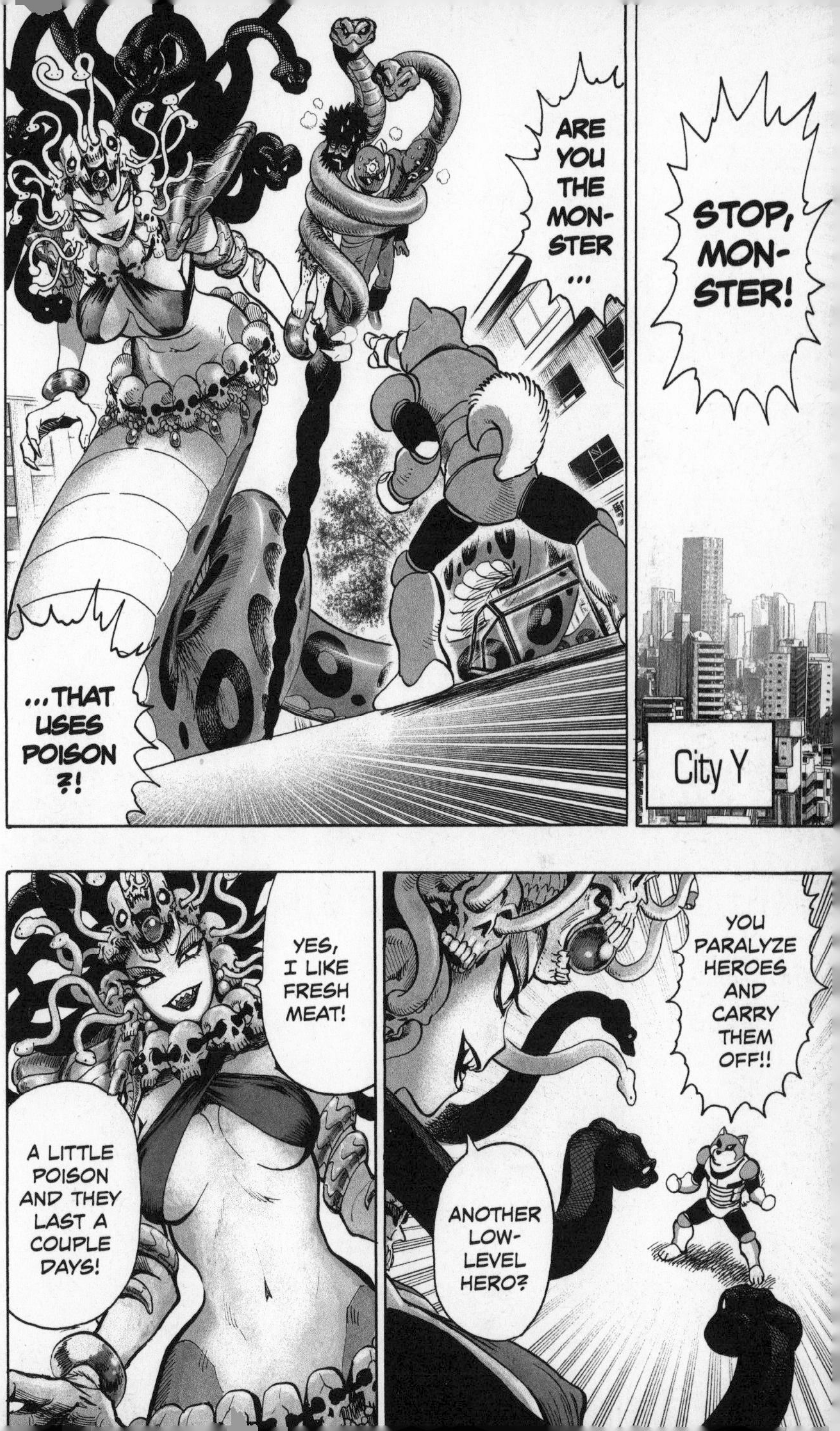
City Y
STOP, MON-STER!
ARE YOU THE MON-STER ...
...THAT USES POISON ?!
YOU PARALYZE HEROES AND CARRY THEM OFF!!
ANOTHER LOW-LEVEL HERO?
YES, I LIKE FRESH MEAT!
A LITTLE POISON AND THEY LAST A COUPLE DAYS!

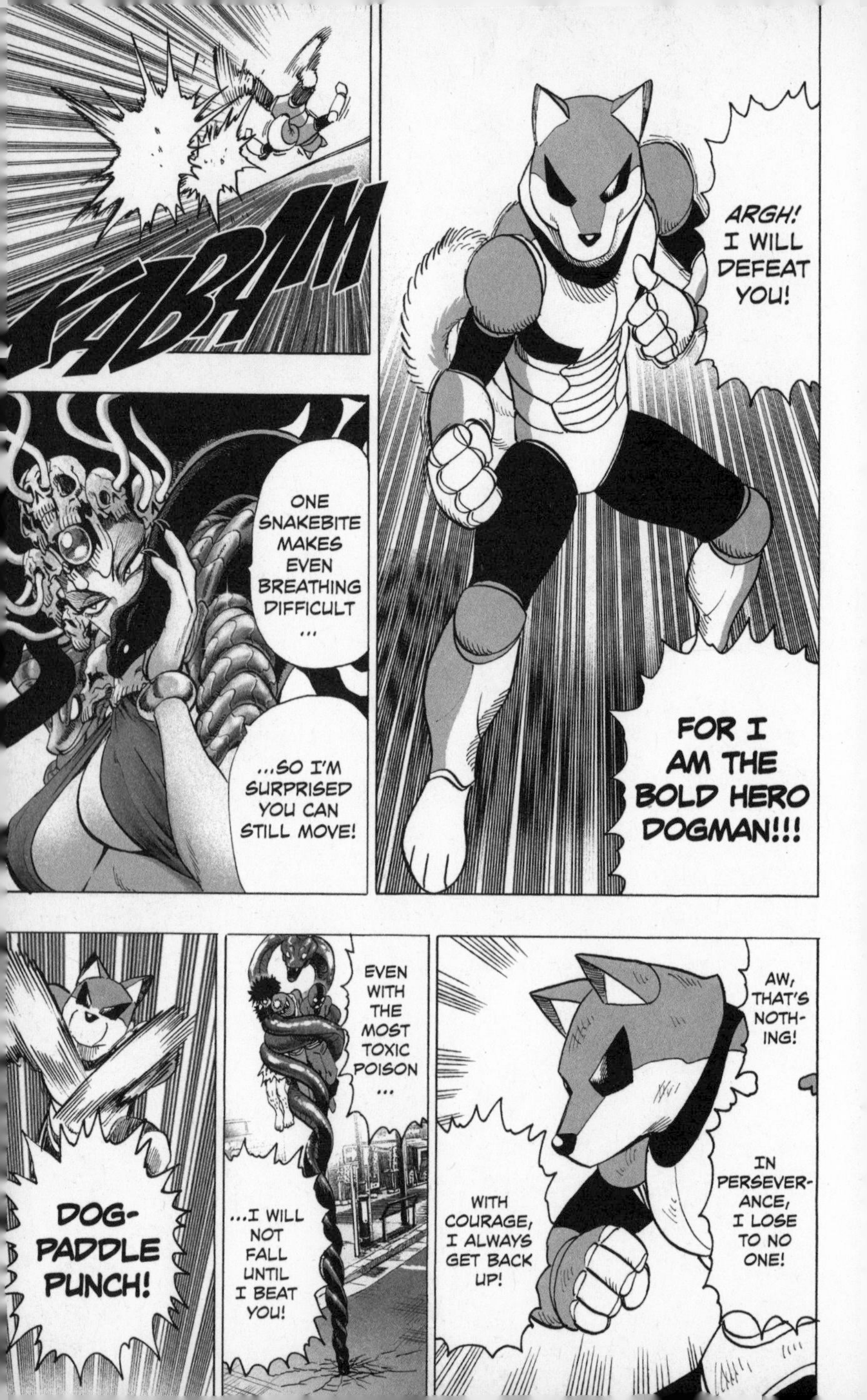
ARGH! I WILL DEFEAT YOU!
FOR I AM THE BOLD HERO DOGMAN!!!
ABRAM
ONE SNAKEBITE MAKES EVEN BREATHING DIFFICULT...
...SO I'M SURPRISED YOU CAN STILL MOVE!
AW, THAT'S NOTHING!
IN PERSEVERANCE, I LOSE TO NO ONE!
WITH COURAGE, I ALWAYS GET BACK UP!
EVEN WITH THE MOST TOXIC POISON...
...I WILL NOT FALL UNTIL I BEAT YOU!
DOG-PADDLE PUNCH!

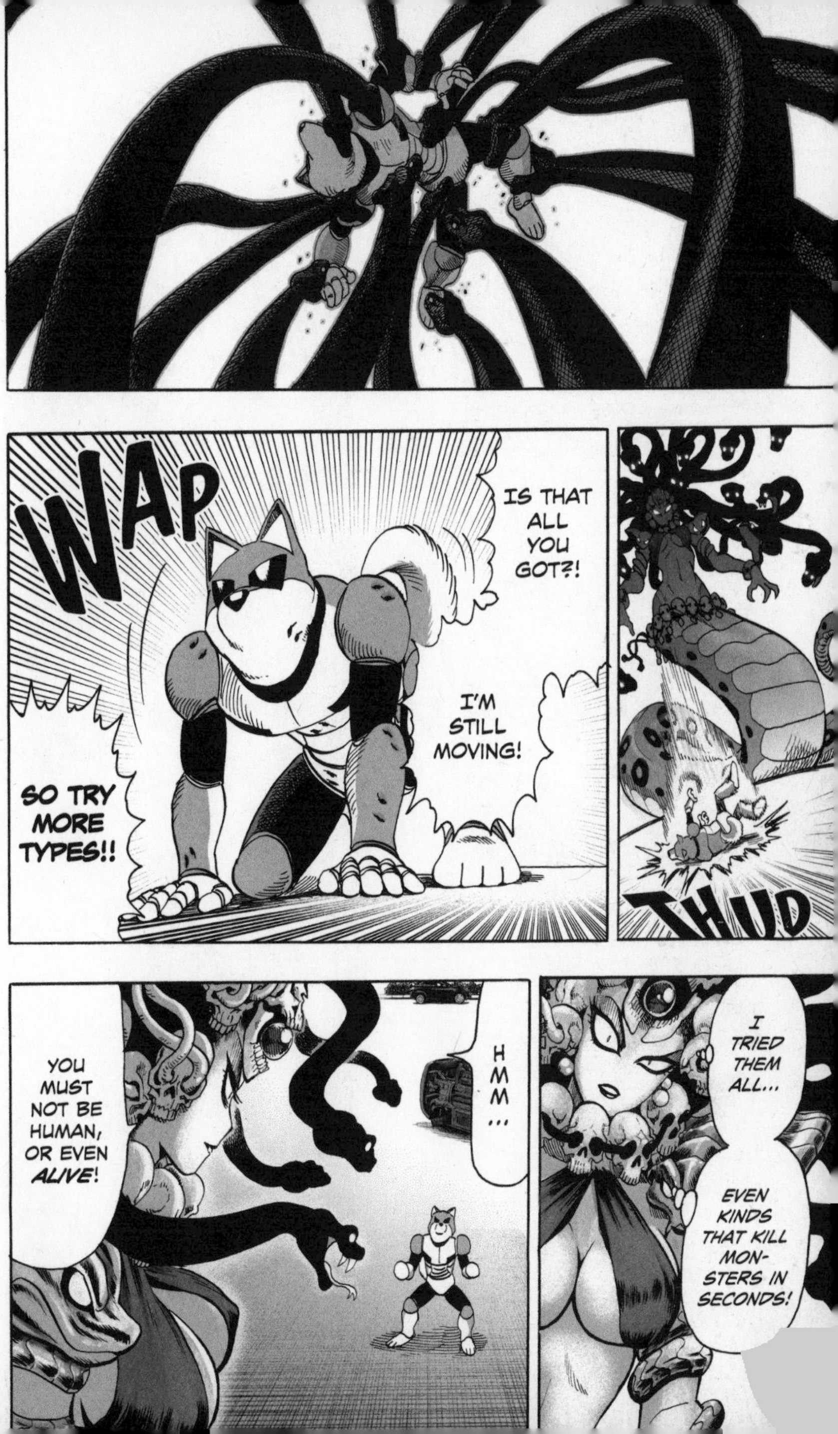
THUD
WAP
IS THAT ALL YOU GOT?!
I'M STILL MOVING!
SO TRY MORE TYPES!!
I TRIED THEM ALL...
EVEN KINDS THAT KILL MONSTERS IN SECONDS!
HMM...
YOU MUST NOT BE HUMAN, OR EVEN *ALIVE*!

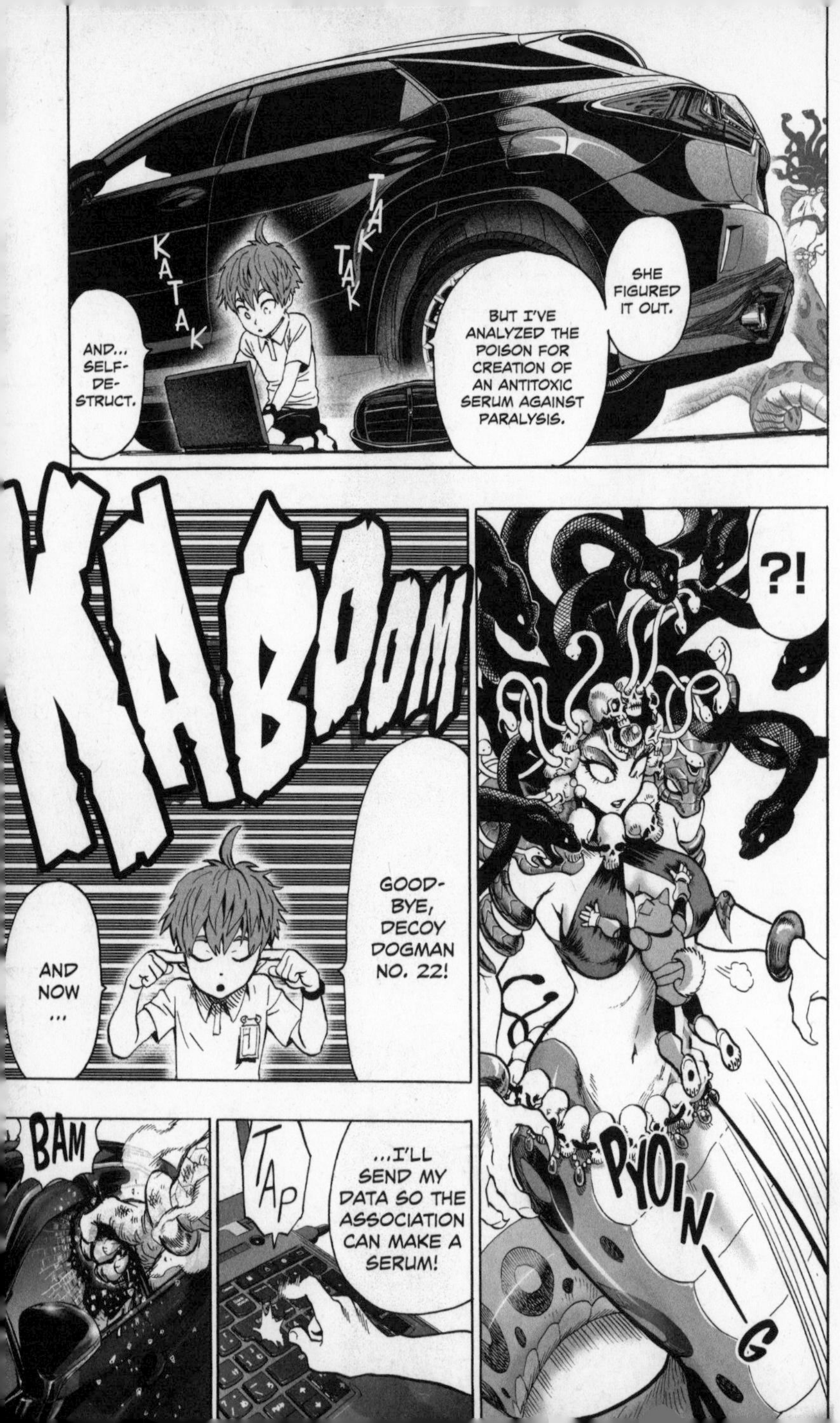
SHE FIGURED IT OUT.
BUT I'VE ANALYZED THE POISON FOR CREATION OF AN ANTITOXIC SERUM AGAINST PARALYSIS.
TAK TAK
KATAK
AND... SELF-DESTRUCT.
?!
PYOIN—G
KABOOM
GOOD-BYE, DECOY DOGMAN NO. 22!
AND NOW ...
TAP
...I'LL SEND MY DATA SO THE ASSOCIATION CAN MAKE A SERUM!
BAM

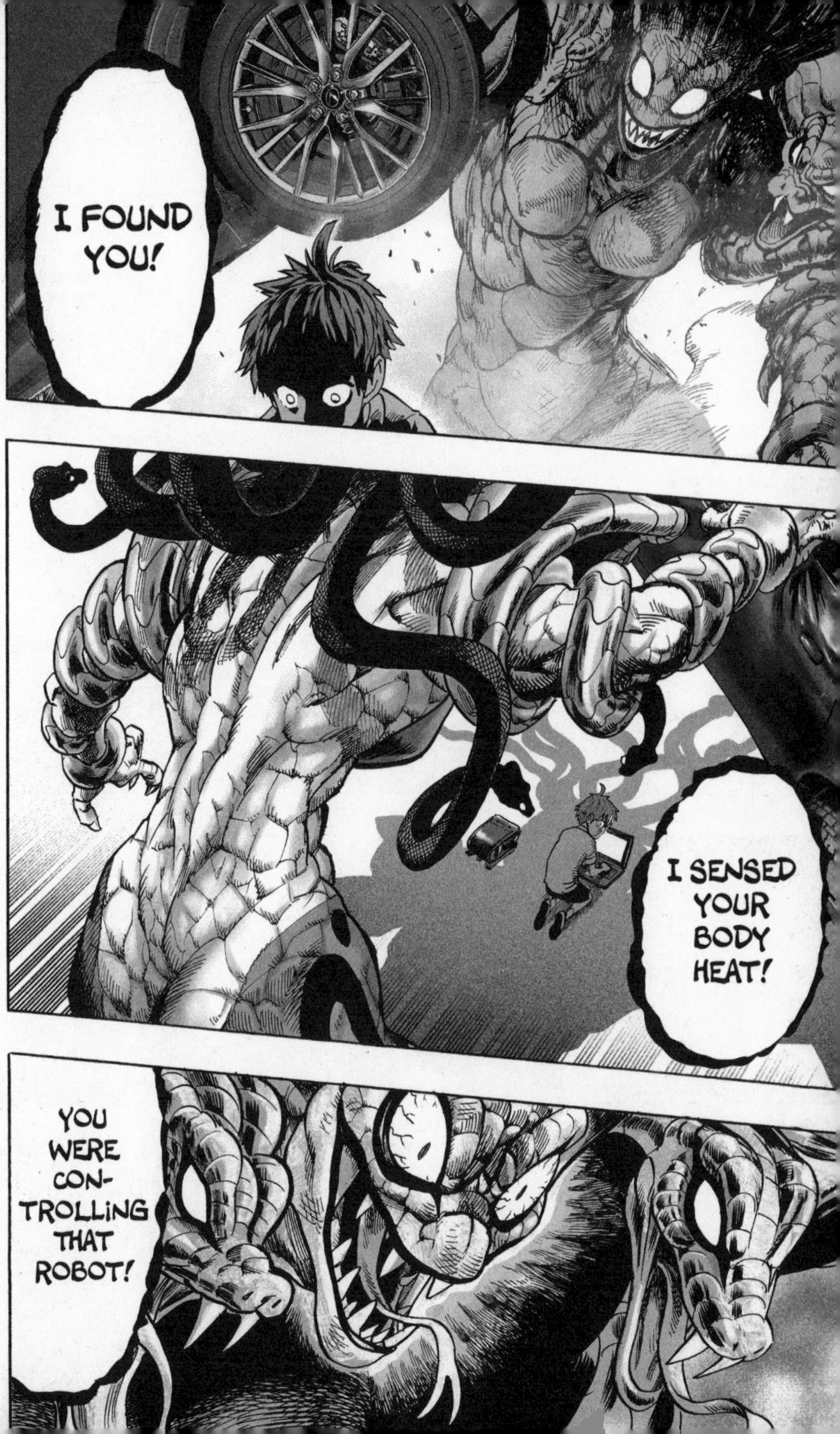
I FOUND YOU!
I SENSED YOUR BODY HEAT!
YOU WERE CON-TROLLING THAT ROBOT!

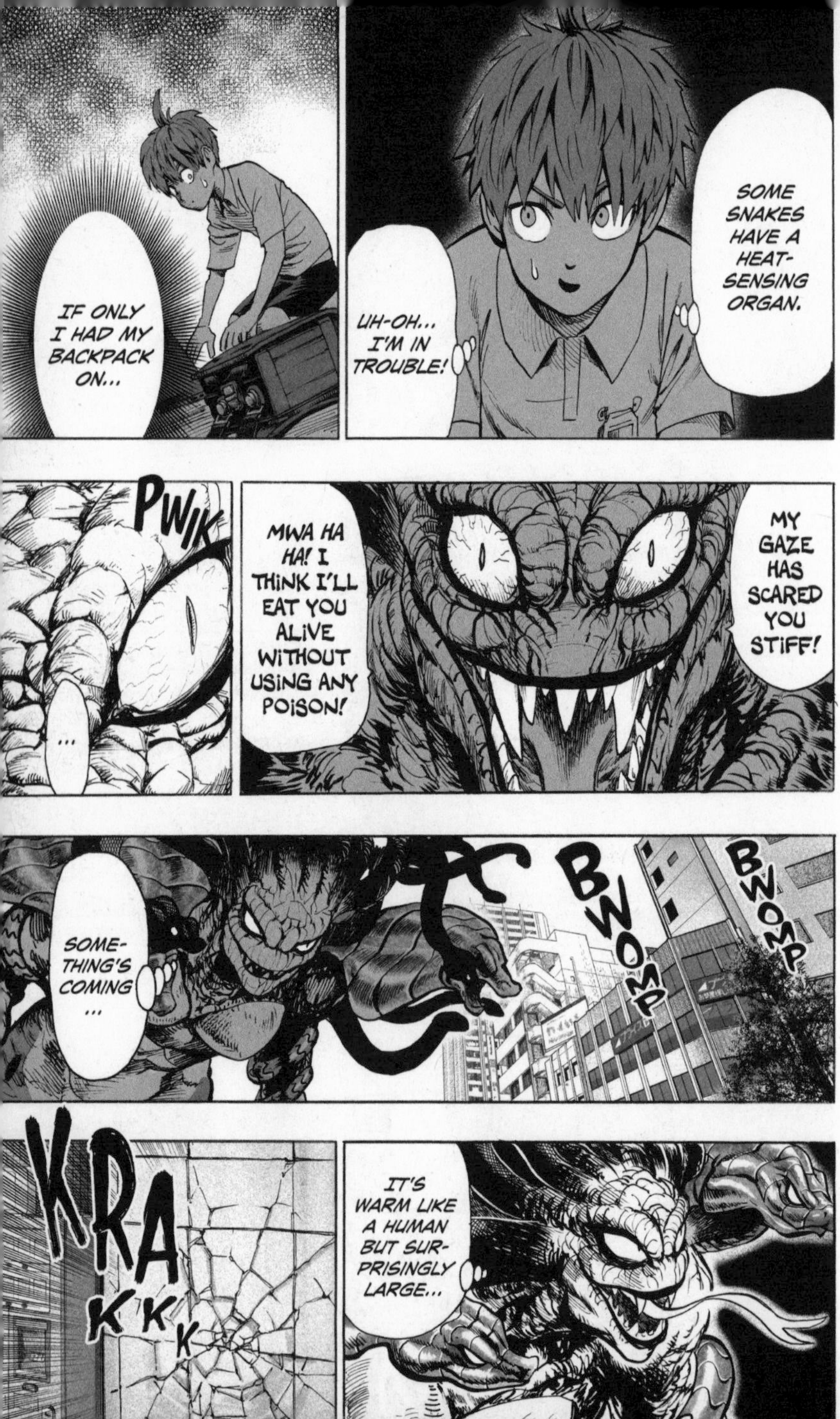
SOME SNAKES HAVE A HEAT-SENSING ORGAN.
UH-OH... I'M IN TROUBLE!
IF ONLY I HAD MY BACKPACK ON...
MY GAZE HAS SCARED YOU STIFF!
MWA HA HA! I THINK I'LL EAT YOU ALIVE WITHOUT USING ANY POISON!
PWIK
...
BWOMP
BWOMP
SOME-THING'S COMING...
IT'S WARM LIKE A HUMAN BUT SUR-PRISINGLY LARGE...
KRAKKK

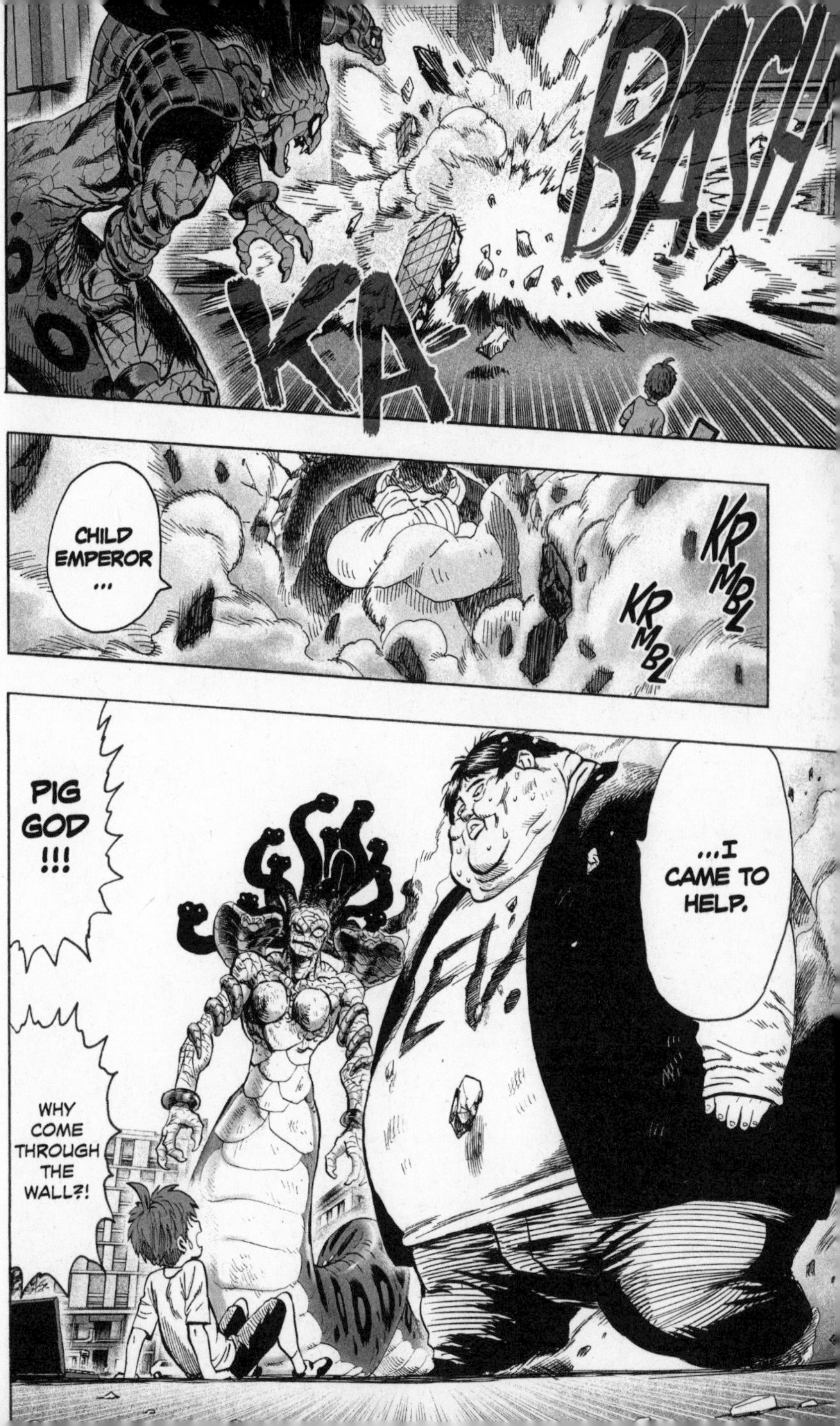
KA
BASH
CHILD EMPEROR ...
KRMBL
KRMBL
...I CAME TO HELP.
PIG GOD !!!
WHY COME THROUGH THE WALL?!

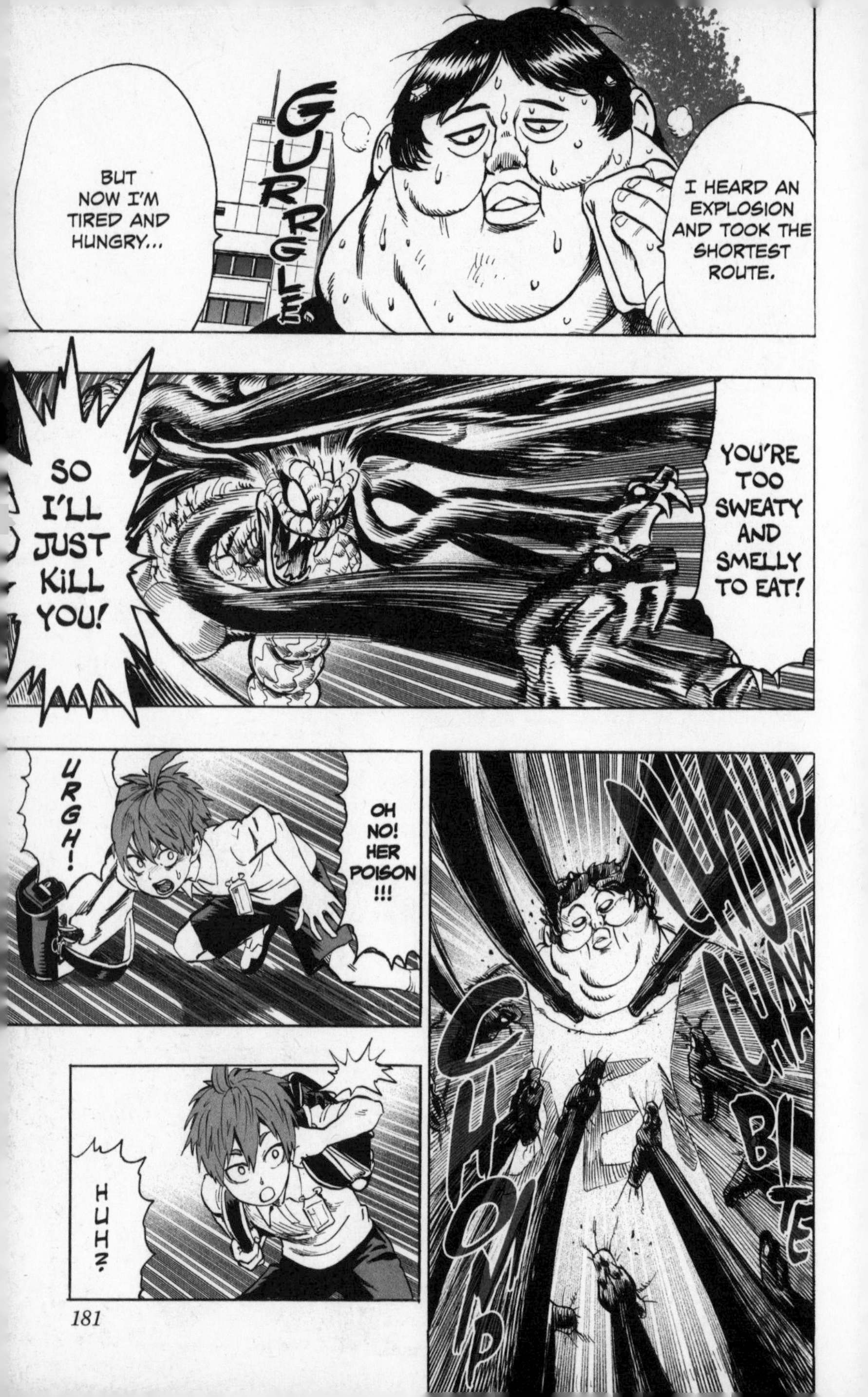
I HEARD AN EXPLOSION AND TOOK THE SHORTEST ROUTE.
GURRGLE
BUT NOW I'M TIRED AND HUNGRY...
YOU'RE TOO SWEATY AND SMELLY TO EAT!
SO I'LL JUST KiLL YOU!
CHOMP
BITE
URGH!
OH NO! HER POISON!!!
HUH?

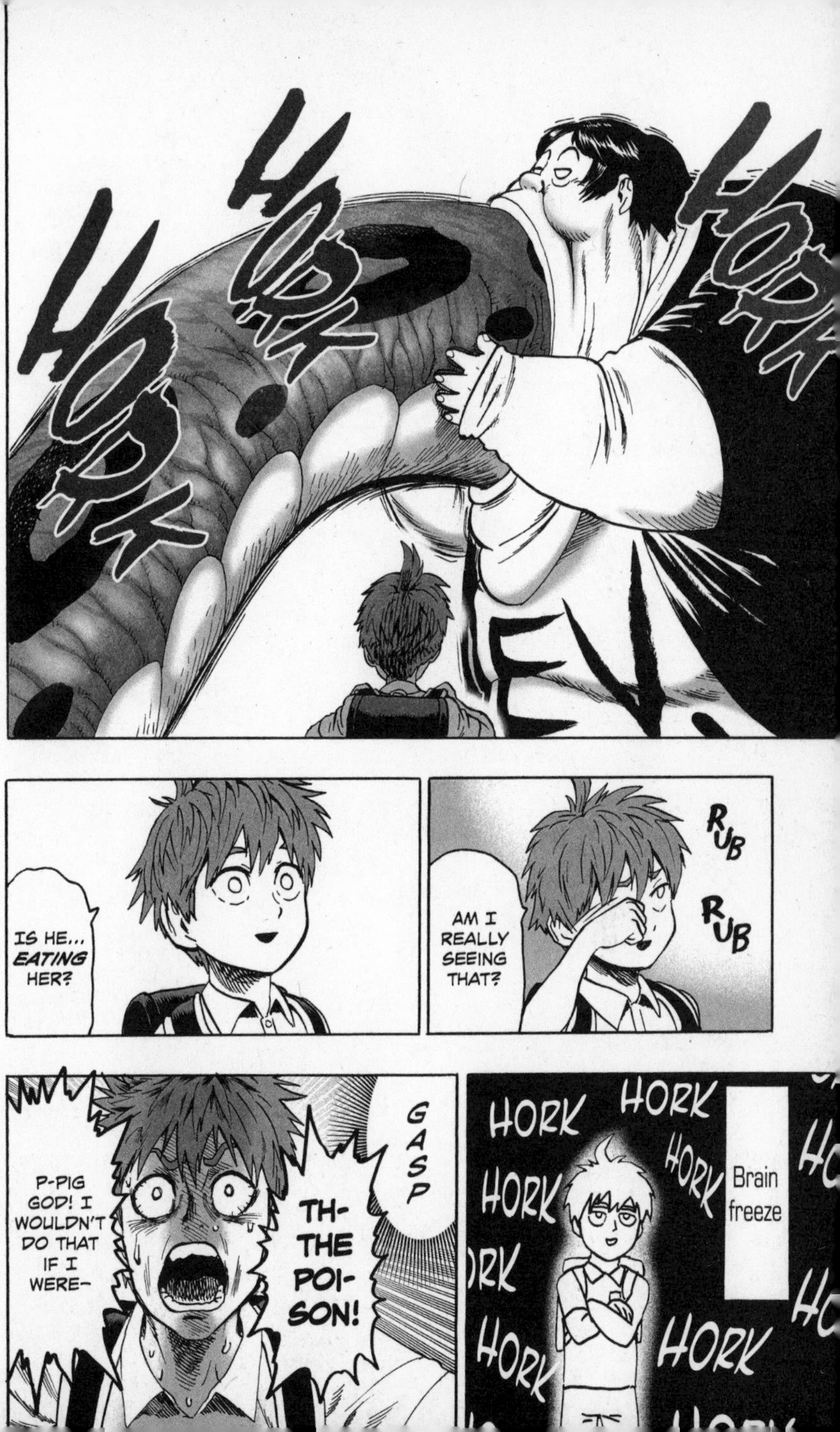
HORK
HORK
HORK
RUB
RUB
AM I REALLY SEEING THAT?
IS HE... *EATING* HER?
Brain freeze
HORK
HORK
HORK
HORK
HORK
HORK
GASP
TH-THE POI-SON!
P-PIG GOD! I WOULDN'T DO THAT IF I WERE—

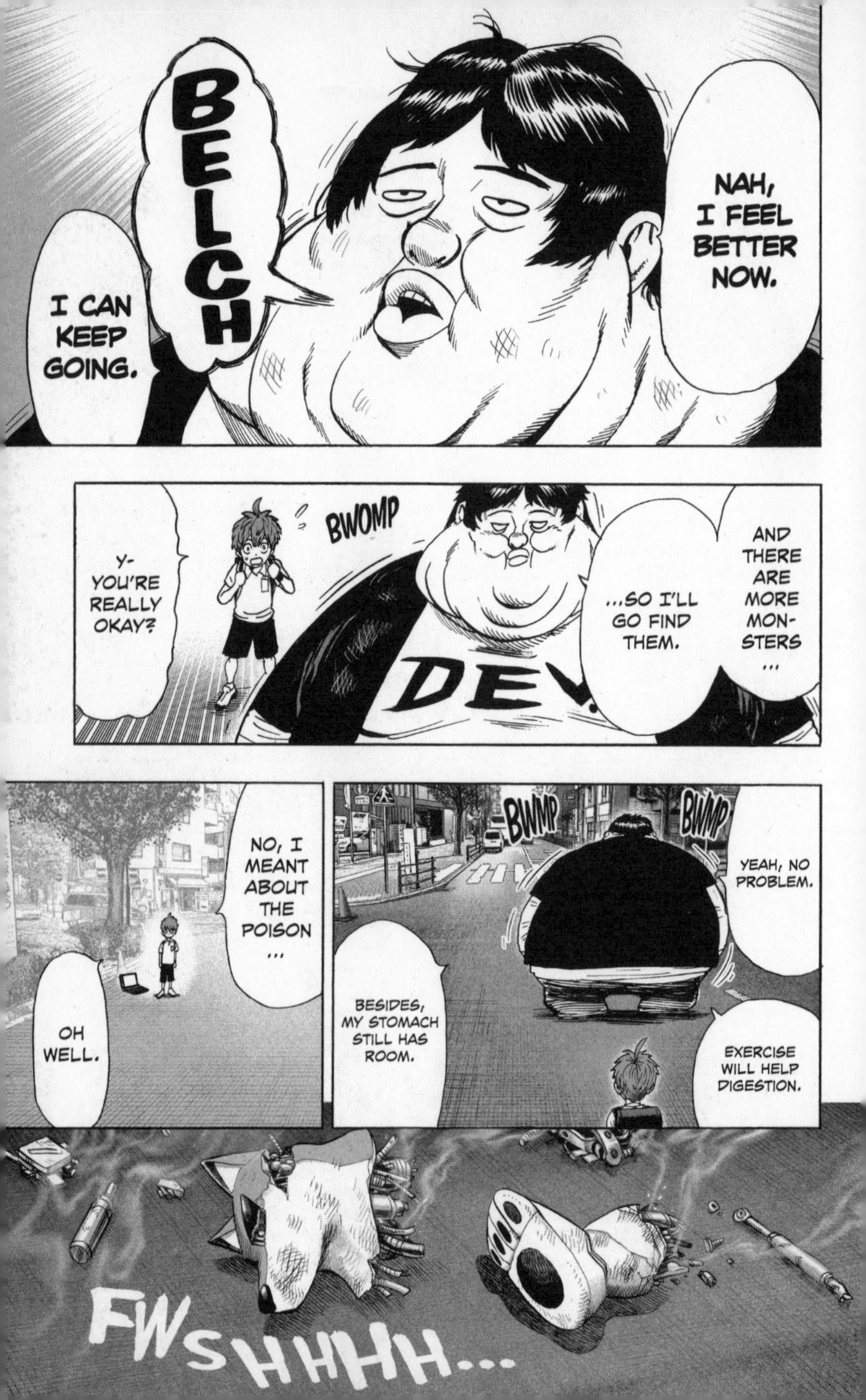
NAH, I FEEL BETTER NOW.
BELCH
I CAN KEEP GOING.
AND THERE ARE MORE MON-STERS ...
...SO I'LL GO FIND THEM.
BWOMP
Y- YOU'RE REALLY OKAY?
BWMP
BWMP
YEAH, NO PROBLEM.
EXERCISE WILL HELP DIGESTION.
BESIDES, MY STOMACH STILL HAS ROOM.
NO, I MEANT ABOUT THE POISON ...
OH WELL.
FWSHHHH...

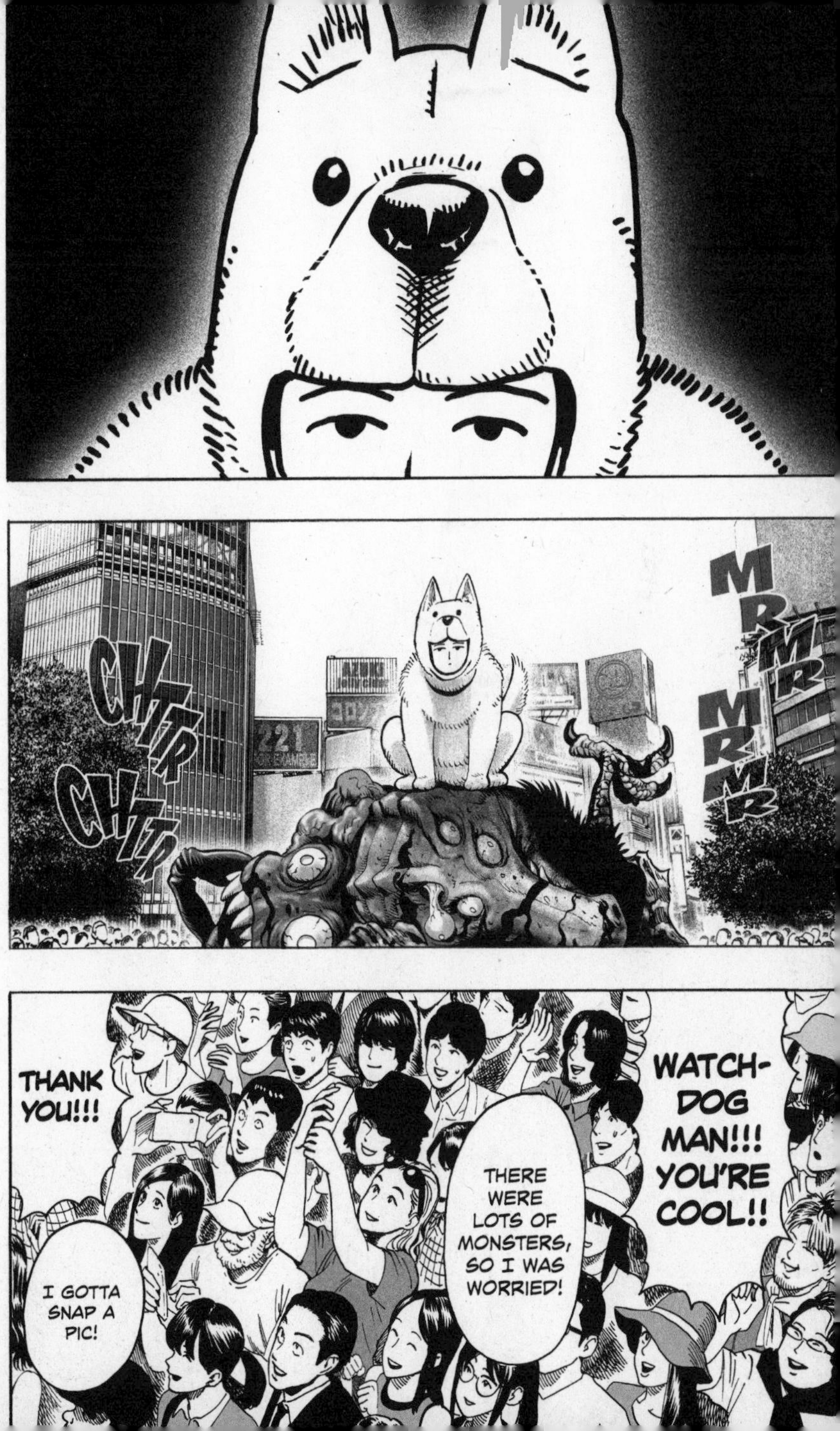
MRMR MRMR
CHTR CHTR
WATCH-DOG MAN!!! YOU'RE COOL!!
THERE WERE LOTS OF MONSTERS, SO I WAS WORRIED!
THANK YOU!!!
I GOTTA SNAP A PIC!

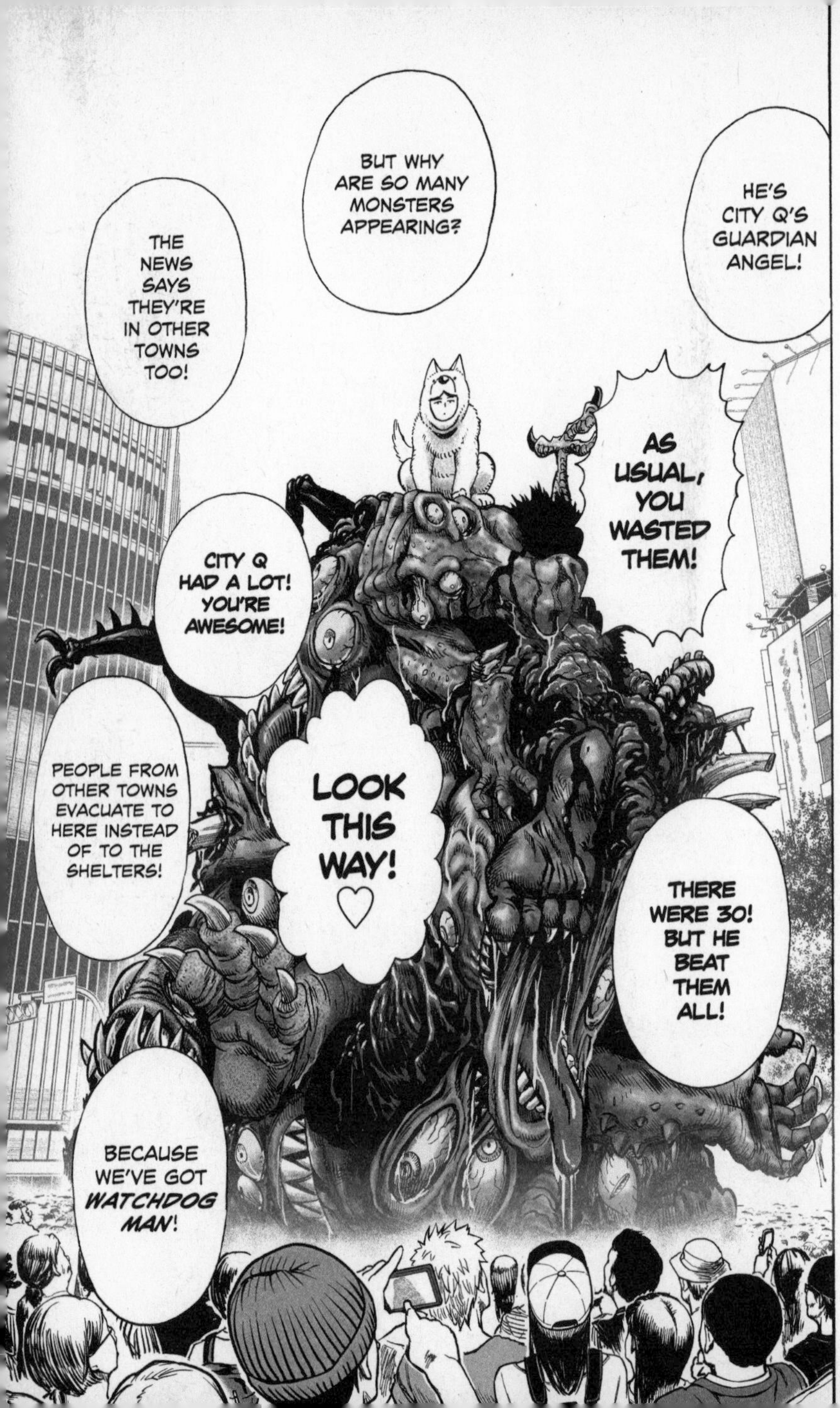
HE'S CITY Q'S GUARDIAN ANGEL!
BUT WHY ARE SO MANY MONSTERS APPEARING?
THE NEWS SAYS THEY'RE IN OTHER TOWNS TOO!
AS USUAL, YOU WASTED THEM!
CITY Q HAD A LOT! YOU'RE AWESOME!
THERE WERE 30! BUT HE BEAT THEM ALL!
LOOK THIS WAY! ♡
PEOPLE FROM OTHER TOWNS EVACUATE TO HERE INSTEAD OF TO THE SHELTERS!
BECAUSE WE'VE GOT *WATCHDOG MAN*!

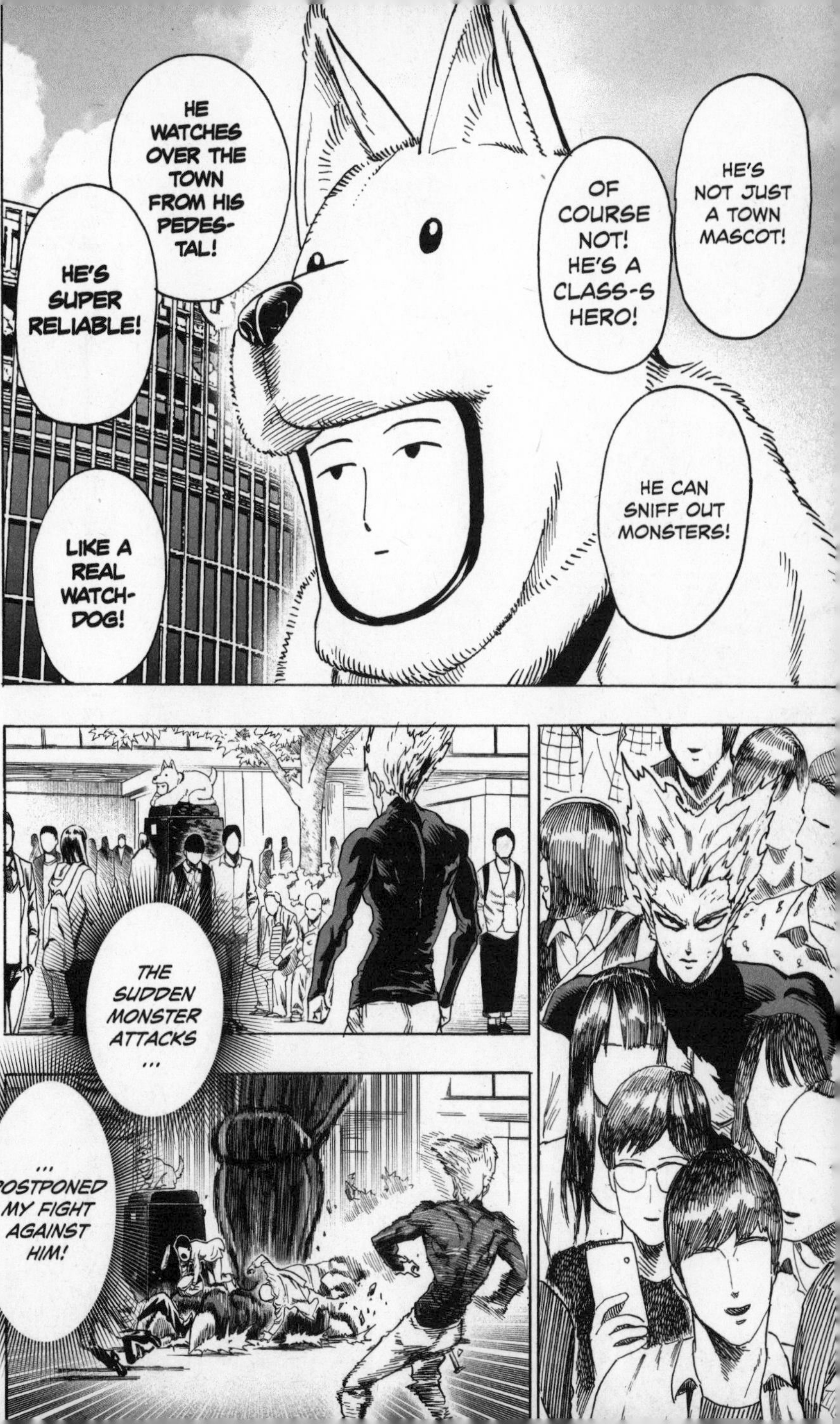
HE'S NOT JUST A TOWN MASCOT!
OF COURSE NOT! HE'S A CLASS-S HERO!
HE CAN SNIFF OUT MONSTERS!
HE WATCHES OVER THE TOWN FROM HIS PEDES-TAL!
HE'S SUPER RELIABLE!
LIKE A REAL WATCH-DOG!
THE SUDDEN MONSTER ATTACKS...
...POSTPONED MY FIGHT AGAINST HIM!

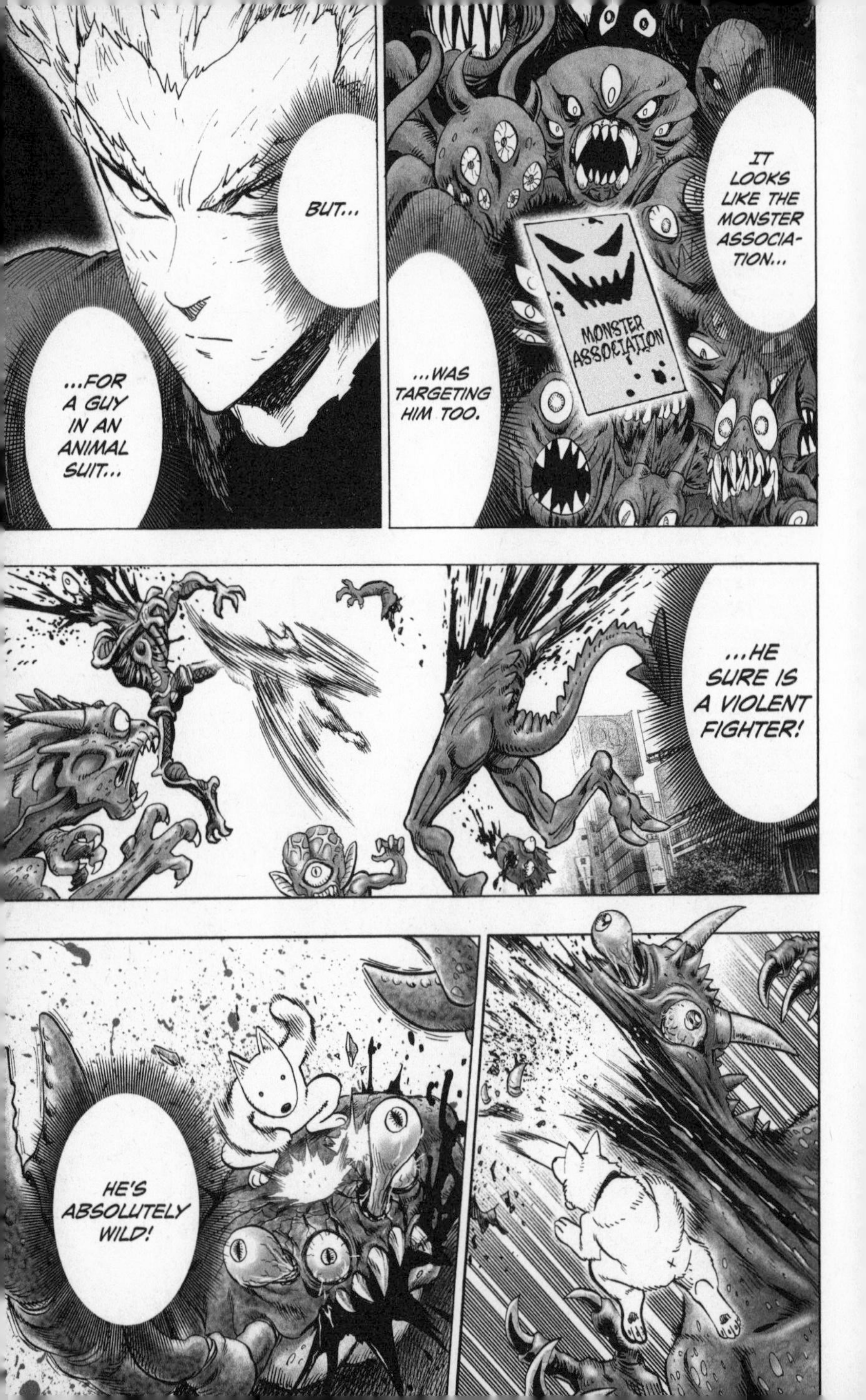
IT LOOKS LIKE THE MONSTER ASSOCIA-TION...
MONSTER ASSOCIATION
...WAS TARGETING HIM TOO.
BUT...
...FOR A GUY IN AN ANIMAL SUIT...
...HE SURE IS A VIOLENT FIGHTER!
...
HE'S ABSOLUTELY WILD!

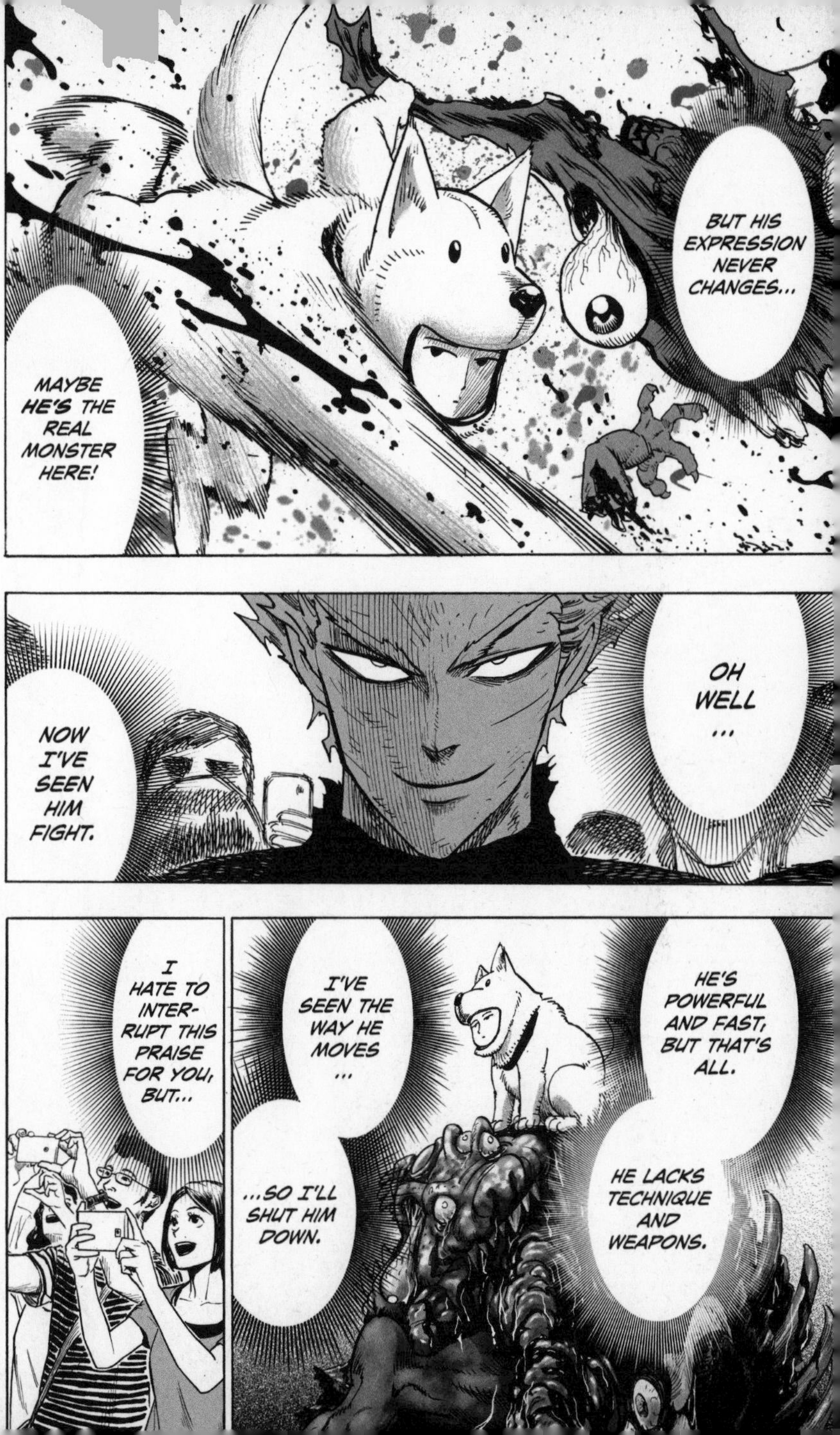
BUT HIS EXPRESSION NEVER CHANGES...
MAYBE HE'S THE REAL MONSTER HERE!
OH WELL ...
NOW I'VE SEEN HIM FIGHT.
HE'S POWERFUL AND FAST, BUT THAT'S ALL.
I'VE SEEN THE WAY HE MOVES ...
HE LACKS TECHNIQUE AND WEAPONS.
...SO I'LL SHUT HIM DOWN.
I HATE TO INTER-RUPT THIS PRAISE FOR YOU, BUT...

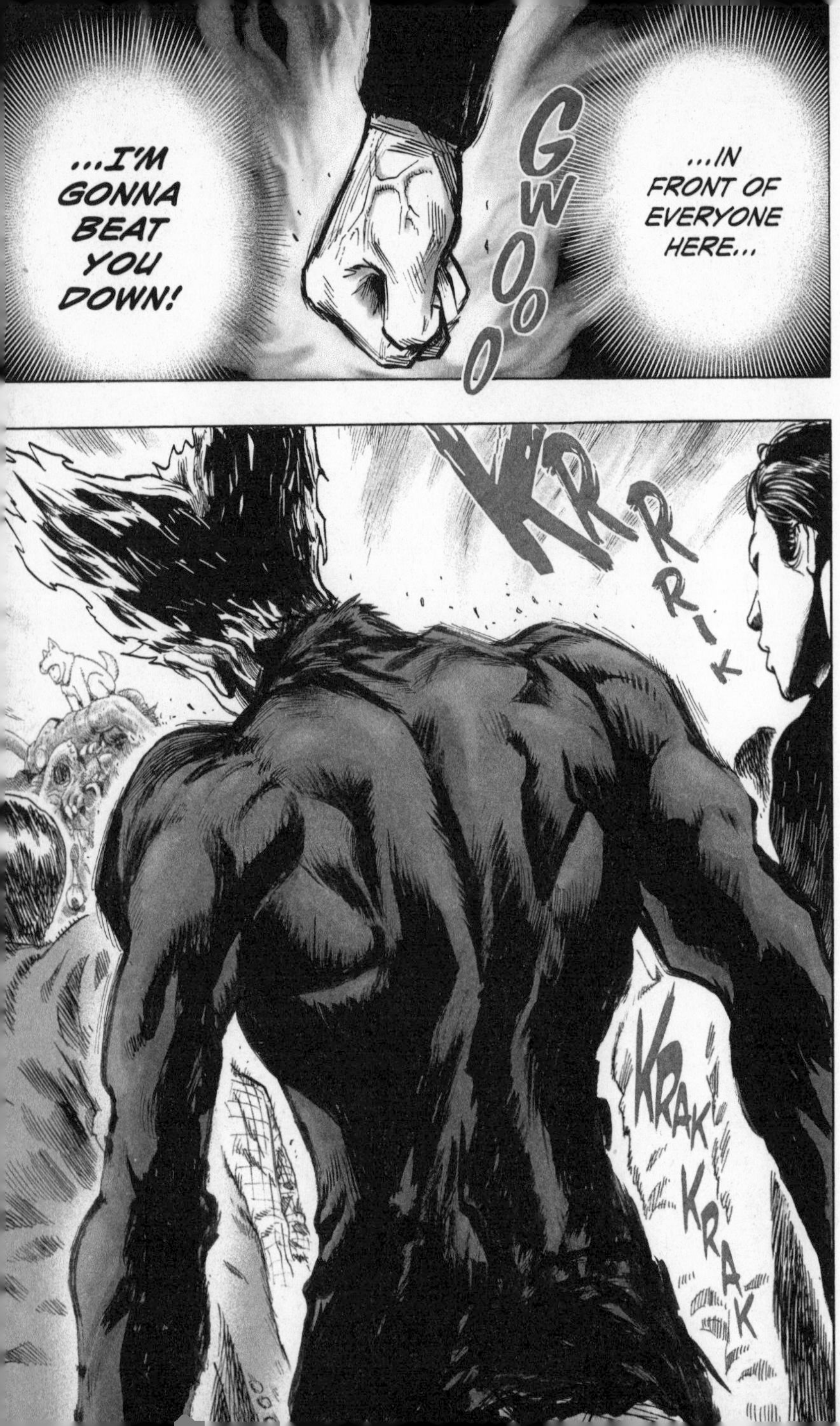
...IN FRONT OF EVERYONE HERE...
GWOOOO
...I'M GONNA BEAT YOU DOWN!
KRRRRIK
KRAK KRAK KRAK

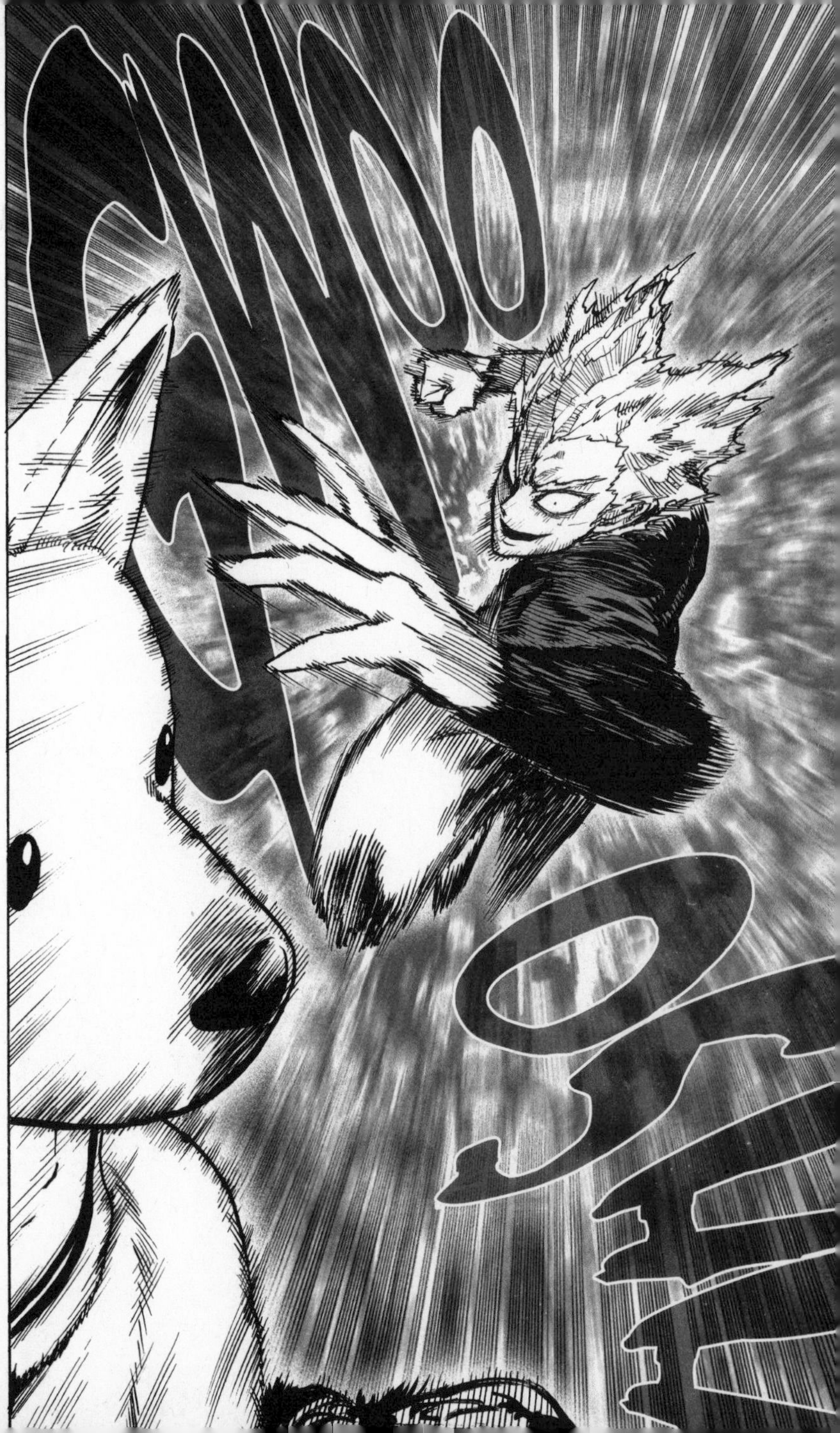

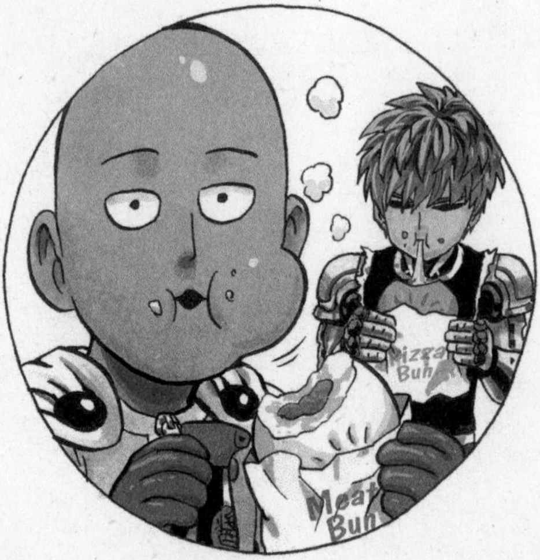
Pizza
Bun
Meat
Bun

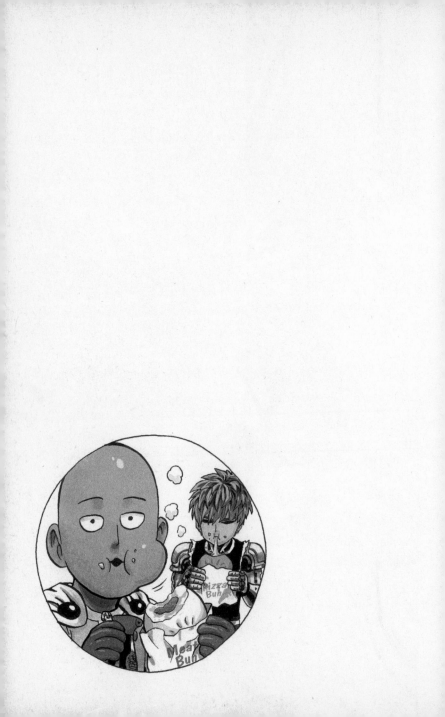

BONUS MANGA: KING'S WEEKDAY OFF

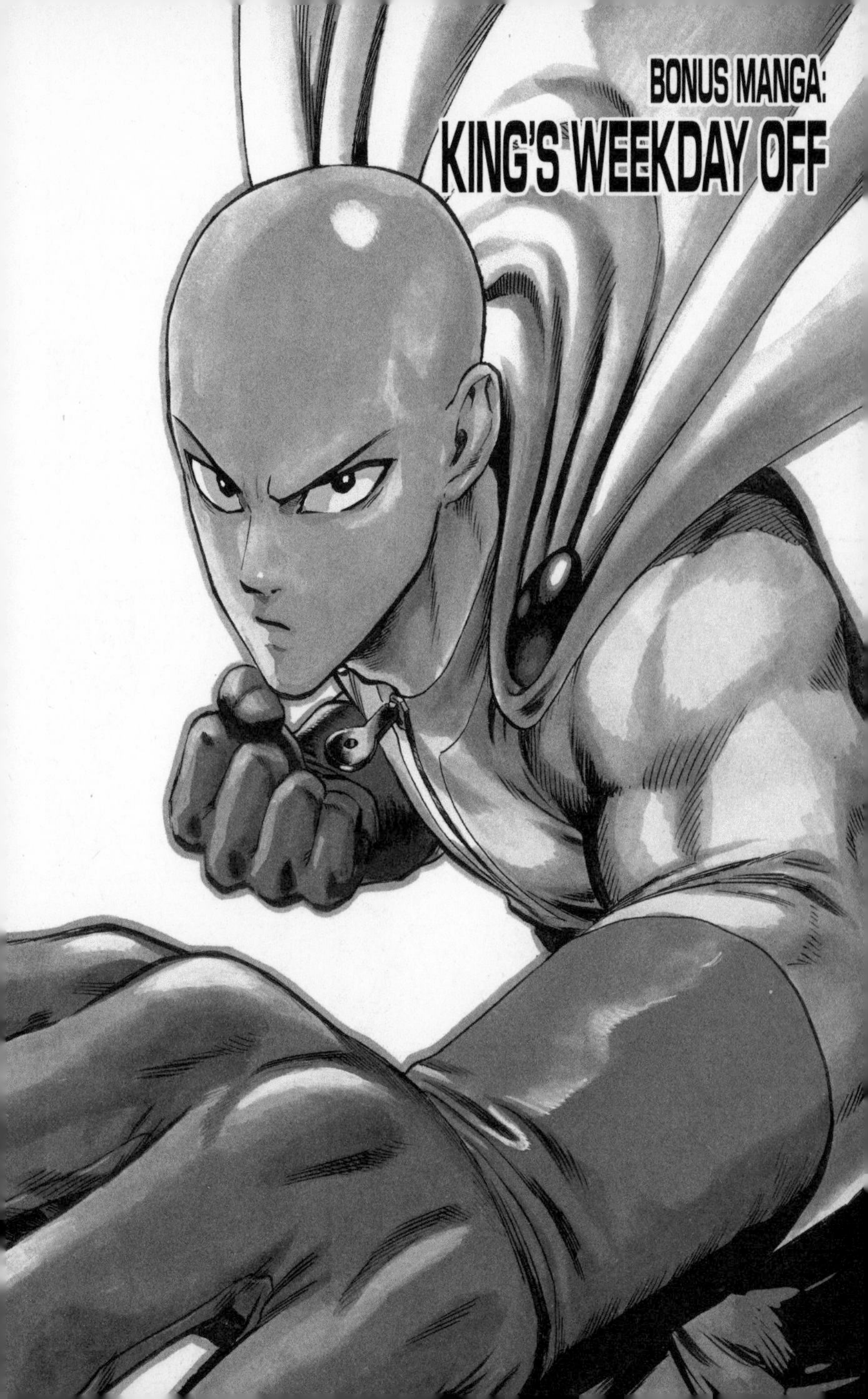

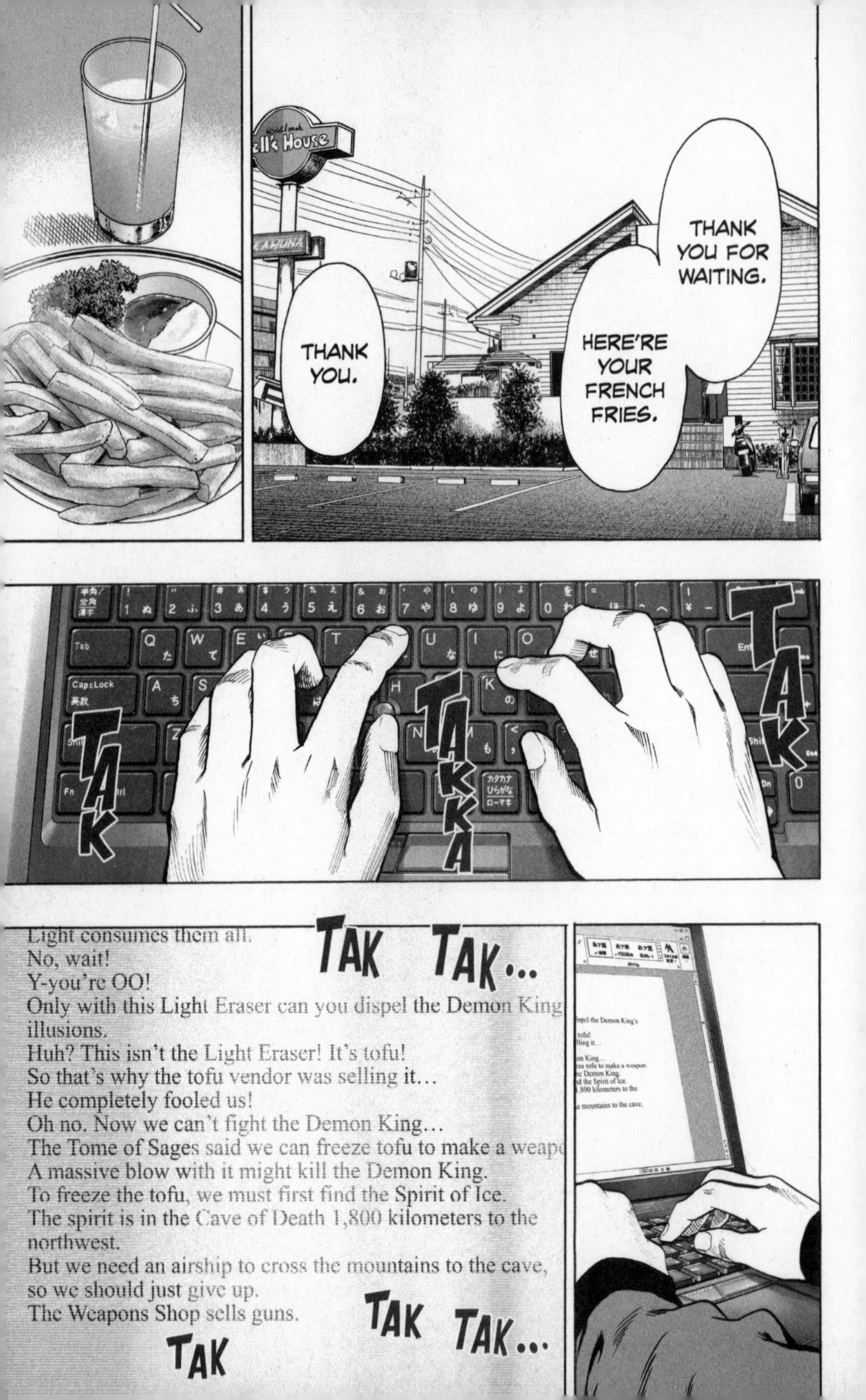
THANK YOU FOR WAITING.
HERE'RE YOUR FRENCH FRIES.
THANK YOU.
TAK
TAKKA
TAK
Light consumes them all.
No, wait!
Y-you're OO!
Only with this Light Eraser can you dispel the Demon King
illusions.
Huh? This isn't the Light Eraser! It's tofu!
So that's why the tofu vendor was selling it…
He completely fooled us!
Oh no. Now we can't fight the Demon King…
The Tome of Sages said we can freeze tofu to make a weap
A massive blow with it might kill the Demon King.
To freeze the tofu, we must first find the Spirit of Ice.
The spirit is in the Cave of Death 1,800 kilometers to the northwest.
But we need an airship to cross the mountains to the cave, so we should just give up.
The Weapons Shop sells guns.
TAK TAK…
TAK TAK…
TAK

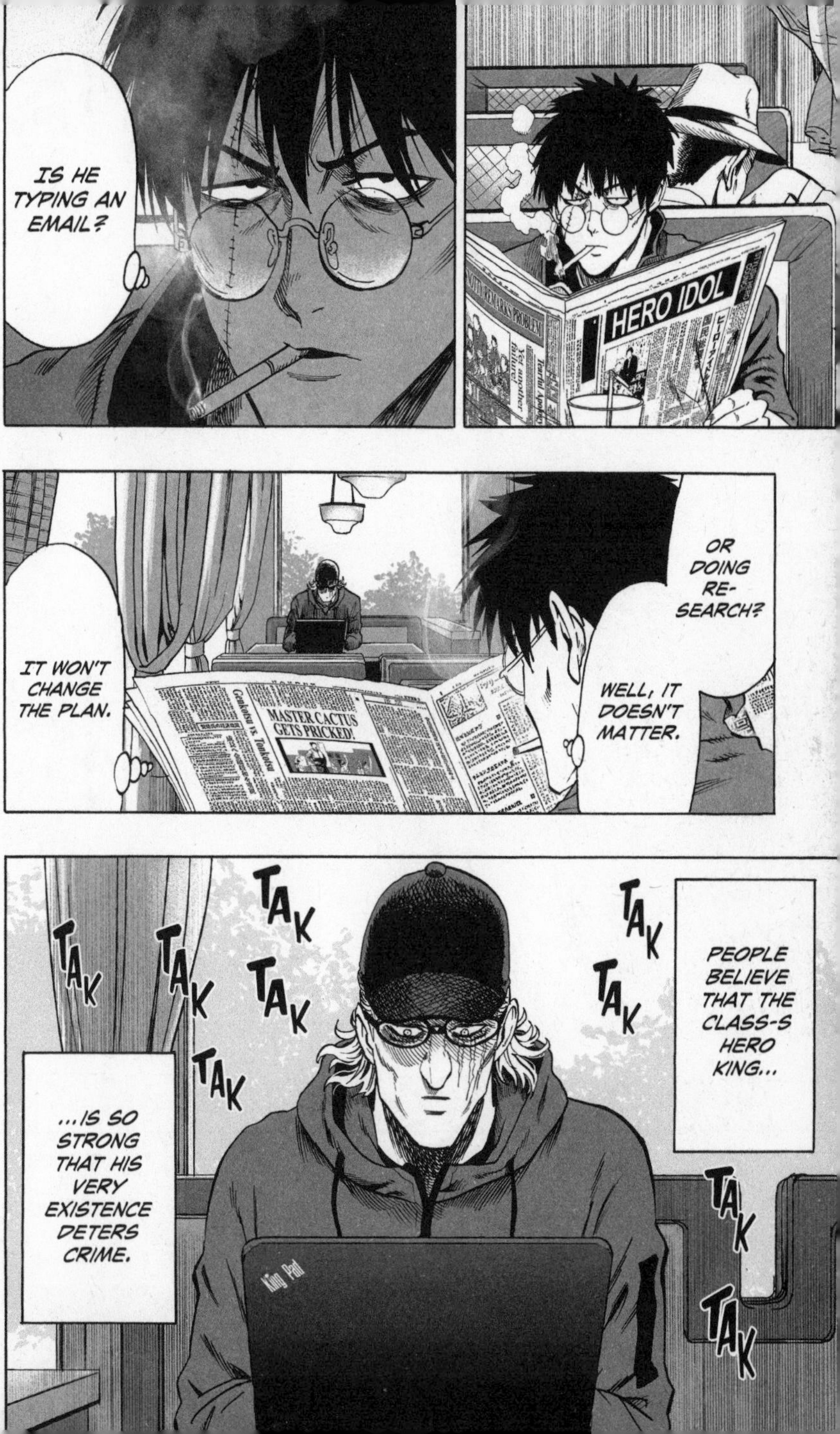
HERO IDOL
IS HE TYPING AN EMAIL?
OR DOING RE-SEARCH?
WELL, IT DOESN'T MATTER.
MASTER CACTUS GETS PRICKED!
Genkotsu vs. Tonkotsu
IT WON'T CHANGE THE PLAN.
TAK
TAK
PEOPLE BELIEVE THAT THE CLASS-S HERO KING...
TAK
TAK
TAK
TAK
TAK
TAK
...IS SO STRONG THAT HIS VERY EXISTENCE DETERS CRIME.
King Pad
TAK
TAK

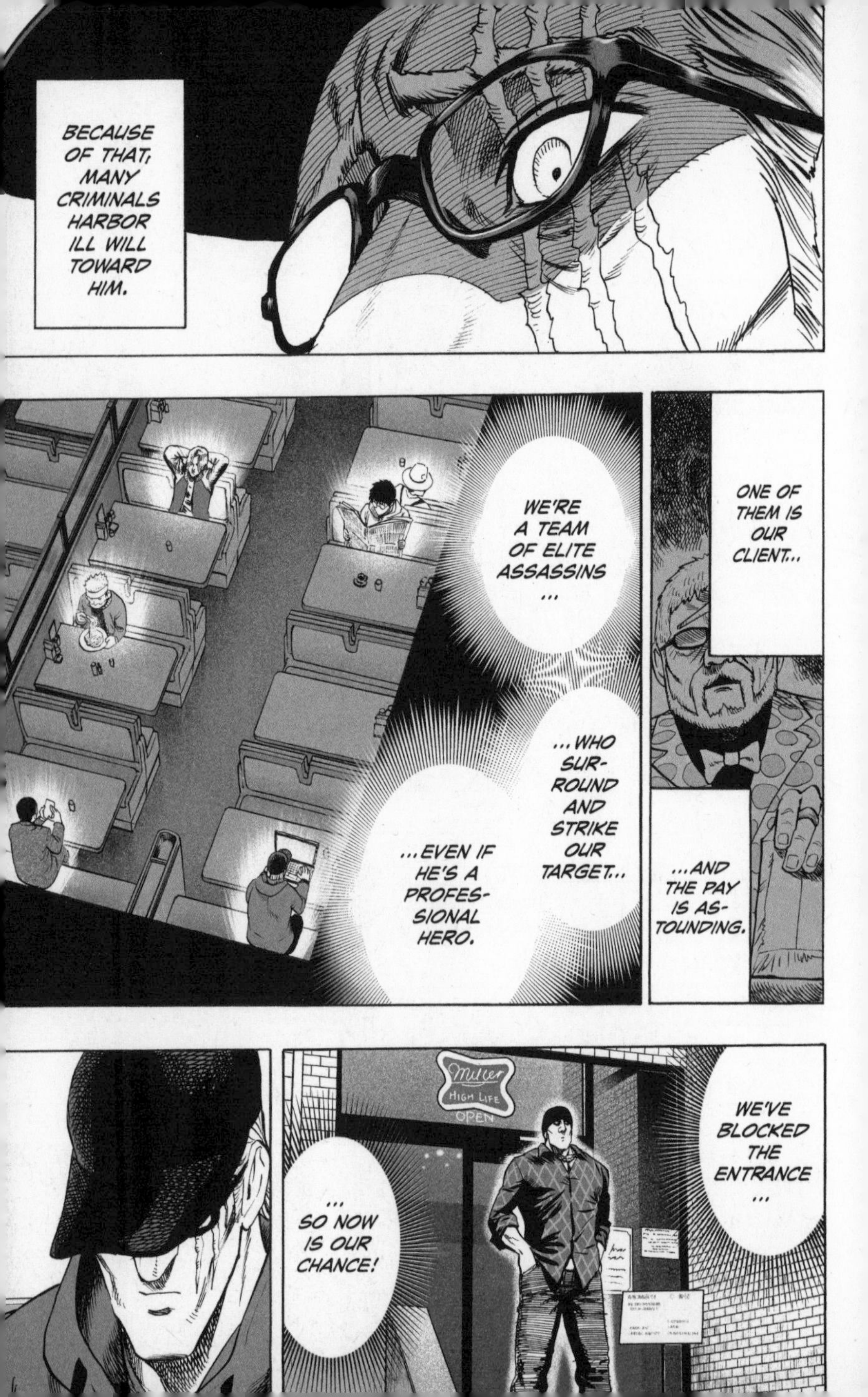
BECAUSE OF THAT, MANY CRIMINALS HARBOR ILL WILL TOWARD HIM.
ONE OF THEM IS OUR CLIENT...
...AND THE PAY IS ASTOUNDING.
WE'RE A TEAM OF ELITE ASSASSINS ...
...WHO SURROUND AND STRIKE OUR TARGET...
...EVEN IF HE'S A PROFESSIONAL HERO.
Miller HIGH LIFE
OPEN
WE'VE BLOCKED THE ENTRANCE ...
... SO NOW IS OUR CHANCE!

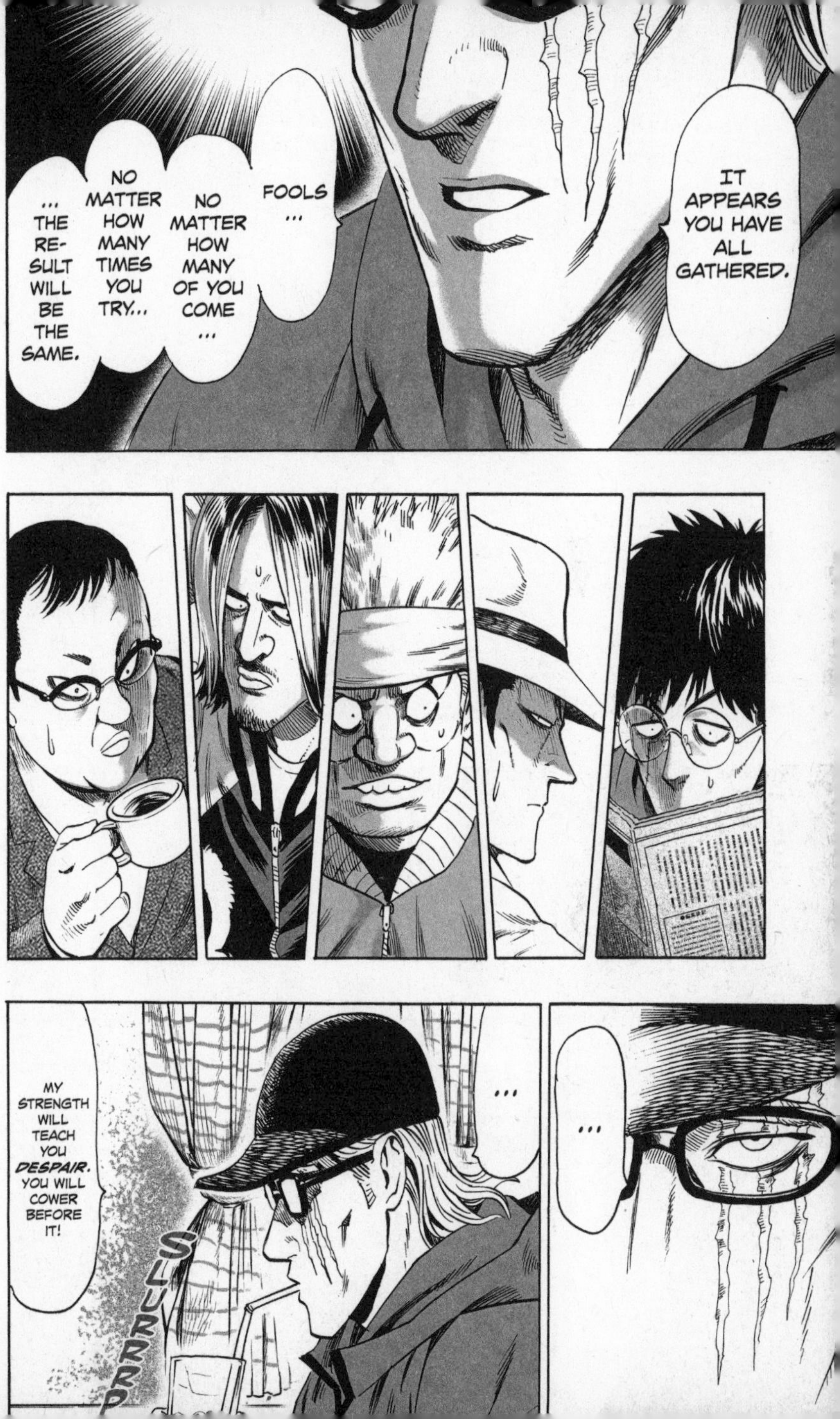
IT APPEARS YOU HAVE ALL GATHERED.
FOOLS ...
NO MATTER HOW MANY OF YOU COME ...
NO MATTER HOW MANY TIMES YOU TRY...
... THE RE-SULT WILL BE THE SAME.
...
...
MY STRENGTH WILL TEACH YOU DESPAIR. YOU WILL COWER BEFORE IT!
SLURRRP

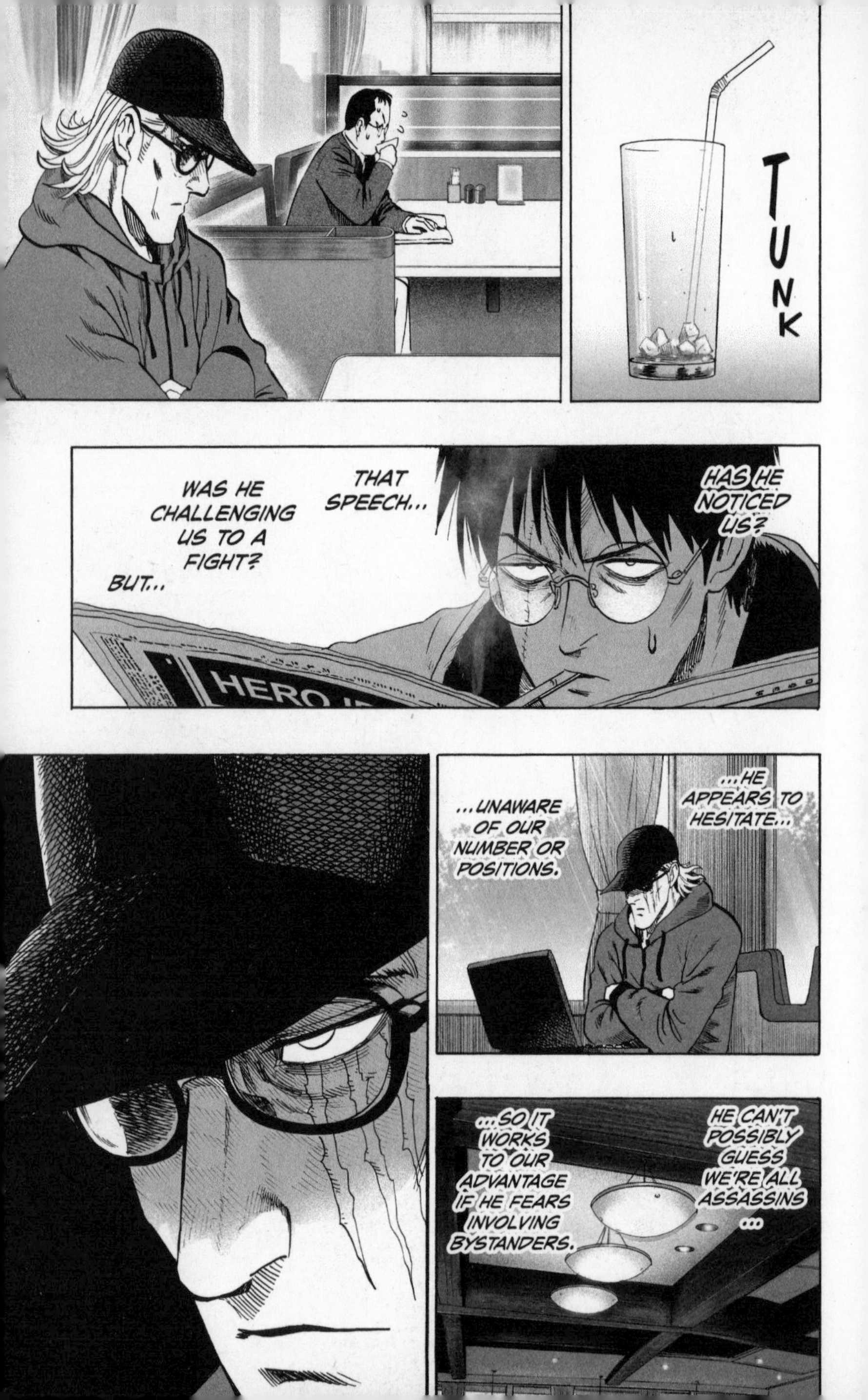
TUNK
HAS HE NOTICED US?
THAT SPEECH...
WAS HE CHALLENGING US TO A FIGHT? BUT...
...HE APPEARS TO HESITATE...
...UNAWARE OF OUR NUMBER OR POSITIONS.
HE CAN'T POSSIBLY GUESS WE'RE ALL ASSASSINS ...
...SO IT WORKS TO OUR ADVANTAGE IF HE FEARS INVOLVING BYSTANDERS.

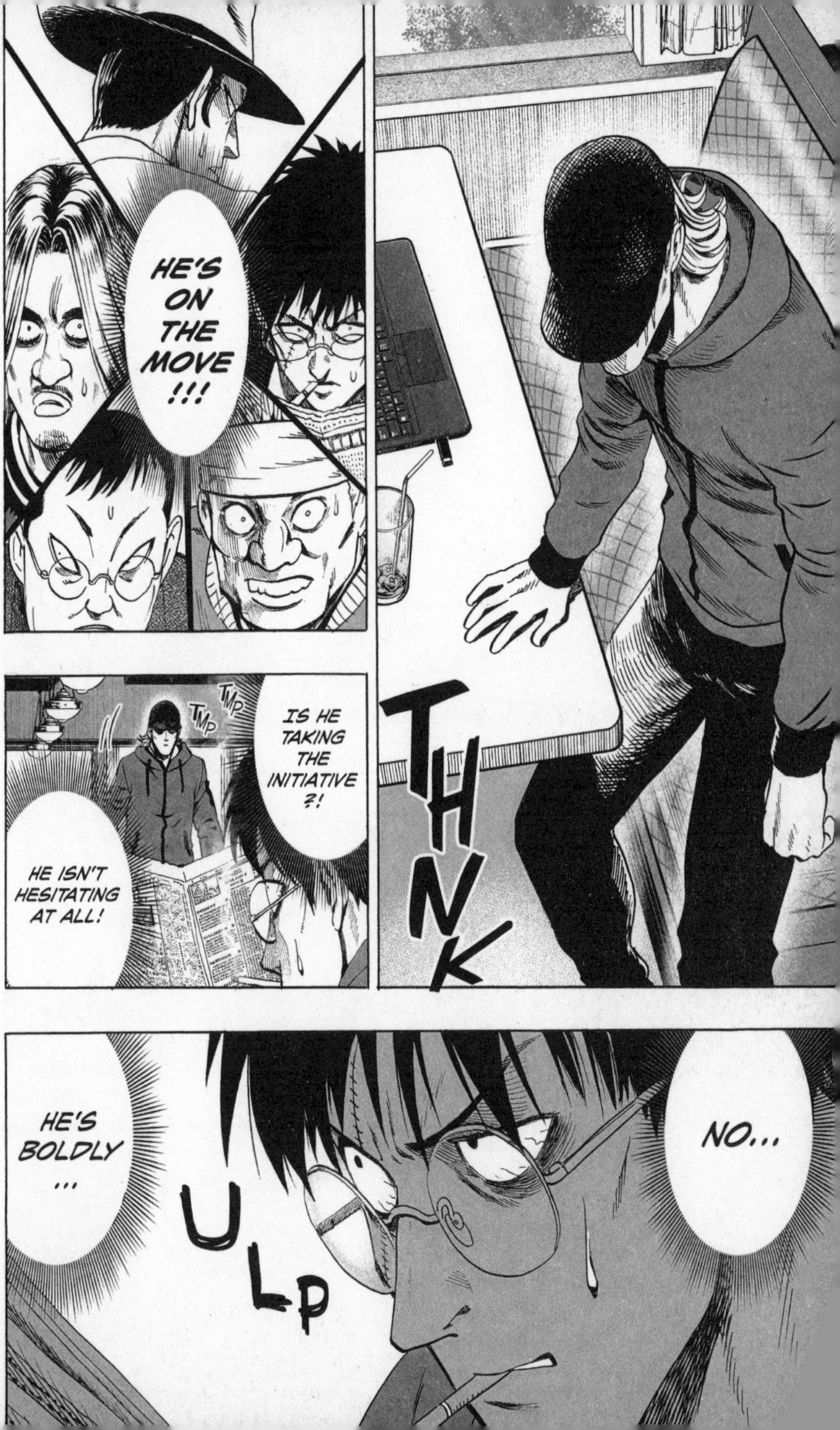
THNK
HE'S ON THE MOVE!!!
TMP TMP
IS HE TAKING THE INITIATIVE?!
HE ISN'T HESITATING AT ALL!
NO...
ULP
HE'S BOLDLY...

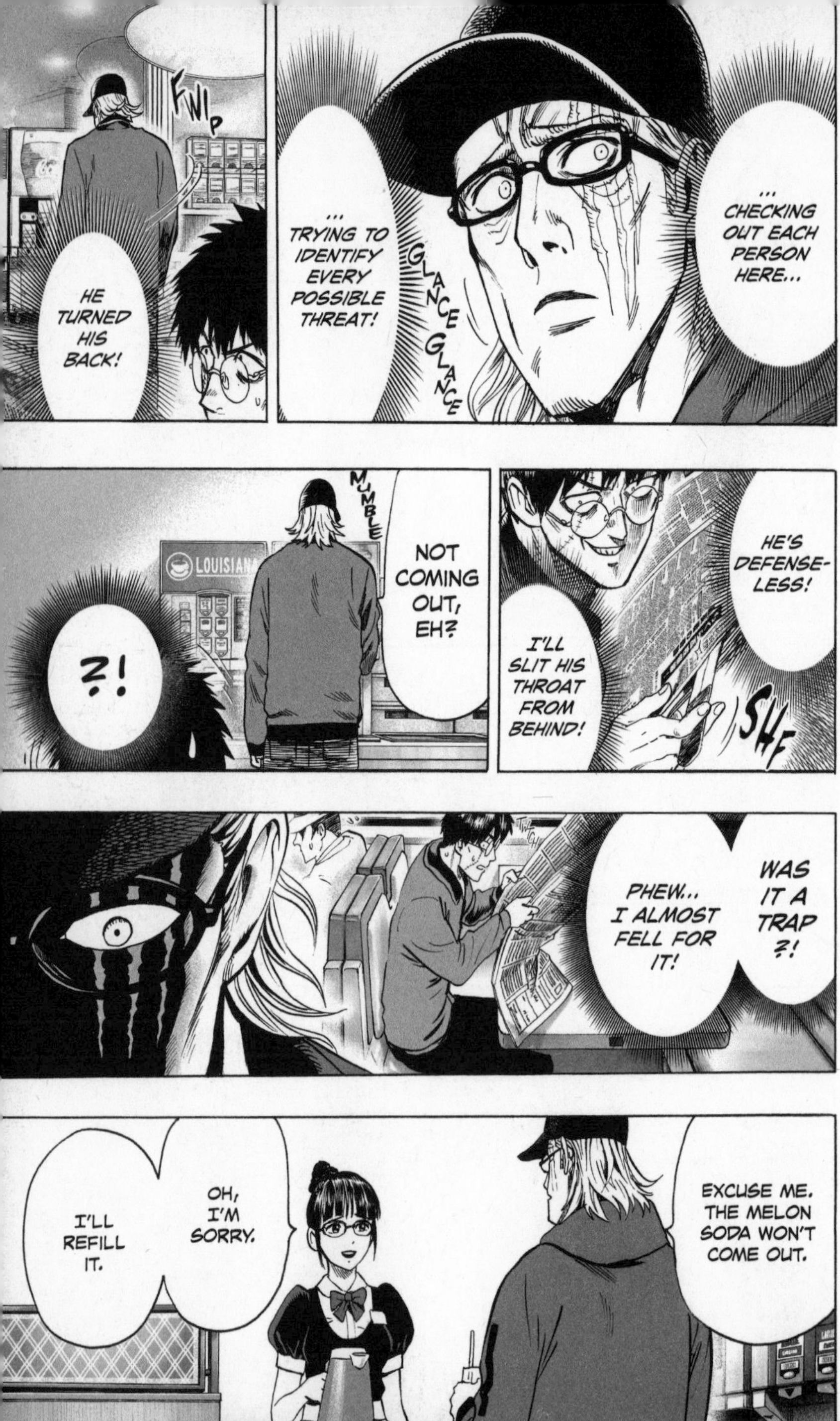
... CHECKING OUT EACH PERSON HERE...
... TRYING TO IDENTIFY EVERY POSSIBLE THREAT!
GLANCE GLANCE
FWIP
HE TURNED HIS BACK!
HE'S DEFENSE-LESS!
I'LL SLIT HIS THROAT FROM BEHIND!
SHF
MUMBLE
NOT COMING OUT, EH?
?!
WAS IT A TRAP ?!
PHEW... I ALMOST FELL FOR IT!
EXCUSE ME. THE MELON SODA WON'T COME OUT.
OH, I'M SORRY.
I'LL REFILL IT.

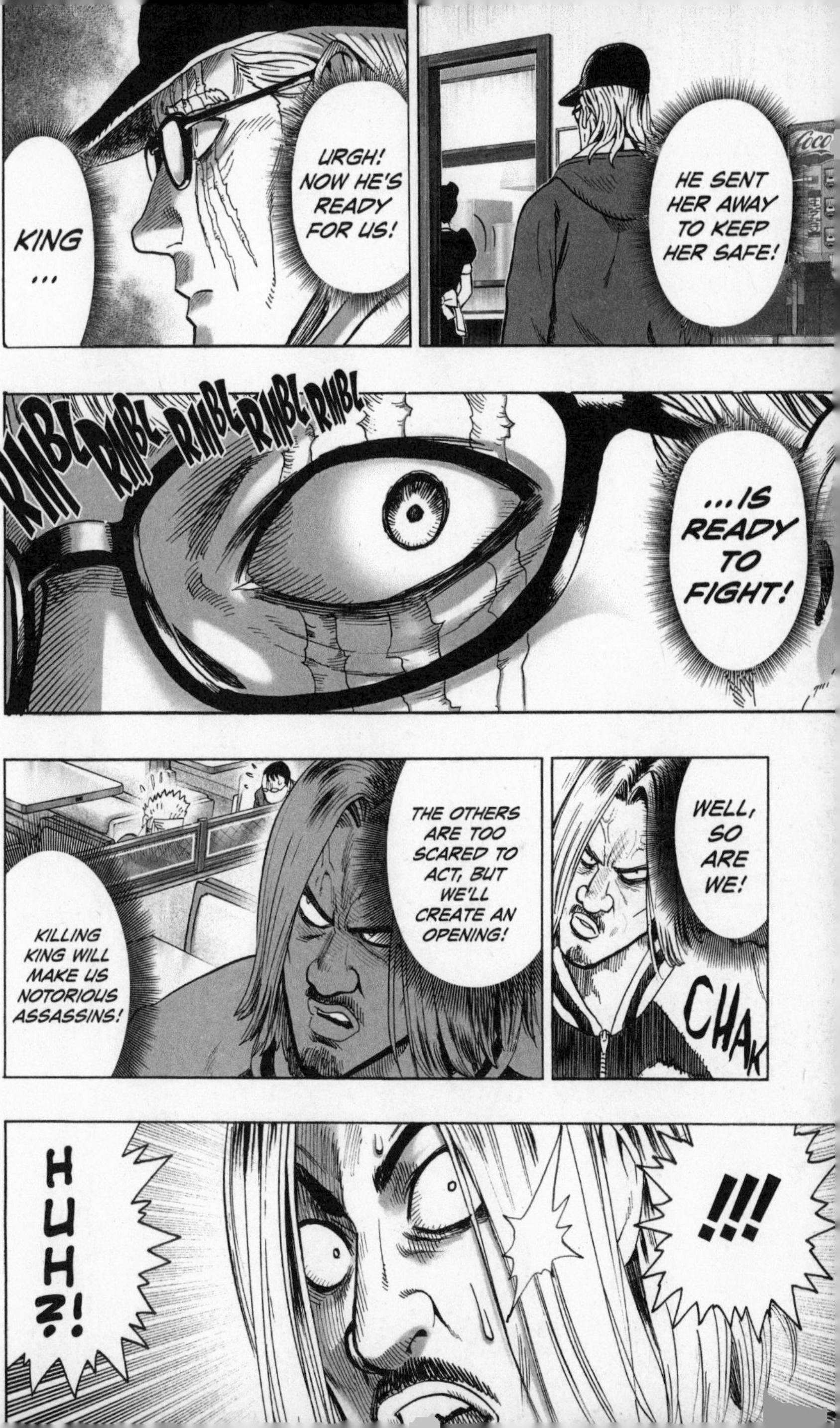
HE SENT HER AWAY TO KEEP HER SAFE!
URGH! NOW HE'S READY FOR US!
KING ...
...IS READY TO FIGHT!
RMBL RMBL RMBL RMBL RMBL
WELL, SO ARE WE!
CHAK
THE OTHERS ARE TOO SCARED TO ACT, BUT WE'LL CREATE AN OPENING!
KILLING KING WILL MAKE US NOTORIOUS ASSASSINS!
!!!
HUH?!

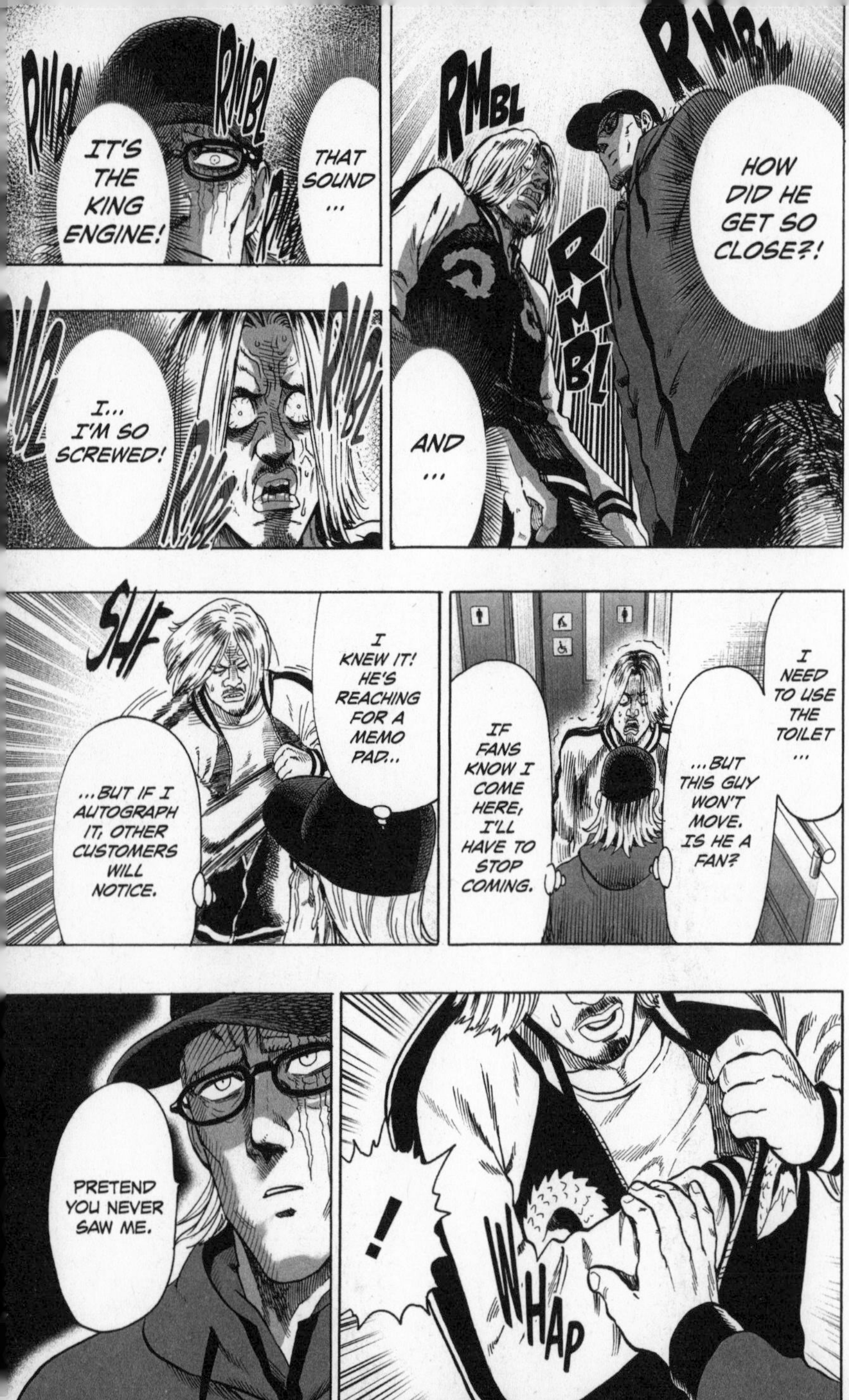
RMBL
RMBL
HOW DID HE GET SO CLOSE?!
RMBL
AND ...
RMBL
RMBL
THAT SOUND ...
IT'S THE KING ENGINE!
RMBL
RMBL
I... I'M SO SCREWED!
I NEED TO USE THE TOILET ...
...BUT THIS GUY WON'T MOVE. IS HE A FAN?
IF FANS KNOW I COME HERE, I'LL HAVE TO STOP COMING.
SHF
I KNEW IT! HE'S REACHING FOR A MEMO PAD...
...BUT IF I AUTOGRAPH IT, OTHER CUSTOMERS WILL NOTICE.
!
WHAP
PRETEND YOU NEVER SAW ME.

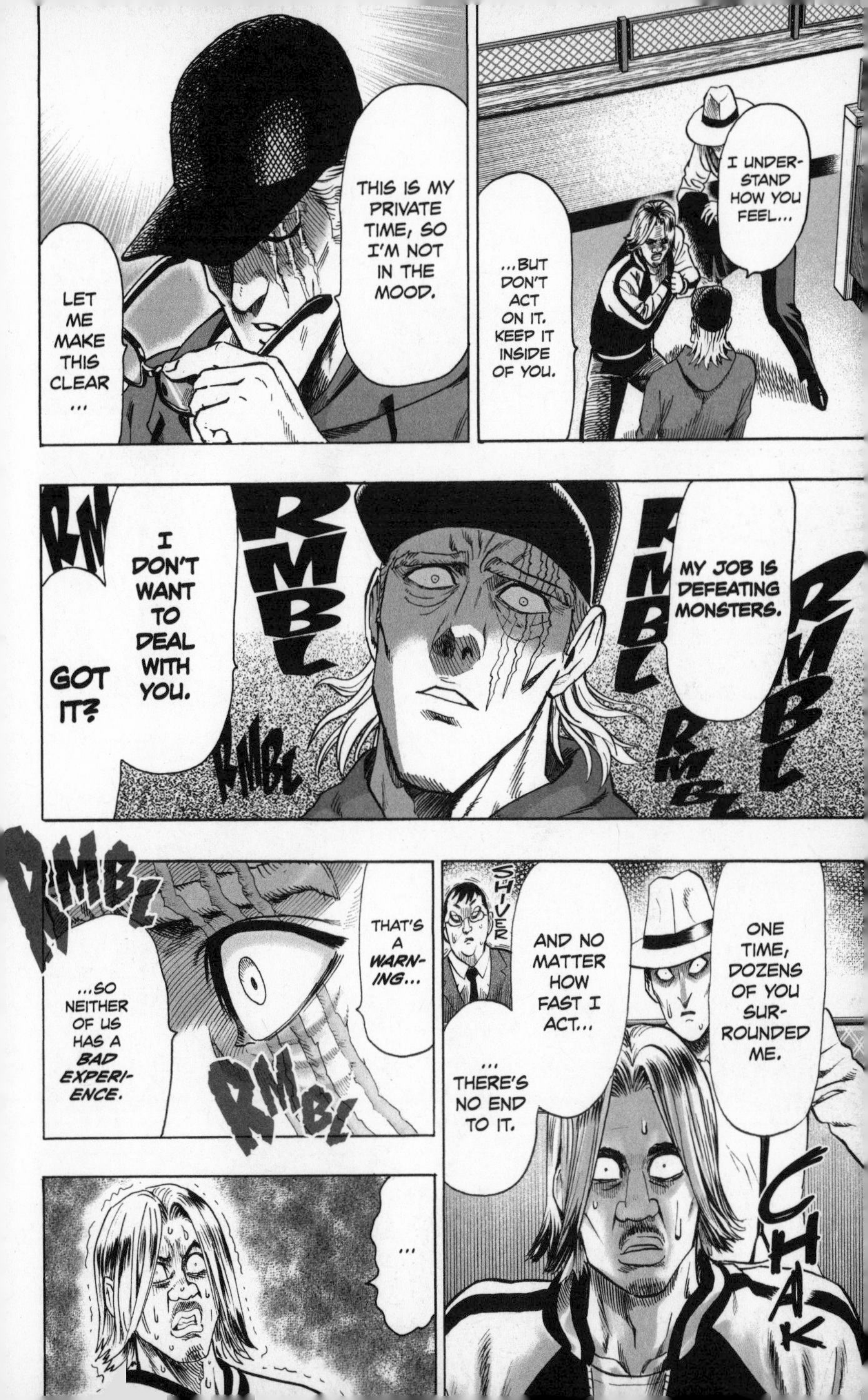
I UNDER-STAND HOW YOU FEEL...
...BUT DON'T ACT ON IT. KEEP IT INSIDE OF YOU.
THIS IS MY PRIVATE TIME, SO I'M NOT IN THE MOOD.
LET ME MAKE THIS CLEAR...
RMBL
RMBL
RMBL
MY JOB IS DEFEATING MONSTERS.
RMBL
I DON'T WANT TO DEAL WITH YOU.
RMBL
GOT IT?
SHIVER
ONE TIME, DOZENS OF YOU SUR-ROUNDED ME.
AND NO MATTER HOW FAST I ACT...
...THERE'S NO END TO IT.
RMBL
THAT'S A *WARN-ING*...
...SO NEITHER OF US HAS A *BAD EXPERI-ENCE*.
RMBL
CHAK
...

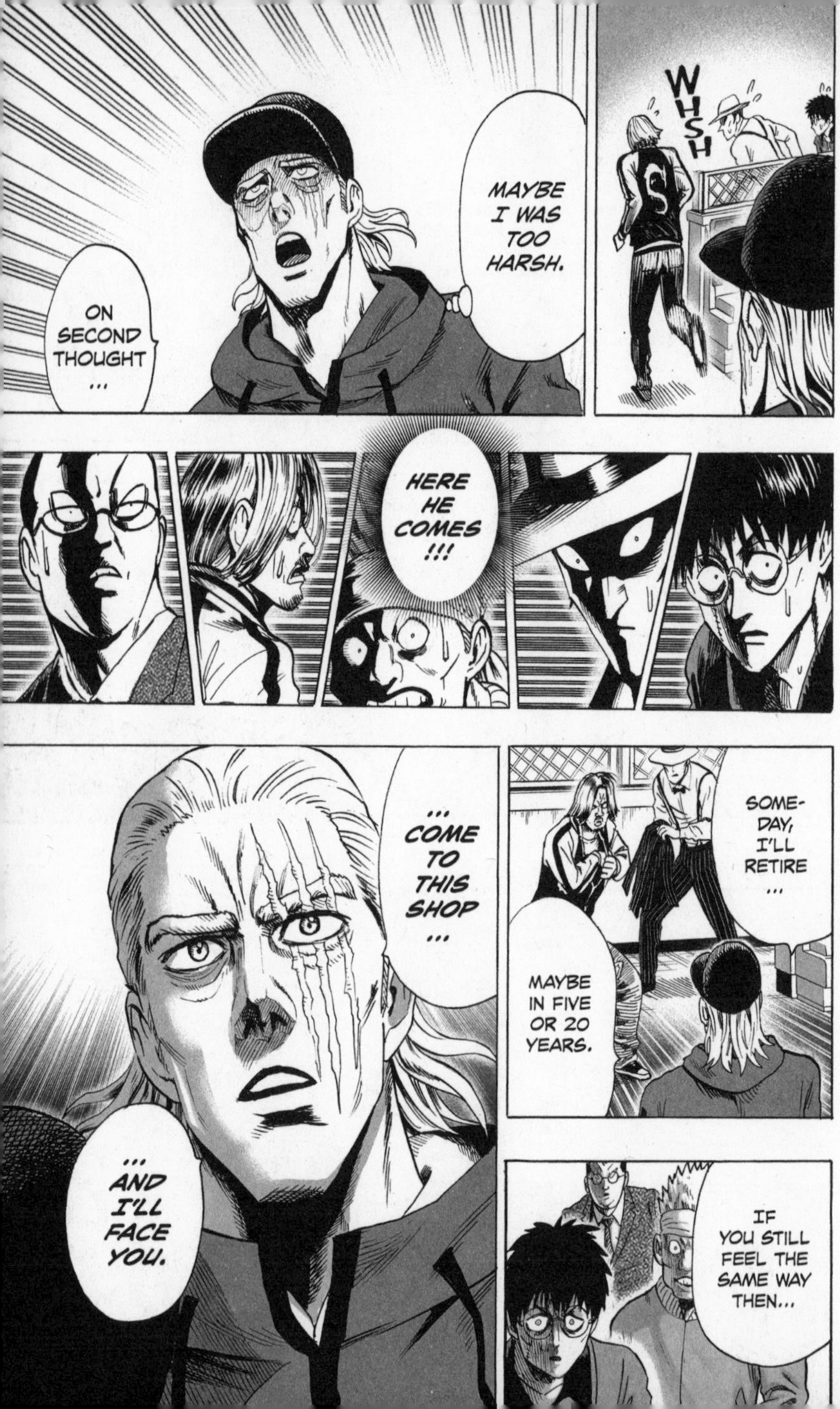
WHSH
MAYBE I WAS TOO HARSH.
ON SECOND THOUGHT...
HERE HE COMES!!!
SOME-DAY, I'LL RETIRE...
MAYBE IN FIVE OR 20 YEARS.
IF YOU STILL FEEL THE SAME WAY THEN...
...COME TO THIS SHOP...
...AND I'LL FACE YOU.

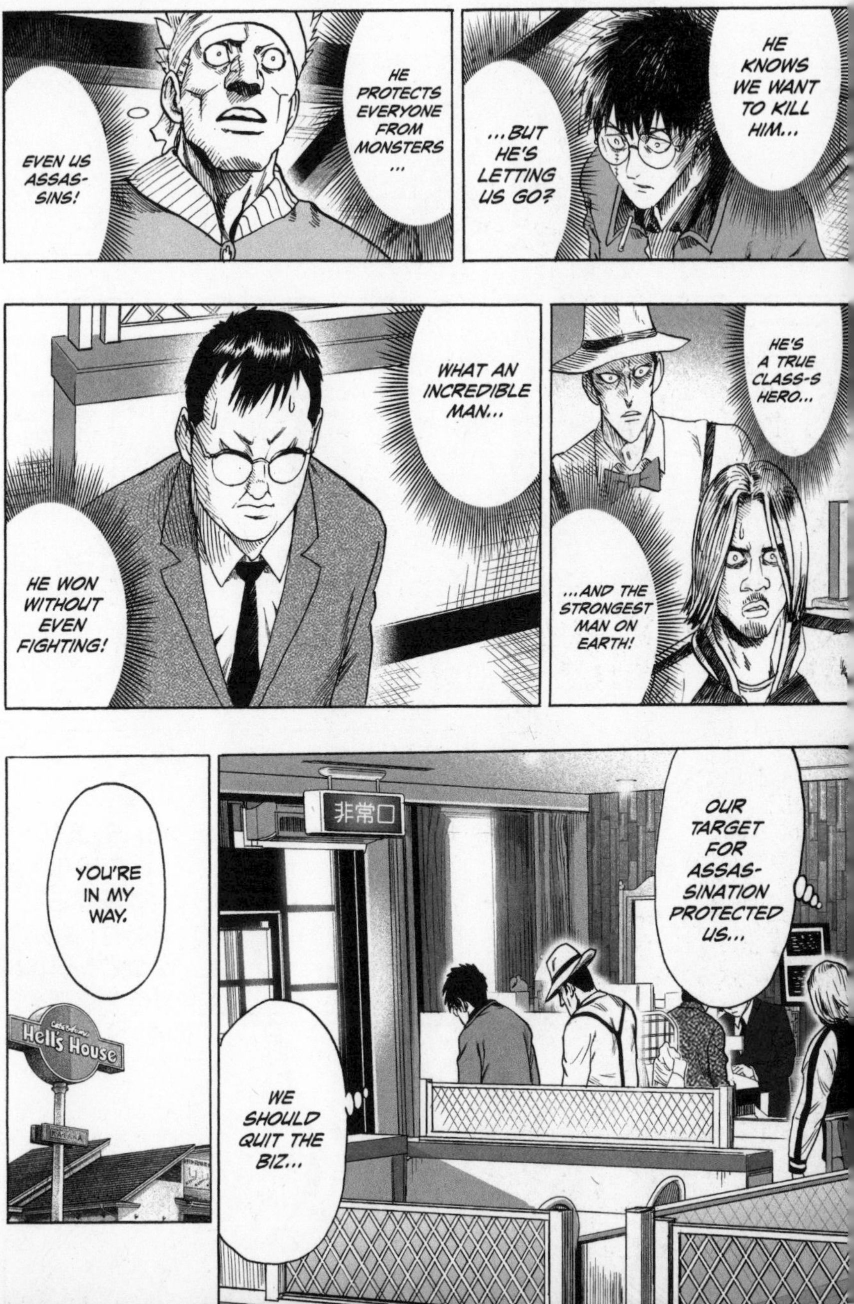
HE KNOWS WE WANT TO KILL HIM...
...BUT HE'S LETTING US GO?
HE PROTECTS EVERYONE FROM MONSTERS ...
EVEN US ASSASSINS!
HE'S A TRUE CLASS-S HERO...
...AND THE STRONGEST MAN ON EARTH!
WHAT AN INCREDIBLE MAN...
HE WON WITHOUT EVEN FIGHTING!
非常口
OUR TARGET FOR ASSASSINATION PROTECTED US...
WE SHOULD QUIT THE BIZ...
YOU'RE IN MY WAY.
Hell's House

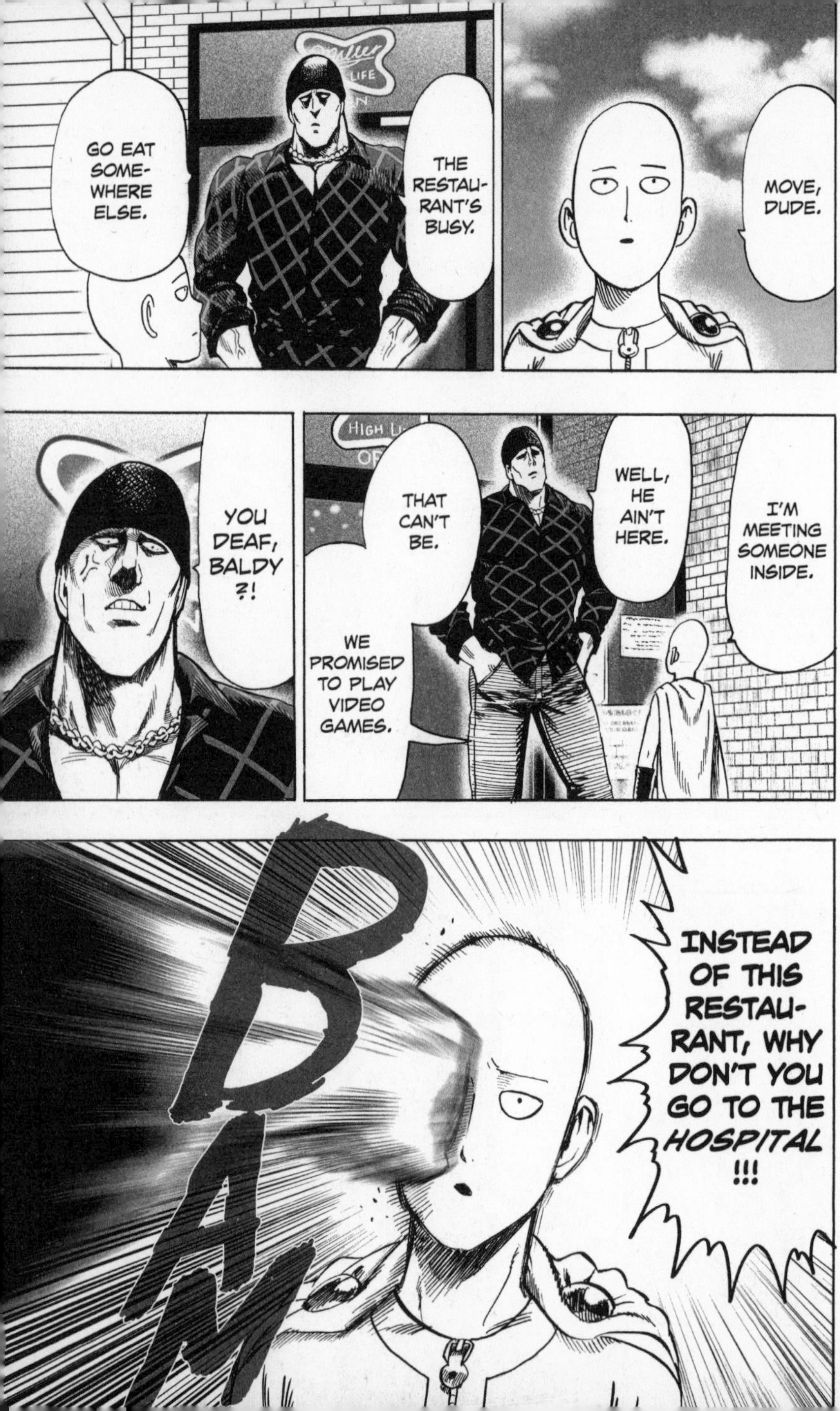
MOVE, DUDE.
THE RESTAURANT'S BUSY.
GO EAT SOMEWHERE ELSE.
I'M MEETING SOMEONE INSIDE.
WELL, HE AIN'T HERE.
THAT CAN'T BE.
WE PROMISED TO PLAY VIDEO GAMES.
YOU DEAF, BALDY?!
INSTEAD OF THIS RESTAURANT, WHY DON'T YOU GO TO THE *HOSPITAL*!!!
BAM

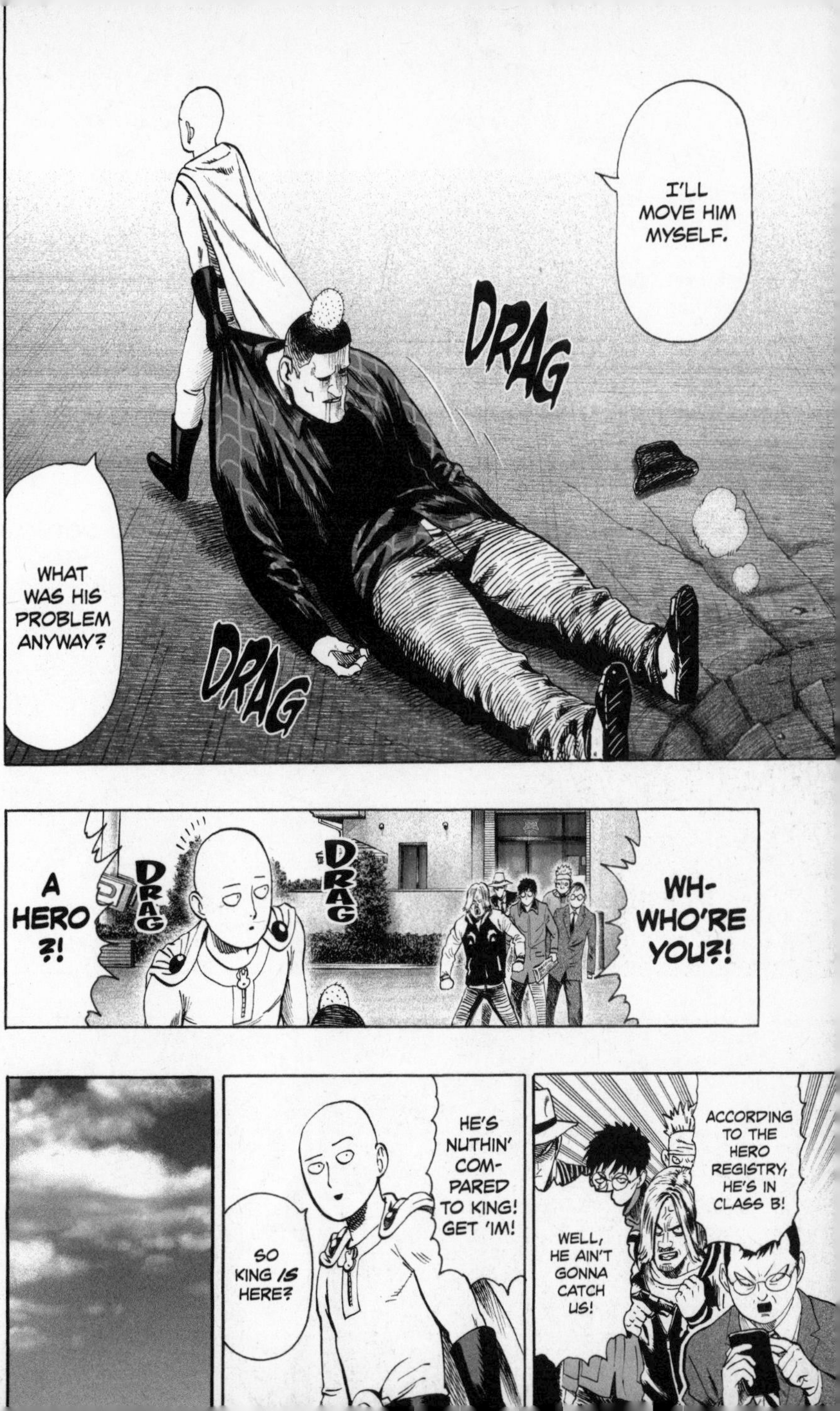
I'LL MOVE HIM MYSELF.
DRAG
DRAG
WHAT WAS HIS PROBLEM ANYWAY?
WH-WHO'RE YOU?!
DRAG
DRAG
A HERO?!
ACCORDING TO THE HERO REGISTRY, HE'S IN CLASS B!
WELL, HE AIN'T GONNA CATCH US!
HE'S NUTHIN' COMPARED TO KING! GET 'IM!
SO KING *IS* HERE?

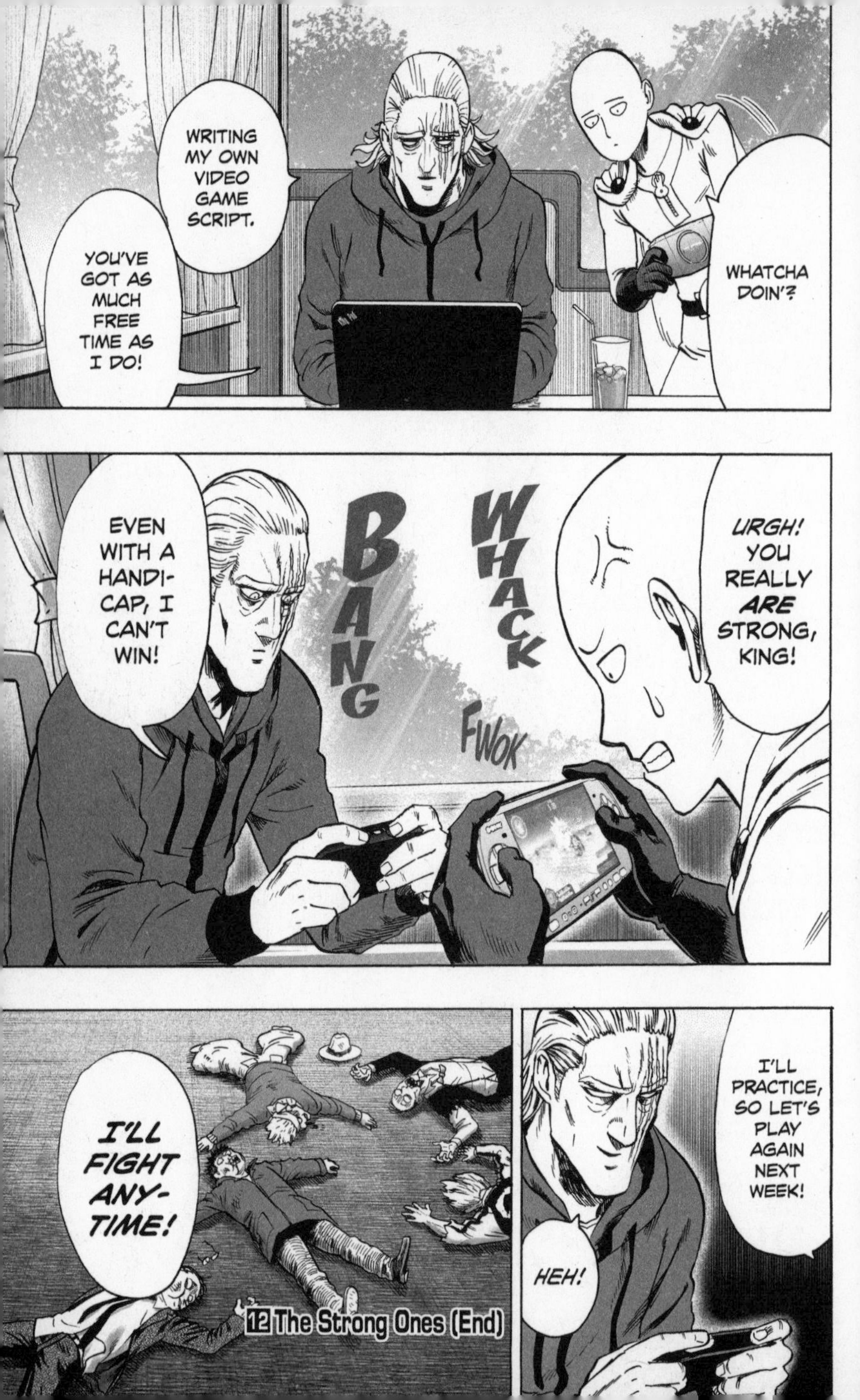
WHATCHA DOIN'?
WRITING MY OWN VIDEO GAME SCRIPT.
YOU'VE GOT AS MUCH FREE TIME AS I DO!
URGH! YOU REALLY *ARE* STRONG, KING!
WHACK
BANG
FWOK
EVEN WITH A HANDICAP, I CAN'T WIN!
I'LL PRACTICE, SO LET'S PLAY AGAIN NEXT WEEK!
HEH!
I'LL FIGHT ANYTIME!
12 The Strong Ones (End)

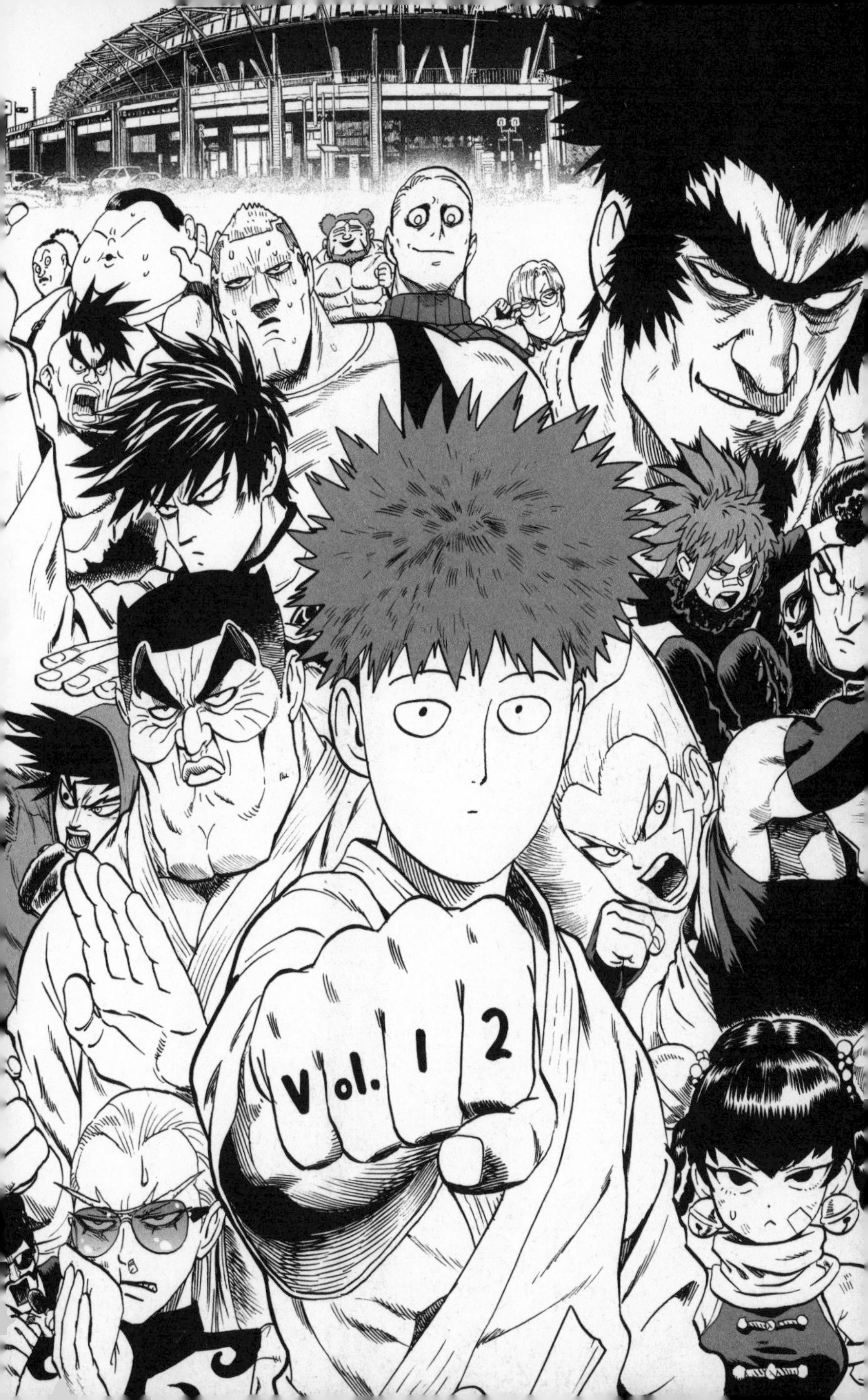
Vol. 12

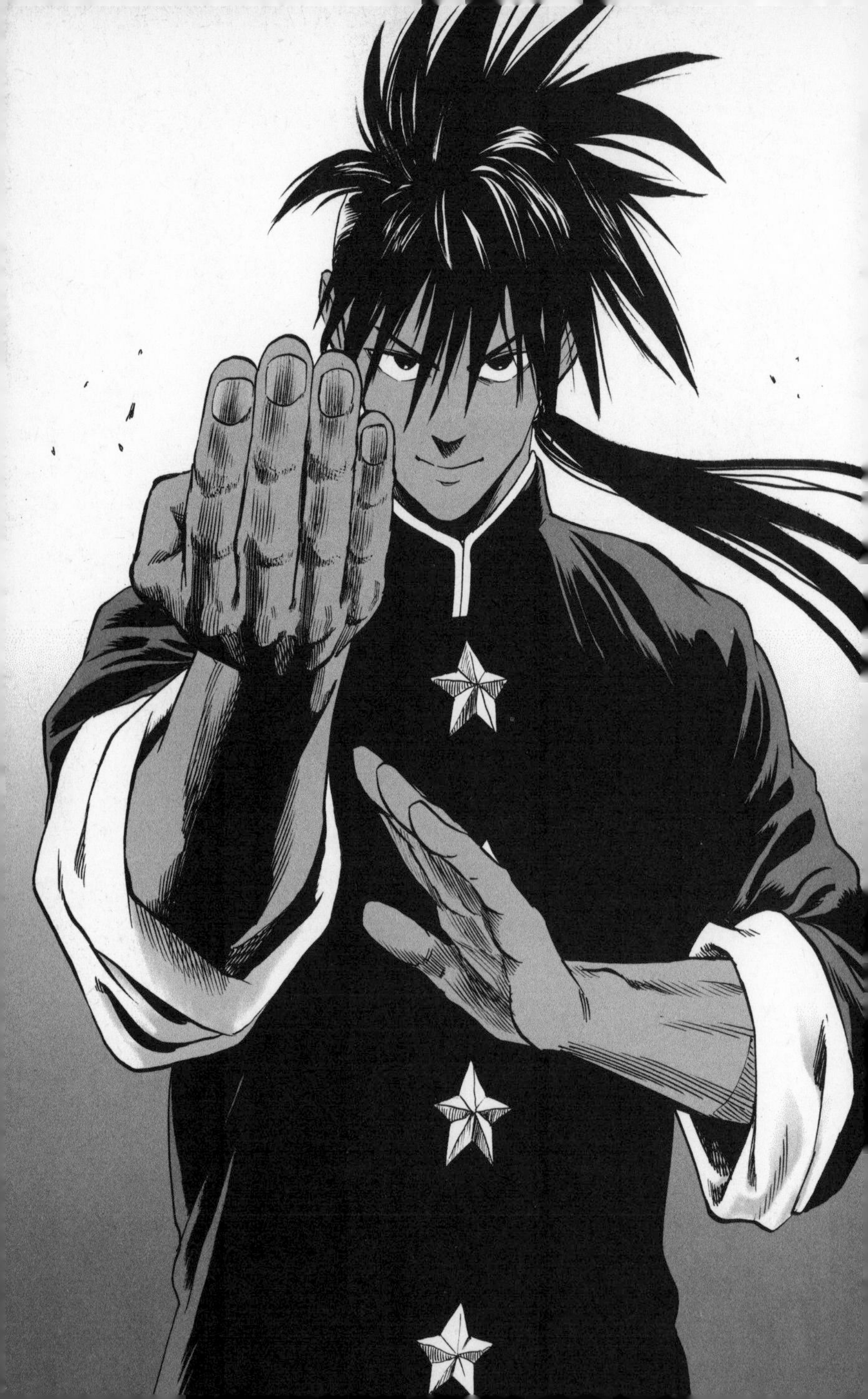

END NOTES

PAGE 78, PANEL 2:
The Japanese romaji on the boy's shirt says "ugly."

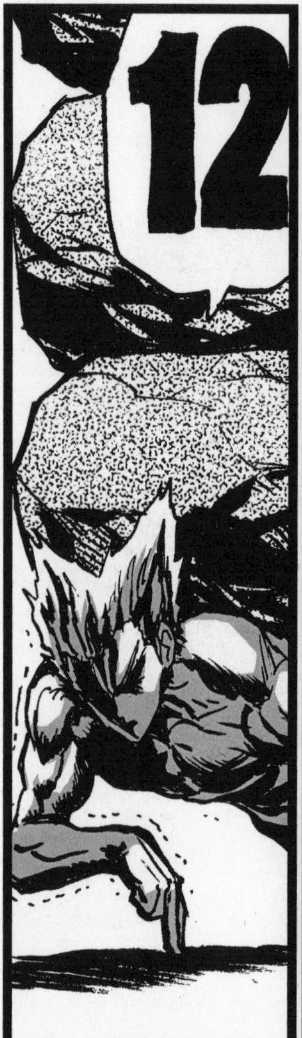
12

ONE-PUNCH MAN

VOLUME 12

SHONEN JUMP MANGA EDITION

STORY BY | ONE
ART BY | YUSUKE MURATA

TRANSLATION | JOHN WERRY
TOUCH-UP ART AND LETTERING | JAMES GAUBATZ
DESIGN | SHAWN CARRICO
SHONEN JUMP SERIES EDITOR | JOHN BAE
GRAPHIC NOVEL EDITOR | JENNIFER LEBLANC

Printed in the U.S.A.

Published by VIZ Media, LLC
P.O. Box 77010
San Francisco, CA 94107

10 9 8 7 6 5 4 3 2 1
First printing, September 2017

www.viz.com

www.shonenjump.com

PARENTAL ADVISORY
RATED T FOR TEEN
ONE-PUNCH MAN is rated T for Teen and is recommended for ages 13 and up. This volume contains realistic and fantasy violence.
ratings.viz.com

EYESHIELD 21

STORY BY RIICHIRO INAGAKI
ART BY YUSUKE MURATA

From the artist of *One-Punch Man!*

Wimpy Sena Kobayakawa has been running away from bullies all his life. But when the football gear comes on, things change—Sena's speed and uncanny ability to elude big bullies just might give him what it takes to become a great high school football hero! Catch all the bone-crushing action and slapstick comedy of Japan's hottest football manga!